CRISIS IN AMERICAN INSTITUTIONS

CRISIS IN AMERICAN INSTITUTIONS

Fourteenth Edition

JEROME H. SKOLNICK

New York University

ELLIOTT CURRIE

University of California, Irvine

Allyn & Bacon

Boston Columbus Indianapolis New York San Francisco Upper Saddle River
Amsterdam Cape Town Dubai London Madrid Milan Munich Paris Montreal
Toronto Delhi Mexico City Sao Paulo Sydney Hong Kong Seoul
Singapore Taipei Tokyo

Publisher: Karen Hanson
Editorial Assistant: Alyssa Levy
Executive Marketing Manager: Kelly May
Marketing Assistant: Gina Lavagna
Production Manager: Wanda Rockwell
Associate Project Manager: Maggie Brobeck
Creative Director: Jayne Conte
Editorial Production and Composition Service: Aptara®, Inc.
Cover Designer: Bruce Kenselaar

Credits appear on Page 401, which constitutes an extension of the copyright page.

Library of Congress Cataloging-in-Publication Data

Crisis in American institutions / [edited by] Jerome H. Skolnick, Elliott
Currie.—14th ed.
    p. cm.
  ISBN-13: 978-0-205-61064-8
  ISBN-10: 0-205-61064-1
    1. United States—Social conditions—1980–   2. United States—Social
conditions—1960–1980.   3. Social problems—United States.   4. United
States—Social conditions.   I. Skolnick, Jerome H   II. Currie, Elliott.
  HN65.C684 2011
  306.0973—dc22

                                                                        2010011732

10 9   16

Allyn & Bacon
is an imprint of

www.pearsonhighered.com

ISBN-10:   0-205-61064-1
ISBN-13: 978-0-205-61064-8

Contents

Preface   ix

Introduction: Approaches to Social Problems   1

SYSTEMIC PROBLEMS

PART ONE *Corporate Power*   17

1 Take the Rich off Welfare   20
Mark Zepezauer

2 Tax Cheats and Their Enablers   27
Robert S. McIntyre

3 The Commercial   33
Neil Postman and Steve Powers

4 Water for Profit   40
John Luoma

PART TWO *Economic Crisis*   47

5 Nickel-and-Dimed: On (Not) Getting by in America   50
Barbara Ehrenreich

6 Generation Broke: The Growth of Debt among Young Americans   62
Tamara Draut and Javier Silva

7 Retirement's Unraveling Safety Net   72
Dale Russakoff

8 The Squandering of America   79
Robert Kuttner

PART THREE *Inequality*   83

9 Increasing Inequality in the United States   86
Dean Baker

v

10 From Poverty to Prosperity: A National Strategy to
Cut Poverty in Half   91
Center for American Progress

11 Day by Day: The Lives of Homeless Women   98
Elliot Liebow

12 As Rich–Poor Gap Widens in the U.S., Class Mobility Stalls   107
David Wessel

PART FOUR *Racism*   *113*

13 The Roots of White Advantage   116
Michael K. Brown, et. al.

14 Schools and Prisons: Fifty Years after *Brown v. Board of Education*   122
Sentencing Project

15 At Many Colleges, the Rich Kids Get Affirmative Action   128
Daniel Golden

16 "They Take Our Jobs!"   134
Aviva Chomsky

PART FIVE *Sexism*   *141*

17 The Conundrum of the Glass Ceiling   143
The Economist

18 Drawing the Line: Sexual Harassment on Campus   150
Catherine Hill and Elena Silva

19 Learning Silence   165
Peggy Orenstein

INSTITUTIONS IN CRISIS

PART SIX *The Family*   *175*

20 Beyond the "M" Word: The Tangled Web of Politics and Marriage   177
Arlene Skolnick

21 The Kids Aren't Alright   186
Sharon Lerner

22 More Than Welcome: Families Come First in Sweden   192
Brittany Shahmehri

PART SEVEN   *The Environment*   *199*

23 A World of Wounds   202
James Gustave Speth

24 Diamond: A Struggle for Environmental Justice in Louisiana's Chemical Corridor   208
Steve Lerner

25 Smoke, Mirrors & Hot Air: How ExxonMobil Uses Big Tobacco's Tactics to Manufacture Uncertainty on Climate Science   218
Union of Concerned Scientists

PART EIGHT   *Work and Welfare*   *227*

26 Doméstica   230
Pierrette Hondagneu-Sotelo

27 Reconnecting Disadvantaged Young Men   239
Peter Edelman, Harry J. Holzer, and Paul Offner

28 The Underclass Label   247
Herbert J. Gans

29 Flat Broke with Children: Women in the Age of Welfare Reform   260
Sharon Hays

PART NINE   *Health and Medical Care*   *271*

30 Sick Out of Luck: The Uninsured in America   274
Susan Starr Sered and Rushika Fernandopulle

31 Why Not the Best? Results from the National Scorecard on U.S. Health System Performance, 2008   281
The Commonwealth Fund

32 The Untold Health Care Story: How They Crippled Medicare   289
Lillian B. Rubin

PART TEN   *The Schools*   **295**

33   **The Shame of the Nation: The Restoration of Apartheid Schooling in America**   **297**
Jonathan Kozol

34   **Class Conflict: The Rising Costs of College**   **303**
Ellen Mutari and Melaku Lakew

35   **Schools as Scapegoats: Our Increasing Inequality and Our Competitiveness Problems are Huge—But They Can't Be Laid at the Door of Our Education System**   **309**
Lawrence Mishel and Richard Rothstein

36   **Hired Education**   **316**
Jennifer Washburn

PART ELEVEN   *Crime and Justice*   **323**

37   **The Myth of Leniency**   **325**
Elliott Currie

38   **Wild Pitch: "Three Strikes, You're Out" and Other Bad Calls on Crime**   **335**
Jerome H. Skolnick

Instant Replay: Three Strikes Was the Right Call   **344**
John J. DiIulio Jr.

Jerome H. Skolnick Replies   **348**
Jerome H. Skolnick

39   **One in 100: Behind Bars in America 2008**   **353**
Pew Foundation

40   **Unjust Rewards**   **364**
Ken Silverstein

PART TWELVE   *America in the World*   **373**

41   **Blowback**   **375**
Chalmers Johnson

42   **Oil, Geography, and War**   **385**
Michael T. Klare

43   **What to Do? A Global Strategy Against Terrorism**   **394**
The 9/11 Commission

Preface

We are, as always, extremely gratified by the positive response to the previous edition of *Crisis in American Institutions*. But once again, we have made many changes for this new edition.

Though we've kept the basic structure of the Thirteenth Edition, we've added a great deal of new material—while dropping many articles that, however compelling, seemed to us to have become dated. In response to the recent, devastating economic crisis that convulsed the United States and the rest of the world, we have added a new article, by Robert Kuttner, that deals with the origins of that global crisis in the meltdown of the American housing market—and added new selections on the dimensions of poverty, the ever-widening gap between the rich and everyone else, and the special plight of disadvantaged youth, who are the worst victims of America's continuing economic troubles. As the country moves toward a long-delayed reform of its health care system, we have updated our coverage of the dismal current state of medical care in America—especially relative to other nations—with two new articles. Our sections on Schools and the Family have been thoroughly updated with two new selections each. New articles on myths about immigration, the corporate effort to deny the importance of global climate change, and the nation's swollen prison population bring this edition up to date on these critical issues. Altogether, more than a third of the selections in this edition are new.

Each edition has provided an opportunity to review the best contemporary writing on social problems, and with each we've regretted having to drop old favorites and omit much promising new work. We invariably find more good writing than we can use—which isn't surprising, since we cover a range of issues, from the economic crisis to racism, from the family to the environment, each of which could profitably occupy a lifetime of study.

We are deeply grateful to the many people who have helped make this new edition a reality. We want particularly to thank Karen Hanson and Alyssa Levy of Pearson Education, Ted Knight of the J.L. Hahn Consulting Group, Jogender Taneja and Aptara®, Inc. for their help (and patience) in facilitating this revision. Special thanks also to Lovely Joy Sangalang, formerly of the University of California, Irvine, for skilled and enthusiastic research assistance. Lauren Healey also provided much-appreciated help with research. We would also like to thank the reviewers for this edition Evan Cooper, *Farmingdale State College*; Gregg Robinson, *Grossmont-Cuyamaca Community College*; and J. Mark Thomas, *Madison Area Technical College*. Once again, we are indebted to our colleagues at New York University and the University of California, Irvine, for providing unfailingly supportive and stimulating environments. We are grateful to the many students and teachers who have continued to educate us about each edition's strengths and weaknesses. And we are grateful, most of all, to the authors of the works we've selected here—without whom, of course, the book would never have been possible. Their continuing effort to make sense of a troubled world and to communicate that understanding accessibly and powerfully is a great source of encouragement in difficult times.

CRISIS IN AMERICAN INSTITUTIONS

Approaches to Social Problems

In the early years of the twenty-first century, American society presents us with some striking paradoxes. We are now the world's only "superpower," and our economic might is admired (and sometimes feared) throughout the world. Yet we are also a nation wracked by widespread poverty on a scale that is unknown in other industrial societies—and that frequently suffers wrenching economic crises that make life precarious and insecure for great numbers of people. We are a country of crowded shopping malls—and crowded prisons; a country of glittering cities inhabited by stubborn legions of homeless people. We are a nation that routinely produces new technological marvels, from Internet software to breakthroughs in high-tech medicine. But we are also a nation in which tens of millions of people have no regular source of health care.

This book explores these paradoxes and others through a collection of some of today's best writing on social problems in America. Our contributors are social scientists, specialists in public health and the environment, and journalists skilled in reporting and analyzing social issues. We don't claim that these articles, by themselves, can resolve all of the complex issues surrounding the causes and consequences of social problems in the United States. We do believe that they challenge readers to think more clearly and more critically about a range of issues that affect us all—from violence against women to racial profiling by police, from homelessness to global warming.

In that sense, these writings fit well with the best traditions in the study of social problems in the United States. Social scientists and others have been studying these problems for a long time, and the study of social problems has never taken place in the antiseptic confines of a scientific laboratory. Social theorists, like everyone else, are deeply influenced by broader trends in the society, the economy, and the cultural and technological setting of social life. As a way of introducing the articles that follow and of placing today's debates in some historical and intellectual context, we want to spend a few pages outlining the way in which the study of social problems has developed over time and how those larger social changes have shaped its basic assumptions and guiding themes.

DEFECTIVES AND DELINQUENTS

The earliest writers on social problems in this country were straightforward moralists, staunch supporters of the virtues of thrift, hard work, sexual purity, and personal discipline. Writing at the end of the nineteenth century, they sought ways of maintaining the values of an earlier, whiter, more Protestant, and more stable America in the face of the new challenges of industrialization, urbanization, and immigration.[1]

This early social science usually concentrated on the problems of what one nineteenth-century textbook described as the "defective, dependent, and delinquent classes."[2] The causes of social problems were located in the physical constitution or moral "character" of the poor, the criminal, the insane, and other "unfortunates." For these theorists, the solution to nineteenth-century social problems lay in developing means of transforming the character of these "defective" classes, in the hope of equipping them better to succeed within a competitive, hierarchical society whose basic assumptions were never questioned. Social reformers working from these theories created, in the last part of the nineteenth and the first part of the twentieth centuries, much of the modern apparatus of "social control" in the United States: reformatories, modern prisons, institutions for the mentally ill, and the beginnings of the modern welfare system.

THE RISE OF "VALUE-FREE" SOCIAL PROBLEMS

During the first decades of the twentieth century, this straightforward moralism was increasingly discarded in favor of a more subtle, ostensibly "neutral" approach to writing about social problems. By the 1930s, the idea that the social sciences were—or could be—purely "objective" or "value-free" had come to be widely accepted. From that point until the present, social problems theory has been characterized by a tortuous attempt to prove that theories and policies serving to support the status quo are actually scientific judgments arrived at objectively. In this view, social scientists do not try to impose their own values in deciding what kinds of things will be defined and dealt with as social problems. Instead, the "scientific" student of social problems simply accepts "society's" definition of what is a problem and what is not. This approach is apparent in these statements, taken from major textbooks and articles, on what constitutes a social problem:

> Any difficulty or misbehavior of a fairly large number of persons which we wish to remove or correct.[3]
>
> What people think they are.[4]

Whenever people begin to say, isn't it awful! Why don't they do something about it?[5]

Conditions which affect sizable proportions of the population, which are out of harmony with the values of a significant segment of the population, and which people feel can be improved or eliminated.[6]

Any substantial discrepancy between socially shared standards and actual conditions of social life.[7]

These definitions share the common idea that social problems are popularly defined. No condition is a problem unless a certain number of people in a society say it is. Because we are merely taking, as our starting point, the definitions of the problem that "other people," "society," or "significant segments of the population" provide, we are no longer in the position of moralizing about objective conditions.

The basic flaw in this happy scheme is that it does not make clear *which* segments of the population to consult when defining problems or deciding between conflicting ideas about what is problematic and what is not. In the real world, societies are divided along class, racial, sexual, and other lines, and the sociologist who proposes to follow "people's" definitions of social problems in fact generally adopts one of several competing ideologies of social problems based on those divisions. In practice, the ideology adopted has usually been not too different from that of the "unscientific" social problems writers of the nineteenth century.

These points are not new; they were raised as early as 1936 in an unusually perceptive paper called "Social Problems and the Mores," by the sociologist Willard Waller. Waller noted, for example, that discussions of poverty in the social problems literature of the 1930s were shaped by the unquestioning acceptance of the ideology of competitive capitalism:

A simpleton would suggest that the remedy for poverty in the midst of plenty is to redistribute income. We reject this solution at once because it would interfere with the institution of private property, would destroy the incentive for thrift and hard work and disjoint the entire economic system.[8]

Waller's question is fundamental: What has been left out in a writer's choice of what are to be considered problems? What features of society are going to be taken for granted as the framework *within* which problems will be defined and resolved? In this case, the taken-for-granted framework is the principle of private property and individual competition. In general, Waller argued, "social problems are not solved because people do not want to solve them";[9] they *are* problems mainly because of people's unwillingness to alter the basic conditions from which they arise. Thus:

Venereal disease becomes a social problem in that it arises from our family institutions and also in that the medical means which could be used to prevent it, which would unquestionably be fairly effective, cannot be employed for fear of altering the mores of chastity.[10]

For Waller, the definition of social problems was, in the broadest sense, a political issue involving the opposed ideologies of conflicting groups.

Waller's points still ring true. Most social problems writers in the United States still tacitly accept the basic structure of American society and restrict their treatment of social problems to maladjustments *within* that structure.

SOCIAL PROBLEMS IN THE 1950s: GRADUALISM AND ANTICOMMUNISM

This is not to say that the literature on social problems since the 1930s has all been the same. Books on social problems, not surprisingly, tend to reflect the preoccupations of the time when they were written. Those conceived in the 1950s, for example, reflect social and political concerns that now seem bizarre. The shadow of McCarthyism and the general national hysteria over the "Communist menace" pervaded this literature. Consider the discussion of "civil liberties and subversion" in Paul B. Horton and Gerald R. Leslie's textbook *The Sociology of Social Problems*.[11] Horton and Leslie saw the "American heritage of liberty" being attacked from both Left and Right, from both "monolithic communism" and overzealous attempts to defend "our" way of life from it. Their position was resolutely "moderate." They claimed a scientific objectivity; yet, they were quite capable of moral condemnation of people whose politics were "extreme," whether Right or Left:

> Most extremists are deviants. Most extremists show a fanatical preoccupation with their cause, a suspicious distrust of other people in general, a disinterest in normal pursuits, recreations, and small talk, and a strong tendency to divide other people into enemies and allies.[12]

The preference for "normal pursuits," even "small talk," over social criticism and action was common in an age noted for its "silent generation," but it was hardly "scientific." Among the other presumably objective features of the book were the authors' "rational proposals for preserving liberty and security," including these:

> *An adequate national defense* is, needless to say, necessary in a world where an international revolutionary movement is joined to an aggressive major power. This is a military problem, not a sociological problem, and is not discussed here.
> *Counterespionage is essential.* Highly trained professional agencies such as the FBI and the Central Intelligence Agency can do this efficiently and without endangering personal liberties of citizens. If headline-hunting congressmen, Legion officials, or other amateurs turn G-men, they merely scare off any real spies and destroy the counterespionage effort of the professionals.[13]

The military and intelligence services themselves were not considered to be problems relevant for social science. Questions about the operation of these agencies were viewed as internal and technical, military rather than sociological, issues.

In a section on "Questions and Projects," the authors asked, "How have conservatives or reactionaries sometimes given unintentional assistance to the Communists? How have liberals sometimes given unintentional assistance to the Communists?"[14]

In the introduction to their book, Horton and Leslie considered the possibilities of social change and the proper role of social scientists in promoting it. They carefully adopted a middle ground between conservatives, to whom social problems were primarily problems of individual character, and "extremists" hoping for sudden or radical changes in social structure. They argued that the resolution of social problems "nearly always involves sweeping institutional changes" but also that such changes are "costly" and "difficult," and that therefore

> it is unrealistic to expect that these problems will be solved easily or quickly. . . . Basic solutions of social problems will come slowly, if at all. Meanwhile, however, considerable amelioration or "improvement" may be possible.[15]

Social change, according to these authors, must be gradual and realistic; it must also be guided by experts. The authors insisted that their own role, and that of social experts in general, was merely to show the public how to get what they already valued. But in this role it was folly for the "layman" to question the expert. Horton and Leslie wrote that "when experts are *agreed* upon the futility of one policy or the soundness of another, it is sheer stupidity for the layman to disagree."[16]

An elitist, Cold War liberalism and gradualism, a fear of extremism and of an international Communist conspiracy—all these were presented not as moral and political positions but as fundamental social scientific truths. The sturdy entrepreneurial and Protestant values described in Waller's paper of the 1930s gave way, in Horton and Leslie's book of the 1950s, to a general preference for moderation, anti-communism, and "normal pursuits."

THE 1960s: AFFLUENCE AND OPTIMISM

A different imagery dominated the social problems literature of the next decade. Robert K. Merton and Robert A. Nisbet's *Contemporary Social Problems*[17] was a product of the beginning of the 1960s, the period of the "New Frontier," which saw a significant shift, at least on the surface, in the focus of social concern. Americans were becoming aware of an "underdeveloped" world abroad and a "disadvantaged" world at home, both unhappily excluded from the benefits of an age of general "affluence" and well-being. New agencies of social improvement were created at home and abroad. A critique of old-style welfare efforts began to develop, along with the notion of "helping people help themselves," whether in Latin America, Harlem, or Appalachia. The idea of inclusion, of participation, in the American way of life became a political metaphor for the age. From a slightly different vantage, the idea emerged as "development" or "modernization." The social problems of the 1960s would be solved by extending the technological and intellectual resources of established American institutions into excluded, deprived, or underdeveloped places and groups. An intervention-minded government combined with an energetic social science on a scale unprecedented in this country.

In this period—very brief, as it turned out—social problems were often seen as problems of being *left out* of the American mainstream: "left behind," as the people of Appalachia were described; "traditional," like the Mexican Americans; or "underdeveloped," like most Africans, Asians, and Latin Americans. In social problems theory, these ideas were manifested in a conservative ideology that celebrated American society as a whole, coupled with a liberal critique of the conditions hindering the extension of the American way to all.

One variant of this view was given in Nisbet's introduction to *Contemporary Social Problems*. For Nisbet, social facts become problematic when they "represent interruptions in the expected or desired scheme of things; violations of the right or the proper, as a society defines these qualities; dislocations in the social patterns and relationships that a society cherishes."[18]

Nisbet's assessment of the American situation was in keeping with the exaggerated optimism of the early 1960s:

> In America today we live in what is often called an affluent society. It is a society characterized by imposing command of physical resources, high standards of private consumption, effective maintenance of public order and security, freedom from most of the uncertainties of life that plagued our ancestors, and relatively high levels of humanitarianism. There are also, of course, squalid slums, both urban and rural; occasional epidemics of disease; sudden eruptions of violence or bigotry, even in the most civilized of communities; people for whom the struggle for food and shelter yet remains obsessing and precarious. Thus, we are not free of social problems, and some of them seem to grow almost in direct proportion to our affluence.[19]

Nisbet was aware that America had not yet solved all its problems; indeed, some seem to come with the generally glittering package that is America in the twentieth century. Yet the problems were viewed as peripheral, as occasional eruptions in the backwaters of society where modern institutions had not fully penetrated.

Like earlier theorists, Nisbet sharply separated the role of the scientific student of social problems from that of other concerned people. The social scientist, as a scientist, should not engage in moral exhortation or political action but instead concentrate on understanding. At the same time, the scientist is

> as interested as the next citizen in making the protection of society his first responsibility, in seeing society reach higher levels of moral decency, and when necessary, in promoting such legal actions as are necessary in the short run for protection or decency.[20]

Here the scientific stance masked a preference for vaguely defined values—"societal protection" and "moral decency"—that, in turn, determine what will be selected as social problems. In this instance, problems were selected according to whether they offended the values of social stability, that is, values associated with the conservative tradition in social thought.

Thus, problems were repeatedly equated with "dislocations and deviations";[21] they were problems of "dissensus," as if consensus might not also be a problem. Indeed, the entire book was divided into two sections, one dealing with "deviant behavior" and the other with "social disorganization." The articles in the text were not all of a piece. A paper by Robert S. Weiss and David Riesman on the problems of work took a different view on what constitutes a problem; the authors declared that "social forms which tend toward the suppression or frustration of meaning and purpose in life are inferior forms, whether or not they tend toward disorganization."[22] But many of the articles simply accepted the purposes of existing institutions and defined problems in terms of combating disorganization *within* those institutions. Perhaps the clearest illustration of this tendency appeared in an essay by Morris Janowitz addressing problems of the military establishment:

> It is self-evident that the military establishment, the armed forces, and their administrative organizations have become and will remain important institutions of United States society. The distinctive forms of military organization must be analyzed in order to understand the typical sources of personal and social disorganization found in military life.[23]

The existence of a large military establishment was defined as outside the critical concern of the sociologist. The focus was not on the effect of the military on national or international life but on the problems of maladjustment within the military apparatus. The increasing scope of military activities was noted, but it was simply accepted as a fact of modern life:

> The armed forces have also become involved in a wide variety of logistical, research, and training activities. In the current international scene, they must take on many politico-military duties, including military assistance of allied powers.[24]

The implication was that the militarization of American society is not itself a problem for social analysis. And the acceptance of the place of the military in American society leads to the enlistment of social science in the service of military ends. Thus, in discussing changes in the requirements of military discipline, Janowitz noted that, in the 1960s, instead of employing "shock technique" to assimilate the recruit into the military, the problem had become how to foster "positive incentives and group loyalties through a team concept."[25] Janowitz didn't ask *what* the recruit is being assimilated *into*. The effect of primary-group relations on morale under Cold War conditions was extensively discussed, but the Cold War itself was not.

Robert Merton's epilogue to *Contemporary Social Problems*, called "Social Problems and Sociological Theory," represented a major attempt to give theoretical definition to the "field" of social problems. Merton was well aware that different interests are present in society and therefore that definitions of social problems were likely to be contested—"one group's problem will be another group's asset"—and more specifically that "those occupying strategic positions of authority and power of course carry more weight than others in deciding social policy and so, among other things, in identifying for the rest what are to be taken as significant departures from social standards."[26]

According to Merton, however, this diversity of perspectives does not mean that sociologists must succumb to relativism or abandon their position as scientific students of society's problems. The way out of the dilemma is to distinguish between "manifest" and "latent" social problems—the latter are problems also "at odds with the values of the group" but not recognized as such. The task of the sociologist is to uncover the "latent" problems, or unrecognized consequences of existing institutions and policies; in this way, "sociological inquiry does make men increasingly accountable for the outcome of their collective and institutionalized actions."[27]

The demand that social science make people accountable for their actions was a healthy departure from the false relativism of some earlier theorists. But the distinction between manifest and latent problems did not do what Merton claimed for it: It did not make the choice of problems a technical or neutral one. Actually, Merton's approach is best seen as providing a rationale for evaluating and criticizing particular policies and structures within a presumably consensual society whose basic values and institutions are not seen as problematic.

We could easily agree with Merton that "to confine the study of social problems to only those circumstances that are expressly defined as problems in the society is arbitrarily to discard a complement of conditions that are also dysfunctional to values held by people in that society."[28] But what about those values themselves? Shouldn't they be examined and, if necessary, criticized? It seems obvious to us, for example, that it is part of the sociologist's task to study and criticize the values held by people in German society during the Nazi era or by slaveholders in the antebellum American South, rather than to confine ourselves to studying conditions that might be "dysfunctional" in terms of those values. To do otherwise amounts to an acceptance by default; the social scientist becomes an expert at handling problems within the confines of an assumed consensus on basic goals and values.

The division of social problems into the two categories of *deviant behavior* and *social disorganization* reflected this acceptance, for both categories were defined as "disruptions" of an existing social order and did not question the adequacy of that social order itself. Thus:

> Whereas social disorganization refers to faults in the arrangement and working of social statuses and roles, deviant behavior refers to conduct that departs significantly from the norms set for people in their social statuses.[29]

It is not, as some critics have suggested, that this kind of analysis suggests that whatever is, is right. But it does imply that whatever *disturbs* the existing social system is the primary problem.

The sociologist's "expert" judgment, of course, may conflict with what people themselves feel to be their problems, and if so, according to Merton, the expert should prevail. Merton argued:

> We cannot take for granted a reasonably correct public imagery of social problems; of their scale, distribution, causation, consequences and persistence or change. . . . Popular perceptions are no safe guide to the magnitude of a social problem.[30]

The corollary, presumably, is that the sociologist's imagery of social problems is at least "reasonably correct," even, perhaps, where segments of the public strongly object to having their problems defined, or redefined, for them. We seem to have come back to the same condescending attitude toward the public expressed by Horton and Leslie and other sociologists of the 1950s.

This kind of attitude wasn't, of course, confined to writers on social problems. It was a major theme in the social thought and government policy of the 1960s, a decade characterized by an increasing detachment of governmental action from public knowledge and accountability—as exemplified in the growth of a vast intelligence apparatus, the repeated attempts to overthrow popularly elected governments overseas, and the whole conduct of the Vietnam War. This process was often excused on the ground that political decisions involved technical judgments that were out of the reach of ordinary people.

The conception of social problems as technical, rather than moral and political, issues was explicit in Merton and Nisbet's text. Thus, Merton suggested that "the kind of problem that is dominated by social disorganization results from instrumental and technical flaws in the social system. The system comes to operate less efficiently than it realistically might."[31]

If the problems are technical ones, then it was, of course, reasonable to view social scientists as technicians and to regard their intervention into social life as free from partisan interest. It is this, apparently, that renders the social scientist a responsible citizen, rather than a "mere" social critic or ideologue:

> Under the philosophy intrinsic to the distinction between manifest and latent social problems, the social scientist neither abdicates his intellectual and professional responsibilities nor usurps the position of sitting in judgment on his fellow men.[32]

It is apparent, however, that this kind of "philosophy" lends itself all too easily to an alignment of expertise and "professionalism" with dominant values and interests masquerading as societal consensus. This is apparent in the choice of topics offered in most textbooks. Merton and Nisbet—whose widely used textbook has gone through several editions—characteristically dealt with mental disorders, crime and delinquency, drug use, alcoholism, suicide, sexual behavior, the population crisis, race relations, family disorganization, work and automation, poverty, community disorganization, violence, and youth and politics. The book did not deal with (to take some examples from our own table of contents) corporate power, sexism, health care, the criminal justice system, and so on. The pattern of these differences is obvious: Merton and Nisbet focused most heavily on those who have, for one reason or another, failed to "make it" within the American system—delinquents, criminals, the mentally ill, drug users—and on disorganization *within* established institutions. Even when individual authors in their book attempted to analyze the system itself, the effort was usually relegated to a peripheral, or merely symbolic, place.

Despite its claim to political neutrality, the social science of the 1960s typically focused on the symptoms of social ills, rather than their sources: the culture of the poor, rather than the decisions of the rich; the "pathology" of the ghetto, rather than the problems of the economy. What "socially shared standards" dictated this choice of emphasis? In the introduction to a newer edition of *Contemporary Social Problems,* Nisbet tried to answer this question. "It may well be asked," he writes, "why these problems have been chosen by the editors," rather than other problems that "for some persons at least might be regarded as even more pressing to national policy."

> The answer is that this is a textbook in sociology. Sociology is a special science characterized by concepts and conclusions, which are based on analysis and research, yielding in turn perspectives on society and its central problems. For many decades now, sociologists have worked carefully and patiently on these problems. In other words this book is concerned not only with the presentation of major social problems but with the scientific concepts and procedures by which these problems have been, and continue to be, studied.[33]

Nisbet seems to be explaining that these problems were selected by the editors because sociologists have studied them, and not other problems, in the past. Such an argument is hardly compelling.

THE 1970s TO THE PRESENT: A HARSHER VISION

Much of the thinking about social problems in the 1960s—and the public policies that flowed from it—tended to assume, at least implicitly, that most of the ills of American society were solvable; that a rich and technologically advanced society should be able to overcome problems like poverty, unemployment, and inadequate health care, if it had the will to do so. And so an active government launched a number of social programs and experiments designed to bring the American reality in closer harmony with the American ideal. In the 1980s, it became fashionable to say that the government attempted too much in those years, throwing vast amounts of money at social problems. In fact, though we did try a multitude of programs, the amounts we spent on them were never large. Our total federal spending on job training, public job creation, and schooling programs for low-income people, for example, never rose to as much as one-half of 1 percent of our gross national product during the 1960s.[34]

But the belief that government had taken on too big a role helped to usher in a harsher, more pessimistic perspective in the 1970s—a perspective that has dominated social policy in the United States ever since. In the context of a deeply troubled economy, the stubborn persistence of poverty and joblessness, and frightening levels of social disintegration in the cities, the moderate optimism of the 1960s began to give way to a new brand of scholarly pessimism arguing that many of these problems were due to "human nature" or defective "culture"—or even genetic deficiencies. The implication was that social concern of the 1960s variety couldn't have much positive impact on social problems—and, in the view of some writers, had probably made them worse.

Writers such as Arthur Jensen resurrected long-discredited hereditary theories of racial inferiority in intelligence to explain why blacks still remained at the bottom of the educational and economic ladder, despite all the equal opportunity programs of the 1960s. Others, such as Harvard's Edward Banfield, explained the persistence of poverty and urban crime as the reflection of a distinctive "lower-class culture" that prevented the poor from thinking ahead or delaying immediate gratification. By the 1980s, Charles Murray and other critics were explaining the stubbornness of poverty as the result of the demoralization of the poor by an overly generous welfare system. The growth of urban violence was similarly explained as the result of excessive leniency with criminals; in the 1980s, when years of "getting tough" with criminals left us with still-frightful levels of crime and violence, some writers began looking for the roots of crime—and of poverty and other social pathologies as well—in faulty physiology or defective genes.

By the 1980s, in other words, American thinking about social problems had just about come full circle; we had returned to something that looked very much like the focus on "defectives, dependents, and delinquents" that characterized late-nineteenth-century social science. And the harsh social policies that flowed from this attitude were also strikingly reminiscent of the Social Darwinism of the late nineteenth century. The belief that many of our social problems (from school failure to juvenile delinquency to welfare dependency) can be traced to deficiencies in the minds, cultures, or genetic makeup of a hard-core few—or to the folly of government intervention—a belief that was so comforting to the complacent thinkers of the nineteenth century, had returned with a vengeance.

As in the past, this outlook—still hugely influential today—serves to explain away some of the most troubling expressions of the crisis in American institutions, including many we address in this book: swollen prisons, the stubborn persistence of deep poverty, minority joblessness that persists at near-Depression levels through "good" economic times and bad. And it is used to justify sharp cutbacks in many of the programs created to address those problems—even successful programs in child health care, job training, and nutrition.

By now, however, this perspective has itself come under growing criticism. Its proponents, after all, have been arguing for a long time that the poor, the jobless, and the sick are largely responsible for their own problems and that they—along with the rest of us—would be better off with less help from government. We have, accordingly, been reducing government's role as well for a long time. But the problems haven't gone away; many have grown. The massive destruction wrought by Hurricane Katrina and the halting response to it by federal and state agencies sharply illustrated the consequences of the decades-long neglect of the most basic government functions. This was an especially stark example, but we see the results of that neglect across many American institutions—in crumbling schools, collapsing public facilities, decaying cities, and a "deregulated" financial system that brought the country (and much of the world economy) to a state of near-collapse. And so the job of developing a fresh and creative approach to social problems is once again on the agenda.

That task is certainly an urgent one. As many of the articles in this book suggest, we have reached what seems to be a crucial turning point in our policies toward social problems. Technological and economic changes are reshaping the conditions of American life with sometimes dizzying speed, and how we choose to deal with those changes will profoundly affect the character of life in the United States for many years to come.

Consider just one example: the rapidly shifting character of work in America. As suggested by several articles in this book, a combination of intense global economic competition and the continuing march of new workplace technology is dramatically affecting the pattern of jobs and incomes in the United States. Whether we can harness these changes to build a more sustaining and fulfilling society will depend on how our social and political institutions respond to them—whether, for example, we are willing to make a sufficient investment in worker retraining and job creation to offset the loss of many traditional jobs, and to provide adequate wages, child care, health care, and other benefits to those now at work in the lower levels of the new economy. And as American lives are more and more affected by the workings of a largely unregulated global economy, we will increasingly need to confront these issues on an international scale. More generally, the increasing interconnection between the United States and the rest of the world—dramatically revealed by the attacks on the World Trade Center in September 2001, and explored in a section at the end of this book—has given new urgency to questions of how we will manage our role as the only "superpower" in a world that is profoundly unstable and wracked by pervasive inequality and insecurity.

These are very big questions, and in this book we can only begin to explore them, not answer them once and for all. But we believe the articles that follow can provide a strong beginning. As in earlier editions, they represent a wide range of styles and perspectives. But most of them fit comfortably within a common overall vision: a critical, democratically inclined approach to social institutions that emphasizes the potential for constructive change.

Within this very broad perspective, there is plenty of room for controversy. Our authors don't necessarily share the same theoretical positions or social or political views. The editors, for that matter, don't always agree—and we think that's as it should be. We frequently argue about many of the issues covered in this book, and this debate has continued through fourteen editions. But we think this tension is fruitful, and we have tried to capture it in our selection of readings.

Our purpose is to raise issues, to provide students with the beginnings of a critical approach to the society they live in and will, we hope, help to improve. This book provides few definitive answers, and it leaves unresolved many basic theoretical and practical questions about the sources and solutions of American social problems. But its purpose will be accomplished if it helps students to begin their own process of confronting those questions.

ENDNOTES

1. C. Wright Mills, "The Professional Ideology of the Social Pathologists," in Irving L. Horowitz, ed., *Power, Politics, and People: The Collected Essays of C. Wright Mills* (New York: Ballantine, 1963).

2. Charles Richmond Henderson, *An Introduction to the Study of Defective, Dependent, and Delinquent Classes* (Boston: Heath, 1906).

3. Lawrence K. Frank, "Social Problems," *American Journal of Sociology*, 30 (January 1925), p. 463.

4. Richard C. Fuller and Richard R. Myers, "The Natural History of a Social Problem," *American Sociological Review*, 6 (June 1941), p. 320.

5. Paul B. Horton and Gerald R. Leslie, *The Sociology of Social Problems* (New York: Appleton-Century-Crofts, 1955), p. 6.

6. Arnold M. Rose, "Theory for the Study of Social Problems," *Social Problems*, 4 (January 1957), p. 190.

7. Robert K. Merton and Robert A. Nisbet, *Contemporary Social Problems* (New York: Harcourt, Brace, and World, 1961), p. 702.

8. Willard Waller, "Social Problems and the Mores," *American Sociological Review*, 1 (December 1936), p. 926.

9. *Ibid.*, p. 928.

10. *Ibid.*, p. 927.

11. Horton and Leslie, *The Sociology of Social Problems*. We refer here to the original edition in order to place the book in its historical context.

12. *Ibid.*, p. 517.

13. *Ibid.*, p. 520.

14. *Ibid.*, p. 523.

15. *Ibid.*, p. 12.

16. *Ibid.*, p. 19.

17. Merton and Nisbet, *Contemporary Social Problems*. Here, too, we refer to the first edition in order to consider the book in historical perspective. The general theoretical perspective in the book has changed little, if at all, as we will note later; there have been some substantive changes, however—for example, the chapter by Janowitz has been dropped and new chapters added.

18. Robert A. Nisbet, "The Study of Social Problems," in *ibid.*, p. 4.

19. *Ibid.*, p. 5. The reader might compare C. Wright Mills's notion, developed during the same period, that the United States should be seen as an "overdeveloped" society; see Irving L. Horowitz, "Introduction," in Horowitz, *Power, Politics, and People*, p. 8.

20. Nisbet, "The Study of Social Problems," p. 9.

21. *Ibid.*, p. 12.

22. Robert S. Weiss and David Riesman, "Social Problems and Disorganization in the World of Work," in Merton and Nisbet, *Contemporary Social Problems*, p. 464.

23. Morris Janowitz, "The Military Establishment: Organization and Disorganization," in Merton and Nisbet, *Contemporary Social Problems*, p. 515.

24. *Ibid.*, p. 516.

25. *Ibid.*, pp. 533–534.

26. Robert K. Merton, "Social Problems and Sociological Theory," in Merton and Nisbet, *Contemporary Social Problems*, p. 706.

27. *Ibid.*, p. 710.

28. *Ibid.*, p. 711.

29. *Ibid.*, p. 723.

30. *Ibid.*, pp. 712–713.

31. *Ibid.*, p. 723.

32. *Ibid.*, p. 712.

33. Robert M. Nisbet, "The Study of Social Problems," in *ibid.*, p. 2.

34. Gary L. Burtless, "Public Spending for the Poor," in Sheldon H. Danziger and Daniel H. Weinberg, *Fighting Poverty: What Works and What Doesn't* (Cambridge, MA: Harvard University Press, 1986), p. 37.

SYSTEMIC PROBLEMS

PART ONE

Corporate Power

The myth of American capitalism is individual "free enterprise"—the vision of the hardworking, thrifty entrepreneur competing with others and constrained by the forces of the market. But the reality of American capitalism is very different: it is an economy that has long been dominated by large and powerful corporations that in many ways have left the "free market" behind.

The Wal-Mart corporation employs more than two million people—a number far greater than the populations of Dallas, San Diego, or Philadelphia: if they were a city, they would be the fifth largest in the United States, barely edged out for fourth place by Houston. The revenue of the largest corporation in America in 2008, Exxon Mobil—roughly $443 billion—was considerably larger than the Gross National Income of Sweden. The American corporation with the most assets—the Citigroup financial empire—had close to two trillion dollars worth, slightly larger than the Gross National Income of Italy. The great size and power of these corporations influences virtually every aspect of life in America—and the world—today.

And as corporate business has become ever larger, it has also become much more entwined with—and dependent on—government. Part of our persistent myth of "free enterprise" is the belief that, unlike poor people on welfare or older people who receive Medicare or Social Security, private businesses must go it alone—earn their own way in the free market—or go under. This belief was, of course, sorely undercut by the recent, massive taxpayer "bailouts" of floundering corporations that were deemed "too big to fail." But the reliance of corporate America on government help predates the recent economic crisis: as the articles here by Mark Zepezauer and Robert S. McIntyre show, corporations are the recipients of an enormous amount of "welfare" of their own, ultimately paid for by American taxpayers. Some of these giveaways come in the form of subsidies to various industries, which, as Zepezauer reveals, vastly overshadow what we spend, as a nation, on all forms of welfare for the poor. The selection we reprint here describes just one of those favored industries—agribusiness—which at this writing received more than $30 billion in subsidies, most of which went to the wealthiest farmers and agricultural corporations. Adding to the illogic, one of the beneficiaries of these government subsidies is the tobacco industry—just as the government is simultaneously trying to discourage smoking, a habit that costs the economy billions every year.

Another way in which government subsidizes corporate business is through an intricate set of tax breaks that are mostly unavailable to ordinary citizens. As Robert S. McIntyre shows, these tax giveaways are increasingly arcane and difficult for even experts to unravel. But they have resulted in a startling decline in the proportion of overall U.S. taxes that are contributed by big corporations. In recent years, indeed, many of the wealthiest corporations have managed to pay little or no federal or state taxes—a situation that is not only patently unfair, but that contributes mightily to the perennial budget crises that have forced repeated cutbacks in schools, public health care, and other critical services. In recent years, Congress has taken some steps to rein in spending on corporate welfare. But these have been far less effective than measures to cut back on public assistance for the poor or working Americans.

These articles suggest that the corporations enjoy an especially privileged position in American society today, supported by an array of special benefits that belie the traditional image of the "free market." The rise of that remarkable combination of private power and public support has been fueled, in part, by the widespread belief that the private sector can do a better job than government in addressing economic needs, and that it should be left alone by government, as much as possible, in order to get the job done most efficiently. The United States has gone much farther in this direction than most countries, with a relatively smaller role for government in economic life than in many other advanced industrial societies. And the dominance of the private sector has increased considerably in recent years, as private companies have moved in to take over many functions that used to be public ones—everything from running schools to operating prisons to providing water, one of the most basic needs of human life.

As John Luoma points out in "Water for Profit," the takeover of water systems in many cities—and countries—by a handful of large corporations was supposed to make the delivery of water more efficient. But in some places, especially in some developing countries, the results have been the opposite. Water, which had been taken for granted even by the poor, suddenly became too expensive for many to afford, and often became unhealthy as well. In the United States, most people still get their water from public utilities, but not for long, if some corporations have their way. Illustrating the reach and complexity of the modern large corporation, among the companies most prominent in the drive to privatize water is the French-based Vivendi Universal, which, among other enterprises, also owns the USA television network and the Universal motion picture studios. Luoma concludes that "If success is measured in terms of delivering an essential commodity to everyone who needs it, then the industry's record is less than encouraging." As we hear calls to turn more and more of our basic needs over to private corporations, we would do well to ponder this example.

The corporate economy, however, cannot function if people do not buy the products and services that corporations sell. Historically, making sure that people do indeed consume enough to keep the economy rolling has long been a challenging task for business—especially because it is often not immediately clear why we need them, or need so many of them. One way in which we are constantly encouraged to buy more is though advertising, which is a more and more ubiquitous part of American life. As Neil Postman and Steve Powers point out in "The Commercial," the average American TV viewer will be exposed to 39,000 minutes of television advertising over the course of a year. The purpose of all that advertising, the authors argue, is not simply to sell specific products: it is about teaching people to believe the more general message that the solution to their problems is to be found in buying the latest consumer goods. That message is surely good for the corporations' bottom line, and hence essential for a profit-driven economy to flourish. Whether it is good for society as a whole—or for the health of the planet—is another question.

CHAPTER 1

Take the Rich off Welfare

Mark Zepezauer

Wealthfare—the money government gives away to corporations and wealthy individuals—costs us more than $815 billion a year. That's:

- 47% of what it costs to run the US government (which is about $1.73 trillion a year, not counting entitlement trust funds like Social Security and Medicare)[1]
- enough money to eliminate the federal debt in just over eight years (the total is now $6.6 trillion, accumulated over 200-plus years)[2]
- more than four times what we spend on welfare for the poor . . .

When agricultural subsidies began during the Great Depression, their main purpose was to keep farmers on the farm by enabling them to earn roughly what people in cities did. Of course, in those days, some 25% of the population lived and worked on farms. Today, only 2% of us do.[1] These days the average net worth of farm households is $564,000—nearly double the $283,000 for nonfarm households.[2] Farmers' household income from all sources (an average of $64,347 in 1999) has exceeded that of nonfarmers' income every year since 1986.[3]

Agricultural subsidies are particularly bizarre these days because they go mostly to relatively few states, for relatively few crops, to benefit relatively few farmers. The wealthiest 10% of subsidized farmers take 74% of the handouts, while the bottom four-fifths get 12% of the total. The bottom half? Just 2%. And 60% of US farmers get nothing at all.[4] Five crops—wheat, corn, rice, cotton, and soybeans—receive 90% of all federal subsidies.[5] Almost two-thirds of total US farm production—including most fruits and vegetables—remains unsubsidized.[6]

Concentrating the subsidies on certain crops also concentrates them geographically. Just 15 states receive 74% of the benefit from federal agriculture programs, while paying only 24% of the cost.[7] In California, the largest agricultural producer, only 9% of the farms received any subsidy at all. (These were mostly big cotton and rice farms, while the state's many orchards and vegetable farms didn't get a penny.)[8] The Northeast gets a particularly raw deal, paying for 30% of the cost of crop subsidies (that is, it contributes 30% of federal taxes), while receiving just 2.4% of the benefit.[9] In an effort to get in on the party, New York's congressional delegation helped create a new subsidy for its dairy farmers in the 2002 farm bill.[10]

Not surprisingly, many of the "luckiest" states are those that can help swing the results of national elections or that have powerful representatives in Congress who help to write farm legislation. The 2002 farm bill gave the most money to Iowa, and the largest increase to Texas. Iowa is the home of Senator Tom Harkin, then the chair of the Senate Agriculture Committee. And Texas sent Republican Larry Combest, chair of the House Agricultural Committee, and Democrat Charles Stenholm, a member of the same committee, to Washington, where they helped double the amount of subsidies for their home state.[11]

And just coincidentally, Representative Stenholm himself is a subsidized farmer, receiving more than $39,000 under the 1996 farm bill (from 1996 through 2002). At least ten of his colleagues, including Senators Grassley (R-IA), Lugar (R-IN), and Lincoln (D-AR), are also on the dole. Representative Marion Berry of Arkansas (not to be confused with the former mayor of Washington, DC) took in more than $750,000 in subsidies between 1996 and 2002. Perhaps you will not be surprised to hear that Berry feels that federal farm subsidy programs are "woefully underfunded."[12]

Not only is the US Department of Agriculture (USDA) generous in its handouts to farmers, it's also quite generous in who it calls a farmer. Making a complete mockery of the supposed aims of the farm subsidies (to help keep 'em down on the farm), the USDA doled out almost $3.5 billion to recipients in urban zip codes between 1996 and 2001.[13] Many recipients aren't even located in the same state as their farms. Among celebrity farmers (outside of Congress) are billionaire David Rockefeller, basketball star Scottie Pippen, broadcaster Sam Donaldson, tycoon Ted Turner, and corporate crime poster boy Kenneth Lay of Enron.[14] In fact, any land that produces $1,000 or more in agricultural products can be officially regarded as a farm.[15] So if you see the word "farmers" in quotes below, you'll know why.

Of course, it's not even necessary to be a human being to qualify as a farmer. One study found farm subsidies going to 413 municipal governments, 44 universities, and 14 prison systems.[16] And such *Fortune* 500 companies as Chevron Oil, John Hancock Life Insurance, Caterpillar Manufacturing, and Eli Lilly Pharmaceuticals are also quote, farmers, unquote—subsidized with your tax dollars.[17] . . .

One last thing before we dive into the details. Despite all the booty being siphoned off to the wealthy, these programs are routinely justified by the need to help combat rural poverty or save small family farms. But there's an alternative that would be a whole lot simpler and cheaper. We could bring the income of every full-time farmer in the United States up to at least 185% of the federal poverty level (about $33,000) for just $4 billion a year.[18] If the agribusiness subsidy's goal were to reduce rural poverty, we could simply write a check to every poor farmer. But of course that's not the goal anymore, is it?

Agribusiness subsidies take several forms:

- With price supports, quasi-governmental agencies or cooperatives buy up "excess" production of a crop to keep the price high. (It's like government-sanctioned price fixing.)
- Production quotas limit who can farm a particular crop (peanut and tobacco farmers, for example, must be licensed by the government).
- Market quotas control how much of a crop can be sold; the "excess" is warehoused (at taxpayer expense) or destroyed.
- Import restrictions limit how much of a crop can be imported into the United States.
- Crop insurance provides low-cost insurance against crop failures and disasters.
- Deficiency payments. . . .

THE "CHEAPER FOOD" RUSE

One rationale for agribusiness subsidies—to the extent that they have any—is that you get cheaper food prices out of the deal. Dream on.

First of all, we pay for many of these handouts with our income taxes, so you'd have to add a portion of those taxes to your food bill to come up with an accurate total. According to one estimate, the average household can tack on $1,805 over the next decade.[19] Besides that, there are indirect subsidies you pay for at the checkout counter without even realizing it.

Price supports, import restrictions, and market and production quotas keep the prices of sugar, dairy products, and peanuts higher in the United States than on the world market. They cost consumers $2 billion a year in higher sugar prices, $1.7 billion in higher dairy prices, and $500 million in higher peanut prices. That's $4.2 billion at the cash register right there.[20]

But crop subsidies actually help drive up the price of many other foods, because they help inflate the cost of rural real estate—by some 25% in 2000 alone.[21] Land that produces subsidized crops is worth more, thus bidding up the price of neighboring land. But more important, because subsidies are paid according to the number of acres planted (instead of farmer need), land becomes overvalued. Land prices are the single biggest contributor to the cost of food.

As a further illustration of the law of unintended consequences, the higher land prices are pushing more small family farms out of business and contributing to the dominance of corporate factory farms. Subsidies push up the price of land beyond what many poor farmers can afford. If they're tenant farmers, their rent goes up, and if they're owner-operators, their property taxes go up. Since neither group can afford to expand their operations, big corporations are able to gobble up more of the available land—which then makes the remaining land that much more valuable. On top of that, the larger agribusiness concerns bid up the price of land in competition with each other, leaving small family farms in the dust.[22]

Even when agribusiness subsidies actually do bring down the cost of food, you typically end up paying for them in other ways. For example, diverting productive salmon streams to grow potatoes in the desert may be great for fast-food outlets and the corporate farmers who supply them, but it's hell on fishermen and recreational workers. Their unemployment insurance is part of the cost of your cheaper meal.

The bottom line is that as agribusiness consolidation has increased, farm employment has declined. There have been jobs created in peripheral sectors, but not as many; employment in these sectors grew by 36,000 from 1975 to 1996, while farm employment dropped 667,000 jobs. More tellingly, the job "growth" in these sectors comes largely at the expense of the environment. Larger farms require more pesticides and machinery, leading to more pollution in our skies and streams as well as our food. So once again, we're subsidizing the deterioration of our environment, and we pay for it in health care costs as well as in taxes.

LIVESTOCK SUBSIDIES

Many Americans are cutting back on meat and dairy products for health reasons. But whatever your diet, you help pay for these products with your taxes (not to mention the Medicare costs for those who over-consume meat and dairy products).

While most farmers have to treat their profits as ordinary income, livestock profits are classified as capital gains and are taxed at a lower rate (now just 15%). But the costs of buying, breeding, and raising livestock are ordinary expenses that can be deducted immediately.[23] This best-of-both-worlds tax treatment encourages people to get into the livestock business, and there are nontax inducements as well.

Cattle ranchers graze their herds on public lands leased to them at about one-eighth of their market value—which works out to pennies per acre. In 2001, the Bureau of Land Management (BLM) took in $4.5 million from grazing leases and spent more than 17 times as much—$77 million—managing the lands. Note that even if the BLM had charged market value, we still would have lost more than $40 million on the deal.[24]

As far as I can tell, the main justification for this seems to be that ranchers are "cultural icons" who maintain a "way of life" that is worth preserving. (There may be a more sophisticated rationale, but I haven't come across it yet.) It's an emotional argument that ignores the facts about how little of the nation's livestock ranching is actually done on public lands—less than 0.1%, according to one study.[25] Besides, maintaining this lifestyle contributes to plenty of destruction.

Cattle trample native plants and grasses, foul local streams, and contribute to erosion. The BLM and the Forest Service have to deal with the effects on wildlife and watersheds in the lands they manage. Add in those environmental factors and the true cost of grazing leases comes to about *$500 million* a year, according to a study by the Center for Biological Diversity in Tucson, Arizona.[26]

Like most agribusiness handouts, cattle subsidies go disproportionately to the very rich—75% of the grazing land leased by the BLM is controlled by fewer than 10% of the lessees. Among these "welfare cowboys" are computer moguls Bill Hewlett and (the late) David Packard of Hewlett-Packard, as well as Jack Simplot, one of the 500 richest people in America. Other handouts go to Texaco, the Mormon Church, and Anheuser-Busch (which presumably grazes its famous Clydesdale horses at your expense). One study of Arizona's Prescott National Forest found that 64% of all leases were held by doctors, lawyers, art dealers, and other business owners—who are hardly dependent on ranching for their livelihoods and certainly aren't clinging to a bygone way of life.[27]

Amazingly, we are paying all this money—and subsidizing the destruction of our public lands—to benefit just 3% of all livestock producers in the United States.[28] This welfare ranching takes up 300 million acres of federally held land. That includes 90% of the BLM's land, 69% of the Forest Service's land, as well as various national parks, wildlife refuges, and nature preserves.[29] But other uses of federal lands contribute far more to local and regional economies. One study of the Kaibab Plateau in Arizona found that recreational activities and hunting licenses generated $1.5 million for the local economy, compared to $46,000 from federal grazing.[30]

Another handout to ranchers is the Western Livestock Protection Program, which spent $9.8 million in 1996 to protect livestock by exterminating predators—in the same year that livestock losses from predators totaled $5.8 million.

In 1998, Congress appropriated $28.8 million for this program, even though the House voted 229 to 193 for the Bass-DeFazio amendment, which would have killed the funding. Supporters of cowboy welfare forced a second vote the next day. As Taxpayers for Common Sense noted,

> After it passed, an inadvertent technical drafting error in the amendment was discovered. On June 24, the technical error was fixed by a unanimous consent request by the amendment's sponsor. Later that same day opponents of the original amendment sought a revote and inaccurately claimed that the error had not been fixed, even though House members were clearly told it had been fixed by Representative Bass. On June 24, the House rejected the amendment, 192–232.[31]

In fiscal year 2003, the program is budgeted at $68 million.

However, the Livestock Protection Program (LPP) is not to be confused with the Livestock Compensation Program (LCP), an emergency program with $750 million to cover drought losses, or the Livestock Assistance Program (LAP), which compensates ranchers for losses not covered by the LCP or the LPP. The LAP kicks in with another quarter billion for FY2003.[32] You'll be relieved to know, though, that nobody is allowed to collect from both the LCP and the LAP at the same time.

Of course, ordinary people have to buy their own insurance to cover losses from natural disasters. The ranchers seem unwilling to shoulder the risks inherent in their chosen business. And once again, it would actually be cheaper to simply write a check to each welfare cowboy for predator losses than to fund these programs.

SUBSIDIES FOR DRUG PEDDLERS

But at least beef and milk are edible. Tobacco, a drug that kills 48 Americans every hour, is also subsidized with a combination of price supports, import restrictions, and production and market quotas.[33]

By keeping foreign tobacco out and limiting domestic production, the government creates a lower supply for the same amount of demand, allowing domestic producers to charge more. There is no rational justification for this; tobacco does far more harm to the economy than any conceivable benefit that could be gained from government support. When the program started in 1933, the health effects of tobacco were not widely known, and there were far more farmers in need of assistance. The program survives today because of sheer political clout. While some tobacco farmers are definitely hurting because of industry outsourcing, the bulk of the subsidy goes to absentee landlords, not farmers. Then again, the mythical promise of a subsidy might keep these smaller farmers producing tobacco, rather than switching to a more useful, though unsubsidized, crop.

In 1996, then-Representative Richard Durbin (now a Democratic senator from Illinois) introduced a proposal to end tobacco subsidies, estimating their direct cost at about $41 million.[34] The price supports also generate higher costs to consumers, at an estimated $857 million. (This doesn't count the additional cost to taxpayers of dealing with smoking-related illnesses through Medicare, Medicaid, veterans hospitals, and government employees' health plans. That costs you an extra $38 billion a year.[35] And that doesn't count the money the Social Security Administration pays out in survivors' benefits to kids whose parents have died from smoking. That puts another $1.8 billion on the tally.[36])

In June 1996, the House of Representatives voted down Durbin's measure by a smoke-thin margin of 212 to 210. There hasn't been a serious effort to end the subsidies since. Usually the tobacco lobby does better than a two-vote margin. Its 13 PACs, among the most generous on Capitol Hill, handed out almost $9.5 million in the 2001–2002 election cycle alone.[37] This is quite a boost from the $10 million distributed between 1986 and 1995.[38] (When you kill off 400,000 of your customers every year, you need all the friends you can get.)

Although the tobacco lobby has made sure that some portion of the federal government supports tobacco farmers, public pressure has forced other parts of the government to discourage smoking. Seeing the writing on the wall, US tobacco manufacturers are making a big push for new customers overseas. US tobacco exports have risen 275% since 1985, when we started threatening countries like Japan, Thailand, South Korea, and Taiwan with trade sanctions unless they opened their markets to US cigarettes.[39]

Taiwan has been trying to restrict smoking in public areas, and to ban cigarette ads and vending machine sales. That should sound familiar, because the same efforts are being made here. But when they do it, we call it an unfair trade practice. If this hypocritical coercion of ours succeeds, the results will be as disastrous for Taiwan as they were for South Korea. One year after the US tobacco giants penetrated that market, the smoking rate for teenage boys had almost doubled (from 18% to 30%), while the rate for teenage girls had more than quintupled (from 1.6% to 8.7%).[40]

Meanwhile, as US tobacco companies have moved more production offshore to service foreign markets, they've also been importing more foreign tobacco to use in domestic cigarettes. This has put the squeeze on US tobacco farmers, the very people these subsidies are supposed to help. At the same time, the USDA has cut tobacco quotas in half in the past few years. To compensate for market losses, the USDA paid out $350 million in direct payments to tobacco farmers in FY2001. This amounts to eight times the previous annual subsidy.[41] (Of course, many of the beneficiaries are absentee landlords who don't farm tobacco but get rich selling their quotas to tenant farmers.) The big payout was not repeated in 2002, but a 2003 farm bill added a new $53 billion program to pay off the farmers again.[42] That brings the current total in tobacco subsidies to $96 million.

Editors' Note: *Notes for this reading can be found in the original source.*

CHAPTER 2

Tax Cheats and Their Enablers

Robert S. McIntyre

You . . . can be a millionaire . . . and never pay taxes! You can be a millionaire . . . and never pay taxes!

You say . . . "Steve . . . how can I be a millionaire . . . and never pay taxes?"

First . . . get a million dollars.

Now . . . you say, "Steve . . . what do I say to the tax man when he comes to my door and says, 'You . . . have never paid taxes'?"

Two simple words. Two simple words in the English language: "I forgot!"

—Steve Martin, *Saturday Night Live*, January 21, 1978

INTRODUCTION

Lots of unscrupulous big corporations and wealthy people are working hard to hide their profits and income from the tax collector. Their schemes are more complicated than Steve Martin's comic infomercial envisioned, but they're just as damaging to our country, and just as reprehensible. In fact, almost three decades after he delivered it, Martin's tax advice needs only minor updating. Add a few zeros to $1,000,000 and change the punch line to "Seven simple words . . . 'I have a note from my lawyer.'"

The culprits are many. The greedy tax dodgers, of course. Their unscrupulous tax advisers, including America's most prestigious accounting firms, biggest banks and many law firms—who make billions of dollars facilitating evasion and avoidance. But most of all, the blame lies with demagogic lawmakers in Washington, who have turned a blind eye to tax evasion, and have refused to give the Internal Revenue Service—the tax police—the resources to stop the abuses.

Tax dodging takes many forms. There are, of course, legal loopholes enacted by Congress in response to lobbying pressure. Generally termed "incentives," they purport to encourage people or companies to do something socially or economically useful. Then there are potentially legal (but often not) tax shelters—what might be called "roll your own" loopholes to cut taxes in ways that Congress never officially intended. And finally, there's outright cheating—simply failing to report your income or making up deductions.

Distinguishing one from the other isn't always easy. Taking a deduction for donating your old car to charity is perfectly legal, for instance. But making up an inflated value for the deduction is cheating. Moving your money offshore and failing to declare the income it earns is clearly cheating if you're a person. But it may be a legal—or at least quasi-legal—tax shelter if you're a multinational corporation. . . .

Far too many investors and business owners are tempted to understate their gross business receipts and/or overstate their expenses, move their investments offshore, fail to report their capital gains accurately, and so forth. Not all succumb, of course. Even for those who do, the actual alchemy of making income disappear for tax purposes is probably often a mystery. That doesn't in any way absolve the tax cheats and aggressive avoiders from blame: they're the demand side of the equation. But without the supply side, the lawyers, accountants and banks that set up the shelters, the demand would go unrequited.

The ethically challenged tax advisers who are willing to help would-be tax evaders are well aware that the chances of their clients being audited by the IRS are extremely low, so long as a tax return doesn't raise obvious red flags. Their chief weapons to win this "audit lottery" are complexity and subterfuge.

In contrast, the vast majority of Americans who make almost all their money from wages have few opportunities for serious tax cheating. Taxes are withheld from paychecks, W-2 forms are easily matched against tax returns, and straightforward deductions for mortgage interest, state and local taxes, and (most) charitable donations are easily checked for accuracy.

So the majority of us who honestly pay our taxes have a major stake in getting the tax dodgers to ante up, too—hundreds of billions of dollars a year, in fact, although no one knows the exact amount for sure.

Taxes, as Supreme Court Justice Oliver Wendell Holmes noted a century ago, are "the price of civilization." Most of us are willing to pay our fair share of the cost of all the things we want and need our government to do—so long as we believe others are chipping in, too. But others—too often those who have gained the most from our society—prefer to shirk their responsibilities and pass the cost onto the rest of us. . . .

> "Is it the right time to be migrating a corporation's headquarters to an offshore location? We are working through a lot of companies who feel that it is, that just the improvement on earnings is powerful enough that maybe the patriotism issue needs to take a back seat to that."
> —Ernst & Young webcast advising its corporate clients to shelter their profits from U.S. taxes by reincorporating in Bermuda—issued in the fall of 2001 soon after the 9/11 terrorist attacks

> "My father said all businessmen are S.O.B.s but I didn't believe it until now."
> —John F. Kennedy, *The New York Times*, April 23, 1962

CORPORATE SHELTERS

Big corporations have an advantage over people in sheltering their income from tax. First of all, of course, they have tremendous lobbying power in Congress. So they can get special tax concessions enacted that ordinary citizens never could. In addition, unlike individuals, corporations are allowed to break themselves into pieces on paper and treat completely phony, non-existent transactions among those pieces as if they really happened. Because large corporations typically operate in many jurisdictions through multiple subsidiaries, they have lots of opportunities to move profits away from where they're actually earned and into places where they're not taxed.

Corporate America, outside of a few industries like oil, was a bit slow to get into the tax-avoidance game. That's why as recently as the 1950s, corporate taxes paid for about a third of the federal government. Indeed, in the early sixties, much of Big Business actually opposed the Kennedy administration's "investment tax credit" as an unwise interference in the marketplace. But by the time that loophole had been repealed in 1969 on grounds of cost and general uselessness, big American companies had gotten a taste of tax dodging and wanted more.

President Nixon was happy to oblige, with expanded depreciation write-offs, tax breaks for exporters and a number of other giveaways. There was a brief tax reform moment in 1976, but it was soon followed by the "supply-side" period that began in 1978 and continued through 1981. Ronald Reagan in his first term was particularly devoted to loopholes. By his second term, however, Reagan (or at least his staff) had come to his senses, and presided over the 1986 Tax Reform Act, which repealed most of the 1981-enacted tax breaks, along with many others, in exchange for lower tax rates.

But tax reform didn't last. Due to enacted loopholes, new tax-dodging schemes and insufficient enforcement, corporate tax sheltering has run amuck. Some of the shelters that corporations use are identical to the tax-avoiding schemes that wealthy people engage in. But corporations can do much more.

For example, a company may make products in one place and sell them in others. If the place it makes the products has low taxes, it may charge its selling subsidiaries, on paper, a lot for the products. That means high profits in the low tax country where the products are made, and low or no profits in the places where the products are sold. Conversely, if the place products are made has the high taxes, then the company will "sell" its products cheaply to its selling subsidiaries, and shift profits to the places where the products are sold.

Or a company may borrow from one of its subsidiaries in a low-tax place. The interest will be deductible against income that would otherwise be taxable in a higher-tax place, and taxed little, if at all by the low-tax place.

Or a company may have a very valuable asset, such as a trade name. If it transfers the ownership of that name to a low-tax place and then charges its taxable operations large royalties to use the name, it can avoid huge amounts in taxes.

One of the more blatant corporate tax shelter schemes that we know about involves a foreign company, the Yukos Oil Company, until recently Russia's biggest oil producer. After the break-up of the Soviet Union, many of Russia's previously state-owned businesses were transferred into private hands, typically at bargain basement prices. Some of the new owners became instant billionaires, and their corruption didn't stop there.

The new Russian tax code was drafted with the help of major American accounting firms, and was, on its face, as full of holes as Swiss cheese. One oddity of the Russian corporate income tax is that its revenues are dedicated to the Russian republics (the rough equivalent of our states), and those republics are authorized to give tax "incentives" to corporations, ostensibly to encourage economic development.

The republics where Yukos pumped and refined its oil weren't about to offer Yukos tax breaks. After all, they didn't need to. They already had the oil and the refineries trapped within their boundaries. But on the advice of its accountants, who included PricewaterhouseCoopers, Ernst & Young and KPMG, Yukos found what it thought was a way around that problem. Yukos went to one of the Russian republics, Mordovia, and sought a tax break for its oil profits. This probably seemed pretty weird at first to Mordovian officials. After all, Mordovia's official website notes:

> "There are no large deposits of natural resources except building materials on the territory of Mordovia. However . . . there are some parts of the Moksha, the Vad and the Sura rivers with deposits of the unique type of resources that is stained oak."

One can imagine the conversation between Yukos and Mordovian officials going something like this:

YUKOS: We'd like a tax exemption for our Mordovian oil profits.
MORDOVIA: But you don't have any oil profits here in Mordovia.
Y: Maybe not yet, but we will soon.
M: What's in it for us?
Y: Well make it worth your while.
M: And if we say no?
Y: Don't even ask.

Once Yukos got its tax exemption in Mordovia it simply transferred its profits, on paper, to that republic, and slashed its Russian income taxes down to near zero.

Unfortunately for Yukos, its thuggish billionaire chief executive, Mikail Khodorkovsky, decided to get involved in Russian politics and television. Russian President Vladimir Putin didn't like the competition and charged Khodorkovsky and Yukos with billions of dollars in tax evasion. Although the Russian tax authorities had previously ignored this misbehavior and the Russian tax code was vague at best, it wasn't a hard case to make.

Yukos's inside-Russia tax shelter was particularly crude, but American companies do much the same thing inside the United States to avoid their state income taxes, with only a patina of added sophistication. Toys "R" Us, for example, transferred the ownership of its trade name to Delaware, which doesn't tax royalties, and then charged its stores around the country hefty fees to use the name. From 2001 through 2003, Toys "R" Us paid no state income tax on its $549 million in reported pretax U.S. profits. Similarly, many Wisconsin banks have avoided taxes by transferring ownership of their income-producing loans to subsidiaries located in Nevada, which has no income tax. Texas-based corporations such as Dell and SBC Communications have shifted the nominal ownership of their companies to partnerships located in Delaware to avoid Texas income taxes. And on and on.

This February, my group, Citizens for Tax Justice, released a study of the state income taxes of 252 of America's largest and most profitable corporations. We found that from 2001 to 2003, these companies avoided paying state income taxes on almost two-thirds of their U.S. profits—at a cost to state governments of $42 billion. Overall, corporate state tax avoidance has led to a 40 percent drop in state corporate income tax collections as a share of the economy from 1989 to 2003.

Shifting profits to no-tax states is just the intramural version of the much larger international tax sheltering that America's big corporations also engage in. The infamous Enron, which paid no federal income tax at all in four of five years from 1996 through 2000, had 881 subsidiaries in foreign tax-haven countries, 692 of them in the Cayman Islands alone, which it used for both tax evasion and financial shenanigans. Halliburton has hundreds of such offshore entities. Famous American logos, such as "Ford" and "Coca-Cola," are now being held by offshore affiliates in the Cayman Islands, in an international version of Toys "R" Us's state tax dodge. Most other big corporations have tax-haven subsidiaries, too, all for the purpose of hiding profits from tax.

To be sure, there are some rules against companies shifting otherwise taxable profits out of the U.S. and into tax-haven countries. Indeed, a major section of the tax code, called "Subpart F," is devoted to curbing such behavior. These rules are full of loopholes, hard to enforce and in need of reform, but they do have some salutary effect. In fact, the reason that Ernst & Young advised its corporate clients in the fall of 2001 to renounce their U.S. citizenship and reincorporate in Bermuda was that it would help get around these restrictions, since the Subpart F rules are harder to enforce or don't apply to "foreign" companies.

Some of the tax schemes that multinational corporations engage in look down-right wacky on their face, but they're very lucrative. For example, one of our biggest banks, Wachovia, used a leasing tax shelter in which it pretended to own a German town's sewer system. That strange scheme allowed Wachovia to eliminate all of its U.S. federal income taxes in 2002.

The list of complicated corporate tax avoidance activities is almost endless, but the effects on federal corporate tax collections is easy to understand.

When Citizens for Tax Justice examined the federal taxes of 275 of the largest U.S. corporations last September, we found that in 2003 these companies, on average, paid only 17.3 percent of their U.S. profits in federal income taxes—less than half the 35 percent rate that the tax code purportedly requires. From 2001 to 2003, 82 of the 275 corporations enjoyed at least one year in which they paid nothing at all in federal income tax, despite pretax U.S. profits in those no-tax years totaling $102 billion.

In 1965, federal and state corporate income taxes in the U.S. equaled 4.0 percent of our GDP, much more than the 2.4 percent average in the other major developed countries. By 2001, the latest year available for international statistics, corporate taxes in those other countries had risen to 3.2 percent of GDP. But American corporate taxes in 2003 had plummeted to only 1.6 percent of GDP. (European countries are becoming increasingly worried, however, about growing corporate tax sheltering in their jurisdictions, too.)

The bottom line is this: Due to enacted corporate tax breaks, rate reductions and tax sheltering, U.S. corporate tax collections at the federal level alone have fallen from 4.8 percent of the gross domestic product in the 1950s to only 1.6 percent in 2004—a drop of two-thirds. To put that in perspective, if corporations paid the same effective tax rate now that they paid in the fifties, corporate tax payments to the U.S. Treasury would be $380 billion a year higher than they actually are.

Some of that decline in federal corporate tax payments since the 1950s reflects a drop in the corporate tax rate from 52 percent to 35 percent. So cracking down on corporate tax evasion and tax sheltering wouldn't restore all of the lost revenue. But it would be a major step toward reducing the budget deficit, maintaining essential government services and protecting honest taxpayers.

CHAPTER 3

The Commercial

Neil Postman
Steve Powers

THE BACKBONE, THE HEART, the soul, the fuel, the DNA (choose whatever metaphor you wish) of nonpublic television in America is the commercial. This is as true of the television news show as it is any other form of programming. To have a realistic understanding of TV news you must consider two dimensions of the commercial. The first concerns money; the second, social values.

Let's talk business first, which means we must begin with the magic initials CPM. CPM is what makes the cash registers sing for news and other programs. It stands for "cost per thousand" (Roman numeral M = thousand). Specifically, it is the cost to an advertiser for each thousand people reached by a commercial. When we last checked, the CPM for the evening newscasts was approximately $6.50 to $7.00 per thirty-second spot, for the broad household audience. That means an advertiser must spend at least $6.50 to reach each thousand people watching the evening weekday news. That works out to a bit more than half a cent for each viewer delivered, as counted by the rating services. The network, in effect, promises to deliver the audience but doesn't promise that any of them will watch the commercials or buy the products. If you use your TiVo to fast-forward through the spots or step out of the room during the commercial to make a salami sandwich, the advertiser still gets charged. But with audiences in the millions, enough people see the commercials and buy enough products to make the system work.

Naturally, programs with high ratings (even if they have a correspondingly high CPM) are attractive to advertisers because they want to reach as many potential customers as possible at one time. News programs fill the bill. On any given weekday evening, around 25 million people are watching the network news, with 60 million more watching local news in the early evening and late night. About 12.5 million people watch morning news programs. For an advertiser who wants to reach a large audience, network news easily surpasses other news media; e.g., newspapers and magazines. *USA Today* boasts the largest daily paper circulation, a little more than 2.5 million. *The Wall Street Journal* is next with 2 million. *Time* magazine has a weekly circulation of 4.1 million people. The Sunday morning news shows *Face the Nation, Meet the Press,* and *This Week* deliver a combined audience of 9 million viewers. *The NewsHour with Jim Lehrer* delivers about 2.4 million viewers each night. Compare all that with the more than 25 million people tuned to the ABC, CBS, and NBC news every weekday evening.

But audience size is by no means the only factor advertisers are interested in. Even more important are demographics. Each news program has a demographic profile; that is, a statistical picture of the age, sex, and income of those who habitually watch the program. Advertisers of skateboards will tend to advertise on news programs with young viewers; advertisers of arthritis medicine will place their commercials on news programs with an "older demographic."

It sounds simple enough but it isn't. Advertising agency spot buyers may have a difficult time trying to figure out where to spend the advertiser's dollar because a show with a small audience can make its news program a good "buy" by lowering its CPM, and a show with the demographics that match the advertiser's target audience may be worth a premium. The time of year will further affect the price (the first and third quarters of the year are less expensive). So news programs try to increase their ratings and attract the coveted demographic. For example, during the week of December 18, 2006, *NBC Nightly News with Brian Williams* was the number-one network news program in the desirable twenty-five- to fifty-four-year-old demo, with a 2.4 rating (each rating point represents 1 percent of the 112.8 million households in the United States). But an advertiser shopping for a bargain might decide to buy the *CBS Evening News with Katie Couric,* with a 1.9 rating in the twenty-five- to fifty-four-year-old demographic, or ABC's *World News with Charles Gibson,* with a 2.2. In that same demographic, NBC delivered 2.888 million people, ABC 2.733 million, and CBS 2.349 million.

Beside sheer numbers of viewers, ratings also purport to tell what percentage of all viewers are watching any given show. Ratings numbers are usually quoted in pairs, such as *NBC Nightly News* total homes delivered: 6.4/13. That means 6.4 percent of the total TV-watching households in the country had the show tuned in and 13 percent of all the households with a TV turned on at that precise moment were watching that show.

After those numbers have been carefully analyzed, spot buyers look at rate cards (which list the price of each news show's commercials) and make their decisions with the help of computers. On NBC News, a thirty-second spot might cost about $60,000. With about eight minutes of commercial time available each night, a network news show can generate about $480,000 a night, or $2.4 million each week. Journalism.org quotes TNS Media Intelligence as estimating that in 2005 NBC's evening news earned $159 million, CBS earned about $162 million, and ABC earned about $168 million, even though NBC had higher overall ratings. The reason given was that much of network advertising is bundled across more than one program or platform, such as NBC network and MSNBC. Moreover, because of the appeal of news programs, commercials placed adjacent to a news show will bring a premium price, as will commercials that lead in to local news programs. Where once there was one hour of news, local and network, many markets now feature two- and three-hour news programs. As we write, a countertrend is under way: reducing evening news program time in favor of double access; that is, one hour of syndicated news preceding and following prime time. Syndicated shows such as *Access Hollywood, Wheel of Fortune, Entertainment Tonight, Oprah, Judge Judy,* and *Primer Impacto* (Spanish language) have replaced many locally produced news programs.

What all of this means is that the stakes in the ad game are astronomical. PricewaterhouseCoopers estimated that the global TV network market in 2003 was $130.7 billion. It also estimated that U.S. broadcast and cable TV networks made $47 billion in 2003 and $52.3 billion in 2004.

It is estimated that NBC, ABC, CBS, and Fox take in at least $4.5 billion a year in prime-time sales. Each rating point is worth about $10,000 for each thirty-second network commercial, but a commercial on a hit series can bring in $32,000 more per commercial that what is charged on an average series. That adds up to $224,000 more per week. Don Hewitt, former producer of the extremely successful *60 Minutes* news program, has boasted that his show makes $70 million a year in profit for CBS (although industry figures estimate that the show earns only $40 million a year). According to 2004 TNS data, annual ad revenue for NBC's ubiquitous *Dateline* franchise was $232.3 million. CBS's *60 Minutes* made $108 million, *60 Minutes II*'s ad revenue was $62 million, and *20/20* took in $77 million. CBS's *48 Hours Mystery,* which premiered as *48 Hours,* had ad revenue of $78 million in 2005. In 2004, *Nightline* took in $75 million. It has since changed its host and adjusted its format to appeal to a younger audience.

With so much money being spent just for airtime, advertisers and their agencies want their messages to be effective. To make sure that happens, they bring in a small army of specialists, people who are experts in making commercials. Over months of work, artists, statisticians, writers, psychologists, researchers, musicians, cinematographers, lighting consultants, camera operators, producers, directors, set builders, composers, models, actors, audio experts, executives, and technicians will toil for one single objective: to make a commercial that will make you buy a product or idea. Time and talent costs can be $500,000 for a short commercial.

There are approximately twenty-five thousand different commercials on network television every year. This is necessary, in part, to keep pace with the two hundred or so new items that appear every week on drugstore and supermarket shelves across the country. This means that advertisers have to produce commercials that will be noticed and will motivate viewers to spend money. The competition is fierce and continuous. At the same time, the costs for advertisers have gotten so high that the sixty-second commercial, once the backbone of broadcast TV, has given way to the shorter thirty-second spot, which is often broken down into ten- and fifteen-second commercials. This "piggybacking" does bring down the cost of each commercial (a fifteen-second commercial will cost about 20 percent less than a thirty-second spot), but it also squeezes four or more commercials into the same time slot that one commercial used to fill. What this means is that next year, if you watch TV as much as the average American, you will be exposed to something on the order of over thirty-nine thousand minutes of commercials.

That number will include commercials that are part of "line campaigns." These are commercials featuring a whole line of products made by one company. For example, Colgate-Palmolive has made commercials that sold Colgate Junior toothpaste, regular Colgate toothpaste, Colgate anticavity mouth rinse, Colgate tartar-control toothpaste, and two kinds of Colgate toothbrushes—all that in one sixty-second commercial. Companies favor the idea of multipurpose spots because they can sell several products for the cost of one commercial. Corporations also believe that the name of their company is as important a selling point as the names of individual products. But it also means more ad clutter for the average viewer, and we are not even considering the promotional spots cajoling you to stay tuned or watch other shows.

In an experimental ad campaign, Phillips Electronics became the sole sponsor for one night's edition of *NBC Nightly News* in December 2006. Instead of the normal seven minutes, Phillips used just over sixty seconds of ad time to emphasize its theme of "sense and simplicity." That freed up an extra six minutes of airtime for news, which resulted in several additional stories. Anchor Brian Williams says the response was highly favorable, with higher ratings and some viewers pledging to buy Phillips's products. ABC's *World News with Charles Gibson* had a single sponsor for each Monday newscast in April 2007. ABC said it would add five minutes to each newscast, during which it would accommodate a series of reports on serious issues around the world.

There is much more that can be said about the economics of commercials, but what we *have* said, we believe, are the basics of the business. It is all about serious money. But commercials are also about the serious manipulation of our social and psychic lives. There are, in fact, some critics who say that commercials are a new, albeit degraded, means of religious expression in that most of them take the form of parables, teaching people what the good life consists of. It is a claim not to be easily dismissed. Let us take as an example an imaginary commercial for a mouthwash, but one that replicates a common pattern. We'll call the product Fresh Taste. The commercial will run for thirty seconds, and, like any decent parable, will have a beginning, a middle, and an end. The beginning will show a man and woman saying good-bye, at her door, after an evening out. The woman tilts her head, expecting to be kissed. The man steps back, in a state of polite revulsion, and says, "Well, Barbara, it was nice meeting you. I'll call sometime soon." Barbara is disappointed. And so ends act 1, which is accomplished in ten seconds. Act 2 shows Barbara talking to her roommate. "This always happens to me, Joan," she laments. "What's wrong with me?" Joan is ready. "Your problem," she says, "is your mouthwash. Yours is too mediciny and doesn't protect you long enough. You should try Fresh Taste." Joan holds up a new bottle, which Barbara examines with an optimistic gleam in her eye. That's act 2. Also ten seconds. Act 3, the final ten, shows Barbara and the once-reluctant young man getting off a plane in Hawaii. Both are in the early stages of ecstasy, and we are to understand that they are on their honeymoon. Fresh Taste has done it again.

Let's consider exactly what it *has* done. To begin with, the structure of the commercial is as compact and well organized as the parable of the prodigal son, maybe even better organized and certainly more compressed. The first ten seconds show the problem: Barbara has trouble with her social life but is unaware of the cause. The second ten seconds show the solution: Barbara has bad breath, which could be remedied by her buying a different product. The last ten seconds show the moral of the story: if you know the right product to buy, you will find happiness.

Imagine, now, a slight alteration in the commercial. The first ten seconds remain the same. The change comes in act 2. Barbara wonders what's wrong with her but gets a somewhat different answer from Joan. "What's wrong with you?" Joan asks. "I'll tell you what's wrong with you. You are boring. You are dull, dull, dull. You haven't read a book in four years. You don't know the difference between Mozart and Bruce Springsteen. You couldn't even name the *continent* that Nigeria is on. It's a wonder that any man would want to spend more than ten minutes with you!" A chastened Barbara replies, "You are right. But what can I do?" "What can you do?" Joan answers. "I'll tell you what you can do. Start by taking a course or two at a local university. Join a book club. Get some tickets to the opera. Read the *New York Times* once in a while." "But that will take forever, months, maybe years," says Barbara. "That's right," replies Joan, "so you'd better start now." The commercial ends with Joan handing Barbara a copy of Freud's *Civilization and Its Discontents.* Barbara looks forlorn but begins to finger the pages.

This, too, is a parable, but its lesson is so different from that of the first commercial that there is no chance you will ever see anything like it on television. Its point is that there are no simple or fast solutions to life's important problems; specifically, there is no chemical that can make you desirable: attractiveness must come from within. This idea, which is a commonplace in the Judeo-Christian tradition, is the exact opposite of what almost all commercials teach.

As we said, the average American TV viewer will see over thirty-nine thousand minutes of commercials next year. Some of them will be quite straightforward, and some funny; some will be spoofs of other commercials, and some mysterious and exotic. But many of them will have the structure of our hypothetical commercial and will urge the following ideas: whatever problem you face (lack of self-esteem, lack of good taste, lack of attractiveness, lack of social acceptance), it can be solved, solved fast, and solved through a drug, a detergent, a machine, or a salable technique. You are, in fact, helpless unless you know about the product that can remake you and set you on the road to paradise. You must, in short, become a born-again consumer, redeem yourself, and find peace.

There are even commercials that show us a vision of hell should we fail to buy the right product. We are thinking, for example, of the 2007 State Farm Auto Insurance commercial, which takes its symbolism straight from Dante's *Inferno.* Some poor guy comes out of a grocery store and finds that the name Brad is scratched on his car door in big letters. He calls his insurance company, and an irritating phone operator explains to him that his low-rate policy only covers scratches of full names. She explains that he'd be covered if Bradley, Bradford, or Brady were scratched on the car but not nicknames. Presumably, the poor guy must drive around forever in perdition with "Brad" etched on his car door, all because he bought his auto policy from the wrong company.

An earlier version of this "wrong product" commercial was the numerous American Express traveler's check spots that showed, for example, a typical American couple checking out of a hotel in some strange city, perhaps Istanbul. The husband reaches for his wallet but cannot find it. He has lost it, along with his traveler's checks. The check-out clerk asks, with hope in his eyes, if the lost checks were American Express traveler's checks, for if they were, they are easily enough replaced. The husband, his voice practically gone, says they were not. The clerk shrugs his shoulders, as if to say, "Then, there is no hope for you." Perhaps you have seen this commercial. Have you ever wondered what happens to these people? Do they wander forever in limbo? Will they always be in an alien land far from home? Will they ever see their children again? Is this not a just punishment for their ignorance, for their lack of attention? The truth, after all, was available to them. Why were they not able to see it?

Perhaps you are thinking we exaggerate. After all, most people don't pay all that much attention to commercials. But that, in fact, is one of the reasons commercials are so effective. People do not usually analyze them. Neither, we might say, do people analyze biblical parables, which are often ambiguous; some, as in the case of the parable of the prodigal son, seem even downright unfair. Like biblical parables, commercial messages invade our consciousness, seep into our souls. Even if you are half-awake when commercials run, thirty thousand of them will begin to penetrate your indifference. In the end, it is hard not to believe.

Whether you call the structure and messages of commercials "religious," "quasi-religious," "antireligious," or something else, it is clear that they are the most constant and voluminous source of value propaganda in our culture. Commercials are almost never about anything trivial. Mouthwash commercials are not about bad breath. They are about the need for social acceptance and, frequently, about the need to be sexually attractive. Beer commercials are almost always about a man's need to share the values of a peer group. An automobile commercial is usually about the need for autonomy or social status, a deodorant commercial about one's fear of nature. Television commercials are about products only in the sense that the story of Jonah is about the anatomy of whales, which is to say, they aren't. Like the story of Jonah, they set out to teach us lessons about the solutions to life's problems, and that is why we are inclined to think of them as a corrupt modality of spiritual instruction.

Boredom, anxiety, rejection, fear, envy, sloth—in TV commercials there are remedies for each of these, and more. The remedies are called Scope, Comet, Toyota, Bufferin, Alka-Seltzer, and Budweiser. They take the place of good works, restraint, piety, awe, humility, and transcendence. On TV commercials, moral deficiencies as we customarily think of them do not really exist. A commercial for Alka-Seltzer, for example, does not teach you to avoid overeating. Gluttony is perfectly acceptable—maybe even desirable. The point of the commercial is that your gluttony is no problem. Alka-Seltzer will handle it. The seven deadly sins, in other words, are problems to be solved through chemistry and technology. On commercials, there are no intimations of the conventional roads to spiritual redemption. But there is original sin, and it consists of our having been ignorant of a product that offers happiness. We may achieve a state of grace by attending to the good news about it, which will appear every six or seven minutes. It follows from this that he or she is most devout who knows of the largest array of products; they are heretics who willfully ignore what is there to be used.

Part of the reason commercials are effective is that they are, in a sense, invisible. When you check the TV listings in your local newspaper or *TV Guide*, do you find the commercials listed? Since there will be more than eleven minutes of commercials, teases, and promotional announcements in a thirty-minute news show, would it not be relevant to indicate what the content of 36 percent of the show will be? But, of course, the commercials will not be listed. They are simply taken for granted, which is why so few people regard it as strange that a commercial should precede a news story about an earthquake in Chile or, even worse, follow a news story about an earthquake in Chile. It is difficult to measure the effect on an audience that has been shown pictures of an earthquake's devastation and immediately afterward is subjected to commercials for Crest toothpaste, Scope, United Airlines, and Alka-Seltzer. Our best guess is that the earthquake takes on a surrealistic aspect; it is certainly trivialized. It is as if the program's producer is saying, "You needn't grieve or worry about what you are seeing. In a minute or so, we will make you happy with some good news about how to make your teeth whiter."

Of course, an argument may be made that a concern over how to make your teeth whiter is far more important than your lamentations about an earthquake; that is to say, advertising fuels a capitalist economy. For a market economy to work, the population must be made to believe that it is in need of continuous improvement. If you are quite satisfied with your teeth, your hair, your 2003 Honda, and your weight, you will not be an avid consumer. You will be especially worthless to the economy if your mind is preoccupied with worldly events. If you are not an avid consumer, the engine of the economy slows and then stalls. Therefore, the thematic thrust of advertising is to take your mind off earthquakes, the homeless, and other irrelevancies and to get you to think about your inadequate self and how you can get better. Of course, the traditional point of journalism is to turn you away from yourself and toward the world. Thus in the intermingling of news and commercials we have a struggle of sorts between two different orientations. Each tries to refute the other. It would be interesting to know which point of view will triumph in the long run.

Water for Profit

John Luoma

Even before the water turned brown, Gordon Certain had plenty to worry about. With his north Atlanta neighborhood in the middle of a growth boom, the president of the North Buckhead Civic Association had been busy fielding complaints about traffic, a sewer tunnel being built near a nature preserve, and developers razing tidy postwar ranch homes to make room for mansions. But nothing compared to the volume of calls and emails that flooded Certain's home office in May, when Georgia's environmental protection agency issued an alert to North Buckhead residents: Their tap water, the agency warned, wasn't safe to drink unless they boiled it first. Some neighbors, Certain recalls, had just fed formula to their baby when they heard the alert. "I had parents calling me in tears," he says. "The things that have happened to the water here have sure scared the hell out of a lot of people." A month later, another "boil water" alert came; this time, when Certain turned on his own tap, the liquid that gushed out was the color of rust, with bits of debris floating in it.

Atlanta's water service had never been without its critics; there had always been complaints about slow repairs and erroneous water bills. But the problems intensified three years ago, says Certain, after one of the world's largest private water companies took over the municipal system and promised to turn it into an "international showcase" for public–private partnerships. Instead of ushering in a new era of trouble-free drinking water, Atlanta's experiment with privatization has brought a host of new problems. This year there have been five boil-water alerts, indicating unsafe contaminants might be present. Fire hydrants have been useless for months. Leaking water mains have gone unrepaired for weeks. Despite all of this, the city's contractor—United Water, a subsidiary of French-based multinational Suez—has lobbied the City Council to add millions more to its $21-million-a-year contract.

Atlanta's experience has become Exhibit A in a heated controversy over the push by a rapidly growing global water industry to take over public water systems. At the heart of the debate are two questions: Should water, a basic necessity for human survival, be controlled by for-profit interests? And can multinational companies actually deliver on what they promise—better service and safe, affordable water?

Already, the two largest players in the industry, French-based conglomerates Suez and Vivendi Universal, manage water for 230 million people, mostly in Europe and the developing world. Now they are seeking access to a vast and relatively untapped market: the United States, where 85 percent of people still get their water from public utilities. Private water providers have positioned themselves as the solution to the developing world's water problems, notes Hugh Jackson, a policy analyst at the advocacy group Public Citizen. "But it's a lot harder for them to make the case when here, in the world's center of capitalism, cities are delivering tremendous amounts of high-quality, clean, inexpensive water to people."

Yet over the past decade, hundreds of U.S. cities and counties, including Indianapolis and Milwaukee, have hired private companies to manage their waterworks. Currently New Orleans; Stockton, California; and Laredo, Texas, are in the process of going private, although opposition has sprung up in all three cities. Water companies have been conducting annual "fly ins" to Washington, D.C., to press their legislative agenda, lobbying for laws that would protect companies from lawsuits over contaminated water and block municipalities from taking back troubled privatized systems. Most recently, a bipartisan group in Congress has been pushing a federal waterworks funding bill, advocated by the National Association of Water Companies, which would require cities to "consider" privatization before they can tap federal funds for upgrading or expanding public utilities and would also subsidize such privatization deals.

At the municipal level the lobbying pressure is equally intense, with water companies actively courting local officials (the U.S. Conference of Mayors' website features a large ad from Vivendi subsidiary U.S. Filter) and spending hundreds of thousands of dollars supporting privatization in local referendums. "It's hard for local guys to turn these companies away," Massachusetts' former water commissioner Douglas MacDonald has said. "They're everywhere, with arms like an octopus."

The argument behind privatization is that only corporate efficiency can rescue the nation's aging waterworks. But if success is measured in terms of delivering an essential commodity to everyone who needs it, then the industry's record is less than encouraging. Around the world, cities with private water-management companies have been plagued by lapses in service, soaring costs, and corruption. In Manila—where the water system is controlled by Suez, San Francisco-based Bechtel, and the prominent Ayala family—water is only reliably available for two hours a day, and rates have increased so dramatically that the poorest families must choose each month between either paying for water or two days' worth of food. In the Bolivian city of Cochabamba, rate increases that followed privatization sparked rioting in 2000 that left six people dead. And in Atlanta, city officials are considering canceling United Water's contract as early as this winter.

"Atlanta was going to be the industry's shining example of how great privatization is," says Public Citizen's Jackson. "And now it's turned into our shining example about how it maybe isn't so great an idea after all."

On a cloudy August day that brought a welcome bit of drizzle to drought-parched Atlanta, Mayor Shirley Franklin lugged a seven-pound bound volume off a shelf and heaved it onto a table in her office. The report, prepared by a committee she appointed shortly after taking office last January, contained the city's case against United Water. It detailed violations of federal drinking water standards, including one instance in which levels of chlorine rose to six times the level the company agreed to in its contract.

The report also listed a string of maintenance problems ranging from broken security cameras and gates to open manholes and water-main leaks that went unrepaired for weeks. Some residents had to wait months for basic repairs, even though the company's contract specifies that some repairs must be made within 15 days. In fact, United failed to complete more than half of all required repairs in 2001, and it allowed rust and debris to build up, so that when the boil-water alerts forced the company to flush the system, brown water flowed from the taps. Finally, the report noted, instead of improving collections of unpaid water bills as promised, United actually allowed collection rates to drop from 98 to 94 percent, costing the city millions of dollars.

United has succeeded at one thing, according to the city: cutting its own operating costs, chiefly by reducing the waterworks staff by 25 percent even as demand for water in burgeoning Atlanta keeps rising. Staff reductions were partly responsible for the company's service troubles, the report indicated, as were higher-than-expected repair expenses: Last year United demanded that the city provide an additional $80 million for unanticipated maintenance costs. The increase was blocked when a lone City Council member refused to sign the revised contract.

In mid-August, Mayor Franklin announced that "United Water has not lived up to its responsibility" and formally notified the company that it had 90 days to fix the problems or the city would terminate its contract. "They keep telling me they are part of a world-class corporation that can bring us world-class service," she says, offering a small smile. "So I'm giving them a chance to prove it." United has offered to spend $1 million on outside inspectors to reassure city officials that it isn't, as Franklin puts it, "cutting any corners."

It wasn't supposed to turn out this way. In 1998, when Atlanta's City Council voted to contract out its water filtration and delivery system, city officials insisted that corporate management would stave off a budget crisis and drastic rate increases, and would lower costs by more than 40 percent while improving service. (Franklin herself, then a management consultant, lobbied for one of the companies bidding on the contract.) It was the largest water-privatization program ever attempted in the United States and was expected to prompt a wave of similar contracts around the country.

Water privatization has been gaining steam since the early 1990s, when market advocates began touting it as the next logical step after deregulating electricity.

Many city waterworks that were built or expanded in the 1970s are now decaying, and the cost of needed repairs is staggering. The U.S. Environmental Protection Agency estimates that U.S. cities will have to spend nearly $151 billion to upgrade or replace pipes, filters, storage tanks, and other infrastructure over the next two decades. Cities will have to spend an additional $460 billion on sewage systems—another area where the corporate water giants are making inroads.

The prospect of skyrocketing infrastructure costs prompted U.S. officials to look overseas, where privatization is already a booming business. Multinational companies now run water systems for 7 percent of the world's population, and analysts say that figure could more than double, to 17 percent, by 2015. Private water management is estimated to be a $200 billion business, and the World Bank—which has encouraged governments to sell off their utilities to reduce public debt—projects it could reach $1 trillion by 2021. *Fortune* has called water "one of the world's great business opportunities," noting that it "promises to be to the 21st century what oil was to the 20th."

The biggest contenders for this emerging market are Suez, a corporate descendant of the company that built the Suez Canal, and the media conglomerate Vivendi Universal, which owns the USA network and Universal Studios. Together, the two companies now control about 70 percent of the world's private water-delivery systems and take in a combined $60 billion in revenues. Both have spent billions in recent years expanding in the United States: In 1999, Suez bought United Water for $1 billion, and Vivendi acquired the then-largest American company, U.S. Filter, for more than $6 billion. RWE/Thames Water, a German/British conglomerate, is currently completing its merger with the biggest remaining domestic company, American Water Works.

The water companies have been expanding even more dramatically in the developing world, where antiquated, often colonial-era, water systems are no match for rapidly increasing populations. More than 1 billion people lack access to clean drinking water, notes Peter Gleick, president of the Pacific Institute for Studies in Development, Environment and Security; a recent report he co-authored points out that "half the world's people fail to receive the level of water services available in many of the cities of ancient Greece and Rome."

Yet corporate water's record in fixing those problems—or even maintaining the industrialized world's systems—has been mixed at best. In 1989 Prime Minister Margaret Thatcher pushed through a program to privatize the United Kingdom's water supply; costs to consumers soared over the following decade, despite billions in government subsidies to the water companies. In some cities, water bills rose by as much as 141 percent in the '90s, while thousands of public-sector jobs were lost. Even the conservative *Daily Mail* declared that "Britain's top ten water companies have been able to use their position as monopoly suppliers to pull off the greatest act of licensed robbery in our history."

Last year the Ghanaian government agreed to privatize local water systems as a condition for an International Monetary Fund loan. To attract investors, the government doubled water rates, setting off protests in a country where the average annual income is less than $400 a year and the water bill—for those fortunate enough to have running water—can run upwards of $110.

BOX **4.1**

Water's Big Three

A handful of global companies have come to dominate the water industry by buying up dozens of smaller competitors. The three top players are based in Europe, but San Francisco-based Bechtel is a close fourth, and Enron's water division, Azurix, was muscling its way into water contracts from Ghana to India before it collapsed. A quick sketch of the Big Three:

SUEZ
- **Number of customers:** 120 million
- **Does business in:** 130 countries, including France, U.K., Argentina, Indonesia, Philippines, and Cameroon; runs water systems in dozens of cities, including Buenos Aires, Casablanca, and Amman, Jordan
- **U.S. activity:** Owns United Water, which manages systems in Atlanta, Puerto Rico, Milwaukee, and Washington, D.C., and is bidding to take over New Orleans' sewer system
- **Also owns:** Waste disposal, electricity, and gas operations; built the Suez Canal in 1858
- **Trouble spots: Nkonkobe, South Africa.** The city went to court late last year to get out of its contract with a Suez subsidiary, arguing that it could save $1.8 million by returning the water system to municipal control.
- **Buenos Aires, Argentina.** In 1992, Suez won a 30-year contract to manage the city's water and sewage systems. But because it failed to install wastewater lines fast enough, sewage has been flooding streets and basements, posing a threat to public health.

VIVENDI UNIVERSAL
- **Number of customers:** 110 million
- **Does business in:** 100 countries, including Hungary, China, South Korea, Kazakhstan, Lebanon, Chad, Romania, and Colombia
- **U.S. activity:** Owns U.S. Filter, the second-largest U.S. water company, best known for its Culligan filters; runs water systems in more than 500 communities
- **Also owns:** Universal Studios, the USA television network, and Houghton Mifflin, as well as waste disposal, energy, and telecommunications operations
- **Trouble spot: Tucuman, Argentina.** Water prices more than doubled after Vivendi took over management of local water systems throughout the province in 1995. Residents protested, and in 1998 the company withdrew from its 30-year contract.

RWE/THAMES WATER
- **Number of customers:** 51 million
- **Does business in:** 44 countries, including U.K., Germany, Turkey, and Japan
- **U.S. activity:** Acquiring American Water Works, which runs water systems in 27 states; the company also owns E'town, a water and sewage company that serves more than 50 communities in New Jersey
- **Also owns:** Electric utilities in Germany, wastewater, gas, recycling, and oil operations
- **Trouble spot: Lexington, Kentucky.** When American Water Works announced its merger with RWE/Thames in September 2001, Lexington indicated that it might try to buy out the conglomerate's local subsidiary, Kentucky-American Water. In response, the company sent letters to each of its 104,000 customers, asking them to fight a "forced government takeover." At present, the utility is still under RWE/Thames' control.

In Bolivia's third largest city, Cochabamba, water rates shot up 35 percent after a consortium led by Bechtel took over the city's water system in 1999; some residents found themselves paying 20 percent of their income for water. Street protests led to riots in which six people were killed; eventually, the Bolivian government voided Bechtel's contract and told company officials it could not guarantee their safety if they stayed in town.

Privatization has also spawned protests and, in some cases, dominated elections in several other countries, including Paraguay—where police last summer turned water cannons on anti-privatization protesters—Panama, Brazil, Peru, Colombia, India, Pakistan, Hungary, and South Africa.

Here in the United States, some municipalities that initially jumped on the privatization bandwagon are now having second thoughts. In Milwaukee, which turned its sewage system over to United Water in 1998, an audit released in July found that a sewer tunnel was dumping raw sewage into local waterways, including Lake Michigan. Vivendi managed Puerto Rico's water and wastewater treatment for seven years, but after a territorial commission cited inaccurate billing and poor maintenance this year, its contract wasn't renewed.

Companies scrambling for lucrative municipal water contracts have also been caught up in corruption scandals. In June, Katherine Maraldo, a New Orleans Sewer and Water Board member, and Michael Stump, the former president of Professional Services Group, which ran the city's wastewater system, were convicted on bribery charges. PSG is now part of Vivendi, which is bidding to take over New Orleans' drinking-water system. And in 2001, two associates of Bridgeport, Connecticut, Mayor Joseph Ganim pled guilty to racketeering, mail fraud, and falsifying tax returns in connection with a $806,000 payment from PSG, which was negotiating for the city's $183 million water contract.

Such incidents point to a fundamental problem with allowing private companies to take over public water systems, says the Pacific Institute's Gleick. In attempting to make attractive bids for long-term contracts, companies often underestimate the cost of maintaining a water system, and so are forced to either skimp on staffing or demand more money to keep turning a profit. "At least when you have public utilities, the money they take in stays in the community," Gleick says. "With the private companies, the profits are going to go out of your community, out of your state, and probably out of your country."

Nevertheless, Troy Henry, the southern regional manager of United Water, is convinced that private water providers can do a better job than public utilities. He readily admits that his company and Atlanta city managers have had problems "dealing with the complexities of the system" in Atlanta and says the company is spending "multiple millions of dollars [to] win back the citizens' and mayor's confidence." A biomedical and electrical engineer and former manager at IBM, Henry argues that private companies can do for water delivery what Big Blue did for computing—revolutionize technology and attract "the best and the brightest and most talented people."

Perhaps Henry can mend fences in Atlanta, which he insists is United Water's—and corporate parent Suez's— "No. 1 priority." But Clair Muller, chair of the City Council's utility committee, contends that even if United Water ends up saving its Atlanta contract, it will merely have proved that privatization can work only under tight city supervision. And if tight supervision is possible, why privatize? "If government is run correctly—and that's always a big *if*—there's no profit motive," she says. "So if this is about saving money, we should always be able to do it cheaper."

In the end, the debate is about more than money. Taking responsibility for a community's water, Muller argues, is simply not the same as running a sports stadium or a cable franchise. "Water is the worst thing to privatize," she says. "It's what we need to live. I think that's key to the whole debate—are we going to lose control over functions that are essential to life?"

PART TWO

Economic Crisis

The United States is the largest economic power in the world: measured in terms of sheer output, we tower over every other country. And when we look around us it is easy to see evidence of the marvels of American productivity: an ever-changing array of high-tech devices, new medical breakthroughs, an economy transformed by computers and the Internet. We are able to communicate almost instantaneously with people around the world. No one would doubt that our economy displays enormous wealth and potential.

But at the same time, we have not been able to translate that economic power and potential into security and well-being for all Americans. Our economy remains volatile and unstable, producing recurring cycles of good times and bad. A long burst of prosperity in the 1990s was followed by a hard fall as the new century began—and, soon after, by the worst economic crisis since the Great Depression of the 1930s. And even in good times, great numbers of people in the United States have been unable to make a living. The articles in this part explore some of the dimensions, consequences, and causes of America's ongoing economic crisis.

One of the most troubling, and enduring, aspects of that crisis is the inability of our economy to ensure a decent standard of living to everyone who works in it. There was a time in our history when Americans assumed that they could attain the "good life" if they got a regular job and stuck with it. But despite our tremendous economic growth, that ideal has never materialized. To be sure, the American economy has produced vast numbers of jobs, and indeed it is sometimes described as a "job machine." But many of these jobs are found in the rapidly growing "service" economy of restaurants, hotels, and other low-paying employers. For people with few skills, these jobs—many paying little more than the minimum wage—may be the only ones they will ever hold. But can they provide a decent and dignified living? Journalist Barbara Ehrenreich spent several weeks working in a restaurant job in order to find out: and her answer is no. The mathematics of the new service economy are simple and harsh: it is virtually impossible to work solely at these low-wage jobs and make enough money to pay the rent and to afford life's basic necessities. As more and more of the jobs we create fit this description, and as we steadily cut back on other sources of income support for poor people—especially poor women—these stark realities should give us pause.

Ehrenreich's article focuses on people at the lower end of the spectrum of jobs and income in America. But they are not the only ones facing difficult economic conditions. Indeed, one of the most troubling changes in twenty-first century America is that economic supports and protections that were once taken for granted have been sharply eroded, even for the middle class and the well-educated. As the next two articles illustrate, economic stress and uncertainty have increased for Americans at every stage of life.

It will probably come as no surprise to many readers of this book, for example, that debt is a growing problem among young adults. But how sharply this burden has risen for young Americans in recent years is startling. As Tamara Draut and Javier Silva point out, credit card debt alone doubled among people aged 18–24 during the last decade of the twentieth century, leaving many students and college graduates "indebted from the start." Rising debt has been driven by many factors, including low wages, unstable jobs, and rising costs for such basics as housing, health and child care, and college tuition (see Chapter 35 for more details on this issue); without systematic efforts to address these underlying issues, the situation is unlikely to improve.

At the other end of the age spectrum, the recent economic shifts are even more momentous. During the long period of economic expansion that began with World War II, many Americans came to expect that they would be well taken care of in their retirement—through some combination of employer pensions, Social Security, and personal savings. That was especially true for workers in the big manufacturing industries that drove the economy in those years of affluence and growth. But today far fewer Americans work in those industries—and even when they do, the companies have often whittled down retirement benefits to a fraction of what they were. As *Washington Post* reporter Dale Russakoff shows, this has led to the odd and disturbing paradox that today's young workers cannot look forward to the kind of secure life after retirement that their grandparents now enjoy. Somehow, in a society of unprecedented wealth, the future prospects of many "ordinary" Americans have moved backward, not forward.

These articles describe an economy that is increasingly insecure—even for those who, in former president Bill Clinton's phrase, "work hard and play by the rules." That fundamental instability was dramatically exposed by the catastrophic economic crisis that consumed the United States (and much of the rest of the world) beginning in 2008. Millions of people lost jobs, opportunities for the future shrank for the educated and the less skilled alike, and whole industries—from banks to the auto industry, traditionally the backbone of the U.S. economy—teetered on the verge of collapse. Why did the world's most powerful economy suddenly find itself in such dire straits? As Robert Kuttner argues, the seeds of the crisis were actually sown long before—in the deregulation of financial institutions and the broader retreat of government from its traditional role of economic oversight. In "The Subprime Scandal," Kuttner focuses on the housing sector, whose sudden implosion set off the larger crisis that brought the world economy to its knees. But the problem is much broader. Economic policy in the U.S., more than in most other advanced industrial countries, has historically been based on the belief that the economy works best when government regulation is least. But the recent crisis makes it painfully clear that a one-sided reliance on the market creates an economy that is not only unjust, but inefficient and unstable.

PART TWO • Economic Crisis

a broader retreat of government from its traditional role of economic oversight. Kuttner focuses on the housing sector whose sudden implosion set off the larger crisis that brought the world economy to its knees. But the problem is much broader: economic policy, more or more in most of the advanced industrial countries, has historically been based on the belief that the market, when is left alone, produces optimum results is least. But the recent crisis the market creates an economy that is not only unjust, but inefficient and unstable.

CHAPTER 5

Nickel-and-Dimed
On (Not) Getting by in America

Barbara Ehrenreich

At the beginning of June 1998 I leave behind everything that normally soothes the ego and sustains the body—home, career, companion, reputation, ATM card—for a plunge into the low-wage workforce. There, I become another, occupationally much diminished "Barbara Ehrenreich"—depicted on job-application forms as a divorced homemaker whose sole work experience consists of housekeeping in a few private homes. I am terrified, at the beginning, of being unmasked for what I am: a middle-class journalist setting out to explore the world that welfare mothers are entering, at the rate of approximately 50,000 a month, as welfare reform kicks in. Happily, though, my fears turn out to be entirely unwarranted: during a month of poverty and toil, my name goes unnoticed and for the most part unuttered. In this parallel universe where my father never got out of the mines and I never got through college, I am "baby," "honey," "blondie," and, most commonly, "girl."

My first task is to find a place to live. I figure that if I can earn $7 an hour—which, from the want ads, seems doable—I can afford to spend $500 on rent, or maybe, with severe economies, $600. In the Key West area, where I live, this pretty much confines me to flophouses and trailer homes—like the one, a pleasing fifteen-minute drive from town, that has no air-conditioning, no screens, no fans, no television, and, by way of diversion, only the challenge of evading the landlord's Doberman pinscher. The big problem with this place, though, is the rent, which at $675 a month is well beyond my reach. All right, Key West is expensive. But so is New York City, or the Bay Area, or Jackson Hole, or Telluride, or Boston, or any other place where tourists and the wealthy compete for living space with the people who clean their toilets and fry their hash browns.[1] Still, it is a shock to realize that "trailer trash" has become, for me, a demographic category to aspire to.

So I decide to make the common trade-off between affordability and convenience, and go for a $500-a-month efficiency thirty miles up a two-lane highway from the employment opportunities of Key West, meaning forty-five minutes if there's no road construction and I don't get caught behind some sun-dazed

Canadian tourists. I hate the drive, along a roadside studded with white crosses commemorating the more effective head-on collisions, but it's a sweet little place— a cabin, more or less, set in the swampy back yard of the converted mobile home where my landlord, an affable TV repairman, lives with his bartender girlfriend. Anthropologically speaking, a bustling trailer park would be preferable, but here I have a gleaming white floor and a firm mattress, and the few resident bugs are easily vanquished.

Besides, I am not doing this for the anthropology. My aim is nothing so mistily subjective as to "experience poverty" or find out how it "really feels" to be a long-term low-wage worker. I've had enough unchosen encounters with poverty and the world of low-wage work to know it's not a place you want to visit for touristic purposes; it just smells too much like fear. And with all my real-life assets— bank account, IRA, health insurance, multiroom home—waiting indulgently in the background, I am, of course, thoroughly insulated from the terrors that afflict the genuinely poor.

No, this is a purely objective, scientific sort of mission. The humanitarian rationale for welfare reform—as opposed to the more punitive and stingy impulses that may actually have motivated it—is that work will lift poor women out of poverty while simultaneously inflating their self-esteem and hence their future value in the labor market. Thus, whatever the hassles involved in finding child care, transportation, etc., the transition from welfare to work will end happily, in greater prosperity for all. Now there are many problems with this comforting prediction, such as the fact that the economy will inevitably undergo a downturn, eliminating many jobs. Even without a downturn, the influx of a million former welfare recipients into the low-wage labor market could depress wages by as much as 11.9 percent, according to the Economic Policy Institute (EPI) in Washington, D.C.

But is it really possible to make a living on the kinds of jobs currently available to unskilled people? Mathematically, the answer is no, as can be shown by taking $6 to $7 an hour, perhaps subtracting a dollar or two an hour for child care, multiplying by 160 hours a month, and comparing the result to the prevailing rents. According to the National Coalition for the Homeless, for example, in 1998 it took, on average nationwide, an hourly wage of $8.89 to afford a one-bedroom apartment, and the Preamble Center for Public Policy estimates that the odds against a typical welfare recipient's landing a job at such a "living wage" are about 97 to 1. If these numbers are right, low-wage work is not a solution to poverty and possibly not even to homelessness.

It may seem excessive to put this proposition to an experimental test. As certain family members keep unhelpfully reminding me, the viability of low-wage work could be tested, after a fashion, without ever leaving my study. I could just pay myself $7 an hour for eight hours a day, charge myself for room and board, and total up the numbers after a month. Why leave the people and work that I love? But I am an experimental scientist by training. In that business, you don't just sit at a desk and theorize; you plunge into the everyday chaos of nature, where surprises lurk in the most mundane measurements. Maybe, when I got into it, I would discover some hidden economies in the world of the low-wage worker. After all, if 30 percent of the workforce toils for less than $8 an hour, according to the EPI, they may have found some tricks as yet unknown to me. Maybe—who knows?—I would even be able to detect in myself the bracing psychological effects of getting out of the house, as promised by the welfare wonks at places like the Heritage Foundation. Or, on the other hand, maybe there would be unexpected costs—physical, mental, or financial—to throw off all my calculations. Ideally, I should do this with two small children in tow, that being the welfare average, but mine are grown and no one is willing to lend me theirs for a month-long vacation in penury. So this is not the perfect experiment, just a test of the best possible case: an unencumbered woman, smart and even strong, attempting to live more or less off the land.

On the morning of my first full day of job searching, I take a red pen to the want ads, which are auspiciously numerous. Everyone in Key West's booming "hospitality industry" seems to be looking for someone like me—trainable, flexible, and with suitably humble expectations as to pay. I know I possess certain traits that might be advantageous—I'm white and, I like to think, well-spoken and poised—but I decide on two rules: One, I cannot use any skills derived from my education or usual work—not that there are a lot of want ads for satirical essayists anyway. Two, I have to take the best-paid job that is offered me and of course do my best to hold it; no Marxist rants or sneaking off to read novels in the ladies' room. In addition, I rule out various occupations for one reason or another: Hotel front-desk clerk, for example, which to my surprise is regarded as unskilled and pays around $7 an hour, gets eliminated because it involves standing in one spot for eight hours a day. Waitressing is similarly something I'd like to avoid, because I remember it leaving me bone tired when I was eighteen, and I'm decades of varicosities and back pain beyond that now. Telemarketing, one of the first refuges of the suddenly indigent, can be dismissed on grounds of personality. This leaves certain supermarket jobs, such as deli clerk, or housekeeping in Key West's thousands of hotel and guest rooms. Housekeeping is especially appealing, for reasons both atavistic and practical: it's what my mother did before I came along, and it can't be too different from what I've been doing part-time, in my own home, all my life.

So I put on what I take to be a respectful-looking outfit of ironed Bermuda shorts and scooped-neck T-shirt and set out for a tour of the local hotels and supermarkets. Best Western, Econo Lodge, and HoJo's all let me fill out application forms, and these are, to my relief, interested in little more than whether I am a legal resident of the United States and have committed any felonies. My next stop is Winn-Dixie, the supermarket, which turns out to have a particularly onerous application process, featuring a fifteen-minute "interview" by computer since, apparently, no human on the premises is deemed capable of representing the corporate point of view. I am conducted to a large room decorated with posters illustrating how to look "professional" (it helps to be white and, if female, permed) and warning of the slick promises that union organizers might try to tempt me with. The interview is multiple choice: Do I have anything, such as child-care problems, that might make it hard for me to get to work on time? Do I think safety on the job is the responsibility of management? Then, popping up cunningly out of the blue: How many dollars' worth of stolen goods have I purchased in the last year? Would I turn in a fellow employee if I caught him stealing? Finally, "Are you an honest person?"

Apparently, I ace the interview, because I am told that all I have to do is show up in some doctor's office tomorrow for a urine test. This seems to be a fairly general rule: if you want to stack Cheerio boxes or vacuum hotel rooms in chemically fascist America, you have to be willing to squat down and pee in front of some health worker (who has no doubt had to do the same thing herself). The wages Winn-Dixie is offering—$6 and a couple of dimes to start with—are not enough, I decide, to compensate for this indignity.[2]

I lunch at Wendy's, where $4.99 gets you unlimited refills at the Mexican part of the Superbar, a comforting surfeit of refried beans and "cheese sauce." A teenage employee, seeing me studying the want ads, kindly offers me an application form, which I fill out, though here, too, the pay is just $6 and change an hour. Then it's off for a round of the locally owned inns and guesthouses. At "The Palms," let's call it, a bouncy manager actually takes me around to see the rooms and meet the existing housekeepers, who, I note with satisfaction, look pretty much like me—faded ex-hippie types in shorts with long hair pulled back in braids. Mostly, though, no one speaks to me or even looks at me except to proffer an application form. At my last stop, a palatial B&B, I wait twenty minutes to meet "Max," only to be told that there are no jobs now but there should be one soon, since "nobody lasts more than a couple weeks." (Because none of the people I talked to knew I was a reporter, I have changed their names to protect their privacy and, in some cases perhaps, their jobs.)

Three days go by like this, and, to my chagrin, no one out of the approximately twenty places I've applied calls me for an interview. I had been vain enough to worry about coming across as too educated for the jobs I sought, but no one even seems interested in finding out how overqualified I am. Only later will I realize that the want ads are not a reliable measure of the actual jobs available at any particular time. They are, as I should have guessed from Max's comment, the employers' insurance policy against the relentless turnover of the low-wage workforce. Most of the big hotels run ads almost continually, just to build a supply of applicants to replace the current workers as they drift away or are fired, so finding a job is just a matter of being at the right place at the right time and flexible enough to take whatever is being offered that day. This finally happens to me at a one of the big discount hotel chains, where I go, as usual, for housekeeping and am sent, instead, to try out as a waitress at the attached "family restaurant," a dismal spot with a counter and about thirty tables that looks out on a parking garage and features such tempting fare as "Pollish [sic] sausage and BBQ sauce" on 95-degree days. Phillip, the dapper young West Indian who introduces himself as the manager, interviews me with about as much enthusiasm as if he were a clerk processing me for Medicare, the principal questions being what shifts can I work and when can I start. I mutter something about being woefully out of practice as a waitress, but he's already on to the uniform: I'm to show up tomorrow wearing black slacks and black shoes; he'll provide the rust-colored polo shirt with HEARTHSIDE embroidered on it, though I might want to wear my own shirt to get to work, ha ha. At the word "tomorrow," something between fear and indignation rises in my chest. I want to say, "Thank you for your time, sir, but this is just an experiment, you know, not my actual life."

So begins my career at the Hearthside, I shall call it, one small profit center within a global discount hotel chain, where for two weeks I work from 2:00 till 10:00 P.M. for $2.43 an hour plus tips.[3] In some futile bid for gentility, the management has barred employees from using the front door, so my first day I enter through the kitchen, where a red-faced man with shoulder-length blond hair is throwing frozen steaks against the wall and yelling, "Fuck this shit!" "That's just Jack," explains Gail, the wiry middle-aged waitress who is assigned to train me. "He's on the rag again"— a condition occasioned, in this instance, by the fact that the cook on the morning shift had forgotten to thaw out the steaks. For the next eight hours, I run after the agile Gail, absorbing bits of instruction along with fragments of personal tragedy. All food must be trayed, and the reason she's so tired today is that she woke up in a cold sweat thinking of her boyfriend, who killed himself recently in an upstate prison. No refills on lemonade. And the reason he was in prison is that a few DUIs caught up with him, that's all, could have happened to anyone. Carry the creamers to the table in a monkey bowl, never in your hand. And after he was gone she spent several months living in her truck, peeing in a plastic pee bottle and reading by candlelight at night, but you can't live in a truck in the summer, since you need to have the windows down, which means anything can get in, from mosquitoes on up.

At least Gail puts to rest any fears I had of appearing overqualified. From the first day on, I find that of all the things I have left behind, such as home and identity, what I miss the most is competence. Not that I have ever felt utterly competent in the writing business, in which one day's success augurs nothing at all for the next. But in my writing life, I at least have some notion of procedure: do the research, make the outline, rough out a draft, etc. As a server, though, I am beset by requests like bees: more iced tea here, ketchup over there, a to go box for table fourteen, and where are the high chairs, anyway? Of the twenty-seven tables, up to six are usually mine at any time, though on slow afternoons or if Gail is off, I sometimes have the whole place to myself. There is the touch-screen computer-ordering system to master, which is, I suppose, meant to minimize server-cook contact, but in practice requires constant verbal fine-tuning: "That's gravy on the mashed, okay? None on the meatloaf," and so forth—while the cook scowls as if I were inventing these refinements just to torment him. Plus, something I had forgotten in the years since I was eighteen: about a third of a server's job is "side work" that's invisible to customers—sweeping, scrubbing, slicing, refilling, and restocking. If it isn't all done, every little bit of it, you're going to face the 6:00 P.M. dinner rush defenseless and probably go down in flames. I screw up dozens of times at the beginning, sustained in my shame entirely by Gail's support— "It's okay, baby, everyone does that sometime"—because, to my total surprise and despite the scientific detachment I am doing my best to maintain, I care.

The whole thing would be a lot easier if I could just skate through it as Lily Tomlin in one of her waitress skits, but I was raised by the absurd Booker T. Washingtonian precept that says: If you're going to do something, do it well. In fact, "well" isn't good enough by half. Do it better than anyone has ever done it before.

Or so said my father, who must have known what he was talking about because he managed to pull himself, and us with him, up from the mile-deep copper mines of Butte to the leafy suburbs of the Northeast, ascending from boilermakers to martinis before booze beat out ambition. As in most endeavors I have encountered in my life, doing it "better than anyone" is not a reasonable goal. Still, when I wake up at 4:00 A.M. in my own cold sweat, I am not thinking about the writing deadlines I'm neglecting; I'm thinking about the table whose order I screwed up so that one of the boys didn't get his kiddie meal until the rest of the family had moved on to their Key Lime pies. That's the other powerful motivation I hadn't expected—the customers, or "patients," as I can't help thinking of them on account of the mysterious vulnerability that seems to have left them temporarily unable to feed themselves. After a few days at the Hearthside, I feel the service ethic kick in like a shot of oxytocin, the nurturance hormone. The plurality of my customers are hard-working locals—truck drivers, construction workers, even housekeepers from the attached hotel—and I want them to have the closest to a "fine dining" experience that the grubby circumstances will allow. No "you guys" for me; everyone over twelve is "sir" or "ma'am." I ply them with iced tea and coffee refills; I return, mid-meal, to inquire how everything is; I doll up their salads with chopped raw mushrooms, summer squash slices, or whatever bits of produce I can find that have survived their sojourn in the cold-storage room mold-free.

There is Benny, for example, a short, tight-muscled sewer repairman, who cannot even think of eating until he has absorbed a half hour of air-conditioning and ice water. We chat about hyperthermia and electrolytes until he is ready to order some finicky combination like soup of the day, garden salad, and a side of grits. There are the German tourists who are so touched by my pidgin "Willkommen" and "Ist alles gut?" that they actually tip. (Europeans, spoiled by their trade-union-ridden, high-wage welfare states, generally do not know that they are supposed to tip. Some restaurants, the Hearthside included, allow servers to "grat" their foreign customers, or add a tip to the bill. Since this amount is added before the customers have a chance to tip or not tip, the practice amounts to an automatic penalty for imperfect English.) There are the two dirt-smudged lesbians, just off their construction shift, who are impressed enough by my suave handling of the fly in the pina colada that they take the time to praise me to Stu, the assistant manager. There's Sam, the kindly retired cop, who has to plug up his tracheotomy hole with one finger in order to force the cigarette smoke into his lungs.

Sometimes I play with the fantasy that I am a princess who, in penance for some tiny transgression, has undertaken to feed each of her subjects by hand. But the non-princesses working with me are just as indulgent, even when this means flouting management rules—concerning, for example, the number of croutons that can go on a salad (six). "Put on all you want," Gail whispers, "as long as Stu isn't looking," She dips into her own tip money to buy biscuits and gravy for an out-of-work mechanic who's used up all his money on dental surgery, inspiring me to pick up the tab for his milk and pie. Maybe the same high levels of agape can be found throughout the "hospitality industry." I remember the poster decorating one of the apartments I looked at, which said "If you seek happiness for yourself you will never find it. Only when you seek happiness for others will it come to you," or words to that effect—an odd sentiment, it seemed to me at the time, to find in the dank one-room basement apartment of a bellhop at the Best Western. At the Hearthside, we utilize whatever bits of autonomy we have to ply our customers with the illicit calories that signal our love. It is our job as servers to assemble the salads and desserts, pouring the dressings and squirting the whipped cream. We also control the number of butter patties our customers get and the amount of sour cream on their baked potatoes. So if you wonder why Americans are so obese, consider the fact that waitresses both express their humanity and earn their tips through the covert distribution of fats.

Ten days into it, this is beginning to look like a livable lifestyle. I like Gail, who is "looking at fifty" but moves so fast she can alight in one place and then another without apparently being anywhere between them. I clown around with Lionel, the teenage Haitian busboy, and catch a few fragments of conversation with Joan, the svelte fortyish hostess and militant feminist who is the only one of us who dares to tell Jack to shut the fuck up. I even warm up to Jack when, on a slow night and to make up for a particularly unwarranted attack on my abilities, or so I imagine, he tells me about his glory days as a young man at "coronary school"—or do you say "culinary"?—in Brooklyn, where he dated a knock-out Puerto Rican chick and learned everything there is to know about food. I finish up at 10:00 or 10:30, depending on how much side work I've been able to get done during the shift, and cruise home to the tapes I snatched up at random when I left my real home— Marianne Faithfull, Tracy Chapman, Enigma, King Sunny Ade, the Violent Femmes—just drained enough for the music to set my cranium resonating but hardly dead. Midnight snack is Wheat Thins and Monterey Jack, accompanied by cheap white wine on ice and whatever AMC has to offer. To bed by 1:30 or 2:00, up at 9:00 or 10:00, read for an hour while my uniform whirls around in the landlord's washing machine, and then it's another eight hours spent following Mao's central instruction, as laid out in the Little Red Book, which was: Serve the people.

I could drift along like this, in some dreamy proletarian idyll, except for two things. One is management. If I have kept this subject on the margins thus far it is because I still flinch to think that I spent all those weeks under the surveillance of men (and later women) whose job it was to monitor my behavior for signs of sloth, theft, drug abuse, or worse. Not that managers and especially "assistant managers" in low-wage settings like this are exactly the class enemy. In the restaurant business, they are mostly former cooks or servers, still capable of pinch-hitting in the kitchen or on the floor, just as in hotels they are likely to be former clerks, and paid a salary of only about $400 a week. But everyone knows they have crossed over to the other side, which is, crudely put, corporate as opposed to human. Cooks want to prepare tasty meals; servers want to serve them graciously; but managers are there for only one reason—to make sure that money is made for some theoretical entity that exists far away in Chicago or New York, if a corporation can be said to have a physical existence at all. Reflecting on her career, Gail tells me ruefully that she had sworn, years ago, never to work for a corporation again. "They don't cut you no slack. You give and you give, and they take."

Managers can sit—for hours at a time if they want—but it's their job to see that no one else ever does, even when there's nothing to do, and this is why, for servers, slow times can be as exhausting as rushes. You start dragging out each little chore, because if the manager on duty catches you in an idle moment, he will give you something far nastier to do. So I wipe, I clean, I consolidate ketchup bottles and recheck the cheesecake supply, even tour the tables to make sure the customer evaluation forms are all standing perkily in their places—wondering all the time how many calories I burn in these strictly theatrical exercises. When, on a particularly dead afternoon, Stu finds me glancing at a *USA Today* a customer has left behind, he assigns me to vacuum the entire floor with the broken vacuum cleaner that has a handle only two feet long, and the only way to do that without incurring orthopedic damage is to proceed from spot to spot on your knees.

On my first Friday at the Hearthside there is a "mandatory meeting for all restaurant employees," which I attend, eager for insight into our overall marketing strategy and the niche (your basic Ohio cuisine with a tropical twist?) we aim to inhabit. But there is no "we" at this meeting. Phillip, our top manager except for an occasional "consultant" sent out by corporate headquarters, opens it with a sneer: "The break room—it's disgusting. Butts in the ashtrays, newspapers lying around, crumbs." This windowless little room, which also houses the time clock for the entire hotel, is where we stash our bags and civilian clothes and take our half-hour meal breaks. But a break room is not a right, he tells us. It can be taken away. We should also know that the lockers in the break room and whatever is in them can be searched at any time. Then comes gossip; there has been gossip; gossip (which seems to mean employees talking among themselves) must stop. Off-duty employees are henceforth barred from eating at the restaurant, because "other servers gather around them and gossip." When Phillip has exhausted his agenda of rebukes, Joan complains about the condition of the ladies' room and I throw in my two bits about the vacuum cleaner. But I don't see any backup coming from my fellow servers, each of whom has subsided into her own personal funk; Gail, my role model, stares sorrowfully at a point six inches from her nose. The meeting ends when Andy, one of the cooks, gets up, muttering about breaking up his day off for this almighty bullshit.

Just four days later we are suddenly summoned into the kitchen at 3:30 P.M., even though there are live tables on the floor. We all—about ten of us—stand around Phillip, who announces grimly that there has been a report of some "drug activity" on the night shift and that, as a result, we are now to be a "drug-free" workplace, meaning that all new hires will be tested, as will possibly current employees on a random basis. I am glad that this part of the kitchen is so dark, because I find myself blushing as hard as if I had been caught toking up in the ladies' room myself. I haven't been treated this way—lined up in the corridor, threatened with locker searches, peppered with carelessly aimed accusations—since junior high school. Back on the floor, Joan cracks, "Next they'll be telling us we can't have sex on the job." When I ask Stu what happened to inspire the crackdown, he just mutters about "management decisions" and takes the opportunity to upbraid Gail and me for being too generous with the rolls. From now on there's to be only one per customer, and it goes out with the dinner, not with the salad. He's also been riding the cooks, prompting Andy to come out of the kitchen and observe—with the serenity of a man whose customary implement is a butcher knife—that "Stu has a death wish today."

Later in the evening, the gossip crystallizes around the theory that Stu is himself the drug culprit, that he uses the restaurant phone to order up marijuana and sends one of the late servers out to fetch it for him. The server was caught, and she may have ratted Stu out or at least said enough to cast some suspicion on him, thus accounting for his pissy behavior. Who knows? Lionel, the busboy, entertains us for the rest of the shift by standing just behind Stu's back and sucking deliriously on an imaginary joint.

The other problem, in addition to the less-than-nurturing management style, is that this job shows no sign of being financially viable. You might imagine, from a comfortable distance, that people who live, year in and year out, on $6 to $10 an hour have discovered some survival stratagems unknown to the middle class. But no. It's not hard to get my co-workers to talk about their living situations, because housing, in almost every case, is the principal source of disruption in their lives, the first thing they fill you in on when they arrive for their shifts. After a week, I have compiled the following survey:

- Gail is sharing a room in a well-known downtown flophouse for which she and a roommate pay about $250 a week. Her roommate, a male friend, has begun hitting on her, driving her nuts, but the rent would be impossible alone.
- Claude, the Haitian cook, is desperate to get out of the two-room apartment he shares with his girlfriend and two other, unrelated, people. As far as I can determine, the other Haitian men (most of whom only speak Creole) live in similarly crowded situations.
- Annette, a twenty-year-old server who is six months pregnant and has been abandoned by her boyfriend, lives with her mother, a postal clerk.
- Marianne and her boyfriend are paying $170 a week for a one-person trailer.
- Jack, who is, at $10 an hour, the wealthiest of us, lives in the trailer he owns, paying only the $400-a-month lot fee.
- The other white cook, Andy, lives on his dry-docked boat, which, as far as I can tell from his loving descriptions, can't be more than twenty feet long. He offers to take me out on it, once it's repaired, but the offer comes with inquiries as to my marital status, so I do not follow up on it.
- Tina and her husband are paying $60 a night for a double room in a Days Inn. This is because they have no car and the Days Inn is within walking distance of the Hearthside. When Marianne, one of the breakfast servers, is tossed out of her trailer for subletting (which is against the trailer-park rules), she leaves her boyfriend and moves in with Tina and her husband.
- Joan, who had fooled me with her numerous and tasteful outfits (hostesses wear their own clothes), lives in a van she parks behind a shopping center at night and showers in Tina's motel room. The clothes are from thrift shops.[4]

It strikes me, in my middle-class solipsism, that there is gross improvidence in some of these arrangements. When Gail and I are wrapping silverware in napkins—the only task for which we are permitted to sit—she tells me she is thinking of escaping from her roommate by moving into the Days Inn herself. I am astounded: How can she even think of paying between $40 and $60 a day? But if I was afraid of sounding like a social worker, I come out just sounding like a fool. She squints at me in disbelief, "And where am I supposed to get a month's rent and a month's deposit for an apartment?" I'd been feeling pretty smug about my $500 efficiency, but of course it was made possible only by the $1,300 I had allotted myself for start-up costs when I began my low-wage life: $1,000 for the first month's rent and deposit, $100 for initial groceries and cash in my pocket, $200 stuffed away for emergencies. In poverty, as in certain propositions in physics, starting conditions are everything.

There are no secret economies that nourish the poor; on the contrary, there are a host of special costs. If you can't put up the two months' rent you need to secure an apartment, you end up paying through the nose for a room by the week. If you have only a room, with a hot plate at best, you can't save by cooking up huge lentil stews that can be frozen for the week ahead. You eat fast food, or the hot dogs and styrofoam cups of soup that can be microwaved in a convenience store. If you have no money for health insurance—and the Hearthside's niggardly plan kicks in only after three months—you go without routine care or prescription drugs and end up paying the price. Gail, for example, was fine until she ran out of money for estrogen pills. She is supposed to be on the company plan by now, but they claim to have lost her application form and need to begin the paperwork all over again. So she spends $9 per migraine pill to control the headaches she wouldn't have, she insists, if her estrogen supplements were covered. Similarly, Marianne's boyfriend lost his job as a roofer because he missed so much time after getting a cut on his foot for which he couldn't afford the prescribed antibiotic.

My own situation, when I sit down to assess it after two weeks of work, would not be much better if this were my actual life. The seductive thing about waitressing is that you don't have to wait for payday to feel a few bills in your pocket, and my tips usually cover meals and gas, plus something left over to stuff into the kitchen drawer I use as a bank. But as the tourist business slows in the summer heat, I sometimes leave work with only $20 in tips (the gross is higher, but servers share about 15 percent of their tips with the busboys and bartenders). With wages included, this amounts to about the minimum wage of $5.15 an hour. Although the sum in the drawer is piling up, at the present rate of accumulation it will be more than a hundred dollars short of my rent when the end of the month comes around. Nor can I see any expenses to cut. True, I haven't gone the lentil stew route yet, but that's because I don't have a large cooking pot, pot holders, or a ladle to stir with (which cost about $30 at Kmart, less at thrift stores), not to mention onions, carrots, and the indispensable bay leaf. I do make my lunch almost every day—usually some slow-burning, high-protein combo like frozen chicken patties with melted cheese on top and canned pinto beans on the side. Dinner is at the Hearthside, which offers its employees a choice of BLT, fish sandwich, or hamburger for only $2.

The burger lasts longest, especially if it's heaped with gut-puckering jalapeños, but by midnight my stomach is growling again. . . .

How former welfare recipients and single mothers will (and do) survive in the low-wage workforce, I cannot imagine. Maybe they will figure out how to condense their lives—including child-raising, laundry, romance, and meals—into the couple of hours between full-time jobs. Maybe they will take up residence in their vehicles, if they have one. All I know is that I couldn't hold two jobs and I couldn't make enough money to live on with one. And I had advantages unthinkable to many of the long-term poor—health, stamina, a working car, and no children to care for and support. Certainly nothing in my experience contradicts the conclusion of Kathryn Edin and Laura Lein, in their recent book *Making Ends Meet: How Single Mothers Survive Welfare and Low-Wage Work,* that low-wage work actually involves more hardship and deprivation than life at the mercy of the welfare state. In the coming months and years, economic conditions for the working poor are bound to worsen, even without the almost inevitable recession. As mentioned earlier, the influx of former welfare recipients into the low-skilled workforce will have a depressing effect on both wages and the number of jobs available. A general economic downturn will only enhance these effects, and the working poor will of course be facing it without the slight, but nonetheless often saving, protection of welfare as a backup.

The thinking behind welfare reform was that even the humblest jobs are morally uplifting and psychologically buoying. In reality they are likely to be fraught with insult and stress. But I did discover one redeeming feature of the most abject low-wage work—the camaraderie of people who are, in almost all cases, far too smart and funny and caring for the work they do and the wages they're paid. The hope, of course, is that someday these people will come to know what they're worth, and take appropriate action.

ENDNOTES

1. According to the Department of Housing and Urban Development, the "fair-market rent" for an efficiency is $551 here in Monroe County, Florida. A comparable rent in the five boroughs of New York City is $704; in San Francisco, $713; and in the heart of Silicon Valley, $808. The fair-market rent for an area is defined as the amount that would be needed to pay rent plus utilities for "privately owned, decent, safe, and sanitary rental housing of a modest (non-luxury) nature with suitable amenities."

2. According to the *Monthly Labor Review* (November 1996), 28 percent of work sites surveyed in the service industry conduct drug tests (corporate workplaces have much higher rates), and the incidence of testing has risen markedly since the Eighties. The rate of testing is highest in the South (56 percent of work sites polled), with the Midwest in second place (50 percent). The drug most likely to be detected—marijuana, which can be detected in urine for weeks—is also the most innocuous, while heroin and cocaine are generally undetectable three days after use. Prospective employees sometimes try to cheat the tests by consuming excess amounts of liquids and taking diuretics and even masking substances available through the Internet.

3. According to the Fair Labor Standards Act, employers are not required to pay "tipped employees," such as restaurant servers, more than $2.13 an hour in direct wages. However, if the sum of tips plus $2.13 an hour falls below the minimum wage, or $5.15 an hour, the employer is required to make up the difference. This fact was not mentioned by managers or otherwise publicized at either of the restaurants where I worked.

4. I could find no statistics on the number of employed people living in cars or vans, but according to the National Coalition for the Homeless's 1997 report "Myths and Facts About Homelessness," nearly one in five homeless people (in twenty-nine cities across the nation) is employed in a full- or part-time job.

CHAPTER 6

Generation Broke
The Growth of Debt among Young Americans

Tamara Draut
Javier Silva

INTRODUCTION

The average credit card debt of Americans aged 25 to 34 years old increased by 55 percent between 1992 and 2001, to a self-reported household average of $4,088. Estimates of card debt based on aggregate data put the dollar amount as much as three times higher.[2] This age group's bankruptcy rate grew by 19 percent over the same period—so that by 2001 nearly 12 out of every 1,000 young adults were filing for bankruptcy.[3] Young adults now have the second highest rate of bankruptcy, just after those aged 35 to 44. Their rate of bankruptcy is higher than it was for young Boomers who were 25–34 years old in 1991.

Why are today's young adults going into debt and going broke? During the boom of the 1990s, the popular media showered attention on the rising fortunes of Generation X, who appeared to be riding the tech boom to great heights. However, in 2001 adults aged 25 to 34 were showing signs that the path to adulthood had become more financially perilous than it was for the previous generation of late Baby Boomers in 1992. The major adult costs that begin to mount between the ages of 25 and 34—housing, child care, and health care—have all increased dramatically over the past decade. And the rising unemployment, slow real wage growth, and skyrocketing tuition and resulting student loan debts have combined to erode the economic security of today's young adults. Additionally, just at this time the newly-deregulated credit industry began aggressively marketing to young people on college campuses. Deregulation also brought higher rates and fees, making it increasingly difficult for young Americans to get out of debt. . . .

DEMOS' FINDINGS ON CREDIT CARD DEBT AMONG YOUNGER AMERICANS, 1992–2001

Prevalence of Credit Cards and Indebtedness. Nearly 7 out of 10 young Americans aged 25 to 34 have one or more credit cards, a level basically unchanged since 1992. Compared to the population as a whole, however, young adult cardholders are much more likely to be in debt: 71 percent of young adult cardholders revolve their balances, compared to 55 percent of all cardholders.

Higher Balances. Credit card debt among young adults has increased significantly since 1992, outpacing the rise among the population as a whole (Table 6.1). The average credit card debt among indebted 25 to 34 year olds increased by 55 percent, to $4,088.

Debt by Income Level. All but the lowest-income young households experienced dramatic increases in credit card debt over the decade. Middle-income young adults experienced the fastest growth of any income group. Credit card debt rose 37 percent among moderate-income young adults earning between $10,000 and $24,999 (Figure 6.1). Middle-income young adults—those with incomes between $25,000 and $49,999—experienced a 65 percent increase in credit card debt. Upper middle-income young adults with incomes between $50,000 and $74,999 experienced a 55 percent increase in debt (Figure 6.2).

Debt Service-to-Income Ratio. The true financial impact of debt is best understood by examining the percentage of income young adults must devote to debt payments, which is typically called the debt service-to-income ratio. Debt service-to-income ratios have been steadily rising for young Americans since 1992, when the average ratio for indebted young adults was 19. By 2001, the average debt service-to-income ratio for 25 to 34 year olds had risen to 24 percent—meaning that the average indebted young American spends nearly a quarter of every dollar earned servicing debt. However, the debt service-to-income ratio severely underestimates the financial burdens facing young Americans in several ways. First, the ratio only measures outstanding mortgage and consumer debt, such as credit cards and auto loans—excluding what is often a young household's largest expense: rent. Second, since the figure doesn't include auto lease payments, the cost of a car may

TABLE 6.1 Average Credit Card Debt among Young Households with Credit Card Debt (2001 dollars)

	1992	2001	% Change 1992–2001
All households	$2,991	$4,126	38%
Aged 25–34	$2,640	$4,088	55%

Source: Demos' Calculations from the 1992 and 2001 Survey of Consumer Finances

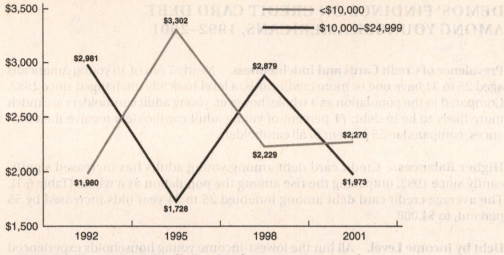

FIGURE 6.1   Average Credit Card Debt among Low- and Moderate-Income Adults Aged 25 to 34 (in 2001 dollars)

not be reflected in the ratio. Finally, the ratio significantly underestimates credit card debt burden because it can only measure the minimum payment burden—which is typically 2½ percent of the total outstanding balance. That means that a credit card debt of $10,000 is counted as $250 in debt service. But the key to paying off credit card debt is making more than the minimum payment. If a young American were to only pay the minimum on a $10,000 balance with a 15% APR, it would take them more than 39 years and cost them over $16,000 in interest charges.

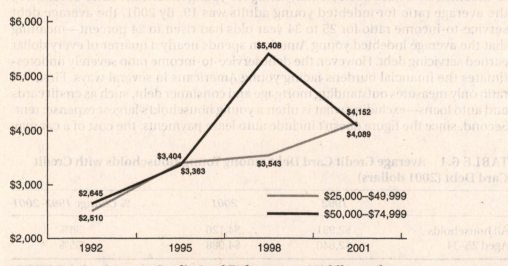

FIGURE 6.2   Average Credit Card Debt among Middle- and Upper-Middle-Income Adults Aged 25 to 34

TABLE 6.2 **Percent of Credit Card Indebted Young Americans Aged 25 to 34 in Debt Hardship (Debt Payment to Income Ratio >40%)**

Income Group (25–34)	1992	2001
Overall	7.9%	13.3%
Income Group		
Under $10,000	37.1%	57.6%
$10,000–$24,999	8.4	22.3
$25,000–$49,999	6.7	13.4
$50,000–$74,999	7.8	5.2

Source: Demos' Calculations from the 1992 and 2001 Survey of Consumer Finances

Debt Hardship. A family spending more than 40 percent of their income on debt payments, including mortgages and student loan debt, is traditionally considered in a state of *debt hardship*. Overall, 13 percent of indebted young Americans experience debt hardship—nearly double the percentage in 1992. Lowest income households are the most likely to be in debt hardship, but middle-income young adults are also experiencing higher levels of debt hardship. About 13 percent of indebted young adults with incomes between $10,000 and $75,000 are in debt hardship (see Table 6.2). Young adults are having a harder time making payments, too. Nearly 1 out of 5 . . . reported being late or missing payments within the last year on any loan, up from 1 out of every 6 in 1992.

WHAT IS DRIVING DEBT?

Several factors may be driving the rise in credit card debt among young adults. In many ways, young families are just like other households—often their paychecks are just enough to cover the rent, groceries and car payment, so that any additional or unexpected expense is financed through credit. But there are unique economic circumstances that may contribute to young adults' greater reliance on credit cards to make ends meet. Young adults are often still servicing student loan debt, have higher unemployment rates and earn lower, entry-level wages. Likewise, today's young adults have come of financial age during an era of banking deregulation that has dramatically increased the availability and cost of credit.

Slow Real Wage Growth. The earnings of 25 to 34 year olds have not kept up with inflation or the costs of basic necessities including housing, healthcare and student loan repayment obligations. Between 1992 and 2001, the median annual earnings of all male workers grew by 5 percent in real terms (see Table 6.3). Female workers made greater gains in their annual earnings, which rose by 6.7 percent in real terms. Both male and female workers with bachelor's degrees made greater gains than their non-degree holding counterparts. However, given the higher amounts of debt borrowed by those attending college in the 1990s, much of the annual earnings advantage by young college workers is diminished by debt service.

In 2001, the average starting salary for college grads was about $36,000, with wide variations among different fields.[4] Salaries in marketing started at $34,000,

TABLE 6.3   Median Annual Earnings of All Wage and Salary Workers Age 25 to 34 (in 2002 dollars)

	Males			Females		
	All Males	**Some College**	**Bachelor's Degree or Higher**	**All Females**	**Some College**	**Bachelor's Degree or Higher**
1992	$34,051	$34,024	$45,756	$27,834	$27,134	$36,177
2001	35,778	35,598	48,782	29,723	26,769	38,331
2002	35,487	35,552	48,955	30,093	26,828	40,021

Source: National Center for Education Statistics, based on data from US Department of Commerce, Bureau of the Census. March Current Population Surveys, 1972–2003.

advertising jobs started at $28,000, and education majors got on average $39,000 out of the gate. It would be valuable to break down the budget for a typical college grad in 2001 (see Figure 6.3).

$2,058	Monthly Take Home Pay
	($36,000 a year, average starting salary of college grads in 2001, minus taxes and a monthly health care contribution of $42)

Absolute Expenses

$182	Student Loan Monthly Payment
	(average monthly student loan payment reported by undergraduate borrowers)
$797	Rent and Utilities
	(median monthly rent for single, college educated adults in 2000)
$456	Food and Groceries
	(average monthly amount spent on food by 25–34 year olds, 2001)
$464	Transportation
	(average monthly amount for car, auto repairs, insurance and gas)
$125	Credit Card Minimum Payment
	(average credit card debt of 25–34 year olds; $4,008 balance at 16% APR)
= $1,933	Total Monthly Expenses

Money Left Over for Everything Else

$34	For child care, entertainment, clothing, furniture, Internet access, etc.

FIGURE 6.3   Sample Budget for Recent College Graduate

The sample budget . . . is for an average college graduate earning about $36,000. The budget makes conservative estimates and does not include expenses for entertainment, clothing, furniture or even household cleaning supplies or toiletries. At the end of the month, our average college grad has just $34 unaccounted for by monthly bills. That money must cover any additional expenses, such as car repairs, new work clothes or even a movie.

Under- and Un-Employment.   Today's young adults are entering a labor market radically different from that of their parents. Many young adults are part of the new contingent labor force, working in temporary jobs that pay less than full-time permanent positions and don't offer health or pension benefits. In 1999, one out of four contingent workers* was between the ages of 25 and 34, a higher percentage than any other age group.[6] College graduates make up the largest percentage of contingent workers, with nearly 38 percent holding bachelor's degrees or higher. Young adults under 24 tend to prefer their contingent arrangement to a full-time job, usually because they're balancing work and school. But the large majority of contingent workers over age 25 would prefer a full-time job.[7]

Not only are young adults frequently *under*-employed, they are also more likely to be unemployed, because young workers have less job tenure. The recent recession has been particularly bad for younger workers, as their unemployment rate rose faster than that of older workers. Almost one in ten young workers were unemployed in mid-2003.[8] Young adults of color face particularly dim prospects in the job market. In 2003, the unemployment rate was 17.9 percent for young African Americans; 9.6 percent for young Latinos and 7.6 percent for young whites.[9] Even during the boom year of 2000, young African Americans' unemployment rate was more than double that of young whites.

Workers with college degrees—who are typically more secure in jobs than those without—have been hit hard since the 2001 recession. In March 2004, the number of unemployed college graduates reached 1.17 million, higher than the number of unemployed high school dropouts. While statistics indicate that college education pays off over the long term, over the short-term many young college grads are finding it difficult to secure jobs.

Student Loan Debt.   This generation is also the first to shoulder the costs of their college primarily through interest-bearing loans rather than grants. Most of the 25 to 34 year olds in the 2001 sample went to college in the 1990s—when college costs increased by an average of 38 percent, borrowing became more common among students, and the amount borrowed grew rapidly.[10] For example, in the 1992–1993 school year, 42 percent of students borrowed money for college. By the end of the decade, almost two-thirds of students had borrowed.[11] A survey of college borrowers conducted by Nellie Mae found that the average college senior graduated with $18,900 in student loans in 2002—taking a big $182 monthly bite out of their paychecks each month.[12] That's more than double the just over $9,000 average loan

---

*The findings presented here are based on the Bureau of Labor Statistics definition of contingent worker: individuals who hold jobs that are temporary and not expected to continue.

amount carried by young adults in the previous generation in 1992.[13] For young adults who pursued graduate degrees, the student loan burdens are even higher: the average combined student loan debt for grad school students is $45,900.[14] Young adults who went to grad school pay an average of $388 per month for student loans, amounting to nearly 13.5 percent of their income.

The average undergraduate student loan debt represents about 9 percent of young adults' income today.[15] The commonly accepted rule, used by credit counselors and lenders, is that total monthly debt payments should not exceed 36 percent of gross income. The debt included would be the rent or mortgage, credit cards, student loans, car leases and any other revolving type of loan. With student loan debt taking up 9 percent of young adults' income on average, that leaves just 27 percent of their paychecks to allocate to rent or a car loan without risking financial hardship —not to mention a damaged credit rating. With one out of every five young adults reporting that they have been late on or missed a loan payment in the past year, it is clear that servicing debt has become increasingly risky, and at a time when credit scores are growing more relevant for employment, housing, and even cell phones.

Aggressive Marketing to College Students.   While many younger Americans are going into debt to make ends meet, aggressive marketing tactics by the credit card industry have helped fuel the use of credit cards. Across college and university campuses at the beginning of each semester, credit card companies engage in "tabling" offering free t-shirts, mugs, pizza, and other incentives for students to fill out credit card applications. These tactics work exceedingly well—a recent study found that 96 percent of college seniors had a credit card. With little or no financial literacy training, many students fall victim to the aggressive marketing tactics offered by credit card companies.

Rising Housing and Transportation Costs.   During the last decade, both home prices and rents have grown faster than inflation. In 2001, 3.2 million households earning between $17,500 and $50,000—which includes the median earnings of today's 25 to 34 year olds—spent more than half their incomes on housing.[16] Compared to the late Boomers in 1992, Generation Xers were spending considerably more on average for rent and transportation, according to Consumer Expenditure Survey data.[17] On average, Gen X renters spent $6,815 annually on rent, about 10 percent more than Boomers of the same age spent in 1992. Young adult households are also spending more on getting around: $8,423 on average for transportation in 2002 compared to $6,820 in 1992 (inflation adjusted dollars).

The Cost of Being Uninsured.   Young adults are much more likely to be uninsured than older workers, putting many young adults at both physical and financial risk. Contrary to popular perception, young adults are not uninsured because they decline coverage from their employer. Only 3 percent of uninsured young workers were offered but declined insurance coverage.[18]

Young adults are more likely to work in jobs that don't offer health care benefits. Nearly half of full-time workers aged 19 to 29 lack job-based health benefits, compared to less than one-third percent of all workers under 65.[19] As a result, young adults are more likely to be uninsured than the population as a whole: approximately

1 in 3 young adults lacks health insurance compared to 1 in 6 Americans overall.[20] Not having health insurance exerts a physical and financial cost on young adults. About half of young adults aged 19 to 29 without health insurance reported having problems paying medical bills.[21]

Child Care Costs.   The ages of 25 to 34 are the prime years when young adults begin to start families. Today, the average woman will have her first child around the age of 25.[22] But unlike three decades ago, today's young families are more likely to have two parents working full-time. Today, mothers with infants are more likely to be working full-time than part-time—adding the expense of child care to the family budget.[23] According to the U.S. Census Bureau, 59 percent of mothers with a child under age 1, and 64 percent of mothers with a child under age 6, are in the workforce. Nationwide, about half of all working families with children under age 13 pay for child care, spending an average of $303 per month, or 9 percent of their earnings.[24] With full-day care ranging from $4,000 to $10,000 a year per child, the cost of child care is a major strain on young families' already tight budgets.

THE YOUNGEST ADULTS: INDEBTED FROM THE START

Today's 18 to 24 year olds are experiencing the pinnacle of two trends fueling the rise in debt: dramatic increases in the cost of college and aggressive marketing of credit cards on college campuses. In this section, we take a closer look at the debt among the youngest adults, those aged 18 to 24.

[P E R S O N A L   S T O R Y]

Randy Carter, Communications Professional, Age 28

Randy Carter got his first credit card from a mail solicitation at age 18. He didn't have to prove any source of income for the $800 credit line, just that he was a student at the University of Wisconsin in Madison. A combination of student loans and a part-time job at a hardware store weren't enough to meet the cost of going to school full-time, so the new Citibank credit card helped make up the difference. After six months of small, steady charges for things like books and meals, Citibank more than doubled Randy's limit to $2,000. Randy then took a new job more in line with his career ambitions that required him to drive around the state. Unfortunately, the non-profit employer didn't reimburse gasoline expenses, so he filled up his tank regularly on his card. "It was clear to the bank that I'd use just about as much credit as they gave me, and that I would make the minimum payment," he realized now. So Citibank doubled his limit again, to $4,000. More offers poured in the mail, and by his senior year, Randy had four cards and was $7,500 in debt. The minimum payments grew to be more than he could handle, so he began using the cash advance checks MBNA sent him to pay Citibank, and vice-versa. These checks carried immediate interest charges in the high twenty percent range, and the result was rapidly rising

(continued)

balances, even when he slowed his purchased. When Randy's older brother learned how deep in debt he was, he took out a low-interest personal loan and paid off most of his debt. "I sent the cards back to be cut up, except for the Citibank card, with a couple thousand dollars on it, because I wanted to take some responsibility for some of my debt," Randy explains.

His first job out of school was with a public television station that could only pay him $9 an hour for 20 hours of work a week, although he put in more than 50 hours a week. "I was committed to the job, and was hoping to translate my effort into a full-time job, which happened, finally, after two years of making under $15,000 a year." Credit continued to fill the gap between his salary and his living expenses, which were low by most standards. His rent in the college town was only $300, but his student loan payments were over $400. He eventually had to put his college loans in forbearance. When Randy finally got his full-time position, the salary was $27,000—lower than expected and with no raise in sight due to a Wisconsin state budget salary freeze.

In September of 2001, Randy decided he needed to take control of his career and his finances and follow a job lead in New York. Taking stock of $18,000 in credit card debt, he paid a $778 establishment fee for a debt settlement company to take $389 a month with the promise of using the savings to settle his debts in three years. Randy's new job at a New York dot com documentary company paid him $650 a week with no benefits, but he was able to live on his brother's couch rent-free. But the city's economy was in a tailspin, and he was laid off four months later. Randy cashed out his retirement savings, taking a substantial penalty to access only a few thousand dollars. He needed the money and couldn't get unemployment benefits for nearly two months because he'd worked in two different states. "I started to have to pay rent, which was a bargain in New York at $500, but with the $389 debt payment, I was left with less than $100 a month to live on. I applied for over 300 jobs and got nothing." When his unemployment ran out, he cobbled together a work week of odd jobs—babysitting, filing, light construction—until finally a temp agency took him on. "By this time, I was severely depressed. I had gone to college and worked hard and had so little to show for it."

After almost a year, he finally got a full-time job in his field, and is now doing better. "It still doesn't pay a fair or sustainable wage for New York, but it is stable and has advanced my career." Randy's bad credit has made getting an apartment of his own nearly impossible. "I've been told to pay the full year's rent up front. If I could do that, would I be so deep in debt?" He's also been told that he would be better off filing for bankruptcy. "I always thought it would be better for me to pay, to honor my debts even when I was unemployed and underemployed. But I've spent over $14,000 in the past 3 years, servicing my debt instead of going to the doctor. I'm 28 years old, and I'm worse than broke."

Credit card debt among 18 to 24 year olds rose sharply over the decade, by 104 percent, to an average of $2,985 in 2001 (see Table 6.4). Although the Survey of Consumer Finances does not survey current students, it is clear that the youngest

TABLE 6.4   Average Credit Card Debt among Young Households with Credit Card Debt (2001 dollars)

	1992	2001	% Change 1992–2001
Aged 18–24	$1,461	$2,985	104%

Source: Demos' Calculations from the 1992 and 2001 Survey of Consumer Finances

adults' increased debt loads are to some extent a result of rising credit card debt among college students. On-campus credit card marketing exploded during the 1990s, as creditors sought to saturate the youth market for the first time.[25] The co-branded college cards and student-conscious advertising and rewards programs were successful: in 2001, fully 83 percent of all undergraduates had at least one credit card. By their senior year, 96 percent of all students have credit cards, carrying an average of six cards. Balances among college students have risen sharply over the last decade. Between 1990 and 1995, one survey found credit debt had shot up 134 percent, from $900 to $2,100.[26] In 2001, college seniors graduated with an average of $3,262 in credit card debt.[27]

Editors' Note: *Notes for this reading can be found in the original source.*

CHAPTER 7

Retirement's Unraveling Safety Net

Dale Russakoff

If it's a clear morning, you can count on seeing 80-year-old Junior K. Paugh strolling streets that tell his life story: Propeller Drive, Fuselage Avenue, Cockpit Street, Compass Road. He's been here more than 60 years, ever since aviation pioneer Glenn L. Martin put him to work making seaplanes and bombers at the defense plant down the road. Franklin D. Roosevelt was president and Martin himself walked the factory floor, urging on workers as the nation went to war.

Out of that perilous time came Paugh's now predictable world. He never is short of money, thanks to Social Security and his company pension that will last as long as he does. Health care costs him next to nothing, thanks to Medicare and retiree health insurance. His Baltimore County home is long paid for, thanks in part to a below-market price of $4,400, a result of wartime subsidies for defense-related housing construction.

"I feel completely secure," says Paugh, no small triumph for the third of 13 children born to farmers in Depression-era Appalachia. The triumph is not only his but also the country's—the fulfillment of a New Deal vision of cradle-to-grave security, underwritten by the federal government and large industrial employers.

That vision is being supplanted by one President Bush calls the Ownership Society, in which the burdens of economic security—and, the president hopes, the rewards—shift back to individuals. Social Security is only one aspect of the shift. The safety net big companies wove for Paugh's generation—long-term employment, pension security, retiree health insurance—has been giving way for so long that its unraveling is mere background accompaniment to Washington's noisy debate over Social Security. But in the lives of most middle-class families, it stays in the foreground, inseparable from the Social Security discussion.

This becomes clear in the company of Junior Paugh, his three children, all in their fifties, and five grandchildren, ages 18 to 35. Their three-generation journey has taken them from Appalachia to suburbia, from government relief to an assembly line to a management track at Sears. Yet, despite the apparent progress, their expectations are sinking: The grandchildren, all three generations agree, have it worse than their parents and grandparents—most dramatically in their prospects for retirement, when all gains and losses come home to roost.

Until now, financial planners have likened retirement security to a three-legged stool: employee pensions, personal savings and Social Security.

For the Paugh grandchildren, the savings leg is effectively gone, reflecting a plunging personal savings rate nationally. In place of Junior Paugh's pension, they have 401(k) plans, under which they—not employers—bear the risk and responsibility of investing enough for retirement. And under Bush's Social Security proposal, their promised benefit could drop significantly.

This is a new order with new givens. Paugh and his co-workers came of age as Democrats who felt protected by their union, their party and their government. His grandchildren are all registered Republicans who feel largely on their own in a world full of risks and responsibilities, and no guarantees. They are willing to give Bush's Ownership Society a try, saying they have no hope that government or employers can or will protect them.

The president is counting on the Ownership Society to do for the Republican Party what the New Deal did for the Democrats—that is, make it the nation's majority party. For now, it is easier to measure what has been lost in security than has been gained in opportunity. But the grandchildren's story is only beginning.

THE WAR GENERATION

If childhood in Western Maryland's Deer Park community during the Depression exposed Paugh early and often to life's hardships, adulthood became one encounter after another with protections government and businesses were erecting against risks his parents had battled on their own.

Paugh got his first job through Uncle Sam, driving a truck for the Civilian Conservation Corps, the New Deal agency that put unemployed people to work preserving natural resources. By the time he went to Glenn L. Martin Co. in 1942, wartime wage controls had led most industrial employers to provide pensions and health insurance—in part to secure their workers' loyalty in an exceptionally tight labor market.

Paugh's job even came with a home. The entrepreneur built whole communities to house his burgeoning workforce, which topped 52,000 in 1942 as military orders soared during World War II. The government subsidized the construction as part of the war effort, and Martin passed on the savings in cheap rent and later, low sales prices.

Initially, Paugh paid $19 a month—including water and electricity—for the house where he still lives at 108 Glider Dr. in Aero Acres, a subdivision built on a former strawberry field. Martin named every street for an airplane part (Left Wing and Right Wing drives had no larger connotation), and everyone lived in an identical 24-by-48-foot bungalow with a hallway, two bedrooms, a bathroom and a spacious living room.

Paugh went off to war in 1943, returning with a Purple Heart for shrapnel wounds in the Battle of Okinawa. He remained faithful to Martin, spurning other offers, including one from the Baltimore Orioles in the 1950s. A lanky lefty, Paugh was a star pitcher for the Martin Bombers, the company's standout industrial league team, but professional baseball had nothing on a factory job in his day. "No security," he explained.

Pitching for the Bombers was its own form of security. Martin was famously fanatical about baseball—he built a verdant field on Eastern Avenue and Wilson Point Road, watching Bombers practices from the wing of a strategically parked airplane. When layoffs began after the Korean War, the Bombers' entire roster was exempt.

In return for this security, Paugh traded away some flexibility. In his days as a "CCC Boy," as he still calls himself, he got $5 of his $30-a-month salary, and the CCC sent the rest home for his parents and 12 siblings.

And he would have received only a small fraction of his $920 monthly pension had he not spent his entire career, 41 years, with one employer—an arrangement dubbed the "invisible handshake." The pension is 40 percent of his retirement income; Social Security pays him $1,373.

Nor would Paugh have retired with lifetime health insurance, under which he pays only $2 for prescription drugs. Because of rising health care costs, retirement experts say, employers now pay as much or more for retiree health insurance—which supplements Medicare—as for pensions.

Another important feature of Junior Paugh's retirement security is his thrift, which was bred into him. "We saved and saved and saved," he said of himself and his wife, who died 10 years ago. Paugh is what his family calls "tight," and proud of it. He does not turn on lights until the afternoon sun all but disappears. "Hey, I'm paying for that," he cracked one day when son Doug stopped by after work and flipped on the living room light. He'd rather sweat than use air conditioning, turning it on only when his children and grandchildren visit. ("It was 110 degrees in the South Pacific and we still won the war," he said.)

In Paugh's day, only the wealthy invested in the stock market; Paugh put his trust in Uncle Sam through the "bond a week" savings plan. He also opened an individual retirement account in the early 1980s, with bank interest rates at 15 percent. Last year, the rate fell below 1 percent. His disappointment with IRAs makes him dubious of young people's faith in the stock market—what goes up, he warns, can come down.

At a recent monthly meeting of the Retirees Association of Martin Marietta, Paugh sat with seven former co-workers whose life experiences were almost identical to his: All 80 or older, all sitting pretty on three-legged retirement stools, and all worried about how their children and grandchildren will get by in old age.

"They spend their money before they make it," Ed Dorsey, 82, said of his children. "I say, 'What do you have for retirement?' They say it's a long way away. But they're all in their fifties!"

All said they regard Social Security as indispensable, and all said they know it cannot sustain their descendants in its current form.

"We're the generation that beat the system," said Elmer Sanders, 83. "Social Security didn't count on us living this long. I tell my wife if I have a stroke, and they put me on life supports, just don't unplug me. If I'm still breathing, the checks keep coming."

THE BOOMERS

For the children of Junior Paugh—Kay, 56, Doug, 54, and Dan, 50—the Social Security debate is only the latest reminder that nowadays few things keep coming.

Doug and Dan followed their father into the Martin Company, which became part of Martin Marietta and then Lockheed Martin until their division of about 700 workers was sold to General Electric Co. several years ago. Now named Middle River Aircraft Systems, still housed in the hangar where Junior Paugh worked, it manufactures thrust-reversers for commercial airplane engines. Dan is a senior buyer; Doug is a painter.

Unlike many who started out with them, the brothers have survived all the reorganizations, and still have the prospect of retiring with full pensions and life-time health insurance, like their father. Typical of companies that still provide these plans, theirs conditions full benefits, which include health insurance for life, on more than 25 years of service—a tenure common in their father's generation, an anachronism in theirs.

"I know we're the fortunate ones," Doug said. "My kids definitely won't get anything like this."

It is not certain that they will either; they know of others who got caught short. Dan had a counterpart in purchasing at the Boeing Co. who had 20 years of service when her division recently was sold to a Canadian company. Her pension benefit was frozen, a 33 percent reduction from the full benefit, and she became ineligible for retiree health insurance. Dan's wife, Joyce, took the same hit in 2001 when her job at Lockheed Martin was eliminated after 21 years. She has since found work at a machine shop, but without a comfortable pension, she said, "It feels like I'll have to work till I die." Last week's news that United Airlines can terminate its pension plans in the largest corporate default in U.S. history sounded to them like more of the same.

So Social Security is hardly the biggest worry.

"As I understand it, people my age could end up getting less than we expect from Social Security, but not too much less, so I feel that it will be there in some form for me. It's not like the government will see you out," Dan Paugh said. "But a company could. As a middle-class person, this scares the daylights out of me."

Their dream, the brothers say, was to do as well as their father: a good job, good wages, a nice-enough house, a family trip now and then. And so far they have. They may even have a similarly secure retirement, buoyed in part by their ballooning home values. Dan's house in Essex has more than tripled in 20 years; Doug's in Cecil County has doubled in five.

Although they and their wives have been contributing to 401(k) plans for 20 years, the brothers say they would not have enough for a comfortable retirement if not for their homes. They may sell them and downsize.

They face a major savings challenge that Junior Paugh didn't: providing for grown-up children. While Junior had 15 years of peak earnings with no child-rearing expenses, Doug has three children, ages 18 to 24, still at home, along with one 4-year-old grandchild. And Junior's daughter, Kay Cody, at 56, is raising her 15-year-old grandson for her daughter, Pamela Cody, 35, a supervisor for a Towson answering service who says she barely can pay her own expenses.

Kay Cody knows the ownership society well, ever since her pension was converted to a 401(k) in the 1990s, forcing her to learn to manage her own retirement savings.

"Growing up, we didn't focus on stocks and mutual funds," she said. "But when they explained the 401(k) to me, I thought, 'That's a darned good idea.' I made sure I understood and kept track of it. Since then, I've taken finance classes, and now I'm on our committee here that monitors how we invest our funds."

In 1996, she suffered a much bigger blow to her security when her husband, a union construction contractor, died of Lou Gehrig's disease. In the process, Cody has learned to tolerate significantly more risk than her father had to. The 2001 stock market plunge following the Sept. 11 terrorist attacks posed no threat to Junior Paugh's pension check, for example, but it savaged his daughter's 401(k) balance. While her funds have mostly recovered, Cody said, "My biggest fear is what if we're hit again and go into another slide?"

Always frugal, she became even more so after her husband's death. Her home in Essex paid for, she put herself on a budget, with a goal of accumulating $5,000 in savings, "in case the washer broke, in case I needed new tires." She created a separate bank account, paying into it from each paycheck, even before buying groceries. When she reached $5,000, she said, $10,000 sounded safer. She passed that, and is still going. She also invested her husband's death benefit and insurance in mutual funds, and invests in a growth fund for her grandson. But she said that her 401(k) and savings amount to $114,000—far short of the $400,000 a financial adviser told her she will need to support herself in retirement.

Her job as an administrator in a medical practice reminds her daily of other risks. Unlike her brothers and her father, she has no expectation of retiring with lifetime health insurance. "I'd like to be like my father and never be sick or have medical needs, but if I'm not, I see every day that Medicare doesn't begin to pay for what health care costs," she said. Her father-in-law, a Bethlehem Steel Co. retiree, lost his retirement health insurance when the company declared bankruptcy, and he had to pay thousands of dollars when he needed a pacemaker, she said.

Amid these rough waters, Social Security represents an island of stability. At 56, Cody is not likely to face benefit reductions, since every proposal so far exempts people 55 and older. But while she supports Bush's call for private accounts, she said she worries more about the system's long-term solvency.

"It does give me huge peace of mind to know I won't have to think about what I have to live off when I'm a certain age," she said. "But of course I worry what will be there for my children and grandchildren. Sometimes I think things look as bleak for them as before Roosevelt started all this."

THE GRANDCHILDREN

One measure of the unraveling of old-fashioned retirement security is that the younger generation of Paughs does not even expect to find it. "Security to me is about having options in case something happens," says Jessica Paugh, 29, an assistant manager at Sears in the Harford Mall in Bel Air.

Daughter of Dan and Joyce, she says she lost confidence in the old order when her mother lost her job of 21 years. "It was heartbreaking," said Jessica, who is now a convert to the Ownership Society. "Now, every day a company is buying another company. So I figure if this works out, great! I love my job, but it could change, and I'll adapt."

Indeed, the Ownership Society looks much like a Sellership Society from the younger Paughs' encounters with it. Sears was sold last spring to Kmart, with potential implications for Jessica. Her cousin Pamela Cody took a cut in benefits when the locally owned answering service where she worked was sold to a national chain. And Jessica's father and uncle know only too well that GE could sell their division, just as Lockheed Martin sold it in the 1990s. Dan Paugh recalls the response of a Lockheed Martin official to workers' surprise about that sale: "For the right price, my best hunting dog is for sale."

In Junior Paugh's day, when experience was valued on the production line, cradle-to-grave security and loyalty to one employer made sense for companies and workers. But for the younger Paughs, who have watched jobs, capital and products cross borders ("Our payroll operation is in India!" Doug exclaimed), the invisible handshake can seem like handcuffs.

Doug's daughter Lindsay, 21, recently left a job as a bank teller to work for a rival bank that offered a raise and promotion, but she forfeited three years toward a pension. The pension was not a factor, she said, because if she hadn't left now, she was certain to leave later. This remark led her mother, Melanie Paugh, who has worked 13 years for BMW, to close her eyes momentarily, as if to steady her spinning head.

"Today, if kids see a $10 raise, they jump," she said. "We were raised to stay put."

Jessica accompanies Junior Paugh to Martin retirees' gatherings sometimes and loves meeting his former co-workers, but cannot believe that all these years later these men still talk about their old company. "They still care about what goes on there—it's just really hard to imagine," she said. "For me, a job is where you work."

Retirement experts say the three-legged stool has only two legs for Paughs grandchildren's generation: Social Security and 401(k)s, which are like a merger of pensions and savings. Jessica's position at Sears comes with a 401(k) into which she tried to put 7 percent of her paycheck, although she said she recently cut back to 3 percent because she couldn't pay her expenses. "If I didn't use my credit card, I wouldn't have eaten some weeks," she said.

Jessica is the only descendant of Junior Paugh to go to college so far. Her parents didn't give her a choice. "They raised me to see college as inevitable, part of being prepared," she said. "Skills are the key. It's in the job description for my position—you need a college degree." Yet another child-rearing expense Junior Paugh did not face.

If Jessica's career goes well and the stock-market cooperates, she could end up as secure as her grandfather is in old age. But for now, even with her recent promotion to assistant manager (salary: $26,000), she and her parents are not counting on it. Her 401(k), now with a balance of $6,000, could reach $308,000 by retirement, according to a calculation provided by the plan, but this is well short of what economists say she would need. She said she hopes to invest more and see more gains.

"I check my balance online every other week," she said. "I have half the money in safe investments. With the rest I'm taking risks, just saying, 'Go! Go! Go!'"

Jessica said she believes firmly she never will be able to afford a house. Her cousin Pamela, who rents an apartment with her husband in Harford County, says the same. And her three younger cousins—Doug's children—have yet to move out on their own. As their parents see it, this is another wobble in the next generation's retirement security stool.

"We did as well and in some ways better than our parents," Melanie said. "I don't see how our kids will."

But Jessica and Lindsay, for their parts, are too optimistic to imagine things won't ultimately go their way, and too young to imagine ever being old.

"In my mind, right now, retirement is a myth. It may exist, but I can't see that far. I have my 401(k), so I'm preparing," Jessica said.

Pamela, the answering service supervisor, sees it differently. On a recent day, when Pamela's 11-year-old Ford Probe broke down, Junior Paugh made the hour-long drive to pick her up and take her to work. A starker contrast in two people's relationship to their government and employers would be hard to conjure.

Here was Junior Paugh at the wheel of his silver Buick LeSabre, having moved out of poverty, into the middle class, and now a secure retirement, with the help of one employer and his government. And here, only two generations behind him, sat Pamela Cody, feeling abandoned by everything her grandfather valued.

"I see how my grandparents were able to get by, but my husband and I just struggle from paycheck to paycheck," she said. "I don't have a pension and I'm not expecting Social Security to hold up long enough for me. Where is all the government's money going? Who is it benefiting? Nothing is benefiting me."

CHAPTER 8

The Squandering of America

Robert Kuttner

THE SUBPRIME SCANDAL

As 2007 dawned, the new year brought a new financial scandal and a new risk of systemic contagion. The so-called subprime mortgage lending sector began incurring large losses, bringing heightened risks to the much larger $6.5 trillion mortgage securities market. "Subprime" is the broad term for credit extended to people who would not ordinarily qualify for loans, either because their income is too low to meet the anticipated payments or because of a poor credit history. In the early 2000s, mortgage lenders introduced ever more complex variants on the traditional home mortgage. These included not just variable-rate mortgages, but mortgage loans with no down payment, mortgages with low "teaser" rates that rose after a brief period even if the prevailing interest rate did not, and mortgages, amazingly, that required no credit check. An estimated 60 percent of subprime loans required either no income verification or only the most cursory check.

Mortgage companies were able to make these loans because they did not bear most of the risk. Typically, these mortgages were sold off as soon as the loan closed, and packaged as securities known as collateralized debt obligations (CDOs). The securities carried rates of return supposedly aligned closely to the risk. According to *The Wall Street Journal,* subprime loans increased more than twelvefold, from about $50 billion in 2001 to over $600 billion in 2005. From 2005 to 2006, the value of high-risk mortgage securities more than doubled.

One might have expected trouble to begin when prevailing interest rates went up, but ominously enough, when the subprime sector got into serious difficulty in early 2007, interest rates were flat or falling. One can only imagine how much more dire the losses—to home owners, lenders, investors, and the larger economy—will be in the next round of interest-rate hikes. One industry study projects that about 32 percent of loans with teaser rates of 4 percent or less will be in foreclosure by 2010.

Rather than higher prevailing rates causing increased defaults, two predictable things happened in early 2007. First, thanks to the lax standards, an increasing number of borrowers had undertaken larger obligations than they could financially bear. Any unexpected slight financial reversal could cause them to default on their loans and lose their homes. For many, the end of the teaser period meant they could no longer afford their payments. Second, subprime lenders looking for quick profits had gone ever farther downward into the pool of risky borrowers, increasing the risk of defaults. By March 2007, about 15 percent of subprime loans were in default.

As in the case of so many other financial bubbles of the past decade, this one was driven by the search for abnormally high returns. Wall Street seemed to have forgotten the most elementary of lessons: higher yield is associated with higher risk. And the subprime mortgage brokers were not some set of shady characters one degree above Mafia lenders—they were bankrolled by the most blue-chip names on Wall Street. But these companies did not bear the full risk—they were middlemen, since most of the securities were sold off to investors such as pension funds.

When one of the biggest of the subprime lenders, New Century Financial Corporation, went bankrupt in April 2007, it was revealed that its own biggest creditor was Morgan Stanley. New Century and other subprime mortgage originators were also heavily financed by hedge funds. And the subprime loan debacle had familiar insider conflicts of interest. New Century originated $60 billion worth of mortgages in 2006, second only to London-based HSBC in its volume of subprime loans. The three founders of New Century, perhaps sensing what was to come, cashed out about $103 million of their own stock in the company over four years at an average price of $42.46 per share, much of it in 2006, even as they continued touting it to investors and analysts. As of April 2007, they were under investigation by the SEC for possible insider trading violations. And even in its bankruptcy, New Century generated profits for investment bankers and Wall Street lawyers on both sides of the case—more sheer economic waste.

The lessons are also familiar from other cases of financial excess over the past decade. Both public and private regulation failed. As the early warnings of this saga were unfolding in the financial pages in 2005 and 2006, the regulatory agencies did nothing. Mortgage companies, as opposed to banks and savings and loan associations, are not directly regulated by the federal government. New Century was given a cursory examination in 2006 by California's regulators, who have a staff of just twenty-five to police 4,100 mortgage origination companies, and was given a clean bill of health. As lightly regulated mortgage brokers have taken increasing market share from traditional thrift and banking institutions, only 23 percent of subprime loans in 2005 were originated by federally regulated lenders. This makes perfect sense, since regulated lenders at least worry about government scrutiny. But in this scandal, little was forthcoming. The Federal Reserve had residual authority to investigate abuses that could disturb financial markets, but as the subprime sector got into ever riskier territory, the Fed undertook no investigation and issued exactly one cease-and-desist order against a subprime lender affiliated with a bank.

In principle, the secondary mortgage market, dominated by Fannie Mae and Freddie Mac, polices the standards. Bad loans, supposedly, are not certified by Fannie and Freddie for resale or securitization But, as we have seen, Fannie Mae was having its own major scandals. And remarkably enough, the agency that monitors Fannie Mae, the Office of Federal Housing Enterprise Oversight, had little interest in the subprime problems. Freddie Mac only tightened its standards in February 2007, after much damage was done. In the meantime, subprime lenders had found ways to package their loans as high-yield securities without Fannie's or Freddie's seal of approval, so the subprime scandal reflected a dual failure. Private markets did not accurately price CDOs and failed to prevent behavior that had serious risks not just for consenting individual investors but for the financial system. And public regulatory agencies, in the hands of close allies on Wall Street who oppose regulation, failed to act.

Only in the spring of 2007 did Congress belatedly begin investigating. And when Congress scheduled hearings, the Mortgage Bankers Association (MBA) defended its most reckless members, using the low-income home buyer as its poster child. Regulating this sector, the association contended, would only deprive some borrowers of credit. When Freddie Mac belatedly tightened standards, MBA chairman John M. Robbins warned that the move "will limit the product options and the access to credit for those individuals most in need, many of whom are first time, underserved or minority homebuyers. The mortgage products that these new standards target are important financial instruments, crucial to helping borrowers get into homes and repair their credit. Regulation that further limits consumer choice is unwarranted."

It was the same argument used to justify the savings and loan excesses of the 1980s. In both cases, the real intent was to make middlemen rich; if some people of modest means got help purchasing homes, that was purely incidental. The mortgage brokers seemed unconcerned that a large fraction of these Americans would lose their homes, as long as the formulas worked and there was good money to be made on average.

If public policy makers wish to help more low-income Americans become home owners, there is a far better approach than relying on sleazy mortgage brokers peddling bait-and-switch products that leave a trail of foreclosure and heartbreak. At other times in our history, the government has offered subsidized mortgages to first-time home buyers, through the VA and FHA. The 3 percent down payment loans offered through FHA have a far lower default rate than those of subprime lenders. Government-backed nonprofits such as Neighborhood Housing Services of America are not in the mortgage business for a quick buck but to counsel low-income home buyers and to work with them for the long haul. Neighborhood Housing Service's foreclosure rate is close to zero.

At times, the government has also stepped in to prevent foreclosures. The Home Owners' Loan Corporation of the mid-1930s worked with homeowners and lenders to encourage forbearance by lenders and renegotiate mortgage terms that allowed hard-pressed home owners to keep their homes in difficult times. Some states, such as North Dakota, created state banks and legislated temporary moratoria on foreclosures. Had the fate of home owners been left to private markets, there would have been a cascade of foreclosures and an even deeper collapse of local housing markets. Today, there is no national Great Depression, but there is a severe depression in some local housing markets requiring more than the tender mercies of private creditors. In early 2007, Ohio, with the nation's highest foreclosure rate, passed a $100 million bond issue to refinance mortgages.

In housing policy, the road not taken includes sound underwriting standards coupled with subsidized mortgages and starter homes, as well as credit counseling, to help new home buyers. Decent housing for moderate-income people requires social subsidy, not just market gymnastics and the quest for the quick buck. Government aid also moderates housing prices, since it adds to the housing supply. But even as markets brace for the wider fallout of this latest financial excess, and regulators belatedly tighten standards, these fundamental lessons seem not to have been learned.

PART THREE

Inequality

Despite recurrent economic crises, the United States remains a wealthy society—by most measures, one of the richest in the world. But that prosperity has not been shared by everyone. One of the most striking features of American society today, indeed, is the stark coexistence of great wealth and widespread poverty. In many respects, economic inequality is more glaring today than ever before in our recent history. But a wide gap between "haves" and "have-nots" has been with us from the beginning, and has stubbornly persisted even during good economic times.

In the 1950s and 1960s, for example, many social scientists described the United States as an "affluent" society—one in which most people could expect a steady improvement in their standard of living, great disparities in income and wealth were fast disappearing, and true poverty was soon to be a thing of the past. These perceptions were based on some undeniable facts. On average, Americans' incomes did rise substantially after World War II, and during the 1960s millions of the poor were lifted above the official poverty line. It was natural to believe that these trends would continue.

But even in the expanding economy of the 1950s and 1960s, there were important limits to what some believed was a steady march toward greater equality. For one thing, the progress in raising the overall standard of living had virtually no impact on the *distribution* of income and wealth in America—the gap between rich and poor. Throughout most of the period since World War II, the upper one-fifth of income earners received roughly 40 percent of the country's total personal income; the bottom fifth, about 5 percent. And although poverty was sharply reduced in many rural areas, it proved to be much more stubborn in the inner cities.

More recently, the trends have become much more discouraging: The limited postwar progress toward economic equality has been reversed. By the early 1980s, the spread of income inequality in the United States had begun to increase as the share of the most affluent rose while the share of the poor fell. In the 1990s, income inequality reached its most extreme level since World War II. By the turn of the new century, the top fifth of income earners took home half the nation's total income.

And the gains at the top have increasingly been concentrated among a very small sliver of the population. Between 1979 and 2006, after-tax incomes rose by 11 percent for the bottom fifth of American households, by 26 percent for the middle fifth, and by 256 percent for the top one percent of income earners. That one percent of Americans took home more than 16 percent of the country's total income in 2006.[1]

But what accounts for the sharp rises inequality in recent years? As the economist Dean Baker argues in "Increasing Inequality in the United States," these growing disparities are not simply a natural result of economic or technological changes. They also reflect the impact of deliberate public policies—on trade, employment, support for unionization, and health care, among others. We have the stark levels of inequality that we do, in short, partly because we have chosen to. And we could choose otherwise.

As Baker makes clear, these policies have been hard on most Americans, except for the very wealthy. But the worst impact has been at the lower end of the economic ladder. As the economic fortunes of the richest Americans have shot upward, those of low-income Americans have deteriorated. At last count, close to 36 million Americans had incomes below the federal government's official "poverty line," something over $20,000 for a family of four in 2008. Today more than one American child in six lives in poverty—a far higher proportion than in most other industrial societies. Many people are aware that poverty is widespread in America, but fewer realize that it is much more prevalent here than in other developed countries. The Luxemburg Income Study, an international comparison of levels of inequality and poverty, shows that, by some measures, American children face risks of poverty that are closer to those of children in Russia or Mexico than to those in other highly developed industrial societies. An American child is more than six times as likely to live in a poor family than a child in Denmark.

As the report we excerpt here from the Center on American Progress makes clear, there is nothing inevitable about this unfortunate record—just as there is nothing inevitable about our extremes of economic inequality. There are clear reasons why poverty in America stands out so starkly among industrial societies and corresponding strategies that we could launch to reduce it dramatically, if we chose to do so.

Poverty is more than a matter of income alone. One of the most devastating, and most visible, consequences of rising poverty (among other causes) has been the growth of homelessness in the United States. Elliot Liebow, an anthropologist, spent several years closely observing homeless women in and around Washington, D.C., and his article paints a compelling picture of what life is really like at the bottom of the American system of inequality. Being homeless, he reveals, means having to struggle every day for the bare essentials of life most of us take for granted— from a place to sleep to somewhere to store our belongings.

Why, when they seem so unfair, do we allow such harsh disparities between rich and poor to persist? One reason is that, as a nation, we have historically believed that, whatever one's present position on the economic ladder, it is always possible to move up—through hard work, pluck, and persistence. The idea that the

United States is a unique land of virtually unlimited opportunity, where who your parents were is far less important than what you achieve on your own, has profoundly shaped our social policies from the beginning—helping to create a society that, in comparison with other advanced industrial nations, has done remarkably little to cushion the impact of inequalities in income and wealth. But as the article we reprint from the business-oriented *Wall Street Journal* suggests, the reality is more complicated. There was probably never as much opportunity to move up in America as we once believed, and the possibilities of moving upward out of poverty have stagnated, or even declined, in recent decades. That doesn't, of course, mean that this kind of upward mobility never happens; it does mean that the wealth and educational level of one's parents matters far more than the myth of unlimited opportunity implies.

ENDNOTE

1. Arloc Sherman, "Income gaps hit record level in 2006, new data show," Washington, DC, Center on Budget and Policy Priorities, April 17, 2009.

CHAPTER 9

Increasing Inequality in the United States

Dean Baker

A SAD STATUS QUO

The United States economy has grown at a reasonably healthy pace over the last quarter century, with GDP growth averaging 3.1 percent annually from 1980 to 2005. However, the benefits of this growth have gone overwhelmingly to the richest 10 percent of families, and among this group, disproportionately to the richest 1 percent. Most households have had very modest gains in income over this period, and the gains they did experience have been largely the result of the growth in two-earner households.

The growth of inequality in the United States is widely acknowledged in policy debates. While there is little dispute about the general pattern of rising inequality, there is considerable debate about the cause. While some policy analysts argue that rising inequality in the United States is an outgrowth of globalization and technology, a strong argument can be made that the driving force has been a series of deliberate policy choices. This article describes some of the key policies that have fostered an upward redistribution of income over the last quarter century.

US TRADE AND IMMIGRATION POLICY—A MAJOR CAUSE OF INEQUALITY?

Perhaps the most basic fact about globalization is that there is vast supply of workers in the developing world who are prepared to work at much lower wages than their counterparts in the developed countries. Trade policies that open up segments of the U.S. labor force to increased competition from workers in the developing world will lower the wages for the workers affected. At the same time, such trade openings will offer gains to the larger economy, since the goods and services produced by these workers consequently will fall in price.

In the United States, trade and immigration policy has been quite explicitly focused on placing less-educated workers that do not have a college degree in competition with workers in the developing world, while leaving the most highly educated workers such as doctors, lawyers, accountants and economists largely protected. This has been done, first and foremost, by making it as easy as possible for companies to establish manufacturing operations in developing countries and ship their output back to the United States. Recent trade agreements have been focused on establishing an institutional structure that protects corporations against expropriations or restrictions on repatriating profits by developing country governments, while also prohibiting tariff and not-tariff barriers that could exclude manufactured goods from the United States. The effect of such agreements is to place U.S. manufacturing workers in direct competition with their counterparts in the developing world.

U.S. immigration policy has also placed downward pressure on the wages of less-educated workers by allowing immigrant workers in many less-skilled jobs such as custodians, restaurant workers, and construction to work in the United States in violation of the law. Although it is illegal, over the last quarter century, employers have knowingly hired millions of immigrant workers, who lack legal authorization to work, for these jobs.

It is important to realize that the United States does not have an "open border" immigration policy. The relatively unskilled workers who work in violation of the law risk deportation any time they encounter a law enforcement officer—for example, if they are stopped for a traffic violation. Similarly, these workers often risk dangerous border crossing to get into the United States. Relatively unskilled workers in Mexico and other developing countries may be willing to take such risks because the wages offered at even low-paying jobs in the United States are so much higher than what they could earn in their native country. Doctors, lawyers, and other professionals in developing countries would not take the same risks, even though they can earn much more in the United States, because they would be sacrificing a relatively comfortable existence in their home country.

If U.S. trade negotiators had a different agenda, they could have constructed trade agreements to place highly educated workers in the United States in competition with their counterparts in the developing world. This could have been accomplished by setting transparent professional and licensing requirements for medicine, law, and other highly paid professions and removing all the legal obstacles that make it difficult for hospitals, universities, and other employers to hire non-citizens. To eliminate concerns about a "brain drain" from developing countries, it would be a simple matter to impose a modest tax on the earnings of foreign-born professionals. This tax would reimburse developing countries for their educational expenses, and could allow them to educate two or three professionals for every one that came to the United States.

A policy that focused on subjecting highly paid professionals to international competition would have allowed for large economic gains in the form of lower prices for health care, college education and many other goods and services in which the wages of highly paid professionals are a sizable portion of the total cost. This sort of trade and immigration policy also would lead to more equality, rather than inequality.

ANTI-INFLATION IN FAVOR
OF SOCIAL POLICIES

A second important cause of rising inequality is the policy and strategy of the Federal Reserve Board, the central bank for the United States. The Federal Reserve Board, or Fed has the responsibility for both sustaining high levels of employment and keeping inflation under control, but in the last quarter century, it has focused much more on combating inflation that it had earlier in the post-war era. This policy relies on keeping unemployment high enough to prevent inflation from rising above the rates it views as acceptable.[2] When the Fed raises interest rates to slow the economy, the people who lose their jobs are disproportionately those at the middle and bottom of the wage distribution. A recent analysis found a strong link between low unemployment and real wage growth for workers in the bottom half of the wage distribution.[3]

In effect, this means that less-educated workers are being called upon to sacrifice by facing higher unemployment rates, and also earning lower wages, in order to keep the inflation rate under control. In prior decades, the government had tried to maintain some equality of sacrifice through wage-price guidelines. As the OECD has recently documented in its new Jobs Strategy, many European countries still effectively use centralized wage bargaining as a mechanism to control inflation without resorting to high levels of unemployment.

ANTI-UNIONISM IN THE UNITED STATES

A third important force placing downward pressure on the wages of large segments of the work force has been the anti-union policies that were put in place in the last quarter century. Partly as a result of these policies, the share of the private sector work force that is unionized fell from more than 20 percent in 1980 to less than 8 percent in 2005. Furthermore, the unions that continue to exist have far less power due to a change in tactics by employers.

In the eighties it became a common practice for employers to fire workers who are involved in union organizing drives. While it is illegal for an employer to fire a worker for their union activity, it is difficult to prove an employers' motivation. Furthermore, the penalties for being found guilty of violating this law are sufficiently trivial that employers risk these penalties in exchange for keeping a union out of their workplace. The ability of employers to fire the leaders of organizing drives has made it extremely difficult for unions to organize new workplaces.

Unions have tried to counter this practice by using outside pressure from various sources—churches, community groups, political figures—to force corporations to recognize unions where the majority of the workers want one. They have also tried to use the bargaining process in sectors of a company where they are organized to force management's neutrality in sectors that they are trying to organize. For example, the Communication Workers have used their bargaining in the traditional sector of the phone industry to force some of the major communications companies to be neutral toward organizing drives in their Internet and mobile phone divisions. However, the tilt toward management in the enforcement of labor laws over the last quarter century has been a major impediment to organizing.

The other major change in labor–management relations during this period has been the practice of hiring replacement workers to take the jobs of workers on strike. This was an extremely rare practice prior to 1980. The turning point came in 1981, when President Reagan brought in military air traffic controllers to replace the civilian air traffic controllers who were out on strike. Most of the striking controllers permanently lost their jobs. Shortly after this strike, there were several highly visible private sector labor disputes in which employers hired permanent replacements for striking workers. This practice made strikes a far less effective weapon against management. As a result, the ability of unions to secure wage gains for their members was further diminished.

THE COSTS OF HEALTH: SKY-HIGH AND EVER INCREASING

A fourth major area of public policy that has led to rising inequality has been the failure to contain the growth of health care costs. While rising health care costs have posed problems in all developed countries, no country has experienced a health care cost explosion comparable to that experienced in the United States. Health care costs rose from 8.8 percent of GDP in 1980 to 15.3 percent of GDP in 2005, in spite of the country's relatively young demographic structure. Health care costs are projected to rise by another 4 percentage points of GDP over the next decade.

Germany and other wealthy countries have been far more effective in keeping their costs under control. One reason that costs in the United States are so high is that it does not have universal health coverage, but rather relies on private insurers to provide coverage for most of the non-elderly population. The insurers have proved largely ineffective in containing costs and incur enormous administrative expenses, with their administrative costs average of 20 percent of the benefits they pay out. Insurers are most profitable when they can find ways to avoid paying benefits to people who are sick and when they can avoid insuring sick people altogether.

Since per person health care costs are largely the same across income groups, which means that health insurance costs the same for a high wage worker and a low wage worker, the rise in health care costs imposed a much larger burden on low and moderate wage earners than it did on high wage earners. If health care costs continue to rise as projected, increases in health care costs are likely to absorb whatever real wage gains that workers at the middle and bottom of the wage distribution are able to earn.

There are other policies that have played a role in the rise of inequality over the last quarter century. For workers near the bottom of the wage distribution, the decline in the real value of the minimum wage has been an especially important factor. The real value of the minimum wage was 30 percent lower in 2005 than it had been in 1980, even though average productivity had risen by more than 70 percent.

Together these policies have led to an economic structure in which the bulk of the gains from economic growth go to those at the top, and disproportionately to those at the very top of the income distribution. Until recently such policies could be justified by the relatively low unemployment rate in the United States, but even this rationale appears to be disappearing. The most recent data from the OECD show the employment to population ratio for prime age workers between 25 and 54 years of age in the EU-15 is almost identical to the ratio in the United States. And, the EU-15 has actually generated jobs at a more rapid pace than the United States since 2000.

CHAPTER 10

From Poverty to Prosperity
A National Strategy to Cut Poverty in Half

Center for American Progress

INTRODUCTION

In February of 2006, the Center for American Progress convened a diverse group of national experts and leaders to examine the causes and consequences of poverty in America and make recommendations for national action. In this report, our Task Force on Poverty calls for a national goal of cutting poverty in half in the next ten years and proposes a strategy to reach the goal.

The Task Force was established in the wake of Hurricane Katrina. When Katrina struck, it revealed that in one of the nation's proudest cities, racial and economic disparities were enormous. Tens of thousands of families were living in severe poverty, jobless and unable to afford transportation out of town or a night in a motel as disaster approached. Many more families and workers were living paycheck to paycheck, able to get by as long as work was steady, but at great risk when the unexpected happened.

The experience of Hurricane Katrina helped spur the creation of this Task Force. Yet this is not a report about why New Orleans' levees broke or about what happened after they did. Our focus is on how we can build a stronger economy, more vibrant communities, and a better nation, in which there are no neighborhoods of extreme poverty, in which steady work is both protection from and a route out of poverty, and in which children and adults can reach their full potential.

Thirty-seven million Americans live below the official poverty line. Millions more struggle each month to pay for basic necessities or run out of savings when they lose their job or have a health emergency.

Poverty imposes enormous costs on society in the lost potential of children, lower worker productivity and earnings, poor health, increased crime, and broken neighborhoods. In a world of increasing global competition, we cannot afford to squander our nation's human resources.

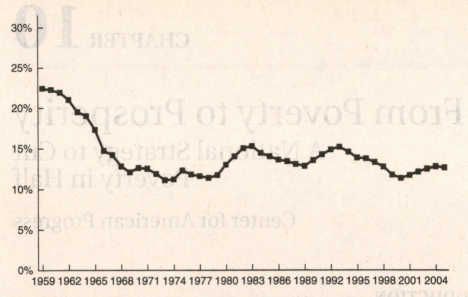

FIGURE 10.1   Poverty Fell by More than Half from 1959–1973, and is Now above 1973 Level

Share of Americans in Poverty, 1959–2005

Source: U.S. Census Bureau, Current Population Survey, 2006 Annual Social and Economic Supplement.

Too often, discussions of poverty are treated as if they're unrelated to the issues facing the middle class. But large numbers of Americans—both low-income and middle class—are increasingly concerned about uncertain job futures, downward pressures on wages, and decreasing opportunities for advancement in a globalized economy. Large numbers of Americans would benefit if high quality early education were more accessible and higher education were more affordable. Large numbers would benefit if more jobs paid enough to support a family. Some issues are distinct, particularly for the smaller group of Americans in long-term, persistent poverty. But much of the agenda to reduce poverty is also one to promote opportunity and security for millions of other Americans, too.

Discussions about poverty often devolve into arguments about who is to blame. Is poverty mainly the fault of the poor or of a society that tolerates poverty and does not provide opportunities for economic mobility? In our view, neither is an adequate answer.

We should expect adults to work and young people to stay in school and not have children before they are able to care for them. We also should expect that jobs be available to those who want to work, that full-time work provide a decent standard of living, that all children grow up in conditions which let them reach their full potential, and that a nation of opportunity should also be a nation of second chances.

Poverty: The Facts

One in eight Americans lives in poverty. In 2005, a family of four was considered poor under the official measures if the family's income was below $19,971. Using this measure, there were 37 million Americans living in poverty, 12.6 percent of the U.S. population.[1]

Nearly one in three Americans is low-income, with an income below twice the poverty line. In 2005, over 90 million people—31 percent of all Americans—had incomes below 200 percent of the federal poverty thresholds, a standard often used as a measure of low income. For a family of four that means an annual income of about $40,000.[2]

One in twenty Americans lives in extreme poverty, with an income below half of the poverty line. In 2005, just under 16 million people—5.4 percent of all Americans—had incomes below half the poverty line, or less than $9,903 for a family of four or $5,080 for an individual.[3] The number of Americans living in such extreme poverty grew by over three million between 2000 and 2005, and the share of poor people living in extreme poverty is now greater than at any point in the last 32 years.[4]

Nearly one-fifth of children are poor. Today, nearly one-fifth of children (17.6 percent) and over one-fifth of children under five years old (20.4 percent) are poor.[5] Children in single-parent families are poorest: 42.7 percent of those in female-headed, and 20.1 percent of those in male-headed families are poor, compared with 8.5 percent of those in married two-parent families.[6]

Minorities are much more likely to be poor than are whites. African Americans (24.9 percent poor in 2005), Hispanics (21.8 percent), and Native Americans (25.3 percent) all have poverty rates far greater than those of whites (8.3 percent). Still, 45 percent of the poor people are non-Hispanic whites.[7] Among African Americans, one key contributing factor is joblessness. The official statistics mask the severity of the problem, because they do not count those who are incarcerated or are no longer looking for work. Columbia University Professor Ronald Mincy has calculated that in 2004, among the civilian population who had not been to college and were between the ages of 22 and 30, only 50 percent of young black men were employed, compared to 79 percent of young white and 81 percent of young Hispanic men. Among high school dropouts, Mincy finds that only 28 percent of young black men were employed.[8]

Immigrants are poorer than natives. Although most poor people in the United States (84 percent) are native-born, foreign-born residents have a significantly higher poverty rate than that of natives (16.5 percent versus 12.1 percent).[9] A major reason is that immigrants are disproportionately likely to be in low-wage jobs; immigrants account for 11 percent of the total U.S. population and 14 percent of the U.S. labor force, but they make up 20 percent of low-wage workers.[10] Low proficiency in English and lack of education are other important factors, as is lack of citizenship status.[11]

Women are more likely to be poor than men. With a 14.1 percent poverty rate, females are substantially more likely to be poor than are males (11.1 percent).[12] One major reason is that women are paid less than men. In 2004, the median hourly wages of women were about 20 percent less than those of men with comparable education and hours of work.[13]

Work among poor families grew dramatically during the 1990s. The share of poor children with a parent working full-time, year-round has grown by 60 percent since 1992. Among poor children, two-thirds (65 percent) have one or more working parents and

(continued)

Poverty: The Facts (*continued*)

one-third (32 percent) have a parent who works year-round, full-time.[14] Among poor adults aged 25-to-54, nearly half (46 percent) work during the year.[15]

Poverty rates are highest in urban and rural areas, but in the largest metropolitan areas, more poor now live in the suburbs than in central cities. Seventeen percent of urban residents, and 14.5 percent of rural residents are poor, compared to 9.3 percent of suburban residents.[16] In the largest 100 metropolitan areas, however, the number of poor living in suburbs exceeds the number living in cities (12 million, compared to 11 million).[17]

More poor people live in the South than in any other region. The South has both the largest number of individuals in poverty and the highest poverty rate. In 2005, 14.9 million poor individuals lived in the South. Fourteen percent of Southern residents were poor, compared to 12.6 percent for the West, 11.4 percent for the Midwest, and 11.3 percent for the Northeast.[18]

Millions of Americans will spend at least one year in poverty at some point in their lives. For most, the experience of poverty is temporary. For some, it is long-term. Task Force member and economist Rebecca Blank has found that over a 13-year period, one-third of all Americans—34 percent of people in a representative sample—experienced poverty. In that 13-year period, about one in ten Americans (9.6 percent) were poor for most of the time, and one in twenty (4.9 percent) were poor for ten or more years. For African Americans, 30.2 percent were poor for most of the time and 16.7 percent were poor for ten or more years.[19]

Poverty in the U.S. is higher than in many other developed nations. In international poverty comparisons, a common approach is to ask what share of the population has income below 50 percent of the nation's median income. Using this measure, the U.S. poverty rate at the turn of the 21st century ranked 24th of 25 countries, with only Mexico having a higher poverty rate.[20] A new UNICEF report on child well-being in rich nations finds that when child poverty is measured in relation to 50 percent of median income, the United States ranks 24th among 24 nations. Another study compared the U.S. with eight other developed countries using the official U.S. poverty line. It found that the U.S. ranked eighth out of nine. Only the U.K. had a higher rate, though U.K. child poverty has fallen substantially since then. The high rates of poverty in the U.S. do not occur because the poor are less likely to be working here. Rather, government does less here to reduce poverty. In a twelve-nation study, the U.S. poverty rate was below average on the basis of market income alone. After taxes and transfers were counted, the U.S. had the highest poverty rate of all twelve nations.[21]

Given the persistence of poverty in recent decades, many Americans may consider it an inescapable reality of modern life. Fueled by years of inaccurate characterizations of past efforts ("We fought a war on poverty and poverty won," as Ronald Reagan stated), many Americans are left to conclude that little can be done beyond providing private charity and urging the poor to do better.

Nothing could be farther from the truth.

The United States has seen periods of dramatic poverty reduction. Amid the strong economy of the 1960s and the War on Poverty, the poverty rate fell from 22.4 percent to 11.1 percent between 1959 and 1973. In the 1990s, a strong economy was combined with policies to promote and support work; the poverty rate dropped from 15.1 percent to 11.3 percent between 1993 and 2000. In each period, a near-full employment economy, sound federal and state policies, individual initiative, supportive civic institutions and communities, and a sustained national commitment led to significant progress.

In the last six years, our nation has moved in the opposite direction. The number of poor Americans has grown by five million. The federal minimum wage has remained flat. Funding for key federal programs that help people get and keep jobs has been stagnant or worse.

At the same time, the wealthiest Americans have received billions of dollars in tax cuts, while inequality has reached historically high levels. A new study by Thomas Piketty and Emmanuel Saez finds that in 2005 the top one percent of American households had the largest share of the nation's income since 1929—19.3 percent.[22] In contrast, the bottom 20 percent of households now have just 3.4 percent of total income, according to the Census Bureau.[23] Between 2003 and 2004, post-tax income of the bottom fifth rose by $200, while income for the top one percent rose by $145,500.[24] The top one percent of households now hold one-third of the nation's net worth, while the bottom 40 percent have less than one percent.[25]

It does not have to be this way. A nation with such enormous resources and capacities need not tolerate persistent poverty.

WHY WE SHOULD REDUCE POVERTY

Poverty violates our fundamental principles as a democratic nation and as ethically conscious individuals. American democracy is built on a simple proposition, declared in our founding documents and developed over centuries of trial and error: All Americans should have the opportunity to turn their aspirations into a meaningful and materially satisfactory life. Our nation is grounded on the idea that together we can create a society of economic advancement for all aided by a government that protects individual rights, ensures fair competition, and promotes a greater common good. The American system is not designed to guarantee that everybody will be the same, think the same, or receive the same economic rewards in life. It simply ensures that people start from a level playing field and have a reasonable shot at achieving success in life and making the most of their abilities.

Economic opportunity has served as the foundation for citizenship and civic engagement throughout our nation's history. As political icons from Thomas Jefferson to Martin Luther King, Jr. have long recognized, core concepts such as freedom and democracy are essentially meaningless for those who lack economic independence. Simply, put, one cannot fully participate in society and help shape the decisions of our government and its priorities if confined to abject poverty.

Beyond our founding principles, the moral imperative to serve the poor is a powerful theme in the social teachings of many major faith traditions in our country. Across faiths, citizens are called upon to press both private and public actors to protect the most vulnerable and help those in need to build economically self-sufficient lives. Judeo-Christian traditions today speak of the ruptured "covenant with God" that leaves our fellow citizens suffering needlessly amid great national wealth.

Addressing poverty and economic security takes on greater urgency in the new economy. Employment for millions is now less secure than at any point in the post-World War II era. Jobs are increasingly unlikely to provide health care coverage and guaranteed pensions. The typical U.S. worker will change jobs numerous times over his or her working years and must adapt to rapid technological change. One-quarter of all jobs in the U.S. economy do not pay enough to support a family of four above the poverty line. It is in our nation's interest that those jobs be filled and that employment rates be high. It is not in our nation's interest that people working in these jobs be confined to poverty.

In the global economy, the greatest potential for success turns on having an educated, healthy, adaptable workforce. It is in all of our interests that children grow up under conditions that prepare them for the economy of the future. Yet an estimated eight percent of all children and 28 percent of African-American children spend at least 11 years of childhood in poverty.[26]

In *The Economic Costs of Poverty in the United States: The Subsequent Effects of Children Growing Up Poor,* Harry Holzer, Diane Whitmore Schanzenbach, Greg Duncan, and Jens Ludwig conclude that allowing children to grow up in persistent poverty costs our economy $500 billion dollars per year in lost adult productivity and wages, increased crime, and higher health expenditures.[27]

Holzer and his co-authors explain that children who grow up in poverty are more likely than non-poor children to have low earnings as adults, reflecting lower workforce productivity. They are also somewhat more likely to engage in crime (though that is not the case for the vast majority) and to have poor health later in life. Holzer and co-authors explain:

> Our results, suggest that the costs to the U.S. associated with childhood poverty total about $500 billion per year, or the equivalent of nearly 4 percent of Gross Domestic Product. More specifically, we estimate that childhood poverty each year:
>
> - *Reduces productivity and economic output by about 1.3 percent of GDP*
> - *Raises the costs of crime by 1.3 percent of GDP*
> - *Raises health expenditures and reduces the value of health by 1.2 percent of GDP.*

Holzer and his co-authors emphasize that these estimates almost certainly understate the true costs of poverty to the U.S. economy. They omit the costs associated with poor adults who did not grow up poor as children. They do not count all of the other costs that poverty might impose on the nation, such as environmental impacts and much of the suffering of the poor themselves.

Reducing poverty would allow more people to contribute to the economic and civic life of the nation, strengthening our economy and fortifying our democracy.

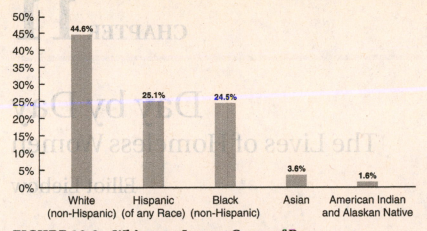

FIGURE 10.2 Whites are Largest Group of Poor

Distribution of Poor by Race/Ethnicity

Categories sum to more than 100 percent because respondents could choose more than one response.

Source: U.S. Census Bureau, Current Population Survey, 2006 Annual Social and Economic Supplement (Three year average from 2003–2005).

CHAPTER 11

Day by Day
The Lives of Homeless Women

Elliot Liebow

On the street or in a shelter, homelessness is hard living. At first sight, one wonders why more homeless people do not kill themselves. How do they manage to slog through day after day, with no end in sight? How, in a world of unremitting grimness, do they manage to laugh, love, enjoy friends, even dance and play the fool? How, in short, do they stay fully human while body and soul are under continuous and grievous assault?

Simple physical survival is within the grasp of almost everyone willing and able to reach out for it.[1] As the women thrash about, awash in a sea of need, emergency shelters, along with public assistance in the form of cash, food stamps, and medical assistance, make it just possible for many of the women to keep their heads above water. Through the use of shelters, soup kitchens, and hospital emergency rooms, it is even possible for most homeless people who do not get public assistance to survive at some minimal level without benefit of a structured assistance program.

At their very best, however, these bare-boned elements of a life-support system merely make life possible, not necessarily tolerable or livable. Serious problems remain. Homelessness can transform what for others are little things into insurmountable hurdles. Indeed, homelessness in general puts a premium on "little things." Just as some homeless women seem to have learned (more than most of us, perhaps) to value a small gesture of friendship, a nice day, a bus token, or a little courtesy that others might take for granted or not notice at all, so too can events or circumstances that would be trivial irritants to others approach catastrophic proportions for the homeless person.[2]

For homeless women on the street, the struggle for subsistence begins at the animal level—for food, water, shelter, security, and safe sleep.[3] In contrast, homeless women in shelters usually have these things; their struggle begins at the level of human rather than animal needs—protection of one's property, health care, and avoidance of boredom. The struggle then moves rapidly to the search for companionship, modest measures of independence, dignity, and self-respect, and some hope and faith in the future. These needs are not particularly sequential or hierar-chical. One can just as easily be immobilized by hopelessness and despair as by hunger and cold. Body and soul are equally in need of nurture, and the women must grab whatever they can get when they can get it.[4]

* * *

For some of the women, day-by-day hardships began with the problem of getting enough sleep. A few women complained they could never get any sleep in a shelter. Grace was one of them. "There's no getting sleep in a shelter," she said. "Only rest."

There was indeed much night noise and movement. There was snoring, coughing, sneezing, wheezing, retching, farting, cries from bad dreams, occasional weeping or seizures, talking aloud to oneself or to someone else who may or may not have been present, and always movement to and from the bathroom. Grace was complaining about noise, and she found a partial remedy in ear plugs. But ear plugs could not help those women like Kathleen who were kept awake not by noise but by questions: Is this it for me? How did I end up here? How will I get out? But eventually, as the night wore on, there was a lot of snoring, and that meant that, Grace and Kathleen notwithstanding, there was a lot of sleeping, too.

Having to get up at 5:30 A.M. and be out of the shelter by 7:00 was a major hardship of shelter life. It was not simply the fact of having to get up and out, but rather that the women had to do this every day of the week, every day of the year (Thanksgiving and Christmas Day excepted), no matter what the weather or how they felt. On any given morning, as the women drifted onto the street, one might see two or three ailing women—this one with a fever or cough or headache, that one with a limp or stomach ache or other ailment—pick up their bags and walk silently into the weather.

The women especially missed Saturday and Sunday mornings, which looked just like Tuesday and Wednesday mornings. The occasional opportunity to stay in bed an extra hour or two was desperately missed. Not being able to sleep in, ever, especially on a weekend, was seen by many as a major deprivation that unfairly set them apart from the rest of the world. At 7:15, on a Sunday morning in the park, several women were looking for benches that offered some protection from the wind. The streets were empty of cars and people and the rest of the world seemed to be asleep. The women talked about how nice it would be to sleep in just one morning, just for the hell of it, or because you don't feel well, and how nice it would be to have *a* place—not even your own place, just a place—where you could go and lie down for a while without having anyone else around telling you to do this or do that.

One bitterly cold Sunday morning Betty announced she was going to the mayor's office the next day to tell him what it was like to live in a shelter and to ask him to order the county-funded shelters to allow people to remain there on Sundays, sleeping, resting, doing their nails or hair, watching TV, or whatever. "Everyone is entitled to a day of rest," she said. "Even homeless women." The women within earshot nodded agreement.

Some of the working women took motel rooms on weekends once or twice a month. Jane regularly disappeared on weekends. "She went to a motel for the weekend so she could sleep in," Judy explained to one of the women who asked about her. Samantha, who was working regularly, used the shelter for eating, washing, and socializing, but when the lights went out on Friday and Saturday nights, she left the shelter to sleep in a car so she could sleep late Saturday and Sunday mornings.

When Vicki learned she would be able to move into her own place in 10 days or so, she talked about her shelter experience as if it were already in the past. The hardest part of living in a shelter, she said, was having to get up every morning, no matter how you felt. The next worse thing was having to go out on the street and kill time—really kill time—until the shelter reopened in the evening.

***

Along with perennial fatigue, boredom was one of the great trials of homelessness. Killing time was not a major problem for everyone but it was high on most women's lists of hardships.* Betty could have been speaking for most of them when she talked about the problem. On a social visit to the state psychiatric hospital where, four years earlier, she had been an inpatient in an alcoholic program, Betty sought out a nurse named Lou. They embraced and Lou asked Betty what she was doing these days. Betty said she was living in a shelter. Lou said that was a shame, and asked Betty how she spent her time.

"I walk the streets," said Betty. "Twelve hours and 15 minutes a day, every day, I walk the streets. Is that what I got sober for? To walk the streets?" Betty went on to say that she sits on a lot of park benches looking for someone to talk to. Many times there is no one, so she talks to the birds. She and the birds have done a lot of talking in her day, she said.

Months later, Betty repeated much of this at her SSI (Supplemental Security Income) hearing. She told the hearing officer about being homeless and sleeping in the night shelter. He asked what her biggest problem was, and Betty said it was staying on the street for 12 hours and 15 minutes every day. She told him about the public library and park benches and the birds. Staying awake with nothing to do was a special problem, she added. You are not permitted to sleep in the library, she said, and she didn't dare fall asleep on a park bench for fear that someone would steal her bags or that a policeman would arrest her for vagrancy.

Some of the women with jobs also had trouble killing time. Like the others, Grace had to leave the shelter by 7:00 A.M. but she couldn't report to work much before 9:00, and her job was less than a 10-minute drive away. "Have you ever tried to kill two hours in the morning, every morning, with nowhere to go and nothing to

---

*DIRECTOR: This world is a place for productive people. The idea of killing time, day after day, was an alien concept to the vigorous, enthusiastic staff. The Refuge volunteers would regularly suggest a plan of action which in a rational world would begin to solve a woman's problems. These solutions were offered with little understanding of the complexity of these women's lives.

do?" she asked. "I have some tapes I can listen to in the car—some Christmas carols and some Bible readings. But two hours? Every day?"

For Sara, leaving the shelter in the morning was by far the worst time of day. That was when being homeless hit her the hardest. You can't decide what to do because it doesn't matter what you do. You're not needed anywhere, not wanted anywhere, and not expected anywhere. Nobody cares what you do.

"I can't go on, walking the streets all day and coming here at night," announced Elsie one evening. "It's not my style. It's just not my style." Some women were better than others at finding relief in a book or TV program or jigsaw puzzle at the day shelter, or in conversation with others, but relief was typically short-lived. Sleeping may also have been tried as a remedy. In the parks, the lobbies of public buildings, and the day shelters, the women did a lot of sleeping. Some of this may have been because they did not sleep well at night, or because of medication, or depression perhaps, but some of it was also a way of killing time, a way of getting through the nothing-to-do present until it was time to do something—go to the soup kitchen, show up for a clinic appointment, or return to the night shelter.

Other kinds of behavior were also aimed at killing time or making it more bearable. Many of the women, for example, regularly appeared at the night shelter or the day shelter or the soup kitchen long before they opened, even when there were no lines to give advantage to early arrivals. It was as if the rush to get to the next "event" was a way of moving from a do-nothing to a do-something state.

For much the same reasons, the women might talk about and plan for an appointment with a doctor or a caseworker that was still several days away. In part, this may have been simply a matter of paying attention to what was most important to them at the moment, but this early anticipation may have also served to bring the event prematurely into present time, thereby giving the otherwise boring and undifferentiated present some sort of focus and direction.

Sometimes the women also made what looked like a deliberate effort to take apart a group of tasks and stretch them out over several days. At any given time, for example, a woman might need to make an appointment with a caseworker, visit a clinic, see a housing office representative, go to the unemployment office, or attend to some personal business. Any two of these tasks could normally be done in a day, one in the morning and one in the afternoon, and three in one day was not always out of the question.

Having a task to do, however, was a precious resource that gave point and structure to the day when it had to be done. To do two or three tasks on the same day would be a waste of resources, so the women often seemed to go out of their way to stretch their tasks over several days.* Thus, what often seemed to be procrastination or laziness or exasperating inefficiency to those looking in from the

---

*KIM: I think this is overstated. Service providers are spread out all over the county. It can take several bus transfers to reach Point B. Bus stop waits and waits in line add up to many hours. Filling out applications everywhere adds up to more. Particularly when dealing with Social Services, a great deal of time is wasted on the way to brick walls and dead ends.

outside may well have been, from the women's point of view, an attempt to distribute structure and meaning over as many days as possible.[5]

* * *

It is all too easy to think of homeless people as having few or no possessions ("How could a homeless person have anything of value?" sneered Kim), but one of the major and most talked-about problems was storage—how to keep one's clothing, essential documents, and other belongings secure and accessible. The preservation and protection of belongings could be a major consumer of one's time, energy, and resources. A principal difficulty was the fact that most emergency shelters had only limited space for individual storage—often space for only two bags or two small cardboard boxes.* And it was not uncommon to find shelters where one could not store anything at all.[6] Even where limited storage space was available, many women were reluctant to use it because there was no guarantee that their belongings would be intact when they returned. Stealing was believed to be common: "You've got to expect these things in shelters" was heard from staff and women alike. The end result was that many homeless women who would have left their belongings behind had they had a safe place to store them were forced to take most of their belongings with them. Some wore them in layers. Others carried them. They had become, in short, bag ladies.[7]

During a discussion of Luther Place, one of the best-run shelters in downtown Washington, one of the women said Luther Place was OK but she didn't like the women there—they were all bag ladies. One of the other women objected that the women at Luther Place were no different from women in other shelters. They were bag ladies, she said, because Luther Place had no storage space.

With some important exceptions, how much "stuff" one had was inversely proportional to the length of time one had been homeless. The longer a woman had been homeless, the more likely it was that she had had to jettison belongings, often stripping down to just what she could carry. For most women, this stripping-down process was a painful exercise in triage. Much of what they carried around in bags, boxes, or suitcases was clothing. Sometimes there was an emergency food ration. Along with toilet articles, some cosmetics, maybe a can opener, a bottle of aspirin or Tylenol or a prescription drug, almost everyone carried a birth certificate, pocket-size ID, varieties of legal documents or official papers, and perhaps some rent receipts or W-2's.

More important, however, were the other, more personal things. Often there were snapshots or framed photographs of children or other family members, personal letters, a color picture of Jesus, a Bible, and other religious and inspirational reading material. There may also have been a teddy bear or a bronzed baby shoe, a swizzle stick perhaps, or a matchbook cover, and some objects that looked like

---

*DIRECTOR: Without question, dealing with the "stuff" of these women was a great source of consternation. There was absolutely no room for the women's personal belongings. There was also an underlying concern that the belongings were a health hazard: some bags were filled with old food and insects.

nothing more than a rag, a bone, a hank of hair, but which were, in fact, tokens of some treasured secret.

Given the contents of their bags, boxes, and suitcases, it is not surprising that the women were fiercely protective and possessive of them, sometimes to the patronizing amusement of outsiders. The importance of clothing and toiletries is self-evident. Moreover, the women had to carry proof of their social existence with them. Without a home address, telephone number, or job as testimony to their existence, they needed their birth certificates and other documents to prove that they existed as legal persons with rights to assert and claims to make on society.

Many of the personal things—the letters, the religious materials, the photographs, and the mementos of people, relationships, and experiences—looked back to earlier, presumably happier times. In effect, the women carried their life histories with them. To lose one's stuff, or to have to jettison some of it, was to lose connections to one's past if not the past itself. Thus, for women who had only the one or two slender boxes they may have been allowed to store in the shelter, along with what they may have carried with them, their more personal belongings tended to be strongly oriented toward the past.[8]

Many other women, however, mainly recent arrivals to homelessness or those with a car or other resources, often had far more belongings than they could carry or store in the shelters. These belongings were typically stored in their cars, public storage warehouses, a church basement, a fellow Alcoholics Anonymous member's garage, or even a garage or attic in the house of a friend or relative.

Most of the time, these nonportable possessions looked forward, not backward. They were things that were being saved for the future rather than remembrances of things past. Here, in the automobiles and the public and private storage spaces, the women kept not only clothing but pots and pans and linens and silverware, lamps and chairs, hat boxes and electric typewriters, and sometimes rugs and other heavy, major household furnishings as well. Sara regularly visited her storage unit to fondle her carefully wrapped crystal and linens. "That sustains her," said Samantha.

Clearly, the main value of these furnishings lay not in sentiment but in the hope, if not the prospect, that they would all be needed tomorrow or next week or next month when the woman would once again set up housekeeping in her own place. So long as she continued to own pots and pans and linens and things, she could remain, in her own mind at least, a temporarily dispossessed homemaker whose return to homemaking was imminent. For the woman who had to give up these furnishings, however, the prospect of returning to homemaking receded into uncertainty and she was plunged deeper into the reality of homelessness.

Past and future, then, and even one's self, were embedded in one's belongings. When Louise could no longer pay for storage and lost her belongings to auction, she was surprised at her own reaction to the loss. Her belongings had been so much a part of her, she said, that now that she's lost them, she's not sure who she is.[9]

Great sacrifices were made to store belongings, and the ever-present threat of losing them was a major source of anxiety and stress. The smallest and cheapest spaces in public storage warehouses were 5' × 5' and rented for $37.50 to $42.50 a month, which meant that some of the women on public assistance spent about 25 percent of their income for storage alone. Others spent much more. During her first couple of years of homelessness, while she still had money from her divorce settlement (her share of the proceeds from sale of the house), Louise paid $156 a month to store her household goods. Kim maintained a storage space in her hometown as well as one in the shelter area. Together, these cost her about $90 a month.

For many women, it was much too easy to fall behind in storage payments, and the penalties built up quickly. The "late charge," invoked one day after the monthly due date, was $10. After 10 days, management put their own lock on the storage bin, denying access to the renter until all due monies had been paid. After 30 days, the stored contents were subject to public auction.

Fierce attachment to belongings meant that many women, storing their things on a month-to-month basis and not knowing how long they would have to continue, ended up making monthly storage payments that totaled many times the original or replacement cost of what was stored. Shirley's experience was a case in point. Shirley had been behind in her storage payments for several months but had managed to stave off the loss of her things to public auction each month by last-minute fund-raising heroics. Eventually, however, she missed another deadline. Suspecting that the auction hammer had come down on the contents of her locker, Shirley and I drove to the storage facility. Yes, the auction had been held, the manager told her, but her stuff was still recoverable because no one had seen fit to bid even $5 for the contents of her $42.50-per-month locker. Shirley was dismayed. This news was probably worse than learning that someone had bought them. "The footlocker alone is worth $50," she protested. "And the chair. Isn't that a nice chair?"

To lighten the financial burden, two or even three women sometimes shared a space, but in a 5' × 5' area, the only way to accommodate additional items was to pile them ever higher. This made for a variety of storage and retrieval problems requiring a strenuous and time-consuming reorganization for each use, especially if—as when June and Peggy doubled up—big or fragile items were involved (a sofa up on end, an old, heavy IBM Selectric typewriter, several lamps, a rug, books, dishes, and more).

So important was secure and adequate storage that women sometimes allowed it to be a determining factor in important life choices. Kim turned down a new job at a much higher salary because her current job allowed her to store her belongings in a locked attic at her place of employment. The higher salary would have more than covered the cost of public storage, but Kim decided the extra money was not worth the loss of convenience and easy access to belongings stored on the job. Elsie planned to prepay six months storage costs when she thought (incorrectly) that she was getting an $800 income tax refund.

Jeanette stored her household furnishings in her 1974 Datsun B-210 station wagon. The car broke down and was towed away by police before Jeanette could assemble the money to repair it. Distraught, Jeanette traced the car to the county's Abandoned Auto Lot. We drove there to salvage some of her smaller, more valued possessions. The lot attendant told Jeanette that the next auction would be the following Friday and that she could probably buy back her car (and everything in it) for $25 or so, the going rate for junk autos. Successful bidders, he told her, would have three days in which to remove their purchases from the lot.

But Jeanette's station wagon had three flat tires, a dead battery, dead license plates, and surely a string of invisible problems as well. The cost of repurchasing the car, having it towed off the lot, and making even minimal repairs would be many times the value of the car, but Jeanette was determined to buy it back. Not for transportation, she explained, but as the only way she could retrieve and afford to keep her belongings. For her, the car had become, purely and simply, a storeroom.[10]

ENDNOTES

1. "Almost" is crucial because the issue is life and death. Some homeless people are killed by hopelessness. Some die quietly and others die violent deaths. Some die from untreated disease or injury, some freeze to death, and still others lose digits or limbs. Here is the sworn testimony of a doctor who treated homeless patients in several Washington, D.C., shelters: "During the winter of 1987/1988, I have personal knowledge that approximately 30 homeless persons . . . had one or more fingers, toes, feet, or legs amputated as a result of gangrene following frostbite. . . . I have been informed that during the winter of 1987/1988, at least 10 homeless persons froze to death." Janelle Goetcheus, MD, *Affidavit (W) in Support of Plaintiff's Memorandum.* . . .

In mild-wintered San Francisco in 1988, the death rate for homeless persons was 58% higher than that for the general population. National Coalition for the Homeless, *Safety Network* 8, no. 2 (February 1989), p. 1.

2. It was from the women that I learned to juxtapose good little things and bad little things in this way. It puts "little things" in a fresh perspective and supports Otto Jesperson's observation that the world is made up of little things; what is important is to see them largely. Cited by Geoffrey K. Pullum, *The Great Eskimo Vocabulary Hoax and Other Irreverent Essays on the Study of Language*, p. 68.

3. Contrary to popular belief, homeless persons do not have secret, ingenious, and sometimes easy ways of getting along. In fact, homeless people on the street have precisely those terrible problems that one would guess them to have. Kathleen Dockett, in her interview study of street homeless persons in Washington, D.C., reports that "a lack of access to bathing (68%) and laundry facilities were the most difficult needs to satisfy. The . . . need for sufficient sleep (63%) and safety in terms of finding a safe place to sleep (58%) were the second most difficult needs to satisfy. . . . There was a strong consensus . . . that shelters were unhealthy, dangerous, stressful." Dockett, *Street Homeless People in the District of Columbia: Characteristics and Service Needs,* pp. viii, ix. When one realizes that many homeless persons—mostly men—often choose street life over shelter life, one begins to get a sense of just how "unhealthy, dangerous, stressful" some shelters can be.

4. The chapter-by-chapter discussion of these needs is not meant to imply a hierarchy.

5. Elderly persons who live alone sometimes resort to much the same strategy of make-work, a sort of remembering to forget. In the morning, a woman goes to the supermarket and buys, say, a carton of milk and a loaf of bread. Later the same morning, she says, "Oh, I forgot to get eggs," and returns to the store. Still later, "I forgot to get potatoes," or "I forgot to go to the post office," and so on through the day, thereby filling it up with things to do.

6. I helped June to move to Mount Carmel, a women's shelter in downtown D.C., and one of the most preferred shelters in the city. She moved in with seven bags, boxes, and suitcases.

The sister in charge explained, almost apologetically, that June would be allowed to store only two such items in the shelter. June went through her things. She threw some of them out and stored the remainder at the Catholic church she used to attend.

7.   Of course not all bag ladies were forced into that status. Some women were or had become bag ladies for less obviously rational reasons, but they were a minority. If affordable, accessible, and secure storage space were available, surely many bag ladies would disappear.

8.   In this discussion of storage, I have attempted to exclude hoarders—those women who hold on to things because they cannot let go of them. It is useful to keep in mind, however, that the storage problems of the occasional hoarder, even if self-inflicted, are as great or greater than everyone else's.

9.   "To lose a home or the sum of one's belongings is to lose evidence as to who one is and where one belongs in this world." Kai T. Erikson, *Everything in Its Path: Destruction of Community in the Buffalo Creek Flood*, p. 177. See the section "The Furniture of Self" in this beautiful book for additional insights into the meanings embedded in one's house and personal possessions.

10.   Jeanette did, in fact, buy back her car for $25, and she found "a Christian gas station owner" who agreed to tow it to his lot and wait for the money. The car never again moved under its own power, but Jeanette was able to keep her things there until, six weeks later, the minister of the church she attended found a church member who allowed her to store her things in his garage.

CHAPTER 12

As Rich–Poor Gap Widens in the U.S., Class Mobility Stalls

David Wessel

The notion that the U.S is a special place where any child can grow up to be president, a meritocracy where smarts and ambition matter more than parenthood and class, dates to Benjamin Franklin. The 15th child of a candle-and-soap maker, Franklin started out as a penniless printer's apprentice and rose to wealth so great that he retired to a life of politics and diplomacy at age 42.

The promise that a child born in poverty isn't trapped there remains a staple of America's self-portrait. President Bush, though a riches-to-riches story himself, revels in the humble origins of some in his cabinet. He says his attorney general "grew up in a two-bedroom house," the son of "migrant workers who never finished elementary school." He notes that his Cuban-born commerce secretary's first job for Kellogg Corp. was driving a truck; his last was chief executive.

But the reality of mobility in America is more complicated than the myth. As the gap between rich and poor has widened since 1970, the odds that a child born in poverty will climb to wealth—or a rich child will fall into the middle class—remain stuck. Despite the spread of affirmative action, the expansion of community colleges and the other social changes designed to give people of all classes a shot at success, Americans are no more or less likely to rise above, or fall below, their parents' economic class than they were 35 years ago.

Although Americans still think of their land as a place of exceptional opportunity—in contrast to class-bound Europe—the evidence suggests otherwise. And scholars have, over the past decade, come to see America as a less mobile society than they once believed.

As recently as the late 1980s, economists argued that not much advantage passed from parent to child, perhaps as little as 20%. By that measure, a rich man's grandchild would have barely any edge over a poor man's grandchild.

"Almost all the earnings advantages or disadvantages of ancestors are wiped out in three generations," wrote Gary Becker, the University of Chicago economist and Nobel laureate, in 1986. "Poverty would not seem to be a 'culture' that persists for several generations."

But over the last 10 years, better data and more number-crunching have led economists and sociologists to a new consensus: The escalators of mobility move much more slowly. A substantial body of research finds that at least 45% of parents' advantage in income is passed along to their children, and perhaps as much as 60%. With the higher estimate, it's not only how much money your parents have that matters— even your great-great grandfather's wealth might give you a noticeable edge today.

Many Americans believe their country remains a land of unbounded opportunity. That perception explains why Americans, much more than Europeans, have tolerated the widening inequality in recent years. It is OK to have ever-greater differences between rich and poor, they seem to believe, as long as their children have a good chance of grasping the brass ring.

This continuing belief shapes American politics and economic policy. Technology, globalization and unfettered markets tend to erode wages at the bottom and lift wages at the top. But Americans have elected politicians who oppose using the muscle of government to restrain the forces of widening inequality. These politicians argue that lifting the minimum wage or requiring employers to offer health insurance would do unacceptably large damage to economic growth.

Despite the widespread belief that the U.S. remains a more mobile society than Europe, economists and sociologists say that in recent decades the typical child

Family Fortune

Where men fall on the scale as adults
when their fathers were in the...

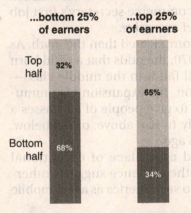

FIGURE 12.1   Family Fortunes

Note: 1995–98 wages for sons born between 1963–68. Figures don't add up to 100% due to rounding.

Source: Bhashkar Mazumder, Chicago Federal Reserve Bank.

starting out in poverty in continental Europe (or in Canada) has had a better chance at prosperity. Miles Corak, an economist for Canada's national statistical agency who edited a recent Cambridge University Press book on mobility in Europe and North America, tweaked dozens of studies of the U.S., Canada and European countries to make them comparable. "The U.S. and Britain appear to stand out as the least mobile societies among the rich countries studied," he finds. France and Germany are somewhat more mobile than the U.S.; Canada and the Nordic countries are much more so.

Even the University of Chicago's Prof. Becker is changing his mind, reluctantly. "I do believe that it's still true if you come from a modest background it's easier to move ahead in the U.S. than elsewhere," he says, "but the more data we get that doesn't show that, the more we have to accept the conclusions."

Still, the escalators of social mobility continue to move. Nearly a third of the freshmen at four-year colleges last fall said their parents hadn't gone beyond high school. And thanks to a growing economy that lifts everyone's living standards, the typical American is living with more than his or her parents did. People today enjoy services—cellphones, cancer treatment, the Internet—that their parents and grandparents never had.

Measuring precisely how much the prosperity of Americans depends on advantages conferred by their parents is difficult, since it requires linking income data across many decades. U.S. research relies almost entirely on a couple of long-running surveys. One began in 1968 at the University of Michigan and now tracks more than 7,000 families with more than 65,000 individuals; the other was started by the Labor Department in 1966.

One drawback of the surveys is that they don't capture the experiences of recent immigrants or their children, many of whom have seen extraordinary upward mobility. The University of California at Berkeley, for instance, says 52% of last year's undergraduates had two parents who weren't born in the U.S., and that's not counting the relatively few students whose families live abroad.

Nonetheless, those two surveys offer the best way to measure the degree to which Americans' economic success or failure depends on their parents. University of Michigan economist Gary Solon, an authority in the field, says one conclusion is clear: "Intergenerational mobility in the U.S. has not changed dramatically over the last two decades."

Bhashkar Mazumder, a Federal Reserve Bank of Chicago economist, recently combined the government survey with Social Security records for thousands of men born between 1963 and 1968 to see what they were earning when they reached their late 20s or 30s. Only 14% of the men born to fathers on the bottom 10% of the wage ladder made it to the top 30%. Only 17% of the men born to fathers on the top 10% fell to the bottom 30%.

LAND OF THE SELF-MADE MAN

Benjamin Franklin best exemplified and first publicized America as the land of the mobile society. "He is the prototype of the self-made man, and his life is the classic American success story—the story of a man rising from the most obscure of origins to wealth and international preeminence," one of his many biographers, Gordon S. Wood, wrote in 2004.

In 1828, a 14-year-old Irish immigrant named Thomas Mellon read Franklin's popular "Autobiography" and later described it as a turning point in his life. "Here was Franklin, poorer than myself, who by industry, thrift and frugality had become learned and wise, and elevated to wealth and fame," Mellon wrote in a memoir. The young Mellon left the family farm, became a successful lawyer and judge and later founded what became Pittsburgh's Mellon Bank. In front, he erected a statue of Franklin.

Even Karl Marx accepted the image of America as a land of boundless opportunity, citing this as an explanation for the lack of class consciousness in the U.S. "The position of wage laborer," he wrote in 1865, "is for a very large part of the American people but a probational state, which they are sure to leave within a longer or shorter term."

Self-made industrialist Andrew Carnegie, writing in the *New York Tribune* in 1890, catalogued the "captains of industry" who started as clerks and apprentices and were "trained in that sternest but most efficient of all schools—poverty."

The historical record suggests this widely shared belief about 19th-century America was more than myth. "You didn't need to be told. You lived it. And if you didn't, your neighbors did," says Joseph Ferrie, an economic historian at Northwestern University, who has combed through the U.S. and British census records that give the occupations of thousands of native-born father-and-son pairs who lived between 1850 and 1920. In all, more than 80% of the sons of unskilled men moved to higher-paying, higher-status occupations in the late 1800s in the U.S., but less than 60% in Britain did so.

The biggest factor, Mr. Ferrie says, is that young Americans could do something most British couldn't: climb the economic ladder quickly by moving from farm towns to thriving metropolises. In 1850, for instance, James Roberts was a 14-year-old son of a day laborer living in the western New York hamlet of Catharine. Handwritten census records reveal that 30 years later, Mr. Roberts was a bookkeeper—a much higher rung—and living in New York City at 2257 Third Ave. with his wife and four children.

As education became more important in the 20th century—first high school, later college—leaping up the ladder began to require something that only better-off parents could afford: allowing their children to stay in school instead of working. "Something quite fundamental changed in the U.S. economy in the years after 1910 and before the Great Depression," says Prof. Ferrie.

One reason that the once-sharp differences between social mobility in the U.S. and Britain narrowed in the 20th century, he argues, is that the regional economies of the U.S. grew more and more similar. It became much harder to leap several rungs of the economic ladder simply by moving.

The paucity of data makes it hard to say how mobility changed for much of the 20th century. Individual census records—the kind that Prof. Ferrie examines—are still under seal for most of the 20th century. Data from the two national surveys didn't start rolling in until the 1970s.

Whatever the facts, the Franklin-inspired notion of America as an exceptionally mobile society persisted through most of the 20th century, as living standards improved after World War II and the children and grandchildren of immigrants prospered. Jeremiads in the 1960s and 1970s warned of an intractable culture of poverty that trapped people at the bottom for generations, and African-Americans didn't enjoy the same progress as whites. But among large numbers of Americans, there was little doubt that their children would ride the escalator.

OLD WISDOM SHATTERS

In 1992, though, Mr. Solon, the Michigan economist, shattered the conventional academic wisdom, arguing in the *American Economic Review* that earlier studies relied on "error-ridden data, unrepresentative samples, or both" and misleadingly compared snapshots of a single year in the life of parent and child rather than looking over longer periods. There is "dramatically less mobility than suggested by earlier research," he said. Subsequent research work confirmed that.

As Mr. Mazumder, the Chicago Fed economist, put it in the title of a recent book chapter: "The apple falls even closer to the tree than we thought."

Why aren't the escalators working better? Figuring out how parents pass along economic status, apart from the obvious but limited factor of financial bequests, is tough. But education appears to play an important role. In contrast to the 1970s, a college diploma is increasingly valuable in today's job market. The tendency of college grads to marry other college grads and send their children to better elementary and high schools and on to college gives their children a lasting edge.

The notion that the offspring of smart, successful people are also smart and successful is appealing, and there is a link between parent and child IQ scores. But most research finds IQ isn't a very big factor in predicting economic success.

In the U.S., race appears to be a significant reason that children's economic success resembles their parents'. From 32 years of data on 6,273 families recorded by the University of Michigan's long-running survey, American University economist Tom Hertz calculates that 17% of whites born to the bottom 10% of families ranked by income remained there as adults, but 42% of the blacks did. Perhaps as a consequence, public-opinion surveys find African-Americans more likely to favor government redistribution programs than whites.

The tendency of well-off parents to have healthier children, or children more likely to get treated for health problems, may also play a role. "There is very powerful evidence that low-income kids suffer from more health problems, and childhood health does predict adult health and adult health does predict performance," observes Christopher Jencks, a noted Harvard sociologist.

Passing along personality traits to one's children may be a factor, too. Economist Melissa Osborne Groves of Maryland's Towson University looked at results of a psychological test for 195 father–son pairs in the government's long-running National Longitudinal Survey. She found similarities in attitudes about life accounted for 11% of the link between the income of a father and his son.

Nonetheless, Americans continue to cherish their self-image as a unique land where past and parentage puts no limits on opportunity, as they have for centuries. In his "Autobiography," Franklin wrote simply that he had "emerged from the poverty and obscurity in which I was born and bred to a state of affluence." But in a version that became the standard 19th-century text, his grandson, Temple, altered the words to underscore the enduring message: "I have *raised myself* to a state of affluence . . . "

PART FOUR

Racism

During the 1960s, the successful struggle for legislation to enforce equal opportunity for minorities—in jobs, housing, and education—created the hope that government action would effectively remove the most important barriers to racial equality in American society. This sense of optimism was enhanced by the expectation of an ever-expanding economy that seemed to promise there would be room for everyone to have a chance at the good life in America.

To some extent, these expectations were borne out—for a while. Blacks and other minorities made significant social and economic progress, particularly in the 1960s, as a result of civil rights protest, government action, and an expanding economy. But the urban riots of the 1960s also showed a more ominous side of the racial picture and revealed that some aspects of racial disadvantage in the United States were relatively impervious to both economic growth and the expansion of civil rights. And during the 1970s and early 1980s, some of the gains made by minorities in earlier years began to be reversed. Minority income fell behind as a proportion of white income, and minority poverty—especially in the inner cities—increased sharply. A combination of unfavorable economic trends, a less generous public policy, and a waning commitment to the vigorous enforcement of civil rights laws has continued to take its toll on minority progress in recent years.

Yet despite these troubling developments, some commentators insist that race is no longer very important in America. No one denies that minorities still suffer a variety of economic and social disadvantages. But it is now sometimes argued that these disadvantages no longer have much to do with outright racial discrimination—which, in this view, has greatly diminished over time. We have, after all, elected an African American as President of the United States. In this argument, the high rates of unemployment and poverty among black Americans, for example, are now mainly due to problems of culture or attitudes, rather than systematic barriers to economic opportunity.

The articles in this section, however, make it clear that this celebration of the end of racial discrimination is decidedly premature. Race still matters in the United

States, and it matters very much. In virtually every realm of American life, minorities must contend with a playing field that remains decidedly unequal.

How can this be true, when we have created so many laws and programs designed to level that field? One reason, as Michael K. Brown and his co-authors argue, is that for generations, the policies of both government and private employers worked in precisely the opposite direction—systematically providing advantages to white Americans that, though sometimes subtle, have shaped the country's racial situation ever since. Most Americans are unaware, for example, that black workers were largely excluded from both Social Security and unemployment compensation for decades—which helped trap them in poverty and economic insecurity and ensured that they fell farther behind whites on the income ladder. At the same time, the housing policies of both private banks and the federal government deliberately supported residential segregation in the cities, which effectively locked many African Americans in impoverished, troubled neighborhoods and robbed them of one of the most important sources of personal wealth—the ownership of a valuable home. In these ways and others, the racial policies of an earlier era have left a legacy of inequality that we have yet to challenge successfully.

The effects of that inequality are disturbingly apparent in the criminal justice system—the site of some of the most dramatic, and divisive, racial disparities in the United States. A half century after the start of the Civil Rights movement, African Americans—especially young African Americans—are far more likely to spend time in jails and prisons than their white counterparts. As the report we reprint from the Sentencing Project notes, there are roughly nine times as many blacks behind bars than at the time of the famous *Brown v. Board of Education* court decision that ended the formal racial segregation of public schools. The reasons for that troubling increase, as the authors point out, are complex—ranging from stubbornly high crime rates to the unequal impact of the war on drugs. But the effects of this unprecedented level of imprisonment are felt in many ways, all of which should concern us. Today a stunning proportion of black children have at least one parent in jail during some part of their childhoods. About one in eight black men cannot vote because they have been convicted of a felony. More generally, the experience of jail or prison has come, in many communities, to seem like an "almost inevitable" aspect of growing up for young black Americans.

The persistence of racial disparities in housing, social benefits, and criminal justice is matched in other institutions as well, including education and jobs. Since the emergence of the civil rights movement in the 1950s and 1960s, there have been many attempts to tackle those inequalities and to promote racial equity and diversity.

One of the most important strategies to combat discrimination has been what is loosely called "affirmative action"—the requirement that institutions make special efforts to ensure a fair chance for historically underrepresented minorities. Many people wrongly believe that this means that colleges, businesses, and other institutions maintain "quotas" mandating that a certain percentage of their employees or students must be from minority groups. In fact, such quotas have been illegal since the 1970s. But universities and other institutions *have* been allowed to devise a variety of ways to increase racial and ethnic diversity.

Affirmative action has become one of most controversial social policies in the United States: many feel that it gives unfair preferences to minorities which have nothing to do with their merit or performance, while others believe that it is an essential tool to maintain a diverse community and to help redress the discriminatory policies of the past. However one feels about that issue in the abstract, it is important to put it in context. What is usually left out in the public debate over affirmative action is that many *other* groups besides minorities receive a variety of preferences in such things as admission to college, and have for a long time. Athletes, for example, have long been able to gain admission to exclusive colleges with lower grades and test scores than other applicants. And, as Daniel Golden shows, many universities now make special efforts to bend the standards in order to admit the children of wealthy parents. This is sometimes euphemistically called "development" admissions, but by whatever name, it is a kind of preference. The fact that, as one student puts it, "Everybody at Duke has something that got them in," helps to put the issue of affirmative action for minority students in better perspective.

The issue of race has become more complex than ever in recent years, because the face of race and ethnicity in American is changing. We are in the midst of one of the most dramatic periods of mass immigration in our history, which has brought millions of people here from all over the world—with especially large numbers coming from Mexico, Latin America, and Asia. As in earlier waves of immigration, the social and cultural changes these newcomers have brought have led to fears and resentments among some of those already here. Much of that response is rooted in the belief that immigrants are hurting the economy and lowering the quality of life for everyone else. In her book *They Take Our Jobs!* Aviva Chomsky shows that these beliefs are more myth than fact. In the excerpt we reprint here, Chomsky examines two myths in particular—that immigrants don't pay taxes and that they are a "drain" on the economy—and finds both to be inaccurate.

CHAPTER 13

The Roots of White Advantage

Michael K. Brown
Martin Carnoy
Elliott Currie
Troy Duster
David B. Oppenheimer
Marjorie M. Shultz
David Wellman

Almost forty years after the civil rights revolution ended, two questions bedevil most discussions of racial economic inequality: (1) Why has deep poverty endured in the black community alongside a burgeoning black middle class? (2) Why do large gaps remain in family income, wages, and employment between blacks and whites? For many people this is the paradox and the bane of the civil rights revolution. How is it, they ask, that civil rights laws ended racial discrimination and left behind an unruly black underclass and substantial racial inequality? . . .

THE ORIGINS OF MODERN STATE-SPONSORED RACIAL INEQUALITY

One need not go back three hundred years to find the antecedents of contemporary white advantage. The New Deal is the most recent benchmark for the accumulation of white privilege and the generation of black disadvantage. Franklin D. Roosevelt's policies were instrumental to both the cause of racial equality and the perpetuation of racial inequality. New Deal agricultural policies paved the way for the mechanization of southern agriculture and precipitated black (and white) migration to the North and the entry of blacks into manufacturing jobs. The Wagner Act legalized unions; minimum wage laws put an economic floor under all workers; the

Social Security Act gave workers a measure of security; and the Employment Act of 1946 codified the government's responsibility for aggregate employment and price levels. These policies, combined with postwar economic growth, undermined the prewar northern racial order, set in motion changes that would dismantle Jim Crow, and reduced black as well as white poverty.

African Americans benefited from New Deal policies. They gained from the growth of public employment and governmental transfers like Social Security and welfare. The Great Society went further, reducing racial inequality, ameliorating poverty among the black poor, and helping to build a new black middle class. But if federal social policy promoted racial equality, it also created and sustained racial hierarchies. Welfare states are as much instruments of stratification as they are of equality. The New Deal's class-based, or race-neutral, social policies did not affect blacks and whites in identical ways. Federal social policy contributed disproportionately to the prosperity of the white middle class from the 1940s on. Whites received more from the New Deal than old-age protection and insurance against the business cycle. Housing subsidies paved the way for a white exodus to the suburbs; federal tax breaks secured union-bargained health and pension benefits and lowered the cost to workers; veterans' benefits were an avenue of upward mobility for many white men. To assume that government policies benefited only blacks or were color-blind, as many white Americans commonly believe, is like looking at the world with one eye.

Three laws passed by Congress in the mid-1930s were instrumental in generating the pattern of racial stratification that emerged during the New Deal: the Social Security Act, the Wagner Act, and the Federal Housing Act. These laws contributed to the accumulation of wealth in white households, and they did more than any other combination of factors to sow and nurture the seeds of the future urban ghetto and produce a welfare system in which recipients would be disproportionately black. It is commonly assumed that the New Deal was based on broad and inclusive policies. While there is some truth to the claim that Roosevelt's New Deal was designed, as Jill Quadagno states it, to provide a "floor of protection for the industrial working class," it was riddled with discrimination. Brokered compromises over New Deal labor and social policies also reinforced racial segregation through social welfare programs, labor policy, and housing policy.[1] How and why did this happen?

Although the Social Security Act created a work-related social right to an old-age pension and unemployment compensation, Congress defied the Roosevelt administration and explicitly excluded domestic and agricultural workers from coverage. It also exempted public employees as well as workers in nonprofit, voluntary organizations. Only 53 percent of all workers, about 26 million people, were initially covered by the old-age insurance title of the Social Security Act, and less than half of all workers were covered by unemployment compensation. Congress subsequently excluded these exempt workers from the Wagner Act and the 1938 Fair Labor Standards Act as well.[2]

Congress's rejection of universal coverage was not a race-neutral decision undertaken because, as some people claimed at the time, it was difficult to collect payroll taxes from agricultural and domestic workers. As Charles Houston, Dean of the Howard University Law School, told the Senate Finance committee, "It [the Social Security bill] looks like a sieve with the holes just big enough for the majority of Negroes to fall through." Almost three-fifths of the black labor force was denied coverage. When self-employed black sharecroppers are added to the list of excluded workers, it is likely that three-quarters or more of African Americans were denied benefits and the protection of federal law. Black women, of whom 90 percent were domestic workers, were especially disadvantaged by these occupational exclusions.[3]

Agricultural and domestic workers were excluded largely because southern legislators refused to allow implementation of any national social welfare policies that included black workers. Roosevelt presided over a fragile coalition of northern industrial workers and southern whites bound to an agrarian economic order. Although blacks began to leave the party of Lincoln for the party of Roosevelt, three-quarters of the African American population still lived in the South, where they could not vote. Southerners feared that federal social policies would raise the pay of southern black workers and sharecroppers and that this in turn would undermine their system of racial apartheid. Black criticisms of the legislation were ignored as Roosevelt acquiesced to southern demands, believing he could not defy powerful southern committee chairmen and still pass needed social welfare legislation.

As black workers moved north into industrial jobs, they were eventually included under the Social Security Act, and Congress ultimately extended coverage of old-age insurance to agricultural workers in 1950 and 1954. Although the Social Security Administration made every effort to treat black and white workers equally, black workers were nevertheless severely disadvantaged by the work-related eligibility provisions of the Social Security Act. Both old-age insurance and unemployment compensation rewarded stable, long-term employment and penalized intermittent employment regardless of the reason. In the name of fiscal integrity, the architects of social insurance in the 1930s were adamant that malingerers, those on relief, or those weakly attached to the labor market be excluded from eligibility and their benefits limited. Due to labor market discrimination and the seasonal nature of agricultural labor, many blacks have not had stable, long-term employment records. Thus, they have had only limited eligibility for old-age and unemployment benefits.

The racial consequences of wage-related eligibility provisions were already apparent in the 1930s. Because labor market discrimination lowers the wages of black workers relative to white workers or denies them employment altogether, blacks receive lower benefits than whites from old-age insurance and unemployment compensation or are denied access at all. By 1939, for example, only 20 percent of white workers who worked in industries covered by social insurance and who paid payroll taxes for old-age insurance were uninsured, but more than twice as many black workers (42 percent) were uninsured.[4] From the outset, Social Security transferred income from African American workers to white workers. This disparity continues today. Even though most black workers are currently covered by

Social Security, on average they still receive lower benefits than whites and pay a higher proportion of their income in Social Security taxes.[5] Like old-age insurance, there is little evidence of overt discrimination in unemployment compensation— eligible black workers are almost as likely as white workers are to receive benefits. But because states imposed strict eligibility requirements during the 1940s and 1950s, black workers were disproportionately excluded.[6] Social insurance is neither universal nor race-neutral.

In combination, labor market discrimination and work-related eligibility requirements excluded blacks from work and social insurance programs in the 1930s, forcing many to go on relief and later on welfare, Aid to Dependent Children (ADC). In fact, most black women were excluded from the unemployment compensation system until the late 1960s. This is because domestic workers were statutorily excluded from unemployment compensation, and as late as the 1950s more than half of all black women in the civilian labor force still worked as domestics. Unemployed black women typically had nowhere to turn but welfare, and this is exactly what they did. By 1960, African Americans accounted for two-fifths of all welfare recipients, a participation rate that did not change much even when the welfare rolls expanded in the 1960s. It is labor market discrimination and New Deal social policies, not welfare, as the conservatives believe, that has harmed black families. The problem cannot be explained by a pathological black family structure.[7]

Social insurance in the United States has operated much like a sieve, just as Charles Houston predicted, and blacks have fallen through the holes. The Wagner Act and the 1937 Housing Act compounded the problem, enlarging the holes in the sieve. Sometimes labeled the Magna Charta of the labor movement, the 1935 Wagner Act was, upon closer inspection, the Magna Charta of *white* labor. Black leaders tried to add an antidiscrimination amendment to the law, but the American Federation of Labor and the white southerners who controlled key congressional committees fought it. As a result, the final version excluded black workers. The law legalized the closed shop, which, as Roy Wilkins of the NAACP pointed out, would empower "organized labor to exclude from employment in any industry those who do not belong to a union." The law also outlawed strikebreaking, a weapon black workers had used successfully to force their way into northern industries. Preventing blacks from entering into newly protected labor unions meant that black workers were subject to the racist inclinations of white workers.[8] One of the consequences of the Wagner Act's failure to protect black workers was that union rules confined them to low-wage unskilled jobs. When these jobs were eliminated as businesses modernized after World War II, black unskilled workers were replaced by automated manufacturing technologies.[9] Thus, the current high levels of black unemployment can be traced directly to New Deal legislation that allowed white workers to deny job opportunities to blacks.

State-sponsored racial inequality was also augmented by a third set of New Deal policies: federal housing and urban renewal legislation. . . .

The mortgage loan programs of the Federal Housing Administration (FHA) and Veterans Administration (VA) were additional boons to white workers. These two federal programs financed more than one-third of all post–World War II mortgages, accounting for more than $120 billion in new housing.[10] The FHA and VA insured home mortgages that allowed lenders to liberalize the terms and conditions of loans. VA mortgages also provided a direct subsidy to home buyers. Unlike the veterans' loans, FHA mortgages were redistributive, aiding working- and middle-class families. Both programs helped extend home ownership to millions of families who otherwise would have been unable to afford it. They also subsidized the development of postwar suburbs. Either the FHA or VA financed almost half of all suburban housing built in the 1950s and 1960s, a benefit that was typically reserved for whites.[11]

As we now know, FHA guidelines for lenders used racist criteria to assess the credit worthiness of loans. Housing expert Charles Abrams accurately concluded that the FHA policy "could well have been culled from the Nuremberg laws." Federal housing administrators were unwilling to insure mortgages in integrated neighborhoods, fearing that anything less than rigid segregation would undermine property values. The FHA underwriting manual warned lenders, "If a neighborhood is to retain stability, it is necessary that properties shall continue to be occupied by the same social and racial classes." Lenders were explicitly told to add restrictive covenants to contracts and deeds. As a consequence, FHA loans favored the suburbs. In a study of St. Louis County, Missouri, Kenneth Jackson compared how FHA loans were distributed in suburban towns with central cities in the same county. His study revealed enormous disparities between the treatment of central cities and suburban jurisdictions. St. Louis County, for example, received five times the number of mortgage loans and dollars as the city of St. Louis.[12] The upshot was that black families living in the city were denied mortgage insurance, and when they did receive a mortgage, the terms were less favorable.

African Americans received only 3 percent of all the home loans underwritten by FHA and VA in 1960, a total that amounted to just 30 percent of all black mortgages. White homeowners, on the other hand, were far more dependent on government-insured and subsidized mortgages: 42 percent of white mortgages in that year were paid for by FHA and VA loans. Black veterans fared somewhat better than black clients of the FHA (African American veterans received two-thirds of all government-sponsored mortgages held by blacks in 1960), but they lagged behind white veterans. By 1950, about 5 percent of black World War II veterans took advantage of a VA loan compared to 13 percent of white veterans.[13] But of course these mortgages could be used only to purchase segregated housing.

Using federal housing policies to sustain segregation is only the best-known instance of this practice. Until the 1960s federal social policy was also integral to propping up southern segregation. Southern states used federal subsidies for public works to reinforce the color line.[14] Veterans' hospitals, for example, were rigidly segregated. Most federal grants contained "nonintervention" clauses that prevented federal officials from supervising or controlling the construction of these buildings. The 1946 Hill-Burton Act contained an explicit exception allowing separate facilities for "separate population groups" if the plan made equitable provision for services of "like quality." Hill-Burton's separate but equal provision was declared unconstitutional in 1963, but by then southerners had used $37 million in federal funds to build eighty-nine segregated medical facilities. In the process, many African Americans were denied medical care, while southern whites benefited from the best medical facilities the federal government could build.[15]

These federal policies underwrote a new pattern of white accumulation and black disaccumulation throughout the country, but especially in the South and in northern cities. White families prospered as suburban developments were constructed, while black families were left holding a losing hand. After World War II, federal housing and urban renewal policies facilitated rigidly segregated neighborhoods and disinvestment in black communities. Blanket federal redlining signaled private investors to avoid making housing or business loans in black communities. One study of Chicago demonstrated that life insurance companies withdrew mortgage money from the city in the 1950s and 1960s for the same reasons the FHA refused to underwrite loans in black neighborhoods. The consequences were severe. As Douglas Massey and Nancy Denton write, "The lack of loan capital flowing into minority areas made it impossible for owners to sell their homes, leading to steep declines in property values and a pattern of disrepair, deterioration, vacancy, and abandonment." This meant that white-owned housing was more valuable than black-owned housing and that the value of white-owned housing largely depended on public policies that created and sustained residential segregation. Compounding these color-conscious, state-sponsored advantages, whites reaped all the benefits of home owning, which, in addition to being cheaper than renting, entitled them to America's major middle-class tax subsidy: the mortgage interest deduction.[16]

The 1950s federal social policies guaranteed the members of an expanding white middle class that they would accumulate considerable wealth with government assistance. Consequently, whites today possess substantially more property and financial assets than black families. In 1993, the median net worth of white households was ten times that of black and Latino households. Blacks have less equity in their homes and fewer investments and Individual Retirement Accounts (IRAs, also known as Keogh accounts). While the ratio of black to white income is 62 percent, the ratio of black to white median net worth is just 8 percent. Perhaps more important, 61 percent of black households have no net financial assets whatsoever. In contrast, only 25 percent of white households find themselves in the same predicament. And even among households with equal incomes, blacks have substantially less wealth than whites.[17]

Editors' Note: *Notes for this reading can be found in the original source.*

CHAPTER 14

Schools and Prisons

Fifty Years after *Brown v. Board of Education*

Sentencing Project

OVERVIEW

The nation is currently celebrating the 50th anniversary of the historic *Brown v. Board of Education* decision that ordered the desegregation of public education. The decision in many ways marked the beginnings of the modern day Civil Rights Movement and during the ensuing half century there has been significant social and economic progress in American society. Much work needs to be done, but many institutions in society have become more diverse and responsive to the needs of African Americans and other people of color.

However, during this period no institution has changed more than the criminal justice system, and in ways that have had profound effects on the African American community. The unprecedented growth in the prison system has produced record numbers of Americans in prison and jail, and has had a disproportionate effect on African Americans. As seen in the figure . . . , there are now nine times as many African Americans in prison or jail as on the day of the *Brown* decision. An estimated 98,000 blacks were incarcerated in 1954, a figure that has risen to 884,500 today (see Figure 14.1).[1]

These absolute numbers translate into dramatic rates for black men in particular. One of every 21 adult black men is incarcerated on any given day. For black men in their late twenties, the figure is one in eight. There are now far more incarcerated black men in this age group (161,600) than the total number of *all* incarcerated African Americans in 1954 (98,000). Given current trends, one of every three (32%) black males born today can expect to go to prison in his lifetime.

The intersection between education and criminal justice is profound as well. In 1954, Chief Justice Warren noted, "In these days, it is doubtful that any child may reasonably be expected to succeed in life if he is denied the opportunity of an education."[2] In an era dominated by information technology where success is measured by one's specialized training, the fact that more than half (52%) of black men

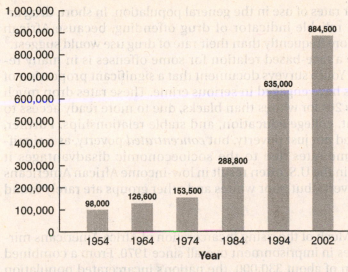

FIGURE 14.1　African Americans in Prison or Jail

in their early 30s who are high school dropouts have a prison record underscores the nation's failure to heed Chief Justice Warren's warning.

　　While the incarceration rates for women are lower overall than for men, the racial disparities are equally dramatic. One of every 18 black females born today can expect to go to prison if current trends continue, or six times the rate for white women. These odds have increased dramatically in recent decades. Black women born today are five times more likely to go to prison in their lifetimes than black women born in 1974.

CAUSAL FACTORS

The factors contributing to the dramatic increase in the number of African Americans in prison and jail are complex, and involve dynamics both within and outside the criminal justice system. Overall, they represent a social policy that has emphasized a punitive response to the problem of crime at the expense of alternative approaches that focus on strengthening families and communities. These include the following:

Crime Rates.　Higher rates of involvement in some crimes explains part of the high rate of black imprisonment. For property offenses, blacks constituted 29.6% of arrests in 2002 and for violent offenses, 38%; these compare to the 12.3% black proportion of the total population. (Note that an arrest may not always be an accurate indicator of involvement in crime, but it often remains the best means of approximating this measure.) However, criminologist Alfred Blumstein, in a study on race and imprisonment, noted that higher arrest rates for drug crimes in particular were not correlated with higher rates of use in the general population. In short, drug arrest patterns were not a reliable indicator of drug offending, because African Americans are arrested more frequently than their rate of drug use would suggest.[3]

What appears to be a race-based relation for some offenses is in many respects one of social class. Youth surveys document that a significant proportion of teenage males of all races have engaged in serious crime. These rates drop much more sharply by the early 20s for whites than blacks, due to more ready access to adult roles—employment, college education, and stable relationships. Further, researchers have identified not just poverty, but *concentrated* poverty, as a significant contributor to crime rates due to the socioeconomic disadvantages it brings. Housing patterns in the U.S. often result in low-income African Americans living in concentrated poverty, but poor whites and other groups are rarely found in such situations.

Rising Imprisonment.   Much of the rising incarceration of Africa Americans mirrors the dramatic increases in imprisonment overall since 1970. From a combined prison and jail population of about 330,000, the nation's incarcerated population has now increased to 2.1 million. This increase is largely attributable to the adoption of "get tough" policies that emphasize harsher sentencing practices, rather than any significant increases in crime rates. An examination of the growth of the prison population from 1992 to 2001 found that the entire increase was explained not by crime rates, but by an increased likelihood that convicted offenders would be sentenced to prison and by longer prison terms.[4]

War on Drugs.   Two overlapping trends since 1980 have contributed to a substantial increase in the number of African Americans in prison. First, the inception of the war on drugs has resulted in a dramatic surge in the number of incarcerated persons, rising from about 40,000 persons awaiting trial or serving a sentence for a drug charge in 1980 to about 450,000 today. The current figure is only slightly less than the total number of incarcerated persons for *all* offenses in 1980.

Second, the prosecution of the drug war has disproportionately affected communities of color. Surveys conducted by the Department of Health and Human Services estimate that blacks constitute 13.3% of monthly drug users, yet blacks represent 32.5% of persons arrested for drug offenses.[5] Of all persons imprisoned for drug offenses, three fourths are black or Latino. These disparities result in large part through a two-tiered application of the drug war. In communities with substantial resources, drug abuse is primarily addressed as a public health problem utilizing prevention and treatment approaches. In low-income communities those resources are in short supply and drug problems are more likely to be addressed through the criminal justice system.

Crack/Cocaine Sentencing.   Federal legislation adopted in 1986 and 1988 provides for far harsher punishment of crack cocaine offenders than powder cocaine offenders, even though crack is a derivative of powder cocaine. Persons convicted of selling 500 grams of powder cocaine are subject to a mandatory five-year prison term; for crack cocaine, the same penalty is triggered by possession of just five grams of the drug. Enforcement of these laws has resulted in African Americans constituting 83% of crack defendants in 2001, despite the fact that approximately two-thirds of users in the general population are white. This represents a policy decision by agencies in the criminal justice system to pursue the "war on drugs" using tactics that have a detrimental impact on the African American community.

In addition, 14 states also maintain disparities in their sentencing differentials between crack and powder cocaine. Widespread concern about these disparities led the U.S. Sentencing Commission to recommend the elimination of the sentencing differential in 1995. This recommendation was overwhelmingly rejected by Congress and the Clinton Administration. A subsequent effort to revise the penalty structure in 2002 was opposed by the Bush Administration's Department of Justice.

"School Zone" Drug Laws.   In recent years many states have adopted "school zone" drug enhancement laws that increase penalties for drug crimes committed near a school. These laws, intended to deter drug-selling to school children, have in practice contributed to extreme racial/ethnic disparities, primarily due to housing patterns. In urban areas, large proportions of most cities are within the typical 1,000–1,500 foot range of these sanctions, whereas in suburban or rural communities, far fewer locations fall within this limit. Since African Americans disproportionately live in urban areas, any such crime (even a drug sale between consenting adults at 3 A.M. near a school) will produce these enhanced penalties. In one recent year, 99% of the juveniles automatically prosecuted as adults in Cook County (Chicago), Illinois, under the school zone law were black and Latino.

"Three Strikes" and Habitual Offender Policies.   Sentencing legislation that imposes harsher prison terms on offenders with prior convictions exerts a disproportionate effect on African Americans. Judges have always had the ability to impose lengthier terms on repeat offenders, but this effect has been magnified through policies such as habitual offender laws and "three strikes and you're out" legislation. Whether one believes that African Americans are more likely to engage in crime or are subject to racial profiling and other discriminatory forms of decision making, the result is that African Americans are more likely to have a prior criminal record than other groups. Therefore, policies that impose harsher penalties based on criminal history will have a disproportionate effect on African Americans. In California, for example, blacks constitute 29% of the prison population, but 44.7% of the persons serving a "three strikes" sentence.[6] These disparities take on added significance due to the extreme disparities created by such policies. A non-violent offense in California that might otherwise lead to no more than a few years in prison becomes a sentence of 25 years to life when treated as a third strike offense.

Inadequate Defense Resources.   Forty years after the historic *Gideon* decision guaranteeing right to counsel in criminal cases, the state of indigent defense remains highly inadequate in many areas of the country. An estimated 80% of criminal defendants are indigent and a 2000 report by the Department of Justice declared that public defense was in a "chronic state of crisis." In Virginia, for example, the maximum payment for attorneys representing a defendant in a felony case that can result in a life sentence is $1,096. In Lake Charles, Louisiana, the public defender's office has only two investigators for the 2,500 new felony cases and 4,000 new misdemeanor cases assigned to the office each year. Since African Americans are disproportionately low-income, they are more likely to suffer the deficiencies produced by these dynamics.

Zero Tolerance Policies.   In response to the perceived problem of school violence, many states and school districts have enacted "zero tolerance" policies for violations of school regulations. Such policies result in automatic suspension or expulsion of students for infractions that in previous times might have been handled by school officials. While ostensibly targeted at gun violence and other serious crimes, in practice these policies have led to disciplinary action for behaviors such as bringing Advil or water pistols to school. Zero tolerance policies contribute to higher rates of suspension and expulsion, and ultimately to increased numbers of school dropouts. Children of color have been disproportionately affected by these policies. According to the Department of Education, 35% of African American children in grades 7–12 had been suspended or expelled at some point in their school careers, compared to rates of 20% for Hispanics and 15% for whites.[7] These figures in turn result in increased risk of involvement in the juvenile and adult criminal justice system.

IMPLICATIONS

At current rates of incarceration, one of every three black males born today can expect to be imprisoned at some point in his lifetime. Whether or not one believes that current crime control policies are "working" to reduce crime, such an outcome should be shocking to all Americans. Imposing a crime policy with such profound racial dynamics calls into question the nation's commitment to a free and democratic society.

Current imprisonment policies affect not only the nearly 900,000 African Americans in prison and jail, but increasingly, their families and communities as well. One of every 14 black children has a parent in prison on any given day; over the course of childhood, the figures would be much higher. Family formation, particularly in urban areas heavily affected by incarceration, is also affected by these trends. In the highest incarceration neighborhoods of Washington, D.C., the absence of black men has created a gender ratio of only 62 men for every 100 women.[8]

Community power is affected by felon disenfranchisement laws as well, which restrict voting rights while serving a felony sentence or in some cases permanently, depending on the state in which one lives. In the coming Presidential election, one of every eight black males (13%) will not be able to vote as a result of a current or previous felony conviction. These laws affect the political influence not only of people with a felony conviction, but of their communities as well. People in these neighborhoods who do not themselves have a felony conviction also have their political voices diluted since fewer residents representing their interests are able to participate in the electoral process.

None of these issues suggests that crime is not a problem for all Americans, or for African Americans in particular. But the approaches taken to address this problem over the past several decades have created a situation whereby imprisonment has come to be seen as an almost inevitable aspect of the maturing process for black men, and increasingly for black women. The social cost of these policies is substantial and growing larger each year. In this 50th anniversary of the *Brown* decision, it is time for the nation to reflect on progress in education, but also to assess how the overall status of the black community has been affected. The dynamics of criminal justice policy suggest that the nation has taken a giant step backward in this regard.

METHODOLOGY

Prison and jail custody data for Figure 14.1 were collected from various Bureau of Justice Statistics publications. Where possible, exact numbers were taken directly from the Bureau of Justice Statistics report. In the case of years in which exact prison or jail data were not available, the numbers were interpolated based on available information for contiguous years. These estimates were most commonly produced by taking the difference between the two points in time and assuming an average annual increase based on the number of years.

This briefing paper was written by Marc Mauer and Ryan Scott King, Assistant Director and Research Associate, respectively, of The Sentencing Project.

ENDNOTES

1. See Methodology section for a description of the population estimates.
2. *Brown vs. Board of Education of Topeka,* 347 U.S. 483, 493. (1954).
3. Blumstein, Alfred. (1993). "Racial Disproportionality of U.S. Prison Populations Revisited," *University of Colorado Law Review,* Vol. 64, 743–760.
4. Karberg, Jennifer C. and Beck, Allen J. "Trends in U.S. Correctional Populations: Findings from the Bureau of Justice Statistics." Presented at the National Committee on Community Corrections Meeting, Washington, DC, April 16, 2004.
5. Substance Abuse and Mental Health Services Administration, Office of Applied Studies, *National Survey on Drug Use and Health, 2002.* Table 1.26A.
6. California Department of Corrections. *Second and Third Strikers in the Institution Population.* Sacramento, CA: Data Analysis Unit. (February 2004).
7. *Status and Trends in the Education of Blacks,* U.S. Department of Education, September 2003, p. 38.
8. Braman, Donald. (2002). "Families and Incarceration," in Mauer, Marc and Chesney-Lind, Meda, (Eds.), *Invisible Punishment: The Collateral Consequences of Mass Imprisonment.* New York: The New Press. P. 128.

CHAPTER 15

At Many Colleges, the Rich Kids Get Affirmative Action

Daniel Golden

Despite her boarding-school education and a personal tutor, Maude Bunn's SAT scores weren't high enough for a typical student to earn admission to Duke University.

But Ms. Bunn had something else going for her—coffeemakers. Her Bunn forebears built a fortune on them and, with Duke hoping to woo her wealthy parents as donors, she was admitted.

Afterward, her parents promptly became co-chairmen of a Duke fund-raising effort aimed at other Duke parents. "My child was given a gift, she got in, and now I'm giving back," says Maude's mother, Cissy Bunn, who declines to say how much the family has contributed to the university.

Most universities acknowledge favoring children of alumni who support their alma mater. But to attract prospective donors, colleges are also bending admissions standards to make space for children from rich or influential families that lack longstanding ties to the institutions. Through referrals and word-of-mouth, schools identify applicants from well-to-do families. Then, as soon as these students enroll, universities start soliciting gifts from their parents.

Duke says it has never traded an admission for a donation. "There's no quid pro quo, no bargains have been struck," says Peter Vaughn, director of development communications. While it won't comment on individual cases, the university notes that financial gifts from parents are used to update facilities and provide financial aid, among other things.

The formal practice of giving preference to students whose parents are wealthy—sometimes called "development admits"—has implications for the legal challenge to affirmative action, which the U.S. Supreme Court will hear April 1 [2003]. Special admissions treatment for the affluent has racial overtones, at least indirectly. Reflecting the distribution of wealth in America, the vast majority of major donors to higher education are white. Defenders of minority preference say such advantages for white applicants are precisely why affirmative action is still needed.

Top schools ranging from Stanford University to Emory University say they occasionally consider parental wealth in admission decisions. Other elite schools, such as Massachusetts Institute of Technology, say parental means don't influence them. "I understand why universities leverage parent contacts to enrich themselves," says Marilee Jones, dean of admissions at MIT. "If somebody's offering them a check, why not take it? But I honestly think it's out of control."

While children of the wealthy have long had advantages getting into colleges, a look at how "development" admissions works at Duke shows how institutionalized the process has become at some major universities.

Under-endowed compared with rivals such as Harvard, Princeton and Stanford, Duke has been particularly aggressive in snaring donors through admissions breaks. Widely considered one of the nation's top ten universities, Duke accepts 23% of its applicants and turns down more than 600 high-school valedictorians a year. Three-fourths of its students score above 1320 out of a perfect 1600 on the SATs.

Yet in recent years, Duke says it has relaxed these standards to admit 100 to 125 students annually as a result of family wealth or connections, up from about 20 a decade ago. These students aren't alumni children and were tentatively rejected, or wait-listed, in the regular admissions review. More than half of them enroll, constituting an estimated 3% to 5% of Duke's student body of 6,200.

The strategy appears to be paying off. For the last six years, Duke says it has led all universities nationwide in unrestricted gifts to its annual fund from non-alumni parents: about $3.1 million in 2001–2002. A university fund-raising campaign recently met its $2 billion goal. While 35% of alumni donate to Duke, 52% of parents of last year's freshman class contributed to the university—besides paying $35,000 in tuition and room and board.

Students admitted for development reasons graduate at a higher rate than the overall student body, Duke says, although their grades are slightly lower. These applicants are held to the same lesser standard as some top athletes; not whether they can excel, but whether they can graduate. "There's never been a case where I think the student can't be successful at Duke, and the student is admitted," says admissions director Christoph Guttentag.

Caroline Diemar, a Duke senior, says she favors maintaining minority preference for college admissions because she knows from experience that well-connected white students get a boost too. The daughter of an investment banker, she applied early to Duke despite an 1190 SAT score. Her candidacy was deferred to the spring.

She then buttressed her application with recommendations from two family friends who were Duke donors, and she was accepted. "I needed something to make me stand out," says Ms. Diemar, a sociology major with a 3.2 grade point average, below the 3.4 average of the senior class. "Everybody at Duke has something that got them in." The lesson she learned: "Networking is how you go about everything."

After she enrolled, Duke recruited Ms. Diemar's parents to serve as co-chairmen of a fund-raising effort. Her father, Robert Diemar, declined to say how much he has given to Duke. "We support all of our five children's schools," said Mr. Diemar, a Princeton alumnus. He said Duke accepted his daughter on merit.

The practice of giving preference to the children of potential donors has caused fissures on Duke's campus, with some worrying that it dilutes the student body's intellectual vitality and undermines racial and economic diversity. In November 2000, a report to the trustees by a university committee on admissions called for a one-third cut in applicants accepted for development reasons. Mr. Guttentag says he plans to reduce such admissions to about 65 this year to achieve "greater flexibility" in shaping next fall's freshman class.

Duke President Nannerl O. Keohane thinks the Supreme Court should uphold affirmative action because preferences for children of potential donors is "disproportionately favorable to white students. . . . The two are definitely linked, and it seems odd to me to allow one sort of preference, but not the other."

The University of Michigan, defendant in the affirmative action case before the Supreme Court, wants to continue to allow preferential treatment for minorities. It also gives preferential admissions treatment to children of potential donors—but only if they're white or Asian.

DISCRETIONARY POINTS

Under the 150-point "Selection Index" Michigan uses for undergraduate admissions, a review committee may award 20 "discretionary" points to children of donors, legislators, faculty members and other key supporters. Minorities underrepresented in higher education—Hispanics, African-Americans and Native Americans—qualify for an automatic 20 points, but they are ineligible for the discretionary points. The university says less than 1% of admitted students receive this edge.

The late Terry Sanford, Duke president from 1969 to 1985, practiced donor preference on a large scale. Mr. Sanford, a gregarious former North Carolina governor, used his wide circle of contacts in business, politics and the media to elevate Duke from a regional to a national university. According to Keith Brodie, Duke's president emeritus, Mr. Sanford would personally meet each year with the admissions and development directors to ensure special attention for 200 of his friends' children applying to Duke. More than 100 would ultimately enroll.

As president from 1985 to 1993, Dr. Brodie says, he removed himself from the admissions process, resisted lobbying by some trustees, and trimmed the number of underqualified students admitted due to donor preference to 20 a year. "A Duke education is too valuable an asset to squander," says Dr. Brodie, a professor of psychiatry, who was criticized as president for a lack of fund-raising zeal. "University presidents are under greater pressure than ever to raise money," he adds. "I suspect many of them have turned to admissions to help that process."

Harold Wingood, who was senior associate director of admissions under Dr. Brodie, recalls that 30 to 40 students per year were upgraded from "rejected" to "wait-list," or from "wait-list" to "admit" due to their family ties. "We'd take students in some cases with SAT scores 100 points below the mean, or just outside the top 15% of their class," says Mr. Wingood, now dean of admissions at Clark University

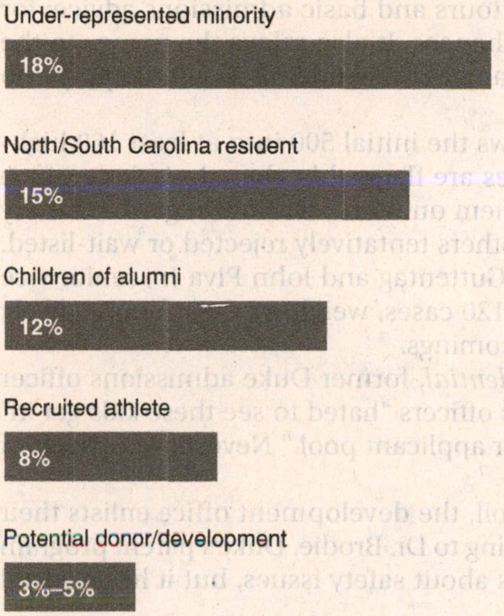

Under-represented minority

18%

North/South Carolina resident

15%

Children of alumni

12%

Recruited athlete

8%

Potential donor/development

3%–5%

**FIGURE 15.1   Study Break:
Proportion of the 1,654 Current Duke
University Freshmen Who Qualified
for Various Admission Preferences**

Note: Some students may have qualified for
more than one preference, or would have qualified for admission on their academic records
regardless of preference.

Source: Duke admissions office.

in Worcester, Mass. "They weren't slugs, but they weren't strong enough to get in on
their own."

The numbers have increased under Ms. Keohane, Duke's current president.
Duke says it admitted about 125 non-alumni children in 1998, and again in 1999,
who had been tentatively rejected or wait-listed prior to considering family connections. It accepted 99 such students in 2000. Similar data aren't available for 2001
or 2002, the school says.

Ms. Keohane says she didn't intentionally increase the number of wealthy applicants given a leg up. She says "it is possible that the numbers drifted upward"
during the recent $2 billion-fund-raising campaign because "more people in devel-
opment expressed interest in candidates. But this was certainly not a policy direc-
tive, or even a conscious choice."

The system at Duke works this way: Through its own network and names supplied by trustees, alumni, donors and others, the development office identifies
about 500 likely applicants with rich or powerful parents who are not alumni.
(Children of major alumni donors are given similar preference in a separate

process.) It cultivates them with campus tours and basic admissions advice; for instance, applying early increases their chances. It also relays the names to the admissions office, which returns word if any of the students forget to apply—so development can remind them.

The development office then winnows the initial 500 into at least 160 high-priority applicants. Although these names are flagged in the admissions-office computer, admissions readers evaluate them on merit, without regard to family means. About 30 to 40 are accepted, the others tentatively rejected or wait-listed. During an all-day meeting in March, Mr. Guttentag and John Piva Jr., senior vice president for development, debate these 120 cases, weighing their family's likely contribution against their academic shortcomings.

In her 2001 book, *Admissions Confidential*, former Duke admissions officer Rachel Toor recalled that most admissions officers "hated to see these kids get in" because they were "the weakest part of our applicant pool." Nevertheless, most of the 120 students are admitted.

Once these children of privilege enroll, the development office enlists their parents as donors and fund raisers. According to Dr. Brodie, Duke's parent program originated as a forum for parent concerns about safety issues, but it has evolved into a fund-raising vehicle.

A committee of more than 200 non-alumni parents provides its volunteer army for the four classes currently at Duke. Committee members usually give at least $1,000 to Duke, and the eight co-chairmen and the national chairman much more—including at least two seven-figure gifts endowing faculty chairs.

Membership in the parents' committee is by invitation only and is overwhelmingly white. Lately, one affluent Chicago suburb—Lake Forest—has dominated its higher echelons. Lake Forest luminaries on the committee have included department-store heir Marshall Field V, who has given at least $100,000 to Duke; Paul Clark, chief executive of Icos Corp., a biotech firm; Robert DePree, chairman of corn-meal maker House-Autry Mills Inc.; and investment banker Willard Bunn III, Maude's father.

The Lake Forest couples are social friends, serve on many of the same Chicago-area boards and several sent their children to the same private elementary school, Lake Forest Country Day. They write recommendations to Duke for each other's children.

'PRETTY INTIMATE GROUP'

Susan DePree, Robert's wife, describes the Duke parents committee as a "pretty intimate group" but not "clubby." She declined to say how much she and her husband have contributed to Duke, but says they solicited at least one six-figure gift from a parent-committee member.

Maude Bunn, whose family lives in Lake Forest, attended an elite boarding school in Lawrenceville, N.J., where the Bunn Library opened in 1996. She says other Lake Forest parents recommended her to Duke.

Cissy Bunn acknowledges her daughter didn't fit the academic profile of a Duke student. "She's bright, she had good grades, but she doesn't meet the superstar status," Mrs. Bunn says. "Did my normal child take the place of somebody who could really make a difference in the world? Sure, yes, to an extent. But there are so many things you can lose sleep over. I'm happy for me and my child."

Maude Bunn says she initially felt very awkward at Duke because her admission "wasn't necessarily on my own merits." But these days, the sophomore says she is thriving. "The more time I've spent here, I feel more and more confident—they didn't have to take me if they didn't think I was equal to all the other students they are admitting," she says. "I'm doing just as well as everybody I know if not better." She is studying art history and wants a career in fashion.

Now her younger sister Meg, a high-school senior, is applying to Duke. Maude says the family likes Meg's chances. "The people my mother works with for fund raising told her, 'It's really hard to get the first child in,'" she says. "After that, sisters and brothers are easier." Duke says it, like many universities, gives some preference to siblings.

Mrs. Bunn says she's not twisting anyone's arm. "I told them, 'If she's qualified at all, that would be lovely,'" she says. "If she gets in, I'd be happy to stay on the parents' committee."

As college admission becomes increasingly competitive, parents try to help their children's chances in any way they can. Duke accepted Jane Hetherington in 2000, despite SAT scores in the mid-1200s and what she calls "average" grades in high school. She attributes her acceptance to a "wonderful recommendation" by Norman Christensen Jr., then dean of Duke's Nicholas School of the Environment and Earth Sciences, a graduate program. She got the recommendation after one meeting with him.

At the time, her father, John Hetherington, was vice president of Westvaco Corp., a paper-products firm that had donated to the school, sponsored research there and hired some of its graduates. Mr. Hetherington asked a family friend on the school's advisory board to have the dean interview Ms. Hetherington.

Mr. Christensen, a Duke professor, says he was impressed by Ms. Hetherington's devotion to environmental studies. The student's father later reciprocated by arranging a meeting between the school's new dean and Westvaco's chief executive officer, hoping the company would increase support for the school. Nothing came of it, says Mr. Hetherington. (Westvaco merged with Mead Corp. last year.)

"I don't feel we benefited from anything you would describe as the traditional white power structure network," says Mr. Hetherington, who is now a Republican state representative in Connecticut and favors a "sunset law" for affirmative action. He doesn't think his position affected his daughter's acceptance into college. "It worked out for some reason," he says. "In all candor, we got lucky."

CHAPTER 16

"They Take Our Jobs!"

Aviva Chomsky

INTRODUCTION

Today's immigration debate is rife with myths, stereotypes, and unquestioned assumptions. I—and we all—hear remarks such as: "Immigrants take our jobs and drive down wages." "Why don't they learn English?" or "I'm not against immigration, only illegal immigration." After twenty years of teaching, writing, and organizing about immigration, it's clear to me that many of the arguments currently being circulated are based on serious misconceptions not only about how our society and economy function, but also about the history of immigration, the law, and the reasons for immigration.

All you have to do is read the papers or listen to the radio to notice that people seem to be extremely distraught and angry about immigration. Immigrants are blamed for a host of social ills and compared unfavorably to previous generations of immigrants. Since they are legally deprived of many of the rights that U.S. citizens enjoy, including the right to vote, elected officials and the general public can marginalize, blame, punish, and discriminate against them with little repercussion. Noncitizens make easy targets and convenient scapegoats. . . .

Today, a large and growing portion of our population lives without the full rights of citizenship. Noncitizens work, pay taxes, go to school, and raise families; they live in our cities and towns; they participate in religious, sports, and community events; they serve (in disproportionately large numbers) in the military. But both the law and popular opinion deem them somehow different from the rest of us, and not eligible for the rights and privileges that 90 percent of the population enjoys.

As of March 2005, more than 35 million people, a little over 10 percent of the total U.S. population, were foreign born. Most of these people had legal permission to be here, but about a third of them did not. About one-third of all foreign-born people (documented and undocumented) came from Mexico, the largest source of immigrants. Over half came from Latin America and the Caribbean as a whole (including Mexico). Another 18 percent came from East Asia. The top ten sending countries were Mexico (10.8 million); China (1.8 million); the Philippines (1.5 million); India (1.4 million); El Salvador (1.1 million); Vietnam (996,000); Cuba (948,000); the Dominican Republic (695,000); Canada (674,000); and Korea (672,000).[1]

During the 1990s the number of immigrants increased rapidly. In 1990, only 19.8 million reported foreign birth. In 2000, the figure was 31.1 million.[2] (These figures do not include the 3.4 million Puerto Ricans who lived in the continental United States according to the 2000 census. They are U.S. citizens, although they are also Latin Americans.) Although one wouldn't guess it from the increasing anti-immigrant agitation in the 2000s, immigration actually slowed significantly after the end of the 1990s.[3] Nativism, or anti-immigrant racism, responded as much to other trends in society as to the actual number of immigrants coming in.

The current influx of immigrants is often compared to the last large and sustained wave, which occurred between 1860 and 1920, when the rate of foreign-born persons in the population ranged from 13 to 15 percent. Because the total population was smaller, this higher percentage represented a smaller number of people. Prior to the 1980s, the highest year for the foreign born was 1930, when 14.2 million people reported foreign birth. Most of these immigrants came from southern and eastern Europe.[4]

During the 1860–1920 immigration wave as well as during that of the late twentieth century, immigration was acompanied by nativist reactions. Nativists worried that immigrants would fail to assimilate, would undermine the perceived linguistic, cultural, and racial homogeneity of the country, would take American jobs, and would lower wages. Commentators in various forums warned that the newcomers would bring disease and crime. Today, Arthur Schlesinger worries about the "disuniting of America," while Samuel Huntington fears the "challenges to American national identity."[5] They seem to be echoing the California attorney general who wrote in 1930 that "only we, the white people, found [America] first and we want to be protected in our enjoyment of it." . . .

IMMIGRANTS AND THE ECONOMY

Some of the most widespread myths about immigration have to do with its effects on the economy. Immigrants are blamed for causing or exacerbating a wide variety of economic ills, from unemployment to low wages to the underfunding of government services. It's undeniable that many Americans feel economically pinched and vulnerable, and that the numbers of Americans in this situation are increasing. But what role does immigration really play in the larger picture of the U.S.—and the global—economy?

IMMIGRANTS DON'T PAY TAXES

Immigrants, no matter what their status, pay the same taxes that citizens do—sales taxes, real estate taxes (if they rent or own a home), gasoline taxes. Some immigrants work in the informal economy and are paid under the table in cash, so they don't have federal and state income taxes, or social security taxes, deducted from their paychecks. So do some citizens. In fact every time the kid next door babysits, or shovels the snow, he or she is working in the informal economy.

Much of the service sector operates in the informal sphere. Nanny jobs and housecleaning jobs—which tend to be held primarily by women—generally use informal arrangements whether the workers are citizen or immigrant, documented or undocumented. But increasingly, jobs that used to be in the formal sector—like factory jobs—have sunk into the informal sector through elaborate systems of subcontracting. Textile and apparel manufacturing are particularly notorious in this regard.[6]

There are some benefits for employers, and for consumers, from this informal sector. Employers can pay lower wages than those required by law. Consumers receive access to cheap products and services provided by these low-wage, untaxed workers.

But workers in the informal economy don't fare so well. They don't have access to any of the worker protections that come with formal employment, like minimum wage or health and safety regulations. Workers in the informal economy can't get unemployment insurance or workers' compensation and generally get no benefits from their employer (like health insurance or sick leave or vacation time).

It's hard to calculate exact numbers for the informal economy because, by definition, it's unregulated. One recent study in Los Angeles estimated that immigrants made up 40 percent of the city's population, and one-fourth of these were undocumented. The informal economy accounted for some 15 percent of the city's workforce, and undocumented workers were concentrated there: 60 percent of workers in the informal economy were undocumented.[7]

Many immigrants work in the formal economy, in which case they have all of the same tax deductions from their paychecks as citizens do. Undocumented immigrants who work in the formal economy generally do so by presenting false social security numbers. The Social Security Administration estimates that about three-fourths of undocumented workers do this.[8]

Public commentary about this practice is often quite angry. In fact, though, the only ones who lose anything when workers use a false social security number are the workers themselves. Taxes are deducted from their paychecks—but if they are undocumented, they still have no access to the benefits they are paying for, like social security or unemployment benefits.

Even with a false social security number, the federal and state taxes that are deducted from a worker's paycheck will go into federal and state coffers. Social security payments are either credited to whoever's number was used, or, if a worker uses a number that doesn't belong to anybody, they go into the Social Security Administration's "earnings suspense file." As of 2005, Social Security was receiving about $7 billion a year through false social security numbers—allowing it to break even, because that's about the same amount as the difference between what it paid out in benefits and what it received in payroll taxes. According to the *New York Times,* "illegal immigrant workers in the United States are now providing the system with a subsidy of as much as $7 billion a year."[9] Yet these workers will never be able to receive Social Security benefits.

IMMIGRANTS ARE A DRAIN ON THE ECONOMY

This is a complicated question that requires us to define "the economy." Generally, those who say immigrants are a drain on the economy are referring to the myth that immigrants use more in public services than they pay in taxes. In fact the majority of immigrants, being of prime working age and ineligible for many public services, tend to contribute more to the public sector than they actually use. However, many of the services they do tap into are local services (schools, transportation, libraries), and the new wave of immigration coincides with federal cutbacks to these services, placing a greater burden on local governments. (The native born, it should be said, *also* tend to use more in local services than they pay in local taxes.)

Several state-level studies have tried to assess the level of state and federal taxes that immigrants, documented and undocumented, pay compared to the level of state and federal services that they receive. Early studies in California and in the Southwest as a whole and more recent studies in the Southeast, which is seeing the highest rates of immigrant population growth now, have come to similar conclusions. Immigrants, documented and undocumented, are more likely to pay taxes than they are to use public services. Undocumented immigrants aren't eligible for most public services and live in fear of revealing themselves to any government authorities. Documented immigrants are eligible for some services—but even they hesitate to use them, since they fear that being seen as a public charge will make it harder for them to stay, apply for citizenship, or bring family members. Nationally, one study estimates that households headed by undocumented immigrants use less than half the amount of federal services that households headed by documented immigrants or citizens make use of.[10]

There are some government services that both documented and undocumented immigrants do benefit from: public schools, emergency medical care, and the public safety system (e.g., police, prisons). These are known as "mandated services," which federal authority requires state government to provide to all people, regardless of immigration status.

The only kind of public service that immigrant households use at higher rates than natives is food assistance programs such as food stamps, WIC, and free or reduced-cost school lunches. However, it's not the immigrants themselves who use this aid—they're usually not eligible—but rather their U.S.-born children, who are citizens.[11]

The Georgia Budget and Policy Institute estimates that undocumented immigrants in the state pay between $1,800 and $2,400 a year in state and local taxes, including sales, property, and income taxes (for those who file W-2 forms with false social security numbers). This brings from $200 to $250 million into state and local budgets.

"Do undocumented immigrants pay enough in taxes to cover the services used?" the report asks.

> For undocumented immigrants, the answer is unclear. However, for legal immigrants, studies have shown that first-generation immigrants pay more in federal taxes than they receive in federal benefits. The same does not hold true for state taxes and services, however, as first-generation immigrants often use more in services than they pay in taxes. However, the descendants of the first-generation immigrant correct that pattern and contribute more in taxes at both the federal and state level than they consume in services at both levels. Each generation successively contributes a greater share due to increased wages, language skills, and education.[12]

Similarly, in Colorado undocumented immigrants were found to pay about $1,850 in state and local taxes if they were working on the books, and $1,350 (in sales and property taxes) if they were working under the table. Thus the estimated 250,000 undocumented immigrants in that state were paying $150 to $200 million in state and local taxes, covering about 70 to 85 percent of the approximately $225 million they used in state and local services.[13]

If immigrants don't make heavy use of social services and they do pay taxes, then why don't their taxes cover all of, or more than, the services they do use? Mostly because they earn such low wages that their tax payments are lower than those of people who earn higher wages. Low wages mean that less is withheld for income taxes, and it means that they have less money to spend, so they pay less in sales and property taxes than people who earn more. In fact, our progressive system of income taxes is designed to take a greater chunk of the income of a high earner than a low earner. So if immigrants are paying less, it's because they're earning less.

A Florida study found similar results: new immigrants tend to have lower levels of education and lower earnings—and thus pay less in taxes—than the U.S. population as a whole. Within fifteen years, immigrants' earnings—and their taxes—have caught up.[14]

Since the 1990s, economists have started to use a more complex model for evaluating the effects of immigration with respect to taxes and public services. Instead of just looking at the cost of educating the children of immigrants, for example, they also look at the potential future tax revenues of those children. This approach, called "generational accounting," is based on the notion that when government spending exceeds tax revenues—that is, when the government operates at a deficit, as is currently the case—future generations essentially have to pay back the debt. So the numbers of new immigrants in future generations will affect how the costs of the debt are distributed—more immigrants means less burden on the native born.[15]

From the perspective of businesses, employing immigrant workers, and workers in other countries, brings some special advantages. Again, a comparison to slavery is enlightening. Slaveholders generally preferred to purchase slaves of prime working age and strength. They discovered that it was cheaper to continually import new slaves and overwork them to death rather than having to pay for the *reproduction* of their slave labor force. Brazilian slaveholders found that they could recover the cost of purchasing a slave with two years of harsh labor, so that any amount of time that a slave survived after that was pure profit. The average was three more years—and the profit could then be used to buy a new slave worker.

When the slave trade was abolished—at the beginning of the nineteenth century in the United States, much later in the century in Brazil and Cuba—slaveholders had to shift their strategies. In order to maintain a slave population, they had to foster reproduction. This meant that they had to invest more in their existing slaves. They had to provide for children who were too young to work, and for the women or elders who cared for the children. They had to increase the level of subsistence so that slaves would *not* die within five years.

Immigration and outsourcing (moving production abroad) fulfill the same logic, from the perspective of businesses. The New Deal social compact put the burden on businesses to give back to their workers, and to society, in order to support the reproduction of the labor force. Wages, benefits, and taxes were all ways in which businesses contributed to social reproduction.

If businesses could find a new source of workers that was reproduced outside of the United States and the New Deal social compact, however, they could save money. If a worker is born and raised in Mexico, works for a U.S. enterprise (either in Mexico or in the United States) between the ages of twenty and forty, then returns to the home community, it is the Mexican family, community, and institutions that bear the costs of reproduction. The U.S. company gets just what the slaveholder got: workers in their prime working years, with no investment in the society that raised them or that will care for them as they age.

Of course some immigrants, even if they originally intended to work for a short time and return home, end up staying. Over time, they lose those special immigrant qualities that make them willing to work for low wages in substandard conditions. In other words, they become more like citizens: they need to work for wages, and in conditions, that will sustain their life here. The opportunities for upward mobility that European immigrants enjoyed may no longer exist, but immigrants do shift in the kinds of jobs they will do, the kinds of conditions they will accept—and the amount of taxes that they pay.

As workers leave the secondary sector—whether because they return home, grow older, or set down roots here—employers remain avid for new immigrants to replace them. A significant exception to the model of economic improvement over time is undocumented immigrants. Unlike "legal" immigrants (refugees, legal permanent residents, and those who become naturalized citizens), whose incomes increase significantly in proportion to their time in the United States, undocumented immigrants tend to remain on the margins of the U.S. economy. Even those who had been in the United States for ten years or more in 2003 had a family income of only $29,900—as compared to natives, whose family incomes averaged $45,900, refugees at $45,200, legal permanent residents at $44,600, and naturalized citizens at $56,500.[16]

It's not surprising, then, that 39 percent of undocumented immigrant children live below the poverty line, and 53 percent lack health insurance.[17] The results of the 1986 Immigration Reform and Control Act, which granted amnesty to a significant portion of the undocumented population then in the United States, are also clear. Once they achieved legal status, migrants were able to improve their levels of education and income.[18] By maintaining arbitrary status differences and excluding millions of people from legal rights, and by ensuring that immigrants will continue to arrive, and that some will continue to be classed as "illegal," U.S. policies guarantee the existence of a permanent underclass.

Editors' Note: *Notes for this reading can be found in the original source.*

PART FIVE

Sexism

The 1960s were known as a decade of civil rights struggles, black militancy, antiwar protests, and campus disturbances. It seemed unlikely that yet another social movement could take hold and grow, but the consciousness of women's oppression could and did grow, with enormous impact over remarkably few years.

Black militancy, the student movement, the antiwar movement, youth militancy, and radicalism all affirmed freedom, equality, and liberation, but none of these was thought to be particularly necessary or applicable to women, especially by radical men. Ironically, it was political experience with radical men that led radical women to the consciousness of women as a distinctly oppressed group and, therefore, a group with distinctive interests.

The feminism that emerged in the 1970s was in fact both novel and part of a long and often painful series of movements for the liberation of women. Women's rights proposals were first heard more than a century ago. But the movement for the equality of women ground to a halt when the emergencies of the Depression and World War II pushed aside feminist concerns. With victory, both sexes resumed the middle-class dream of family, security, and upward mobility. These years of the late 1940s and early 1950s were the years of "The Feminine Mystique,"[1] when the *domestic* role of women dominated American culture.

When women began, in the 1970s, to once again reassert themselves and claimed to be able to be doctors and lawyers and bankers and pilots, they were met with derision. The "Long Amnesia" had taken hold and stereotyped women's roles into those of the 1940s and 1950s. Nevertheless, women persevered, and, in what was historically a brief period, it became inconceivable to see no female faces broadcasting the news, granting loans, and training to be jet pilots at the U.S. Air Force Academy.

By the twenty-first century most young women in American were growing up in a world so greatly changed from the 1950s that for many these battles seemed like pieces of a long-ago past. But the struggle for real equality between the sexes is hardly over, for reasons suggested by the readings in this part. Although the idea of male supremacy may be on the way out in most industrialized nations, there is still, in many respects, a long way to go.

How much this is true at the top of the economic scale is shown in the *Economist* magazine's discussion of the persistence of the "glass ceiling" that blocks women from anything like equal participation at the highest levels of American business. Women today in many countries, including the United States, are more likely to be corporate executives than they were a generation ago, but progress has stalled in recent years. Though women are almost half of the American workforce, they still make up only about 8 percent of top managers in American business, and less than 1 percent of chief executive officers; and these proportions have barely changed at all over the past decade.

What accounts for the stubborn persistence of the "glass ceiling"? The *Economist* cites three key reasons: the exclusion of women from the informal social networks through which men have traditionally gotten influence and promotions, a pervasive stereotyping of women as less capable of leadership, and the lack of role models to guide women upward in the corporate hierarchy. Why, in a society supposedly committed to equality between the sexes, do these obstacles still persist? Part of the problem is the stubborn persistence of sexist norms and expectations that, though often subtle, still shape the lives of men and women in very different ways. As Peggy Orenstein shows in "Learning Silence," these attitudes begin very early. Orenstein observed a California school that enjoys an exemplary curriculum. But she also found operating in the school a "hidden curriculum" that delivers unstated lessons—a "running subtext"—undermining girls' confidence in their ability to learn, especially in crucial subjects like science and math. Girls and boys are also given subtle but effective cues on how to behave in the classroom and where to locate themselves in the school's culture and social organization. Orenstein concludes that these faint but compelling lessons have the effect of teaching students their proper place in the status hierarchy of the larger society.

The early development of these gender expectations helps explain what the *Economist* calls the "glacially slow" pace of change in opportunities for women at the upper levels of the American economy.

But, of course, the economy is not the only realm in which women face special risks and disadvantages. Sexual harassment and violence, for example, remain ever-present threats to women at all points on the social spectrum, and are far more widespread than official statistics indicate—and more widespread than most authorities are willing to acknowledge. The survey we excerpt here from the American Association of University Women charts some of the dimensions and consequences of the problem of sexual harassment on college campuses. The survey makes clear that this is a problem that crosses gender boundries—but also that it is both more severe and more pervasive for women.

ENDNOTE

1. Betty Friedan, *The Feminine Mystique*, New York: Norton, 1963.

CHAPTER 17

The Conundrum of the Glass Ceiling

The Economist

WHY ARE WOMEN SO PERSISTENTLY ABSENT FROM TOP CORPORATE JOBS?

It is 20 years since the term "glass ceiling" was coined by the *Wall Street Journal* to describe the apparent barriers that prevent women from reaching the top of the corporate hierarchy; and it is ten years since the American government's specially appointed Glass Ceiling Commission published its recommendations. In 1995 the commission said that the barrier was continuing "to deny untold numbers of qualified people the opportunity to compete for and hold executive level positions in the private sector." It found that women had 45.7% of America's jobs and more than half of master's degrees being awarded. Yet 95% of senior managers were men, and female managers' earnings were on average a mere 68% of their male counterparts'.

Ten years on, women account for 46.5% of America's workforce and for less than 8% of its top managers, although at big *Fortune* 500 companies the figure is a bit higher. Female managers' earnings now average 72% of their male colleagues'. Booz Allen Hamilton, a consulting firm that monitors departing chief executives in America, found that 0.7% of them were women in 1998, and 0.7% of them were women in 2004. In between, the figure fluctuated. But the firm says that one thing is clear: the number is "very low and not getting higher."

In other countries the picture is similar. Not a single woman [was] featured in *Fortune* magazine's list this June of the 25 highest-paid CEOs in Europe. Although Laurence Parisot, the chief executive of Ifop, an opinion pollster, was chosen recently to head Medef, the French employers' association, she is a rare exception. Corinne Maier, an economist with EDF, a French energy group, gave a scathing description of French corporate life in last year's best-seller, "Bonjour Paresse." "Among the well-heeled battalions of executives," she wrote, "only 5% are women." Equality in the French workplace, claimed Ms. Maier, "is a far-off dream."

It is even farther off in Japan where, until 20–30 years ago, it was generally unacceptable for women to stay in the office after 5pm. One ambitious employee of a foreign multinational dared to hide in the ladies room until the men had left before returning to her desk to finish her work. There has been some progress since. This year two women have been appointed to head big Japanese companies. Fumiko Hayashi is now chairman and CEO of Daiei, a troubled supermarket chain; and Tomoyo Nonaka, a former newscaster, has been appointed boss of Sanyo Electric. Nissan has a general manager for "diversity development" who, when asked recently what has changed least in Japanese business in the past 20 years, replied: "The mindset of Japanese gentlemen."

In Britain, the number of female executive directors of FTSE100 companies rose from 11 in 2000 to 17 in 2004, according to Cranfield, a business school—17 women as against almost 400 men. A larger sample of British quoted companies found that 65% had no women on their board at all in 2003. No British woman has yet headed a big British company, although 44% of the workforce is female. Marjorie Scardino, CEO of Pearson, owner of the *Financial Times* which owns 50% of *The Economist,* is American, as is Laura Tyson, who heads the London Business School. Clara Furse, boss of London's stock exchange, was born in Canada.

It is progress of a sort—but of a glacially slow sort. The glass-ceiling phenomenon is proving peculiarly persistent. The top of the corporate ladder remains stubbornly male, and the few women who reach it are paid significantly less than the men that they join there.

This is despite the fact that companies are trying harder than ever to help women to climb higher. So-called "diversity programmes" (which are aimed at promoting minorities as well as women) are as common as diversity on the board is rare, and not just among service industries such as finance and retailing. No-nonsense formerly male clubs such as IBM (where two decades ago blue-suited identikit white men drove the company close to bankruptcy), GE (where the culture was not exactly female-friendly during the long rule of its legendary leader Jack Welch) and BP (where long hours at sea on windy oil rigs were a career booster), have appointed senior executives to be in charge of diversity. The three firms were the unlikely joint sponsors of a recent conference on "Women in Leadership."

DIVERSITY PAYS

Such companies no longer see the promotion of women solely as a moral issue of equal opportunity and equal pay. They have been persuaded of the business case for diversity. It has long been known that mixed groups are better at problem solving than like-minded ones. But the benefits of diversity are greater than this. Research by Catalyst, an American organisation that aims to expand "opportunities for women and business," found a strong correlation between the number of women in top executive positions and financial performance among *Fortune* 500 companies between 1996 and 2000.

For some companies the push towards greater diversity has come from their customers. Lou Gerstner, the man who turned around IBM partly by promoting diversity within the company, has said "we made diversity a market-based issue . . .

it's about understanding our markets, which are diverse and multicultural." Lisa Bondesio, head of diversity in Britain for Deloitte, a big firm of accountants, says that diversity is "about how we differentiate ourselves in the marketplace."

Other companies surprisingly fail to reflect the diversity of their customers. Procter & Gamble (P&G), for example, the manufacturer of Pampers nappies, Max Factor and Tampax, boasts in its 2004 annual report that it was ranked "among the top companies for executive women" by the National Association for Female Executives. Yet it has only two women on its 16-person board, both of them non-executives, and out of the 45 people it lists as its top "corporate officers" only three are women—ie, 93% of them are men. P&G is an enormously successful company and its management programmes are widely admired. Its shareholders may wonder if it would do even better if the gender ratios at the top were less skewed.

Many companies have been motivated by a desire to broaden the pool of "talent" that their human-resources departments can fish in. They worry in general about the ageing populations of the developed world. But particular industries have other reasons for broadening their recruitment trawl. The big accounting firms, for example, had their reputations seriously dented by the demise of Enron and its auditor Arthur Andersen just before they had an unprecedented increase in business as a consequence of the extra duties imposed by the Sarbanes-Oxley act. They became the "employer of choice" for far fewer graduates at a time when they needed to attract far more. A consequence is that they have had to extend their recruitment and promotion efforts to more women.

The management-consulting business, where firms tend to follow the career strategy of "up or out," would like to hold on to many more of its women. But up or out can scarcely accommodate maternity leave, so it is no surprise that the industry loses twice as many women as men from the middle rungs of its career ladder.

Booz Allen Hamilton, a leading consulting firm, regularly wonders how to alter the fact that only 1–2% of its partners are women. Orit Gadiesh, the chairman of Bain, a rival, is a notable exception to the general exclusion of women from the top ranks. However, an earlier career in the Israeli army may have provided essential skills for her to reach the top.

Some firms' diversity programmes are working. At IBM, there are now seven women among its 40 top executives. GE says that 14% of its "senior executives" are now women, although none of them featured in the chief executive's recent reshuffle at the very top. The firm's six new business divisions are all headed by men.

By contrast, Alcan, a Canadian multinational metal manufacturer, has made extraordinary progress. Three out of its four main businesses are now headed by women (including the bauxite and alumina business). Steven Price, the company's HR director, says "it's been a long journey" to reach this point. Crucial has been "the tone at the top" and a determination to break down the perception that working long hours and wearing air miles like a "battle medal" are ways to get ahead in the company.

Why is it proving so difficult for women to reach the top of corporations? Are they simply less ambitious, less excited by the idea of limitless (albeit first-class) travel, late nights and the onerous responsibilities imposed by mounting regulation?

A 2002 survey of top executives in American multinationals around the world did find them to be less ambitious, at least for the very top job: 19% of the men interviewed aspired to be CEO, whereas only 9% of the women did. At a slightly lower level there was less difference: 43% of women hoped to join a senior management committee, compared with 54% of the men. Catalyst, on the other hand, says that its research shows that women and men have equal desires to have the CEO job. "Ambition knows no gender," says Ilene Lang, the president of Catalyst and once a senior executive in Silicon Valley.

WHO'S IN THE CLUB?

Top businesswomen in America give three main explanations for why so few of them reach "C-level"—that group of executives who preface their titles with the word "chief." First comes the exclusion from informal networks. In many firms jock-talk and late-night boozing still oil the wheels of progress. In America and elsewhere it has become almost traditional for sales teams to take potential clients to strip clubs and the like. These activities specifically exclude most women.

Yasmin Jetha, a Muslim of Asian origin who made it to the board of Abbey, a British bank and a FTSE100 company until it was taken over last year by Spain's Banco Santander, says that although she neither drinks alcohol nor supports a rugby team, she made a point in her career of participating in industry-wide events where the opportunities for exclusion are less. More and more women in business are forming their own networks, which also help to counter male clubbishness.

The second hurdle is what Ms. Lang calls "pervasive stereotyping of women's capacity for leadership." Everyone is unconsciously biased and there is strong evidence that men are biased against promoting women inside companies. This was a central point in the landmark 1989 case in America of *Price Waterhouse v Hopkins*, where Ann Hopkins sued her employer when she was not given a partnership. She eventually won her case in the Supreme Court. Since then some companies have begun to take special steps to guard against bias. Deloitte, for example, carefully scrutinises its pay and promotion decisions for bias, especially its list of new partners announced annually in June.

The third hurdle is the lack of role models. There are too few women in top jobs to show how it is done. Helen Alexander, the chief executive of The Economist Group and one of very few female CEOs to have succeeded a female CEO (Ms. Scardino) says, however, that the role models that matter come earlier in life—at school or in the family. In addition, it seems to be important for many successful businesswomen to have had a supportive father.

Chris Bones, a senior human-resources executive with Cadbury Schweppes before he took over as head of Henley Management College at the beginning of this year, suggests another reason. The flattening of organisations in recent years, as layers of management have been stripped out, has meant that promotions now are far steeper steps than they used to be. This leaves fewer opportunities for people to reenter the workforce at higher levels. And many women inevitably need to take time off during their careers. In America, there is evidence to suggest that more women with children under the age of one are taking time off work than was the case some years ago.

More and more too are withdrawing to care for elderly parents at a time when they are on the cusp of the higher echelons. Ben Rosen, a professor at the Kenan-Flagler Business School in North Carolina who has done research on the topic, says that many women bail out of corporate life to become self-employed consultants and entrepreneurs, roles where they can have greater freedom and autonomy to manage the rest of their lives. This may be reinforcing companies' long-held belief that they should invest less in women's careers because they are unlikely to stay the course.

Ms. Maier's Gallic analysis of the issue is that French men spend more time at work than women, which "can be explained by their insatiable predatory instincts as well as by their casual approach to banal household chores." This leaves women with so much to do at home that they are more than twice as likely as men to work part-time, "which makes it all the more impossible to break the glass ceiling." In America a survey by the Centre for Work-Life Policy found that 40% of highly qualified women with spouses felt that their husbands did less work around the home than they created.

Another finding of the study was that qualified women leave work for a mixture of reasons—some pull them away (home and family life), and some push them away (the type of work, the people they are working with). In business, the push factors were found to be particularly powerful, "unlike, say, in medicine or teaching." The vast majority of women (93%) said they wanted to return to work, but found the options available to them "few and far between, and extremely costly." Across sectors, women lost 37% of their earning power when they spent three or more years out of the workforce.

Very few (5%) wanted to return to the companies they had left, claiming the work they had been doing there was not particularly satisfying. In Britain, women are increasingly dissatisfied with work. A recent study by the University of Bath of female workers between 1992 and 2003 showed an overall decline in their stated levels of job satisfaction. For full-time female managers the decline was an above-average 6%. For men, job satisfaction over the same period went up.

The only category of female workers with a significant rise in satisfaction (of 19%) was that of part-time craft workers. It has become a lot more rewarding to blow glass or design gardens than to strive forever in a vain bid to reach the boardroom.

CHANGE NEEDED

Will time alone erode the gap between men and women? The steep decline among women in the popularity of MBA degrees, the *sine qua non* (at least in America) of a fast-track corporate career, suggests not. What is more, women with MBAs are fast dropping out of the workforce. One study in America found that one out of every three such qualified women is not working full-time. For men, the comparable figure is one in 20.

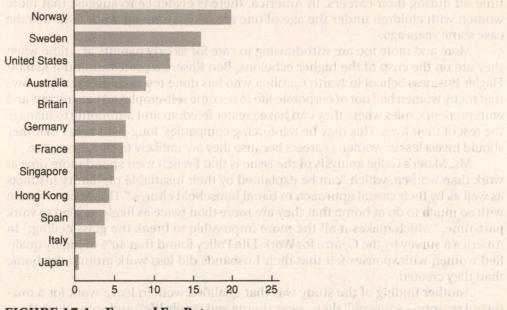

FIGURE 17.1   Few and Far Between

Source: Ethical Investment Research Service

What can be done to improve the gender balance at the top? In Norway, legislation has been passed decreeing that by the end of 2006 all companies must have at least two women on their boards. Norway already leads the world in the number of women on its company boards (see [Figure 17.1]).

In Britain a group of businesswomen has set up an organisation called WDOB, or Women Directors on Boards, whose aim is "to change the face of UK plc." Jacey Graham, its director, hopes to see the almost static percentage of female executive directors in Britain more than double (to 10%) by 2010.

Ms Graham says that such change "won't just happen." It needs specific intervention within companies—intervention that is led from the top. Opportunities for flexible working are particularly helpful in keeping women in the workforce. KPMG, one of the Big Four accounting firms, is aiming to double the percentage of its partners who are women (currently 13%). It says flexible working is a key measure to help it achieve this goal. Three-quarters of all requests for flexible working over the past 12 months have been from women.

Mentoring is also helpful. The WDOB has initiated a programme in which the chairmen and CEOs of 25 FTSE100 companies have agreed to mentor women who have been identified from other companies among the group as having boardroom potential. "The sad thing," says Ms. Graham, "is that some companies could not find a woman to put forward for mentoring." Women are enthusiastic mentors of each other. Colleen Arnold, the general manager of IBM Europe, Middle East and

Africa, mentors 27 people formally and more than 100 informally. "Mentoring," she says, "is penalty-free."

Chief executives are appointed by sub-committees of companies' boards, often advised by headhunters. More of them will be women when more members of the sub-committees are women and when fewer headhunters are old white men. As Catalyst's Ms. Lang puts it "There are so many women qualified to be on boards who are out there, under the radar screen." Heidrick & Struggles, a firm of headhunters, says that boards may need to look beyond the top-management structures from which non-executive directors are usually drawn if they are "to increase markedly the ratio of female to male directors."

Some think the task is particularly urgent. Chris Clarke, the America-based CEO of Boyden, a firm of headhunters, and a visiting professor at Henley Management College in England, argues that women are superior to men at multi-tasking, team-building and communicating, which have become the essential skiffs for running a 21st-century corporation. Maria Wisniewska, who headed a Polish bank, Bank Pekao, and is an international adviser to the Conference Board, says: "The links between the rational and emotional parts of the brain are greater in women than in men. If so, and if leadership is about making links between emotion and intelligence, then maybe women are better at it than men."

CHAPTER 18

Drawing the Line
Sexual Harassment on Campus

Catherine Hill
Elena Silva

Sexual harassment is a part of college life, so common that, according to one student, "it seems almost normal." Most college students (89 percent) say that sexual harassment occurs among students at their college, with one-fifth (21 percent) saying that peer harassment happens often. When asked about specific kinds of harassment, two-thirds of students (62 percent) say that they have been sexually harassed, and a similar number (66 percent) say that they know someone personally (such as a friend or classmate) who has been sexually harassed. That means that about six million college students encounter sexual harassment at college. Expressed another way, on a campus of 10,000 undergraduate students, about 6,000 students will be harassed.

This chapter examines the prevalence of sexual harassment on campus. It describes what types of sexual harassment occur, where they occur, who is harassed, and who is harassing. For the most part, students indicate that verbal and visual kinds of sexual harassment are common, but incidents involving contact or physical threat are not rare. In addition, a sizeable number of students—41 percent—admit that they have sexually harassed someone. In most cases, these students say that they thought it was funny, the other person liked it, or it is "just a part of school life." On this final point, both harassed and harassing students agree: Sexual harassment is indeed a common part of campus life.

WHAT TYPES OF SEXUAL HARASSMENT OCCUR?

According to college students, unwanted comments, jokes, gestures, and looks are the most common type of sexual harassment on campus (see Figure 18.1). About half of college students have been the target of unwanted sexual comments, jokes, gestures, or looks, and a similar number know someone personally

	Experienced Themselves	Know Someone
Experienced any sexual harassment	62	66
Received sexual comments, jokes, gestures, or looks	53	51
Were flashed or mooned	28	35
Had someone brush up against them in a sexual way	25	33
Were touched, grabbed, or pinched in a sexual way	25	31
Were called gay, lesbian, or a homophobic name (such as faggot, dyke, or queer)	24	42
Received sexual pictures, photographs, web pages, illustrations, messages, or notes	18	19
Had sexual rumors spread about them	16	30
Had their clothing pulled in a sexual way	15	21
Had someone block their way, corner them, or follow them in a sexual way	11	15
Had sexual messages posted about them on the Internet, e-mail, instant message, or text message	9	13
Were forced to kiss someone	7	12
Had their clothing pulled off or down	7	11
Were asked to do something sexual in exchange for giving them something (e.g., a better grade, a recommendation, class notes, etc.)	6	7
Were forced to do something sexual other than kissing	5	8
Were spied on as they dressed or showered at school (e.g., in a dorm, in a gym, etc)	5	7

Base = All qualified respondents (*n* = 2,036); 1,096 female and 940 male college students ages 18 to 24.

FIGURE 18.1   Percentage of College Students Who Have Been Sexually Harassed or Know Someone Personally Who Has Been Sexually Harassed

who experienced this type of harassment. Being called gay, lesbian, or a homophobic name is also a common experience among college students. More than one-third know someone who has been called gay, lesbian, or a homophobic name, and about one-quarter of students have had this happen to them. Physical forms of harassment are also prevalent. For example, one-quarter of college students have been touched, grabbed, or pinched in a sexual way, and nearly one-third of students know someone personally who has experienced this kind of harassment. Other common types of sexual harassment include flashing or mooning, intentionally brushing up against someone in a sexual way, and spreading sexual rumors about individuals.

While the percentage of college students experiencing some types of sexual harassment is relatively low, the number of implied incidents is quite high. For example, the 5 percent of undergraduate students ages 18 to 24 who say that they have been forced to do something sexual other than kissing translates into about half a million students nationwide, and the 11 percent of students who say they have been physically blocked, cornered, or followed in a sexual way translates into about a million students nationwide.[1] Put another way, at a campus with 10,000 undergraduate students, 500 students will experience some form of sexual assault while at college, and about a thousand students will be blocked, cornered, or followed in a sexual way during their college lives—no trivial matter for colleges and universities. . . .

WHO IS HARASSED?

Both Male and Female Students Are Harassed, But in Different Ways Male (61 percent) and female (62 percent) students are equally likely to encounter sexual harassment in their college lives. Important differences between men and women are evident, however, when the types of harassment—as well as reactions to these experiences—are considered (see Figure 18.2). Female students are more likely to experience sexual harassment that involves physical contact (35 percent versus 29 percent).

Among all students, more than one-third of females (41 percent) and males (36 percent) experience sexual harassment in their first year of college. Among harassed students, 66 percent of females and 59 percent of males encounter sexual harassment in their first year.

Differences by Sexual Identity and Race/Ethnicity Some groups of students are more likely to be sexually harassed than are others. Lesbian, gay, bisexual, and transgender (LGBT) students are more likely than heterosexual students to be sexually harassed in college and to be sexually harassed often (see Figure 18.3). LGBT students are at higher risk for both contact and noncontact types of sexual harassment.[2] Harassers come from all quarters of the academic community. Among students who have experienced harassment, LGBT students are more likely to have been harassed by peers (92 percent versus 78 percent), teachers (13 percent versus 7 percent), and school employees (11 percent versus 5 percent).

The survey reveals racial/ethnic differences in the prevalence of sexual harassment among college students (see Figure 18.4). White college students are more likely than black and Hispanic students to experience sexual harassment. White students are more likely to experience verbal and other noncontact forms of harassment. Specifically, white students are more likely than their black and Hispanic peers to hear sexual comments, jokes, gestures, or looks (54 percent

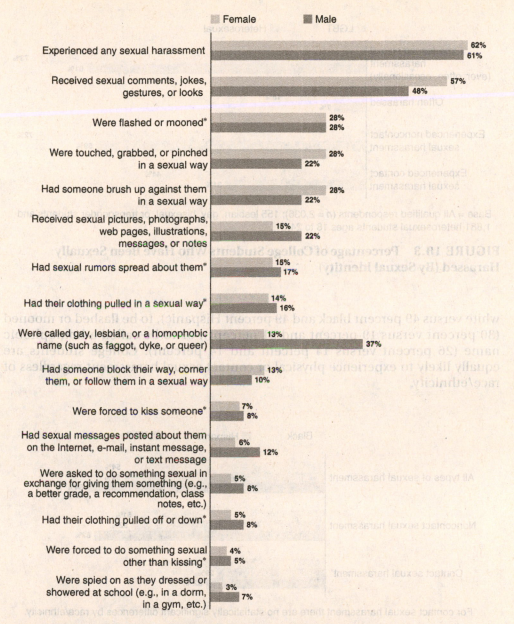

Female   Male

Experienced any sexual harassment
Female: 62%
Male: 61%

Received sexual comments, jokes, gestures, or looks
Female: 57%
Male: 48%

Were flashed or mooned*
Female: 28%
Male: 28%

Were touched, grabbed, or pinched in a sexual way
Female: 28%
Male: 22%

Had someone brush up against them in a sexual way
Female: 28%
Male: 22%

Received sexual pictures, photographs, web pages, illustrations, messages, or notes
Female: 15%
Male: 22%

Had sexual rumors spread about them*
Female: 15%
Male: 17%

Had their clothing pulled in a sexual way*
Female: 14%
Male: 16%

Were called gay, lesbian, or a homophobic name (such as faggot, dyke, or queer)
Female: 13%
Male: 37%

Had someone block their way, corner them, or follow them in a sexual way
Female: 13%
Male: 10%

Were forced to kiss someone*
Female: 7%
Male: 8%

Had sexual messages posted about them on the Internet, e-mail, instant message, or text message
Female: 6%
Male: 12%

Were asked to do something sexual in exchange for giving them something (e.g., a better grade, a recommendation, class notes, etc.)
Female: 5%
Male: 8%

Had their clothing pulled off or down*
Female: 5%
Male: 8%

Were forced to do something sexual other than kissing*
Female: 4%
Male: 5%

Were spied on as they dressed or showered at school (e.g., in a dorm, in a gym, etc.)
Female: 3%
Male: 7%

*The difference between female and male students is not statistically significant.

Survey question: During your whole college life, how often, if at all, has anyone...done the following things to you when you did not want them to? Possible answers: never, rarely, occasionally, often, or decline to answer.

Base = All qualified respondents (*n* = 2,036); 1,096 female and 940 male college students ages 18 to 24.

FIGURE 18.2   Percentage of College Students Who Have Been Sexually Harassed (By Gender)

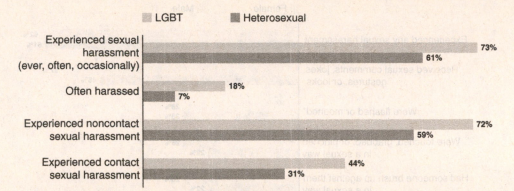

Base = All qualified respondents (*n* = 2,036); 155 lesbian, gay, bisexual, or transgender students and 1,881 heterosexual students ages 18 to 24.

FIGURE 18.3   Percentage of College Students Who Have Been Sexually Harassed (By Sexual Identity)

white versus 49 percent black and 49 percent Hispanic), to be flashed or mooned (30 percent versus 19 percent and 21 percent), or to be called a homophobic name (26 percent versus 14 percent and 14 percent). College students are equally likely to experience physical or contact sexual harassment regardless of race/ethnicity.

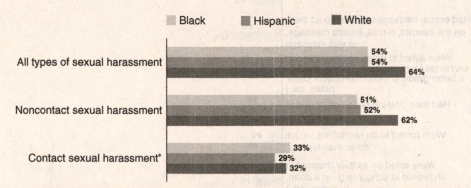

*For contact sexual harassment there are no statistically significant differences by race/ethnicity.

Note: Differences between black and Hispanic populations are not statistically significant for any category.

Base = All qualified respondents (*n* = 2,036); 340 black, 316 Hispanic, and 1,183 white students ages 18 to 24. The remaining 197 students chose a different category, such as Asian or Pacific Islander, mixed racial background, or other race, or declined to answer.

FIGURE 18.4   Percentage of College Students Who Have Been Sexually Harassed (By Race/Ethnicity)

Student Voices

Types of Student-to-Student Sexual Harassment

"There is a guy in all my classes who consistently touches me in a sexual way that I really don't appreciate."
—Female, 2nd year

"Just at a party where someone tried to get me to kiss them and I didn't want to but was forced to." —Male, 1st year

"Phone harassment calling me derogatory homosexual names [and] leaving messages." —Male, 4th year

"A lewd joke about rape directed to me during a soccer game." —Female, 2nd year

"A girl kept trying to show off her breasts to get my attention." —Male, 3rd year

"Joking around with other guys calling each other gay." —Male, 3rd year

"Someone tried to force me to kiss them and pushed me into a room."
—Female, 4th year

"I got mooned and made fun of."
—Male, 1st year

"Another student forced me to do things I did not want to do."
—Female, 4th year

"People who lived in the same hall as me in the dorms started spreading rumors about my sex life, which were not even close to true. They also spread condoms around my room."
—Female, 3rd year

"Just a female grabbing me in a sexual way." —Male, 4th year

"Being sent unwanted pornographic images through e-mail." —Male, 4th year

"Getting whistled [at] and/or had sexual related comments made to me outdoors on campus grounds."
—Female, 2nd year

WHO IS HARASSING?

Student-to-Student   Student-to-student harassment is the most common form of sexual harassment on campus. More than two-thirds of students (68 percent) say that peer harassment happens often or occasionally at their college, and more than three-quarters of students (80 percent) who experienced sexual harassment have been harassed by a student or a former student. Given that students comprise the vast majority of the campus population, it is perhaps not surprising that most sexual harassment occurs between and among students. Still, the prevalence of peer harassment among college students suggests a student culture that accepts or at least seems to tolerate this type of behavior.

Faculty/Staff-to-Student   Sexual harassment of undergraduates by faculty and staff is less common than peer harassment, but it does occur.[3] Almost one-fifth of students (18 percent) say that faculty and staff often or occasionally sexually harass students. Conversely, only one-quarter of students (25 percent), say that faculty and staff never harass students.

About 7 percent of harassed students have been harassed by a professor. Only a small number of students cite resident advisers, security guards, coaches, counselors, or deans as harassers. While faculty/staff-to-student sexual harassment does not typically happen, these percentages imply that roughly half a million undergraduate students are sexually harassed by faculty or other college personnel while in college.

Sexual harassment by faculty can be especially traumatic because the harasser is in a position of authority or power. One indication that students find sexual harassment by a faculty or staff member especially objectionable is that the majority of students (78 percent) say that they would report an incident if it involved a professor, teaching assistant, or other staff member, whereas less than half (39 percent) say they would report an incident that involved another student. Students may feel safer reporting faculty and staff harassment because it feels more egregious than peer harassment, which may present the possibility of ridicule and may be seen as something students should be able to handle on their own.

Male and Female Harassers Among students who have been harassed,[4] both male students (37 percent) and female (58 percent) students have been harassed by a man. More than half of these female students (58 percent) have been harassed by one man, and a little less than half (48 percent) have been harassed by a group of men. Female-to-female student sexual harassment appears to be the least common combination. Less than 10 percent of female students have been sexually harassed by another woman (9 percent) or group of women (6 percent).

Student Voices

Types of Faculty/Staff-to-Student Sexual Harassment

"One of my professors always makes sexually offensive jokes towards women. He doesn't speak about anyone within the class in particular, but his jokes are always about sexual favors women should perform."
—Female, 4th year

"It was with a professor and he suggested that my grade could be better if I was more interested in him."
—Female, 2nd year

"One of my supervisors tells me often that she wishes that I liked older women and that she wishes I was her age or vice versa, says we would be perfect."
—Male, 2nd year

"I was in a class where telling off-color jokes was acceptable and encouraged by the professor." —Female, 5th year

"I had a professor who used an example of a prostitute, and he used me as the prostitute." —Female, 3rd year

"When I attended [university], one professor [name] told me to my face that he wanted to have a sexual relationship with me." —Male, 4th year

"A teaching assistant offered me a better grade for a sexual favor."
—Female, 4th year

"When I lived in a dorm, the RA would ogle my roommates and I when he saw us." —Female, 3rd year

For male students who have been sexually harassed, the picture is more complicated. About one-third have been harassed by one man (37 percent) or one woman (33 percent), and about one-fifth have been harassed by a group of men (21 percent) or a group of both men and women (23 percent).

A relatively large number of students (13 percent total, 20 percent male, 7 percent female) are not sure who harassed them. Presumably, these incidents (e.g., spreading rumors, posting messages) were conducted anonymously.

About four in 10 college students (41 percent) admit to harassing someone. Among these students, noncontact types of sexual harassment are most common. For example, one-third of these students (34 percent) say they made unwanted sexual comments, jokes, gestures, or looks, and 17 percent admit to making homophobic remarks (see Figure 18.5).

More than half of male college students (51 percent) admit that they have sexually harassed someone in college, and more than one-fifth (22 percent) admit to harassing someone often or occasionally. One-fifth of male students (20 percent) say that they have physically harassed someone.

Although men are more likely to be cited as harassers and to admit to harassing behaviors, the problem of campus sexual harassment does not rest solely with college men. Of the students who have been harassed, one-fifth (20 percent) have been harassed by a female. Almost one-third of female students (31 percent) admit to committing some type of harassment. These findings remind us that not all men are sexual aggressors and not all women are passive victims. Both male and female students can and do behave in ways that are viewed by others as overly sexually aggressive.

The distinction between harasser and victim is also not so clear, as many students who admit to harassing others have been harassed themselves. Among students who have been the target of sexual harassment, a majority (55 percent) say that they have harassed others. In contrast, of students who have never been harassed, only 17 percent say they have harassed others. More than one-fifth of students (21 percent) who have been harassed say that they have harassed others often or occasionally.

These patterns reflect, in part, differences in the willingness of students to recognize unwanted sexual conduct in themselves and others. These patterns also suggest a cycle of sexual harassment.

WHY DO STUDENTS HARASS?

Harassers give the following reasons for their behavior:

- I thought it was funny (59 percent)
- I thought the person liked it (32 percent)
- It's just a part of school life/a lot of people do it/it's no big deal (30 percent)
- I wanted a date with the person (17 percent)
- My friends encouraged/"pushed" me into doing it (10 percent)
- I wanted something from that person (7 percent)
- I wanted that person to think I had some sort of power over them (4 percent)

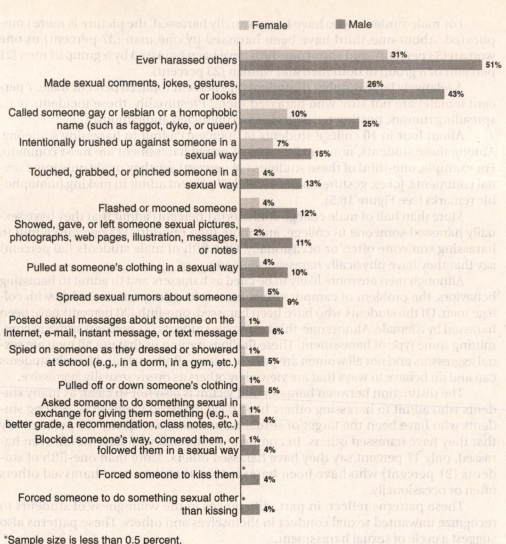

*Sample size is less than 0.5 percent.

Survey question: During your whole college life, how often, if at all, have you done the following things to someone...when that person did not want you to? Possible answers: never, rarely, occasionally, often, or decline to answer.

Base = All qualified respondents (*n* = 2,036); 1,096 female and 940 male college students ages 18 to 24.

FIGURE 18.5   Percentage of College Students Who Say They Have Sexually Harassed Others (By Gender)

Male students (63 percent) are more likely than female students (54 percent) to think sexual harassment is funny. Some differences are also evident among racial/ethnic groups. White students (36 percent) are more likely than black or Hispanic students (25 percent each) to say that they made unwanted sexual comments, jokes, gestures, or looks to another person. White students (61 percent) are also more likely than black students (46 percent) to say they harassed because they thought it was funny, whereas black students (45 percent) are more likely than white students (30 percent) to say they harassed because they thought the person liked it.

Student Voices

Sexual Harassment Made Me Feel . . .

"Upset and embarrassed."
—Female, 2nd year

"Belittled, alone, uncomfortable."
—Female, 5th year

"Slightly uncomfortable, but not threatened." — Male, 3rd year

"Self conscious, pissed off, and concerned, in that order." —Female, 3rd year

"They happen so often that I've become very immune to them. I get more annoyed by it than anything." —Male, 2nd year

"Annoyed but they don't seem to be something to take seriously."
—Male, 1st year

"It makes me feel like I have no control over my life." —Female, 4th year

"Annoyed, frustrated, embarrassed, violated." —Male, 4th year

"Angry, self conscious, ashamed."
—Female, 3rd year

"It was funny at first, but then they kept doing it." —Male, 4th year

"I don't really like them but I don't feel threatened or anything."
—Female, 4th year

"I begin to question my morals and what I stand for." —Female, 1st year

"It has made me feel threatened. It has made me afraid of being raped."
—Female, 3rd year

"In general [it] makes you feel embarrassed and hurt."
— Male, no year given

"They made me feel pretty cheap . . . like a piece of meat but I guess you expect behavior like this at college."
—Female, 2nd year

"It makes me feel horrible. It makes me feel like a second-class citizen."
—Female, 2nd year

"Hurt and sad." —Female, 1st year

"Bad at first but you learn to laugh it off." —Male, 5th year

Differences between male and female reactions to sexual harassment are most evident when students are asked about their personal experiences. The majority of female students (68 percent) say they have felt very or somewhat upset, compared to a third of male students (35 percent). The remaining two-thirds of male students (61 percent) say they have been either not very or not at all upset. In contrast, more than one-fifth of female students (23 percent) say that they have been not very upset and only 6 percent say that they have been not at all upset by their experiences.[5]

Student Voices

Sexual Harassment Affects My Education Because . . .

"It makes me feel very uncomfortable and it affects my willingness to accept the advice or lectures offered by professors." —Female, 4th year

"Uncomfortable, did not want to be in class." —Female, no year given

"They distract from the working environment and make it harder to concentrate because you become paranoid." —Male, no year given

"In school if you let things get to you, you aren't able to perform. Best thing is to just shake it off and keep going."
—Male, no year given

"I felt violated and could not focus on my classes. I also felt limited in where I could go on campus." —Female, 4th year

"Embarrassed and slightly uncomfortable going to that class."
—Male, 4th year

Student Voices

I Didn't Tell Anyone About Sexual Harassment Because . . .

"Don't know. Didn't know who to tell or how to say it." —Female, 4th year

"It wasn't a big deal." —Male, 2nd year

"There's no one to tell. Besides if I decided to tell someone other than a fellow student it would probably be questioned or ignored." —Female, 4th year

"I've had bad sexual experiences in the past that make me more likely to not want to tell anyone." —Female, 3rd year

"Not sure . . . I guess [I was] scared or felt it wouldn't be taken seriously."
—Female, 1st year

"Felt I was probably being paranoid. It was rare and infrequent occurrences and never escalated to anything even moderate, so I just brush it off and try to forget about it."
—Female, 2nd year

"I was embarrassed." —Female, 2nd Year

"Not that big of a deal. I could take care of it myself." —Female, 5th year

"Thought it best to handle the situation on my own." —Male, 5th year

"It wasn't serious enough to report."
—Male, 4th year

"It wasn't that big a deal and I didn't want anyone to get in trouble or to make myself look childish." —Female, 3rd year

"I didn't think it was serious, just another part of the daily grind." —Male, 2nd year

"It didn't seem like a big enough deal and I wasn't confident anything could/would be done about it." —Female, 2nd year

"It was annoying, creepy, unwanted and uncomfortable, but not threatening enough to complain." —Female, 5th year

Differences in Emotional Reactions   Female students are more likely than male students to feel embarrassed, angry, less confident, afraid, confused, or disappointed with their college experience as a result of sexual harassment (see Figure 18.6). Female students are also more likely to worry (at least a little) about sexual harassment. Only one-fifth of male students (20 percent) say they worry, compared to more than half of female students (54 percent). Very few male or female students (1 to 2 percent), however, say they worry about sexual harassment often.

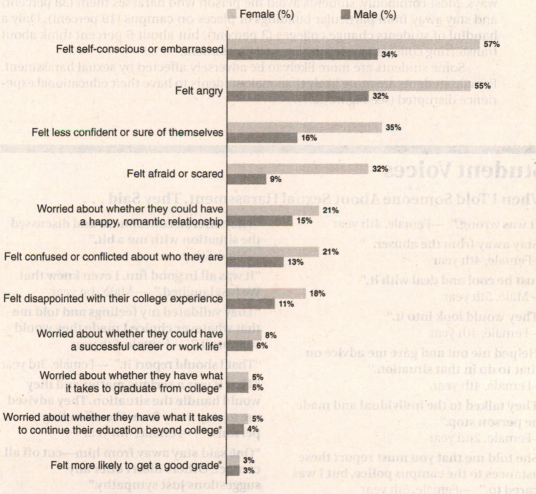

Female (%)   Male (%)

Felt self-conscious or embarrassed — 57% / 34%

Felt angry — 55% / 32%

Felt less confident or sure of themselves — 35% / 16%

Felt afraid or scared — 32% / 9%

Worried about whether they could have a happy, romantic relationship — 21% / 15%

Felt confused or conflicted about who they are — 21% / 13%

Felt disappointed with their college experience — 18% / 11%

Worried about whether they could have a successful career or work life* — 8% / 6%

Worried about whether they have what it takes to graduate from college* — 5% / 5%

Worried about whether they have what it takes to continue their education beyond college* — 5% / 4%

Felt more likely to get a good grade* — 3% / 3%

*This difference is not statistically significant.

Survey question: Has sexual harassment of any type related to your college life ever caused you to ...? All possible answers are listed above.

Base = Respondents who experienced harassment (*n* = 1,225); 659 female and 566 male college students ages 18 to 24.

FIGURE 18.6   Reactions to Sexual Harassment Experiences (By Gender)

Differences by emotional reaction also occur between lesbian, gay, bisexual, and transgender students (LGBT) and heterosexual students. While equally upset by hypothetical examples, LGBT students are more likely to feel upset by their actual experiences with sexual harassment than are heterosexual students.

IMPACT ON EDUCATION

Sexual harassment has an impact on the educational experience in large and small ways. Most commonly, students avoid the person who harasses them (38 percent) and stay away from particular buildings or places on campus (19 percent). Only a handful of students change colleges (3 percent), but about 6 percent think about transferring colleges as a result of sexual harassment.

Some students are more likely to be adversely affected by sexual harassment. Female students are more likely than male students to have their educational experience disrupted (see Figure 18.7).

Student Voices

When I Told Someone About Sexual Harassment, They Said . . .

"It was wrong." —Female, 4th year

"Stay away from the abuser. " —Female, 4th year

"Just be cool and deal with it." — Male, 5th year

"They would look into it." — Female, 4th year

"Helped me out and gave me advice on what to do in that situation." —Female, 4th year

"They talked to the individual and made the person stop." —Female, 2nd year

"She told me that you must report these instances to the campus police, but I was scared to." —Female, 5th year

"Confront the person and ask them never to do it again." —Male, 3rd year

"I spoke to a therapist and from there I was able to start coping with the situation." —Female, 3rd year

"They offered consolation and discussed the situation with me a bit." —Male, 5th year

"It was all in good fun. I even knew that. We just laughed." —Male, 1st year

"They validated my feelings and told me that whatever choice I made they would support it." —Female, 5th year

"That I should report it." —Female, 3rd year

"That it was a serious matter and they would handle the situation. They advised me to stay away from the offending persons." —Female, 4th year

"One said stay away from him—cut off all contact. Others didn't offer any suggestions just sympathy." —Female, 2nd year

"Friends and family urged me to tell a campus police officer. The campus police officer contacted the offending employee's supervisor." —Female, 3rd year

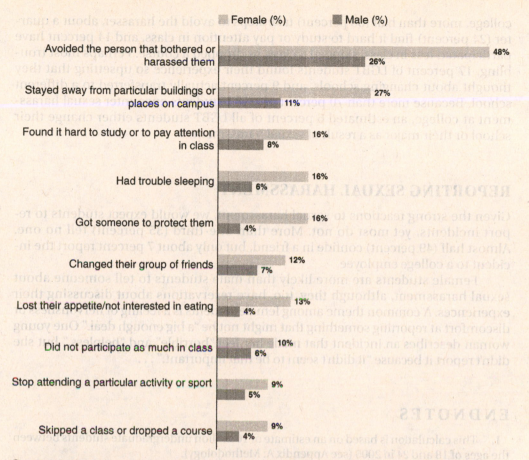

■ Female (%)   ■ Male (%)

Avoided the person that bothered or harassed them: 48% / 26%

Stayed away from particular buildings or places on campus: 27% / 11%

Found it hard to study or to pay attention in class: 16% / 8%

Had trouble sleeping: 16% / 6%

Got someone to protect them: 16% / 4%

Changed their group of friends: 12% / 7%

Lost their appetite/not interested in eating: 13% / 4%

Did not participate as much in class: 10% / 6%

Stop attending a particular activity or sport: 9% / 5%

Skipped a class or dropped a course: 9% / 4%

Survey question: Has sexual harassment of any type related to your college life ever caused you to ...? Possible answers included the answers listed above plus the following: think about changing schools, avoid a study group, make a lower grade on a test or paper than you think you otherwise would have, not go to a professor's/teaching assistant's office hours, avoid the library, change your school, think about changing your major, change your major, and not sure. Only those answers in which the difference between males' and females' responses is statistically significant are displayed.

Base = Respondents who experienced harassment (*n* = 1,225); 659 female and 566 male college students ages 18 to 24.

FIGURE 18.7   Effects of Sexual Harassment on the Educational Experience (By Gender)

Female students are more likely to avoid their harassers, find it hard to study or pay attention in class, avoid particular buildings or places on campus, or have trouble sleeping due to sexual harassment. Female students are also more likely to get someone to protect them.

LGBT students are especially likely to have their educational experience disrupted by sexual harassment. Among LGBT students who encounter harassment at college, more than half (60 percent) take steps to avoid the harasser, about a quarter (24 percent) find it hard to study or pay attention in class, and 14 percent have participated less in class, skipped a class, or dropped a course. Perhaps most troubling, 17 percent of LGBT students found their experience so upsetting that they thought about changing schools, and 9 percent actually transferred to a different school. Because more than 70 percent of LGBT students encounter sexual harassment at college, an estimated 6 percent of all LGBT students either change their school or their major as a result of sexual harassment.

REPORTING SEXUAL HARASSMENT

Given the strong reactions to sexual harassment, we would expect students to report incidents, yet most do not. More than one-third (35 percent) tell no one. Almost half (49 percent) confide in a friend, but only about 7 percent report the incident to a college employee.

Female students are more likely than male students to tell someone about sexual harassment, although they, too, have reservations about discussing their experiences. A common theme among female students is a feeling of nervousness or discomfort at reporting something that might not be "a big enough deal." One young woman describes an incident that made her feel "horrible" and "helpless," but she didn't report it because "it didn't seem to be that important." . . .

ENDNOTES

1. This calculation is based on an estimate of 10 million undergraduate students between the ages of 18 and 24 in 2005 (see Appendix A: Methodology).
2. The one exception is "forced sexual contact," where the size of the sample was not sufficient to draw conclusions.
3. In part, faculty-student harassment may be relatively uncommon compared to peer-to-peer harassment due to the broad definition of sexual harassment used in this report. For example, we wouldn't expect a professor to moon students—the second largest type of sexual harassment reported by students.
4. This question referred to any experiences with sexual harassment at college and could include multiple incidents; therefore, percentages do not add up to 100.
5. A small percentage of male and female students say that they were not sure.

CHAPTER 19

Learning Silence

Peggy Orenstein

Weston, California, sits at the far reaches of the San Francisco Bay Area. The drive from the city takes one through a series of bedroom communities, carefully planned idylls in which, as the miles roll by, the tax brackets leap upward, the politics swing right, and the people fade to white. But Weston is different: once an oddly matched blend of country folk and chemical plant workers, this is an old town, the kind of place where people still gather curbside under the bunting-swathed lampposts of Maple Street to watch the Fourth of July parade. Many of the businesses in Weston's center—doughnut shops, ladies' clothing stores, a few hard drinkers' bars, and picked-over antiquaries—haven't changed hands in over thirty years. There are a few fern bars and one café serving espresso here, but if people want high tone, they go to the city.

Not that Weston has remained suspended in time. The ramshackle houses downtown may still be populated by the families of mechanics, plant workers, and, in shoddy apartment complexes, a small community of working poor, but the hills that ring the town's edge have been gobbled up by tract homes where young professionals have hunkered down—a safe distance from urban ills—to raise their children. There's even a clean, modern supermarket by the freeway, built expressly for the new suburbanites, with a multiplex cinema across the street for their occasional evenings out.

The only place where Weston's two populations converge regularly is at Weston Middle School, a crumbling Spanish-style edifice just up the street from the post office, city hall, and, more important to the student body, a McDonald's. This is the town's sole middle school, and as such, it serves nearly nine hundred students a year from this disparate population. The bumper stickers on the cars dropping off the children reflect the mix: Toyota vans advertising the local NPR affiliate pull up behind rusty pickups that proclaim: "My wife said if I buy another gun she'll divorce me; God, I'll miss her!" There is also a staunch Christian population here—Mormons, Seventh-Day Adventists, and other, less austere sects whose cars remind other residents that "Jesus Loves You!"

In recent years, Weston Middle School has fulfilled its mandate well: the school entrance is draped with a "California Distinguished School" banner, earned last year by the students' estimable standardized test scores as well as the staff's exemplary performance. The teachers are an impressive, enthusiastic group who routinely seek methods of instruction that will inspire a little more engagement, a little more effort on the part of their pupils: an eighth-grade history teacher uses a karaoke microphone to juice up his lessons; an English teacher videotapes students performing original poems to bring literature to life; a science teacher offers extra credit to students who join him in cleaning up the banks of a local river. There is also some concern about gender issues in education: Weston's history teachers have embraced the new, more inclusive textbooks adopted by the state of California; in English, students write essays on their views about abortion and read, among other books, *Streams to the River, River to the Sea*, a historical novel which recasts Sacagawea as an intrepid female hero.

Yet the overt curriculum, as fine as it may be, is never the only force operating in a classroom. There is something else as well. The "hidden curriculum" comprises the unstated lessons that students learn in school: it is the running subtext through which teachers communicate behavioral norms and individual status in the school culture, the process of socialization that cues children into their place in the hierarchy of larger society. Once used to describe the ways in which the education system works to reproduce class systems in our culture, the "hidden curriculum" has recently been applied to the ways in which schools help reinforce gender roles, whether they intend to or not.

THE DAILY GRIND: LESSONS IN THE HIDDEN CURRICULUM

Amy Wilkinson has looked forward to being an eighth grader forever—at least for the last two years, which, when you're thirteen, seems like the same thing. By the second week of September she's settled comfortably into her role as one of the school's reigning elite. Each morning before class, she lounges with a group of about twenty other eighth-grade girls and boys in the most visible spot on campus: at the base of the schoolyard, between one of the portable classrooms that was constructed in the late 1970s and the old oak tree in the overflow parking lot. The group trades gossip, flirts, or simply stands around, basking in its own importance and killing time before the morning bell.

At 8:15 on Tuesday the crowd has already convened, and Amy is standing among a knot of girls, laughing. She is fuller-figured than she'd like to be, wide-hipped and heavy-limbed with curly, blond hair, cornflower-blue eyes, and a sharply up-turned nose. With the help of her mother, who is a drama coach, she has become the school's star actress: last year she played Eliza in Weston's production of *My Fair Lady*. Although she earns solid grades in all of her subjects—she'll make the honor roll this fall—drama is her passion, she says, because "I love entertaining people, and I love putting on characters."

Also, no doubt, because she loves the spotlight: this morning, when she mentions a boy I haven't met, Amy turns, puts her hands on her hips, anchors her feet shoulder width apart, and bellows across the schoolyard, "Greg! Get over here! You have to meet Peggy."

She smiles wryly as Greg, looking startled, begins to make his way across the schoolyard for an introduction. "I'm not exactly shy," she says, her hands still on her hips. "I'm *bold*."

Amy is bold. And brassy, and strong-willed. Like any teenager, she tries on and discards different selves as if they were so many pairs of Girbaud jeans, searching ruthlessly for a perfect fit. During a morning chat just before the school year began, she told me that her parents tried to coach her on how to respond to my questions. "They told me to tell you that they want me to be my own person," she complained. "My mother *told* me to tell you that. I do want to be my own person, but it's like, you're interviewing me about who I am and she's telling me what to say—that's not my own person, is it?"

When the morning bell rings, Amy and her friends cut off their conversations, scoop up their books, and jostle toward the school's entrance. Inside, Weston's hallways smell chalky, papery, and a little sweaty from gym class. The wood-railed staircases at either end of the two-story main building are worn thin in the middle from the scuffle of hundreds of pairs of sneakers pounding them at forty-eight-minute intervals for nearly seventy-five years. Amy's mother, Sharon, and her grandmother both attended this school. So will her two younger sisters. Her father, a mechanic who works on big rigs, is a more recent Weston recruit: he grew up in Georgia and came here after he and Sharon were married.

Amy grabs my hand, pulling me along like a small child or a slightly addled new student: within three minutes we have threaded our way through the dull-yellow hallways to her locker and then upstairs to room 238, Mrs. Richter's math class.

The twenty-two students that stream through the door with us run the gamut of physical maturity. Some of the boys are as small and compact as fourth graders, their legs sticking out of their shorts like pipe cleaners. A few are trapped in the agony of a growth spurt, and still others cultivate downy beards. The girls' physiques are less extreme: most are nearly their full height, and all but a few have already weathered the brunt of puberty. They wear topknots or ponytails, and their shirts are tucked neatly into their jeans.

Mrs. Richter, a ruddy, athletic woman with a powerful voice, has arranged the chairs in a three-sided square, two rows deep. Amy walks to the far side of the room and, as she takes her seat, falls into a typically feminine pose: she crosses her legs, folds her arms across her chest, and hunches forward toward her desk, seeming to shrink into herself. The sauciness of the playground disappears, and, in fact, she says hardly a word during class. Meanwhile, the boys, especially those who are more physically mature, sprawl in their chairs, stretching their legs long, expanding into the available space.

Nate, a gawky, sanguine boy who has shaved his head except for a small thatch that's hidden under an Oakland A's cap, leans his chair back on two legs and, although the bell has already rung, begins a noisy conversation with his friend Kyle.

Mrs. Richter turns to him, "What's all the discussion about, Nate?" she asks.

"*He's* talking to *me*," Nate answers, pointing to Kyle. Mrs. Richter writes Nate's name on the chalkboard as a warning toward detention and he yells out in protest. They begin to quibble over the justice of her decision, their first—but certainly not their last—power struggle of the day. As they argue, Allison, a tall, angular girl who once told me, "My goal is to be the best wife and mother I can be," raises her hand to ask a question. Mrs. Richter, finishing up with Nate, doesn't notice.

"Get your homework out, everyone!" the teacher booms, and walks among the students, checking to make sure no one has shirked on her or his assignment. Allison, who sits in the front row nearest both the blackboard and the teacher, waits patiently for another moment, then, realizing she's not getting results, puts her hand down. When Mrs. Richter walks toward her, Allison tries another tack, calling out her question. Still, she gets no response, so she gives up.

As a homework assignment, the students have divided their papers into one hundred squares, color-coding each square prime or composite—prime being those numbers which are divisible only by one and themselves, and composite being everything else. Mrs. Richter asks them to call out the prime numbers they've found, starting with the tens.

Nate is the first to shout, "Eleven!" The rest of the class chimes in a second later. As they move through the twenties and thirties, Nate, Kyle, and Kevin, who sit near one another at the back of the class, call out louder and louder, casually competing for both quickest response and the highest decibel level. Mrs. Richter lets the boys' behavior slide, although they are intimidating other students.

"Okay," Mrs. Richter says when they've reached one hundred. "Now, what do you think of one hundred and three? Prime or composite?"

Kyle, who is skinny and a little pop-eyed, yells out, "Prime!" but Mrs. Richter turns away from him to give someone else a turn. Unlike Allison, who gave up when she was ignored, Kyle isn't willing to cede his teacher's attention. He begins to bounce in his chair and chant, "*Prime! Prime! Prime!*" Then, when he turns out to be right, he rebukes the teacher, saying, "*See,* I told you."

When the girls in Mrs. Richter's class do speak, they follow the rules. When Allison has another question, she raises her hand again and waits her turn; this time, the teacher responds. When Amy volunteers her sole answer of the period, she raises her hand, too. She gives the wrong answer to an easy multiplication problem, turns crimson, and flips her head forward so her hair falls over her face.

Occasionally, the girls shout out answers, but generally they are to the easiest, lowest-risk questions, such as the factors of four or six. And their stabs at public recognition depend on the boys' largesse: when the girls venture responses to more complex questions the boys quickly become territorial, shouting them down with their own answers. Nate and Kyle are particularly adept at overpowering Renee, who, I've been told by the teacher, is the brightest girl in the class. (On a subsequent visit, I will see her lay her head on her desk when Nate overwhelms her and mutter, "I hate this class.")

Mrs. Richter doesn't say anything to condone the boys' aggressiveness, but she doesn't have to: they insist on—and receive—her attention even when she consciously tries to shift it elsewhere in order to make the class more equitable.

After the previous day's homework is corrected, Mrs. Richter begins a new lesson, on the use of exponents.

"What does three to the third power mean?" she asks the class.

"*I know!*" shouts Kyle.

Instead of calling on Kyle, who has already answered more than his share of questions, the teacher turns to Dawn, a somewhat more voluble girl who has plucked her eyebrows down to a few hairs.

"Do you know, Dawn?"

Dawn hesitates, and begins "Well, you count the number of threes and . . ."

"*But I know!*" interrupts Kyle. "*I know!*"

Mrs. Richter deliberately ignores him, but Dawn is rattled: she never finishes her sentence, she just stops.

"*I know! ME!*" Kyle shouts again, and then before Dawn recovers herself he blurts, "*It's three times three times three!*"

At this point, Mrs. Richter gives in. She turns away from Dawn, who is staring blankly, and nods at Kyle. "Yes," she says. "Three times three times three. Does everyone get it?"

"*YES!*" shouts Kyle; Dawn says nothing.

Mrs. Richter picks up the chalk. "Let's do some others," she says.

"Let me!" says Kyle.

"I'll pick on whoever raises their hand," she tells him.

Nate, Kyle, and two other boys immediately shoot up their hands, fingers squeezed tight and straight in what looks like a salute.

"Don't you want to wait and hear the problem first?" she asks, laughing.

They drop their hands briefly. She writes 8^4 on the board. "Okay, what would that look like written out?"

Although a third of the class raises their hands to answer—including a number of students who haven't yet said a word—she calls on Kyle anyway.

"Eight times eight times eight times eight," he says triumphantly, as the other students drop their hands.

When the bell rings, I ask Amy about the mistake she made in class and the embarrassment it caused her. She blushes again.

"Oh yeah," she says. "That's about the only time I ever talked in there. I'll never do that again."

BAD CHEMISTRY: "GUYS LIKE IT WHEN YOU ACT ALL HELPLESS"

It is another late-fall morning under the oak tree at Weston. Amy, Becca, and Evie huddle together slightly apart from the other students, the intimate turn to their shoulders making it clear that they're exchanging the juiciest gossip. A squadron of seventh-grade boys on bicycles zips by and the girls look up, annoyed, sidling to the left to avoid being hit.

A few seconds later, Becca, usually the most reserved of her friends, shrieks.

"Get that away from me!"

The bikers are forgotten as the girls scatter, screaming, their faces flushed, revealing Carl Ross, a boy from Evie's math class, whose feet are firmly planted where the girls once stood. An uncapped jar labeled "Felicia" dangles from his left hand. Until a minute ago, it held a large spider he'd captured for extra credit in science class. Felicia is currently hanging from a dead pine needle in his other hand, her legs tucked in and body contracted in fear.

Becca runs about ten feet and turns around. When she smiles, she reveals a mouth full of braces. "I'm *deathly* afraid of spiders," she says, her eyes shining as she looks back at her tormentor.

The other two girls run up to her. "God, me too!" Amy says breathlessly, clutching her friend's arms. "When I saw *Arachnophobia* my dad had to go check my room for me. He had to look under the bed!"

Evie's cheeks are pink and her dark hair is falling from its bun. She tucks the wayward wisps back in place as a second boy lets the bug drop from his finger by a lengthening strand of web. "Yuck, how disgusting," she says, widening her eyes. "I hope he doesn't come near me with that."

As a woman standing among these girls, I wasn't sure how to react. I desperately wanted them to stand up to the boys who increasingly joined in the game. I wanted them to be brave, to marvel at the spider's jewel-green body, to ask for a turn at holding it and watching it try to spin its escape. But I felt the pressure too: a real girl, a girl who wants a boy to like her, runs screaming from spiders. The more she likes a boy, the more she allows him to terrorize her, and the more helpless she pretends to be. Showing any real interest in spiders would've been imprudent for the girls, a denial of their newly important femininity. During my year at Weston, I saw girls run from spiders innumerable times; with each flight toward traditional femininity, I thought about who has permission, who has the right in our culture, to explore the natural world, to get dirty and muddy, to think spiders and worms and frogs are neat, to bring them in for extra credit in science. In fact, to be engaged in science at all.

"I'm not *really* afraid of that stuff, except snakes and blood," Amy admits later, after the hoopla. "But guys like it if you act all helpless and girly, so you do."

As with math, there is a circular relationship among girls' affection for science, their self-esteem, and their career plans. But unlike in math, the achievement gap between girls and boys in science is actually widening: the National Assessment of Educational Progress found that, for thirteen-year-olds, gender differences in all areas of science performance except biology actually increased during the 1980s, with boys' skills improving and girls' slipping during that time. This is particularly disturbing when one considers that today's young people are growing up in an era of rapid technological change; without a solid grounding in science, girls will not only be unable to participate in shaping that change, they will be helpless in the face of it.

Certainly, the culture outside the classroom discourages scientific competence in girls. Boys still have more casual exposure to science—whether it's light meters, chemistry sets, or, like Carl and his friends, spiders—and they're more likely to have computers at home. Science toys are still marketed almost exclusively toward boys, with boys featured on packages (or, worse still, girls *watching* boys) and the world of video games seems constructed with an entirely male audience in mind.

In school, girls opt out—or are pushed out—of science at every stage of advancement. In high school, boys and girls take introductory biology and chemistry in similar numbers, but far more boys go on to physics or advanced chemistry, while girls, if they take science at all, continue with biology. And although the numbers of women who pursue the sciences has skyrocketed, there were formerly so few that even huge jumps yield small results: for instance, the number of female engineers grew 131 percent during the 1980s, but women still make up only 8 percent of that field. In fact, a scant 16 percent of currently employed scientists are female, and that figure may well have peaked: by the late 1980s, the numbers of women pursuing degrees in science and engineering (excluding the social sciences) had leveled off and was dropping, especially in advanced physics and computer science.

Nonetheless, in spite of the achievement gap, today's girls believe that they can excel in science; the trouble is, boys (perhaps prejudiced by the overreaction to spiders and snakes) do not share that belief about their female classmates. Because of that disparity, science laboratory groups—in which boys grab equipment from girls, perform experiments for them, and ridicule girls' contributions—can become less an opportunity for partnership than a microcosm of unintended lessons about gender.

Amy's science class is taught by Mr. Sinclair, a mustachioed fellow with a receding hairline, who chose teaching as a profession during what he describes as his idealistic youth in the late 1960s. He periodically considers changing careers, mostly for financial reasons, but he enjoys his work too much to quit. Instead, he stays sharp by attending conferences on science instruction, subscribing to newsletters, seeking out new ways to teach. He tries hard to be creative because, he says, the kids tend not to like physical science very much. But judging from what happens in his classroom, it's really the girls who don't like it.

Like Mrs. Richter, Mr. Sinclair never intentionally discriminates against the girls in his class; both he and the other eighth-grade science teacher at Weston— who is also male—are quick to point out the few girls who do participate (although in further conversation I found that many of those girls felt neither affection nor affinity for the subject). What I saw instead, even more than in the math classes I observed, was a kind of passive resistance to participation by the girls that went unquestioned by the teacher. Call it gender bias by omission. When, week after week, boys raised their hands to ask or answer questions in far greater numbers than girls, when only boys shouted out responses, when boys enthusiastically offered up extra-credit demonstrations, the teacher simply didn't notice.

The very morning that Amy flees shrieking from Felicia the spider, Mr. Sinclair invites me to observe as her section of his physical science class performs an easy, fun experiment called "The Cartesian Diver." Each group of three students is given an empty dishwashing liquid bottle, an eyedropper, and a beaker of water. The idea is to fill the bottle with water, drop in the dropper, and, through some magical process that the students must determine (which turns out to be placing a little water in the dropper in advance, then squeezing the bottle to cause mass displacement), make the dropper sink and float at will.

In Amy's lab group there is another girl, Donna, and a boy, Liam, who sits between them. Liam performs the experiment as the two girls watch, occasionally offering encouragement, but no criticism. When he is successful, Amy squeals and pats him on the arm. Eventually Liam lets Donna and Amy each try the diver exactly once; then he recovers it and continues to play.

In another group of two girls and one boy directly behind Amy, Roger stands behind the girls, supervising . . . sort of.

"You're doing it wrong, ha-ha," he taunts in a singsong voice. Roger has a long rattail and a pierced ear; he wears an oversized tie-dyed T-shirt. The girls, who have styled their long blond hair identically, huddle together, trying to ignore him, and continue to attempt the experiment. Roger watches them a moment longer, then grabs the bottle from them, pours the water into the beaker and walks away with the dropper. The girls do not protest. When he comes back a few minutes later, the girls have refilled the bottle, but, still uncertain about how to proceed, have decided to empty it again and start over.

"Oh, smart," Roger says sarcastically. "*Real* smart." He grabs the bottle again. "*I'll* do it." He refills the bottle, puts the dropper in, and completes the experiment while the girls watch in silence.

I wander to the far corner of the room, where Allison, from Amy's math class, and Karla, a round-faced Latina girl with deep dimples and black hair pulled into a topknot, are having trouble with their diver. There are several girls sitting around them, yet they have asked a boy for help.

"I told him he could do it for us because he has man's hands," Karla, who once told me she wants to be an astronaut, tells me, smiling.

A second boy is watching the scene. When his friend completes the experiment, he pumps his fist in the air. "Yes!" he says. "A *man* had to do it!"

"But *how* did you do it?" Allison asks.

"I have magic hands," the first boy answers. "*Man* hands," and he laughs.

The girls laugh too—acting appropriately "helpless and girly"—but they never learn how to do the experiment. Instead, like the girls in the other groups, they have become outsiders in the learning process, passive observers rather than competent participants. In truth, "man hands" do complete most of the experiments in the room.

INSTITUTIONS
IN CRISIS

PART SIX

The Family

I s there a crisis in the American family? Certainly it is a time of change for the family, and for many families it is also a time of trouble. The "traditional" family, with the husband as the sole source of financial support and the wife as a full-time homebody, still exists, of course, but it is now a statistical minority. Increasingly large numbers of women, married or not, have entered the labor force. Others live in unconventional intimate arrangements and contribute to the increasing diversity of American family lifestyles. All of this diversity, this permissiveness, if you will, seems to many to be menacing the integrity and stability of the American family.

These changes do not, however, necessarily signal decline or decay. To conclude that the family is declining, one must point to a historical era when things were rosier. Certainly, the ideal of home, motherhood, and apple pie is part of our romantic mythology, but the myth did not always match the experience.

Nevertheless, many Americans—men and women, husbands and wives, parents and children—are experiencing marked uncertainties and anxieties. We have known deep changes in family life and in society. But our understanding of how to interpret these changes—and to deal with them—has been impaired by lack of knowledge about the relationship between family life and society, particularly about the impact of social forces upon the everyday workings of family life.

In "Beyond the 'M' Word," Arlene Skolnick examines how these changes have affected the institution of marriage—which has become a "major combat zone" in the heated debates about the state of the family as well as many other social issues, including poverty, welfare, and gay rights. Marriage has been declared to be obsolete many times in American history, but Skolnick shows that, despite these periodic claims, the institution is "very much here to stay." Most Americans still look to marriage as the "gold standard" for personal relationships, and most will eventually enter into it. Those who believe that the family is disintegrating may be confusing decline with diversity. It is true that the American family today looks different than it did in the past, and the culture has come to accept a wider range of family types. But in one form or another, the family has shown itself to be remarkably resilient.

That doesn't mean, however, that all is well with American families, as Skolnick's discussion makes clear. The volatile global economy, in particular, has taken a heavy toll on families all across the social and economic spectrum. America has become a high-risk, high-stress society, and family life has been feeling the strain. Economic booms and recessions, the trade-offs between time spent at work and family time generate pressures for families and those living within them. This is especially true as economic inequality and homelessness have hardened into stubbornly persistent features of American life. But the middle-class family has also been hit uncommonly hard by economic decline. Layoffs among blue- and white-collar workers have resulted in downward social mobility for suburban as well as inner-city families, while others have prospered.

Part of the problem for all too many American families is that we lack anything approaching a comprehensive national policy that could ease the strain between parenting and work. In the 1990s, some steps were taken to develop new national policies regarding family leaves and child care. But were these efforts adequate? The next two articles suggest that they weren't.

The United States stands out among the world's advanced nations—and even many less-developed ones—in the stinginess of our supports for families and children. A recent survey, for example, finds that only four of 173 countries studied failed to provide some form of leave with income for women at childbirth: the four were Liberia, Papua New Guinea, Swaziland, and the United States.[1] Something similar holds for the provision of child care. Most advanced industrial nations have some established policy providing safe and largely affordable child care as a matter of right. But in the United States, as Sharon Lerner's article shows, all too many families have to scramble to find child care at all, and often can't afford to pay for it if they do, and the quality of care they ultimately receive, when they do, is sometimes abysmal. The consequences for children and their parents are both troubling and costly in the long run. What is especially frustrating, as Lerner points out, is that fixing this glaring child care deficit would be both relatively simple and relatively inexpensive.

We know that better, more supportive family policies are possible because a number of other countries have them. In her article "More than Welcome," Brittany Shahmehri, an American journalist living in Sweden, gives us an in-depth description of that country's extensive supports for families, which are among the most generous in the world. The centerpiece of the Swedish approach is a guaranteed leave of absence from work for new parents when their children are born, which is not only far longer than our own brief parental leave, but is also paid. The generous parental leave, moreover, is only one of many "family-friendly" policies in Sweden, which provides an approach to nurturing families and children that contrasts conspicuously with the distinctly minimal efforts in the United States. The heart of the difference is that in Sweden, as in some other European countries, it is assumed that society as a whole has an interest in—and a responsibility for—the well-being of *all* children.

ENDNOTES

1. Jody Heymann, Alison Earle, and Jeffrey Hayes, *The Work, Family, and Equity Index: How Does the United States Measure Up?* Montreal, Project on Global Working Families, 2007.

CHAPTER 20

Beyond the "M" Word
The Tangled Web of Politics and Marriage

Arlene Skolnick

THE THIRTY YEAR DETOUR

At the end of 1992, the media summed up the major events of the year. These included the obvious: the presidential election, and a major race riot in Los Angeles, touched off by the acquittal of police officers who had been filmed beating an unarmed black suspect named Rodney King. But another event to make onto at least one list was the birth of a fictional baby to a popular television sit-com character named "Murphy Brown."

The three events were linked in the mixture of trivia and tragedy that marked the struggle for America's political future that year. In June, in the wake of the Los Angeles riots, then Vice President Dan Quayle addressed the Commonwealth Club in San Francisco. "The lawless social anarchy which we saw," he argued, "is directly related to the breakdown of family structure."

At the very end of speech, he denounced the "Murphy Brown" character, played by Candace Bergen, for having a child out of wedlock. She and her "Hollywood elite" creators were "mocking fatherhood," thereby encouraging family disintegration among the poor.

Quayle's attack backfired. Instead of stirring up righteous anger, he launched a torrent of late-night talk-show jokes and a frenzy of ridicule in the media. A chastened Quayle denied that he had ever criticized single mothers.

Presidential candidate Bill Clinton captured the national mood with a vision of "an America that includes every family. Every traditional family and every extended family. Every two-parent family, every single-parent family, every foster family."

Yet the Murphy Brown episode turned out to be merely the misfired opening shot in a real political/cultural war. Clinton had barely settled into the White House when a barrage of op-eds, articles, books, and talk-show appearances argued that, as a cover story in *The Atlantic Monthly* put it, "Dan Quayle Was Right" after all: the rise of single parenthood would have terrible consequences for the nation's children and for all the rest of us, too. And it didn't matter whether the cause was divorce or illegitimacy.

Though conservatives led and funded the new crusade, Democrats and many liberals joined up. No more was heard about "all our families" no matter what their form. Instead, Clinton advisers hailed the two-parent family as the "best anti-poverty program." In the media, pundits of all political hues warned that single parenthood had become the number one threat to the country because it was the root cause of all the rest: poverty, crime, drugs, juvenile violence, and failing schools—what Joe Klein called "a nauseating buffet of social ills."

Since the early 1990s, then, marriage has been a major combat zone in the culture wars, at the center of debates over poverty, welfare, sexuality, divorce, race, gender, and gay rights. It has also been a focus of governments at all levels. In 1996, Congress passed, and President Clinton signed, the Defense of Marriage Act (DOMA). The law declared that the federal government may not consider same sex relationships as marriage, even if one or more states do. It also declared that states need not consider same sex couples as married even if other states do.

In addition, state and local governments became involved in a range of marriage-promotion efforts—high school courses on the benefits of marriage, premarital counseling, bonuses for poor couples who agree to marry, covenant marriage, among many others. And when the 1996 welfare reform was renewed, the bill included, along with numerous cuts to safety net programs such as food stamps, $750 million over five years to promote "healthy marriage" and "responsible fatherhood."

In addition, a self-described "marriage movement" began in the 1990s, a broad crusade to "arrest America's moral decay" by restoring both a "marriage culture," traditional fatherhood, discouraging alternative family forms, and reviving the stigma and a sense of shame to divorce and single motherhood.

Following the money, sociologist Scott Coltrane has shown that the marriage movement has been a joint project of the religious and economic conservatives, funded by an array of right-wing foundations. Nevertheless, many of the leading marriage movement organizations typically describe themselves as nonpartisan and nonsectarian. And they recruited a politically motley collection of clergy, marriage and family therapists, social scientists, judges, lawyers, and policy analysts to take part in their various activities.

Further, in their conferences and in their many reports, articles, op-eds, and books they speak the language of social science to support their claims that traditional marriage is the remedy for poverty and the only setting in which children can develop into healthy adults.

The marriage movement has never faced a coherent and politically effective opposition. Social scientists have challenged conservative claims that we live in a "post-marital society"; that Americans, especially the poor, must be persuaded that marriage is a good thing, that marriage is the cure for poverty and other social ills, that a bit of marriage education or counseling, without any other supports, can result in stable "healthy" marriages. Simplistic notions about the long, stable history of marriage, and its supposed demise at the hands of feminists and the 1960s counter-culture, are also at odds with what historians of the family have found. Families have always been in flux.

The political aims of the marriage movement, however, are served by framing the marriage issue as a two-sided debate between those who are valiantly trying to save the institution and the liberals and feminists whose agenda is to destroy it. But there is no such agenda. Conservatives demonize anyone who questions their social science or doubts the need for vigorous action to "save" marriage as being against marriage. They also count as opponents anyone who points to the injustice of government efforts to penalize single parents, gay families, and other "deviant" family forms without regard for the children who live in them.

Nevertheless, there really are a number of left intellectuals and activists who do have a problem with marriage. Some argue that it is a white, middle-class thing, irrelevant to the poor, the nonwhite, the non-heterosexual. Farther out on the political spectrum, marriage is actually a fighting word; echos of "smash monogamy" can still be heard, joined now by gay and lesbian liberationists who denounce gay marriage as a kind of assimilation to patriarchal normality.

And some law professors and other academics argue that the state should not be in the marriage business at all—in other words, that legal marriage should be abolished. Whatever merits these arguments may have in the abstract, they have no relevance to current political and social realities.

Claims about the decline of marriage resonate precisely because Americans, in contrast to other Western countries, care so much about the institution. The death of marriage has been proclaimed countless times in American history; and yet no matter how many times it fails to die, the threat never seems to lose its power.

Although the institution is much changed since the 1960s, it is at the same time very much here to stay. As sociologist Steven Seidman put it in a defense of gay marriage against the gay liberationists who oppose it, "This reality must be the starting point for any serious political discussion."

In addition, we need some historical perspective to understand how we got to the current predicaments of marriage and family life and where we are likely to go in the future. We need to counter the simplistic before-and-after story conservatives tell about the long, unchanging history of marriage and its sudden demise at the hands of feminists and the 1960s counterculture. No reputable historian endorses this talk. Families have always been diverse and they have always been in flux.

We also need to replace the moral decline narrative with an alternative explanation of the remarkable transformations in family, gender, sexuality, and personal life that people have seen with their own eyes, as well as the stress, uncertainty, and disorientation these shifts have brought about. We need to move the terms of debate from the moral failings of individuals to the wider structural changes of society. I suggest a story of historical transition, culture lag, and family sustainability.

This is not the first time Americans have had to rewrite the scripts of family life. The current wave of family change resembles previous eras when economic transformation destabilized existing social arrangements. Indeed, the breadwinner-caregiver family model that people think of as "traditional" is a nineteenth-century product—an adaptation to the industrial age. The separation of home and work undid the earlier "family economy" of farmers, craftsmen, and shopkeepers. In the post-industrial era the distinctive "separate spheres" family arrangement, with its rigid gender roles, has become obsolete. A more flexible, egalitarian model of marriage and family is struggling to be born.

In short, we are passing through a historical watershed—an unsettled period of several decades when, as Peter Drucker put it, a society has to "rearrange" itself—"its worldview, its social and political structures . . . its key institutions." We know from the past that remaking the cultural blueprints for family life is no easy task. Such "rearrangements" do not happen without distress, disruption, and political and cultural conflict. There is no use trying to restore the family patterns of the past, but the inevitable "rearrangement" is stalled by a cultural and political stalemate.

But that is not the only challenge families face in postindustrial America: the new globalized and deregulated economy has unraveled the social contract that sustained working- and middle-class families in the postwar era. As sociologist Frank Furstenberg reported, ensuring the well-being of children has far less to do with the marital status of the family they live in than with the resources—financial, psychological, and social—their parents bring to the task of raising them. In recent years, marriage has become a "luxury item," available only to those with steady jobs and good incomes.

Here is the contradiction at the heart of conservative ideology. Despite their professed reverence for family values, conservatives oppose in principle the economic arrangements that enable families to flourish, and they work hard to advance the economic forces that disrupt them.

And here is a second contradiction: the Republican Party has abandoned its long-standing (if only formal) commitment to equal rights for women and has sold its soul to religious fundamentalism—while its economic policies undermine the "traditional" male breadwinner role to which the fundamentalists are committed.

To support families in the new era we will need to rethink deeply embedded ideas concerning men, women, and work—as well as the relationship between families, government, and the private sector.

HOME ECONOMICS

Many of the family problems Americans worry about—delays in marriage, poor unmarried women having children, young adult offspring moving back home, seemingly unable to launch themselves into adulthood—are rooted in economic factors far more than in psychological or cultural ones. One of the most significant but least talked about features of American society over the last twenty-five years is the growth of economic inequality and insecurity.

We do hear about time squeezes and money squeezes—often blamed on the bad choices of women who flee home for work or on consumerism run amok. But the big picture has gone surprisingly unreported. Not only is there a growing gap between the "haves" and "have-nots," but there is a widening gulf between the middle and the top of the income scale. And economic insecurity is increasingly affecting the middle class.

Neither party has focused on the implications of the new economic landscape for family life, much less on what to do about it. Yet a few maverick conservatives were the first to warn that the American or neoliberal version of globalization may be unsustainable without a better balance between free market values and social responsibility. "Through its effects on the family," warned John Gray, a former adviser to Margaret Thatcher, in 1998, "the American free market weakens one of the social institutions through which a liberal capitalist civilization renews itself."

Although the media feature stories on the "mommy wars" and professional women who supposedly "opt out," the reality is that the majority of mothers, even of very young children, are in the workforce—by necessity. But media preoccupations might be changing. The polls are showing increasing levels of public concern with economic security, even as basic economic indicators improve. And there is beginning to be a substantial literature on the economic underpinnings of American families, or the lack thereof.

Economic pressures begin to take their toll early in life, delaying the transition to adulthood. "Drowning in student loan and credit card debt? Can't afford to get married, buy a home, have children? At last, a book for the under-35 generation. . . ." So reads the jacket blurb for *Strapped: Why America's 20- and 30- Somethings Can't Get Ahead*, by Tamara Draut, one of a number of new books on the obstacles young Americans face in the harsh new economic landscape.

Yale political scientist Jacob Hacker has been writing about what he calls "the great risk shift," the "massive transfer of risk from corporations and the government onto families and individuals." His research has revealed that family incomes have become wildly unstable over the past twenty years. One symptom of this instability is higher levels of debt. Elizabeth Warren, of Harvard Law School, has illuminated a little noticed but surprisingly widespread phenomenon: more people declare bankruptcy than file for divorce; one out of seven children in America will live through a family bankruptcy by the end of the decade. But the problem is not "affluenza" or "luxury fever." In *The Two-Income Trap*, Warren and her daughter Amelia Tyagi demolish the "myth of overconsumption," beloved by social critics of the left as well as the right. Rather, families are going deeper and deeper into debt to meet basic, fixed expenses—mortgage payments, taxes, tuition for nursery school and college, health insurance, and the like.

The decline of the steady job and the rise of the mass layoff are the subjects of *The Disposable American*, an important new book by Louis Uchitelle, the economics writer for the *New York Times*. He debunks the myths that sustain the practice: that layoffs are a business necessity, that there will be benefits in the form of a stronger economy and better jobs. In addition, he argues, layoffs impose severe human costs in the form of family instability, depression, and other mental health problems and contribute to a general deterioration of American life.

Clearly, there is an opportunity here for Democrats and progressives to speak to the middle class and those lower down the income scale. Even Thomas Friedman, one of the best-known boosters of globalization, worries that inequality and insecurity may be the Achilles' heel of the new capitalism. He has called for a "politics of sustainable globalization" and a domestic "new New Deal." Liberals and the left should be able to put together a coherent and appealing political program based on our own traditional values: fairness, opportunity, enabling individuals and families to cope with the hazards of postindustrial life.

THE (NEW) TROUBLE WITH MARRIAGE

The other dilemma of the twenty-first century, even more fraught than the economic challenge, is sustaining families in the midst of a major shift in gender relations. "There has never been a society, so far as we know," writes Anthony Giddens, ". . . in which women have been even approximately equal to men." At the turn of the twenty-first century, the United States is on the verge of becoming such a society. Moreover, this challenge to the traditional gender hierarchy is not confined to one country or the West, but extends around the globe, along with varying degrees of resistance to it.

The prevailing assumption is that feminism, along with the hedonism and sexual excess of "the sixties," lured women—and men—away from marriage and home. In fact, the gender revolution is rooted in trends that reach back a hundred years, to the turn of the twentieth century, if not earlier. We need to distinguish feminism from the economic and social transformations whose unintended consequence is the erosion of gender inequality. The shift to a service economy has drawn women into the workplace. Educational levels have risen for both sexes. A series of life-course revolutions has reduced the period of active child care in a woman's life to a small segment of an eighty-year span.

Women actually started moving into the paid workforce in the 1890s, but it was not until the 1970s that a tipping point was reached and gender change became a contentious public issue. The old marriage bargain, whereby he brought home the bacon and wore the pants and she offered sex, babies, and housekeeping in return, is no longer possible or desirable for most Americans. Yet the United States is far from the post-marital society the alarmists describe. It remains central to American culture, an expected life event for virtually everyone. For years, the Census Bureau has been projecting that 90 percent of Americans will marry at some point in their lives, and in 1994, 91 percent of women had actually been married by the age of forty-five. Surveys show that generations X and Y are even more enthusiastic about marriage than their predecessors. What really bothers people in the marriage movement is that while Americans prefer marriage over any other lifestyle, they resist the scarlet letter morality that the movement militants would like to restore.

There is no evidence that Americans have become indifferent to marriage. Studies that look at popular attitudes, across racial, class, and ethnic groups, show that marriage remains the gold standard for couple relationships. Nor is there any evidence that the values and marital expectations of welfare recipients and other poor women differ significantly from those of the middle class. Some of the statistics cited by marriage militants—that the two-parent-married-with-children household is only a quarter or less of the total number of households or that most Americans spend half their lives outside of marriage—reflect the dramatic increase of longevity over the past century rather than the decline of marriage.

WHAT ABOUT DIVORCE?

The marriage movement insists that rising divorce rates since the 1950s clinch the case that Americans no longer value lifelong marriage. But divorce rates peaked between 1979 and 1981 and have declined moderately since then. The current estimate is that about 43 percent of marriages will break up. Most family researchers see the combination of high marriage rates and high divorce rates as the paradoxical outcome of the high expectations Americans bring to marriage. These expectations, contrary (again) to the marriage movement, can't be blamed on the counterculture. Americans have always valued companionship between spouses and never defined marriage as an unbreakable contract. Indeed, divorce literally came to America on the Mayflower, along with other revisions of traditional marriage arrangements made by the Protestant reformers.

Today's divorce rates may well reflect the difficulties of moving to a more gender-equal family and society. Legally, marriage is a much-transformed and reformed institution, and feminists and gays have had much to do with the changes. What historian Hendrik Hartog calls "the long nineteenth century" lived on in the laws of marriage until the 1970s. Legal marriage remained a major institution for the perpetuation of gender inequality, turning individual men and women into husbands and wives with sharply different roles and responsibilities. Despite a series of reforms over the years, the laws of marriage continued to impose restrictions and disabilities on women until feminist lawsuits challenged the status quo. Laws against marital rape, for example, were once unthinkable. We are not finished with gender inequality, but at least in the eyes of the law, husband and wife are now assumed to be equal.

The push for gay marriage, far from undermining the institution, is its best advertisement. Most significantly, the gay experience shattered the cliché that legal marriage is "just a piece of paper." Heterosexual couples may not be aware of the thousands of rights that legal marriage bestows on spouses, but gay couples are sorely aware of their absence. For example, in his book on the roots of the gay marriage movement, George Chauncy describes the painful vulnerability of gay partners who lack legal recognition of their relationship and so can't be considered "next of kin" when dealing with hospitals, schools, banks, and other institutions. The challenge of making a deeply gendered institution into a union of intimate equals may take another generation or so to work out.

Emily Post and the New Silent Majority.   In 1992, when the moral panic over single parenthood and divorce erupted, other disturbing trends, such as crime and drug use, were slowing down or in reverse. The proportion of children born to unwed parents was holding steady. Teenage pregnancy had started to decline. As Nicholas Lehman put it in 1997, the sense of crisis over moral decline and social disintegration was "a phenomenon floating free of reality, driven by no actual contemporary developments."

A decade and a half ago, E. J. Dionne argued that the public was frustrated with the moralizing and the personal attacks that had come to dominate American politics. "If ever there were a set of issues on which Americans wanted less polarization and political posturing," he wrote, "it was surely those involving families, children, and sexuality." Yet the posturing and polarization continue, and Democrats continue to be stymied by it. Not since Bill Clinton's "all our families" response to Dan Quayle has a leading politician challenged the divisiveness that pervades current political discourse about family matters. Yet mainstream American attitudes have not shifted rightward in recent years. The symbiotic relationship between the right-wing message machine and the insatiable appetite of today's media for high decibel conflict has driven political discourse far to the right, but there remains a large and diverse center that is simply drowned out by all the noise.

Every once in a while, however, the voice of the tolerant majority is heard in the land. It happened in the backlash against the Clinton impeachment and again when conservatives tried to exploit the Terri Schiavo case. But the implicit views that underlie these responses are rarely articulated. Recently, however, I came across an explicit defense of tolerance and pluralism from a surprising source—three new books on etiquette. One was the seventeenth edition of Emily Post's American classic, first published in 1922; the others were a fiftieth anniversary revision of Amy Vanderbilt's etiquette guide and Letitia Baldrige's revision of her own earlier volume.

The commonsense voices in these three works offer a refreshing antidote to the pervasive moral decline narrative. They agree that the world we live in has been transformed over the past four decades—"Since the early 60s it's as if some Superman-like character has been hurling us through time," Baldrige writes. But she goes on to argue that "we must be clear-eyed about the changes that have taken place—and alert to those to come—and arm ourselves with knowledge of how to handle them in today's terms."

The Post book even offers a historical perspective on today's family changes. In a note to the reader, Emily's great-granddaughter-in-law Peggy Post writes, "Times are changing so rapidly it's a challenge for most of us to keep up. But I'm happy to assure you that helping people adapt has been a mainstay of the Emily Post tradition from the beginning." She goes on to note that the first edition of the book was also written at a time of rapid social change, the 1920s. "As Victorianism gave way to the jazz age, the more informal approach to things foreshadowed the casualness that infuses every aspect of everyday life in the twenty-first century . . ."

The books still tell you how to set a formal dinner table and how to deal with weddings, funerals, and the other life cycle rites and rituals. But they emphasize dealing with new situations and with the new diversity in people's personal lives: How, for example, "to arrange the seating at a wedding when both sets of parents have divorced and remarried and are still acrimonious," how to plan for a wedding when the bride is pregnant or the couple is gay, how to teach teenagers about safe sex, and how to adjust to "the new codes concerning sex and dating and women taking the initiative romantically and men and women traveling together on business."

In sum, they blend the traditional values of civility and kindness, with newer values of tolerance, and a live-and-let-live respect for diversity. Here, for example, is Amy Vanderbilt: "Luckily for us, we have been raised in a society in which democratic principles filter down to the private level."

Here is Emily Post on the same subject: "Today's 'ideal' family is found anywhere that love grows, respect is nurtured among individuals, and kindness and consideration flourish." And "If you've ever wondered why families in commercials look so much alike. . . [it's because] married couples make up half of American households, but account for two-thirds of all consumer spending. . . . Media images have a way of creating norms that don't reflect reality. . . . This can lead to stereotyping, prejudice, and ill-mannered treatment of families that are regarded as different." I can't recall a better moral defense of America's diverse families.

CHAPTER 21

The Kids Aren't Alright

Sharon Lerner

Alexandria, a pudgy 10-month-old with pink bows clipped to her tiny ponytails, is waiting. Propped up on a pillow in the tidy living room of her apartment in Palm Beach, she's calmly swigging warm formula while her mother gets ready for work. Soon she'll be buckled into her car seat and whisked off. To where? She must wait to find out. Most days she goes to a lady's house a few minutes away, but sometimes she winds up at her uncle's apartment or with a friend of her mom's. If she could, Alexandria might tell you that what she's really waiting for is one safe place to be every day while her mother works. And she might have to wait a very long time.

Alexandria is on a waiting list for subsidized care along with more than 45,000 other children in Florida and almost half a million around the country. Countless families would welcome a break in childcare costs. Working parents now spend more on childcare than they do on college tuition, food, car payments or, in many states, rent. But even to make it onto a waiting list, families must meet strict income criteria set by states to sift out all but the neediest of needy families. Alexandria's mother, Denise, for instance, is raising four children while working full-time as an assistant case worker for a family service agency. Having earned just $19,000 last year, Denise is eligible for aid—and she made sure to request it right after her daughter was born. But still they wait.

Across the country, families in dire financial situations qualify for help—but don't get it because the funds aren't there. Of the more than 15 million children entitled to childcare help nationwide in 2000, only one out of seven received it, according to the Washington-based advocacy group the Center for Law and Social Policy. The government has been offering some of the poorest working families subsidies to care for their children since at least 1974. Yet, while both the number of women in the workforce and the price of care relative to wages have shot up since then, government spending on daycare hasn't risen accordingly. And the backup appears to be worsening. Because there has been no increase in funding for childcare since the Bush Administration took power, some 300,000 children are expected to lose childcare assistance by 2010.

What happens to these babies, toddlers and school-aged kids while their parents work? For Alexandria, the usual setup is far from ideal. The woman who cares for her is elderly, leaves the TV on for much of the day and charges $150 a week, which strains Denise's tight budget. Perhaps most frustrating, she's sometimes unavailable, as she is today. Denise has a plan B: Alexandria's uncle agreed to look after the baby this morning. But when she calls him from her car as she heads toward his apartment, he doesn't answer his phone.

What's a woman who's late for work to do when her baby sitters go AWOL? Denise pulls into a gas station to ponder this question. If she brings Alexandria to work, which begins with three hours of driving to pick up a child in foster care and bring him to visit his mother, she risks losing her job. But she doesn't know any other trustworthy baby sitters. And the choice between endangering her job or her baby is an easy one. So, as she's done on more than one occasion in the past, she heaves a big sigh and drives off to work with her infant daughter in the back seat.

Other children on Florida's waiting list, like little 1-and-a-half-year-old Valerie, a smiley toddler whose dark hair is in a pageboy, go to decent preschools at great expense to their parents. Four out of ten single mothers who pay for childcare spend half or more of their income on it, and many can only afford the dicier options. But Valerie's mom, Glabedys, is pleased with the center where her daughter spends her days. When she drops Valerie off at Busy Bees Pre-School, housed in two toy-filled buildings in Wilton Manors, she runs off to play instead of crying and clinging to her mother, as she used to when she was left with neighbors. She's been learning about colors and shapes. And she clearly likes her teachers.

But while Valerie remains on the waiting list for a subsidy to pay for her care, Glabedys pays her preschool fees with money she would have spent on groceries. Though she works full-time at a factory that makes hurricane protection gates, Glabedys couldn't even afford her apartment after the $135-a-week outlay to Busy Bees. So she rented storage space for most of her things and a small room in a house where the two now live. They survive on donations from a local food pantry.

Some other parents who can't afford care go into debt, putting the fees for childcare on their credit cards. Still others leave their children home with older siblings—a phenomenon that contributes to the state's truancy problem, according to local child advocates. And some stay home with their children despite a desperate need for income. Not surprisingly, research has shown that parents who receive help paying for childcare are more likely to be employed and have higher incomes.

Conversely, those who don't are more likely to stay home with their children and scrape by on next to nothing.

Such was the case for Heather Tomlinson. When I interviewed her, Tomlinson, her 16-month-old son Ian and her school-aged daughter were living on the extremely variable paycheck of her boyfriend, who installs leather upholstery in cars and is paid by the car. Even on good weeks, his income barely covered the family's expenses. So Tomlinson applied for help with childcare when Ian was born. Stuck on the waiting list, she couldn't envision how to afford care that would enable her to interview for a job, let alone keep it. Yet because she didn't work, she was labeled a low priority on the waiting list. So the family was squeaking by. She mentioned that she recently had only eight diapers to last her son for three days. "I had to leave each one on a little longer than I should have," she said. "Eventually he got a rash."

Unfortunately, Ian's diaper rash and Valerie's donated food get no airtime in the national shouting match over childcare, or at least the mainstream media's coverage of it, which seems to be an endless loop of condemnations and defenses of both daycare and working mothers. Earlier this year, researcher Jay Belsky warned parents that children who spent time in the care of anyone except their mothers were more likely than those cared for by stay-at-home moms to exhibit bad behavior as preschoolers and kindergartners. Even though the study found only a slight connection between time spent in daycare and bad behavior, and the behavior was all within the normal range, the link between daycare and bad behavior made it into the headlines. And a chorus of conservatives quickly declared daycare a bad thing. Meanwhile, there was little mention of the fact that there are great variations in childcare—or that children in good care tend to do better.

In fact, the clear association between better care and better outcomes is one of the major truths to emerge from Belsky's research, *Study of Early Child Care and Youth Development*. This finding has two important corollaries, both of which the country seems to have a hard time stomaching. First, the good care in which children do well costs money. There's plenty of research on what that good care should entail. Among other things, preschoolers need one-on-one attention, consistent relationships with trained, knowledgeable adults, and safe settings complete with educational toys and books—all of which are expensive.

The second reality that is perhaps even more difficult to confront, especially for proponents of childcare, is that without these expenditures, childcare can be pretty bad. And it's not just poor kids on the waiting list who are in lousy care. Parents who are lucky enough to get subsidies can use them to pay any state-regulated center- or home-based daycare, which, thanks to underfunding, runs the gamut from decent to worrisome to horrendous.

Florida may offer some of the starkest examples of low-quality care because of the rates providers are paid for subsidized kids, which vary from county to county but are shockingly low throughout the state. In Miami/Dade Country, for instance, providers are paid just $1.76 an hour for each subsidized toddler and $2 for an infant. Not surprisingly, there is a severe, chronic shortage of qualified people who have the patience, skills and willingness to work with young children. Denise, Alexandria's mom, is already well aware of the problem. Two years ago, she moved her three older children out of a center where they were getting subsidized care after they complained repeatedly of being hit by a teacher.

The eight babies in cribs at the Discovery Me Pre-School in the Kendall section of Miami are too young to complain, though they make it clear with their tears and outstretched arms that they'd much rather be held or played with than confined to their tiny beds. Discovery Me, located in a large, windowless space behind a mall in Kendall, a suburban community in the southwest part of the city, provides care to fifty-two children. Officially, there should be no more than four infants for every adult. But here there were eight alone with a single caretaker, each whiling away the hours in only a diaper.

Indeed, a few unannounced visits to some of the centers that accept subsidized children in southern Florida revealed that it's not unusual for such absurd numbers of children to be in the care of a lone adult. In the Sunshine State, one childcare provider can legally look after as many as eleven 2-year-olds, fifteen 3-year-olds or twenty 4-year-olds. You might think it'd be impossible to surpass these state-set limits, which are the laxest in the nation. Yet even these ratios are routinely violated.

At the Peter Pan Child Development Center in Pompano Beach, for example, nineteen 3- and 4-year-olds and a school-aged girl were in a small room with an elderly woman in a wheelchair on the afternoon of my visit. Though it's supposed to be nap time, several children have strayed from their sleeping mats. Across a small walkway, another classroom full of children at the center was also under-staffed, with two adults overseeing four infants and thirteen 1- and 2-year-olds.

Meanwhile, at Discovery Me, it wasn't just the babies who were having a difficult day. According to Olga Ceballos, the center's director, thirty-eight 2-, 3- and 4-year-olds were in the care of just two adults. Ceballos says one of her teachers had a doctor's appointment on this particular day, leaving the preschool more under-staffed than usual.

There is no pool of substitute teachers for Ceballos to draw on—with the piddling pay, it's hard enough to find regular staff. So the director stepped in to look after the children. "There were just so many kids, I had to put the TV on," she says. Afterward the children went into the playground adjoining the parking lot. Being responsible for more than two dozen playing toddlers was so stressful that Ceballos talks about the stint as a physical trauma. "By the time I had to leave for my meeting, I was shaking all over," she says.

Even the best-run centers struggle to find qualified adults to hire. At the A-Plus Early Learning Center, in a small Tudor-style building in the middle of a housing complex in Miami, director Linda Carmona Sánchez struggles to make the work enticing to potential staff. Teachers there and most everywhere in the state receive no health benefits, paid vacation or sick leave. And even though they are subject to fingerprinting and background checks and required to take a forty-five-hour training course and ongoing education, most Florida childcare workers make only the state's minimum wage, $6.67 an hour, which adds up to about $14,000 a year for full-time work. Just across the street from A-Plus, they could easily make more serving up fries at Burger King or McDonald's. Stocking the shelves at the local Wal-Mart pays more, too. Even Sánchez, who has run the center for ten years and works a minimum of sixty hours a week, earns just $17,680 a year.

Some of Florida's childcare woes are its own. The state has relatively high poverty levels. And thirty-two regional networks dole out the federal dollars—as opposed to one state agency—which creates unnecessary administrative costs. But the crisis is also clearly a national one. More than twenty-five states have lowered their eligibility caps. In several, a family of three with income of $20,000 now earns too much to qualify for subsidies. Others leave their income thresholds higher and simply cap the numbers on waiting lists. Or they put parents on lists but give them a number in the high tens of thousands that would mean their children might finally get subsidized care sometime in their teenage years. And because of the lack of federal funds, childcare providers cut workers' pay; scrimp on books, toys and crayons; and struggle to pay their rent.

Part of what's so frustrating about the nation's childcare mess is that it would be so simple to solve. It would cost $30 billion per year to boost the quality of childcare and also guarantee to help pay for it for everyone with an income below twice the poverty level, according to estimates by Mark Greenberg of the Center for American Progress. That would mean extending benefits to almost 1 million more low-income working families than now get childcare subsidies, since some states now cap the eligibility for help just above the poverty line. While Greenberg's plan would mean adding $18 billion to the state and federal money already paying for childcare for low-income families, that's less than 5 percent of what we've already frittered away in Iraq.

Or we could follow in the steps of countries such as France, Belgium, Denmark and Sweden, which provide high-quality universal or near-universal childcare. The United States spends only about $200 on care for every child under 15, according to Janet Gornick, an expert in international social welfare policy. That's one-fifth of per capita spending on childcare in France, where 99 percent of 3-, 4- and 5-year-olds are enrolled in publicly provided care, and one-tenth of that in Sweden and Denmark, where virtually all preschool-age children of working parents can immediately access a spot. In fact, a 1971 bill, the Comprehensive Child Development Act, would have created a universal system in the United States, establishing childcare as a right for all families, regardless of income. The broadly supported legislation was to have established national quality standards and provided money for training of childcare providers and the purchase of facilities. Families making up to about 44 percent of the median income were to have received free care, and those earning up to 74 percent would have been charged on a sliding scale. But, alas, though the bill passed both the House and the Senate, Nixon killed it, delivering a veto speech penned by Pat Buchanan that warned against "communal approaches to childrearing."

Since the bill's 1971 defeat, engineered in part by Phyllis Schlafly, the idea of a comprehensive approach to childcare has been dormant—if not dead—in the United States. Substantially underfunded, what exists of federally subsidized childcare is vulnerable to the conservative criticism that low-quality government services are unworthy of expansion. (As with healthcare, who wants second-rate services for their children, right?) And so the cycle of neglect has continued. Indeed, there has been no increase in federal funding for childcare in six years.

The best hope for improvement in childcare looms on the 2008 horizon. Presidential hopefuls Hillary Clinton, Christopher Dodd and Barack Obama are all members of the Health, Education, Labor and Pensions Committee, which oversees much of the funding for childcare. And all have paid lip service to the difficulty of affording childcare. In speeches Obama has noted its rising costs. In mid-October, as part of her Agenda for Working Families, Clinton came out with what her press release referred to as a "bold new effort" to provide $200 million in federal funding for training and benefits for childcare workers. While a much-needed first step in drawing attention to the issue, $200 million is far too little to make a significant dent in the nation's childcare crisis. Meanwhile, Dodd, with the least name recognition, has accomplished the most on the issue, having created the Family and Medical Leave Act as well as legislation similar to what Clinton just proposed, which has been knocking around Congress without traction for almost ten years.

Historically, twin arguments have defended public spending on childcare: parents need to work, and children benefit from education before they hit school age. With two-thirds of mothers of young children now employed, the necessity of work has never been clearer. The parents waiting for subsidies in Florida and elsewhere arguably understand the importance of work better than anyone. Were they on welfare, they'd be guaranteed low-cost childcare along with their workfare assignment, at least until the time limits kick in. So by having a low-wage job, they're already fighting a disincentive to find work and subsist on it.

The need for early education is also increasingly obvious. These days, scientists usually explain the importance of teaching young children—rather than just baby-sitting them—by talking about rapid brain growth in the first three years of life, when the critical window for learning is wide open. But there may be no better illustration of the need, or hunger, for developmental help than the children who regularly try to climb the fence surrounding the Irma Hunter Wesley Fort Lauderdale Child Development Center. A one-story building on a run-down stretch of Sistrunk Boulevard in Fort Lauderdale, the center has an unmistakably homey feel. There are several wooden rocking chairs in the nursery and, in the back, a sunny library filled with everything from pop-up to board books. Reading nooks are decorated with stuffed animals and posters. And there's even a tiny couch, where a toddler might curl up to read. But the kids out front, some as young as 5, can't afford to attend the center. And without a safe place to play, they scale the fence daily with the hope of riding on the playground's toy cars and swings.

As it turned out, this fall, little Alexandria—now 17 months old—finally made her way to the top of the list and now receives the coveted reimbursement she and her mother had been awaiting. But there's no sane reason it should have taken almost a year and a half for that to happen. She shouldn't have been dragged along to her mother's work. The kids on Sistrunk Boulevard, still without anything constructive to do, should have a decent place to play. Glabedys should be able to afford food. And the babies at the Discovery Me center should have someone to pick them up. Instead, the children are scrambling to make it over the fence, holding onto the sides of their cribs—and waiting.

CHAPTER 22

More Than Welcome
Families Come First in Sweden

Brittany Shahmehri

Recently, my husband's laptop needed repair, and he called technical support to arrange for service. When he explained the problem, the phone representative at the multinational computer company said, "I'm going to recommend level-two support, but the technician will have to call you tomorrow to schedule an appointment. Today he's home with his sick kid."

When we still lived in the US, my husband might have wondered what a sick child had to do with his laptop. But last year we moved to Sweden, where parents not only are legally entitled to stay home with their sick children, but also get paid for doing so. Most amazing is that there's no shame in it. For fathers as well as mothers, it is assumed that when your child is sick, you are going to take care of him or her. That's more important than fixing someone's laptop on the spot. The computer company knows it and my husband's employer knows it. In almost every circumstance, the laptop can wait a day.

Even visiting tourists can see that Sweden has a child-friendly culture. A stroller logo is as common as the wheelchair logo in public restrooms and elevators. Buses accommodate strollers, and trains have places for children to play. (By the way, the children ride free.) Gas stations often have tiny working toilets as well as the standard toilets, as do zoos and other places that cater to children. "Amazing," I thought, the first time I visited.

But on closer examination, all of this is just window dressing. Sweden has one of the most generous parental leave policies in the world. Parents of each newborn or newly adopted child share 450 paid days to care for that child. The childcare system is of extremely high quality, offers a wide range of options, and is subsidized for all families. Parents are legally entitled to work reduced hours at their current jobs until their children reach the age of eight (when they formally enter school), and can take up to 60 paid days to take care of sick children. Toss in protected time to nurse a baby on the job and tuition-free universities, and to an American working parent, it sounds like utopia!

WHY SUCH WIDESPREAD SUPPORT?

According to Dr. Irene Wennemo, a Swedish family policy expert, the question of supporting families in Sweden is generally framed in terms of how the state should implement policies and what level of resources should be invested. "It's very accepted here that the state should be responsible for the living standard of children," Wennemo told me. "Children aren't a private thing; society has a responsibility for part of the cost."

Most of the reasons for this are self-evident. Children are members of society. It's not good for people, especially children, to live in poverty. Children should have equal opportunities. It's necessary for society that people have children, so it should be easy to combine working and having children. It's good for men and women to have equal access to both work and family.

"If you want a society in which it is accepted that both partners go out and work, then you have to take people's needs seriously," states Gunnar Andersson, a sociologist at Lund University. "Both school and child care must be really good, and there must be much more flexibility for all."[1]

"This is what our parents worked for," explains Anneli Elfwén, a Swedish midwife with two young sons. In the 1950s most Swedish women stayed home with the children. When women began to enter the workforce in the late 1960s, the need for stronger family policy became clear. The modern versions of parental leave policy and subsidized child care were implemented in the early 1970s and met with wide popular support. When I asked Elfwén why support for family policy was so widespread, she laughed, "Maybe we get it in the breastmilk. It's very natural for us."

HOW IT WORKS

When Elfwén's first son, Simon, was born in 1995, Elfwén was entitled to the same parental leave benefits that are offered to all Swedish families. She and her husband could share the 450 days of leave as they pleased, though one month was reserved for her, and one for her husband; and if either of them chose not to take their individual time, they would forfeit it.

One of the most unique aspects of Swedish parental leave is that it can be taken part time. Elfwén and her husband used the flexibility in their schedules to extend the time Simon spent at home with one of his parents. Between paid leave, flexible jobs, and the help of grandparents, the Elfwéns juggled a two-career, two-parent family. When their second son, Olle, was born in 1998, he, too, was entitled to 450 days of his parents' time. This made it possible for Elfwén to maintain the career that she loves, while keeping her children home until they were about three. The parental leave made all the difference.

Parents can continue to work reduced hours until their children reach the age of eight. This option was chosen by a couple I know, both schoolteachers. The mother took one day a week off, the father one day, and they staggered their hours on remaining days, so that their children spent less time in child care. Both parents were able to maintain professional lives while sharing the responsibility for raising their children.

CHOICES IN CHILD CARE

When it was time for the Elfwéns to decide on a preschool for Simon, they selected a Waldorf school with low student–teacher ratios and organic vegetarian meals. There are also traditional preschools, Christian schools, Montessori schools, cooperative schools, and even daycare centers that focus on gender equality. Families pay the county rather than the childcare center, and the amount depends on each family's household income. This means that, with few exceptions, parents can send their child to any childcare center without consideration to finances. So a single mother studying at university might pay $30.00 a month for her child to attend a school, while a family with three children and a household income of $40,000 would pay around $240 a month to have their three children in the same school. As of 2002, there will be a cap of $115 a month for the first child, ramping down according to income.

Of course, things are not perfect. It can be difficult to find a spot in the middle of the year, so it's necessary to plan ahead. The school we chose for my four year old did not suit him, so we kept him home while waiting for a place in a new school. In looking at the options, however, we were impressed with the low student–teacher ratios at all the preschools we visited, and the consistently high quality of care.

SEPARATE TAXATION AND CHILD ALLOWANCES

A few other odds and ends round out the package. People are taxed individually in Sweden, so a woman's income won't fall into a high tax bracket just because the household income is high. In addition, cash payments take the place of tax deductions for children. Each month, about $95.00 per child is deposited into the account of every family with a child, from the unemployed to the royal family. Families with more than two children receive a small bonus, so for my three children, we get a cash payment of $300 a month. Many families turn the money over to their children when they reach the age of 15 so they can learn to handle a checking account and manage their clothing and leisure purchases.

THE EMPLOYER'S ROLE

In Sweden, creating balance between work and family life is not left solely to the government and individual families. Section five of the Swedish Equal Opportunity Act reads, "An employer shall facilitate the combination of gainful employment and parenthood with respect to both female and male employees." Employers, in other words, are legally obligated to help employees combine parenthood and work. Employees who believe that an employer has directly violated this principle can take their case to the office of the Equal Opportunity Ombudsman (JämO).

Claes Lundkvist filed one of the eight cases registered with JämO last year regarding parenthood and employment. Lundkvist, a broadcast journalist for Swedish Radio, generally took his children to daycare each morning, and his wife, a physiotherapist with her own business, picked them up at the end of the day. But a new contract required Lundkvist to transfer to a branch more than an hour away. His working hours were inflexible as well. "My wife was very stressed taking all the responsibility," Lundkvist says. "It didn't work." After looking at JämO's Web page, he decided to pursue the issue.

The involvement of fathers as parents should be encouraged, according to JämO: "Employers may have an old-fashioned view of parenthood, or think that 'your wife can take care of that,' when the husband wants to be free to care for sick children or asks for more flexible working hours in order to combine work and family."[2] Changing the attitude of such employers is one of JämO's goals. JämO accepted Lundkvist's case, recognizing that without some adjustment in his new situation, his ability to combine work and family would be seriously impaired. The case initially met with resistance from Lundkvist's employers, and as he was a contract worker, JämO's power was limited. Lundkvist has since, however, negotiated a solution that does offer some flexibility.

With each case filed, the resulting publicity strengthens the public debate about men's rights and responsibilities as fathers. "It's hard to change gender roles," says Tommy Ferrarini, a PhD student at the Institute of Social Research in Stockholm who is currently doing research on family policy. But Ferrarini believes measures such as parental leave time allotted for the father shift social expectations: "It puts pressure on the employers when something becomes a right. It's all very individualized. . . . [This means] increased individual autonomy for the mother, the father, and the children. You give both parents the possibility of self-fulfillment."

WHAT FAMILY POLICY MEANS FOR WOMEN

Swedish mothers don't think they are doing it all, and they don't think the system is perfect. Some women have jobs that are more flexible than others; some are happier with their child care than others. While men are doing a larger share of the housework than in the past, couples still fight about who does the laundry. You'd be hard-pressed to find a Swedish mom who would call herself a superwoman.

Observing the situation, however, I see women who come pretty close to fulfilling the American "superwoman" myth. The vast majority of women have careers. With the help of their partners, they juggle children and work and birthday parties and still manage to make it to aerobics every week.

In the US, in contrast, the superwoman myth operates in a male-dominated corporate culture, and society views accepting help as a weakness. If you are granted a day off, you should be grateful. If your husband takes two unpaid weeks at the birth of a child, he should be grateful. If his company calls after a week and asks him to come back early (as my husband's company did), he should apologize when he says no, and then thank them for understanding.

In Sweden, you can certainly say "thank you" if you like, but no one has done you any favors. Among CEOs and entrepreneurs, you may see a more male-dominated culture, but even there, people are still likely to take a good portion of the five to eight weeks vacation they receive annually.

Swedish women face many of the same problems as their American counterparts. Their career advancement slows while children are young, and juggling everything can be very challenging. But women in Sweden do not have to do it alone. Families are supported by society, both financially and culturally. This means that women also give back to society, and not just in tax dollars—though even there, their contribution is substantial. Having women in the workplace changes the culture. Today, 43 percent of representatives in the Swedish Parliament and half of all State Ministers are women. In the long run, that will have an effect on the tone of the government as well as the laws that are passed.

CHILDREN ARE PEOPLE, TOO

Children in Sweden are not considered merely a lifestyle choice. They're members of society in their own right. Flexibility and support for families means that parents are better able to meet the needs of their children, something the children deserve. This approach offers myriad benefits to children, both emotionally and physically. Recent studies have suggested that "parental leave has favorable and possibly cost-effective impacts on pediatric health."[3] The same studies also indicate that with longer parental leaves, child and infant mortality rates go down.[4]

Respect for children is an important aspect of Swedish culture. Sweden has a Children's Ombudsman who represents children and young people in public debates, the ultimate goal being that young people can make their voices heard and gain respect for their views. In line with this, corporal punishment of any kind is illegal. Though controversial when it was first proposed, a Parliamentary Minister put the issue into context: "In a free democracy like our own, we use words as arguments, not blows. . . . If we can't convince our children with words, we will never convince them with violence."[5]

Children in Sweden are people, not property. Family policy is very much about creating a better situation for men and women who choose to have families, but at its core, family policy is all about children. A society that cherishes and respects children must make it possible for every child to be raised with certain minimal standards. Ensuring healthcare coverage, making sure children have enough to eat, and keeping children free of the risks that inevitably accompany poverty are a few modest goals. In Sweden, every child is entitled to be home with his or her parents for the first year of life. That is the minimum standard the society has chosen.

What that means is that any child you see on the street had access to her parents for the most important time in her development and has access to free, high-quality medical and dental care. You know that she has enough food to eat, and that she likely attends a well-run preschool. That child has advocates in government and the support of society. Who will that child become? Right now it doesn't matter. The bottom line is that she lives in a society that values her just the way she is.

ENDNOTES

1. Kristina Hultman, "A Step Away from a Childless Society?" *New Life: A Gender Equality Magazine for New Parents* (Stockholm: Swedish Government Division for Gender Equality, 2001): 10.

2. "What Is JämO?," a brochure published by the Equal Opportunity Ombudsman's office; see *www.jamombud.se.*

3. C. J. Ruhm, "Parental Leave and Child Health," *NBER Working Paper* no. W6554 (Cambridge, MA: National Bureau of Economic Research, 1998): 27.

4. Sheila Kamerman, "Parental Leave Policies: An Essential Ingredient in Early Childhood Education and Care Policies," *Social Policy Report 14,* no. 2 (2000): 10.

5. Louise Sylwander, "The Swedish Corporal Punishment Ban—More Than Twenty Years of Experience," Barnombudsmannen website, www.bo.se (choose the British flag for English).

For additional information about Sweden, see the following article in a past issue of *Mothering:* "Swedish Parents Don't Spank," no. 63.

PART SEVEN

The Environment

I t's sometimes said that in America today, everyone has become an environmentalist. If so, this represents a large change in a relatively short time. The environmental movement in the United States only took off in the 1960s and 1970s. Yet today many practices that seemed revolutionary in those days are now routine. Schoolchildren learn about the virtues of recycling in the classroom; corporations run magazine advertisements urging the public to recognize their commitment to clean air and water. The vast majority of Americans, according to opinion polls, believe that maintaining a clean environment is worth whatever it costs.

These changes have been so pervasive and so rapid that some now insist that the battle against environmental destruction has been largely won and we can now relax our concern. Others think that we've already gone too far in the pursuit of environmental quality, to the point where cumbersome regulations are hobbling the economy and lowering our standard of living.

But as the articles in this part make clear, any complacency about the state of the environment is unwarranted. It's true that important gains have been made against some environmental problems. But for others, progress is slow at best, and at the same time, new and gravely threatening problems have emerged that were largely unforeseen only a few decades ago. One recent report, for example, estimates that more than half of the American population "live and breathe in communities with dangerously high levels of air pollution."[1] Another tells us that there may no longer be *any* streams or rivers left in the United States that are free from chemical contamination.[2]

As James Gustave Speth makes clear, these are not isolated problems. They reflect a much larger and more fateful transformation of the relationship between human beings and the natural environment—one that has been going on for centuries, but has radically accelerated in recent years. Huge surges in population and economic activity, in particular, have made the "human footprint" much heavier than it was in the past, and this process can only continue in the coming years, especially as formerly poor nations push to become part of the developed industrial world. The great increases in population, production, and consumption around the world have dramatically increased older, familiar environmental problems—like industrial pollution and sewage—and also fostered new and, if anything, even more critical ones—like global climate change and the massive depletion of natural resources. In the long run, these may turn out to be the most formidable problems that human societies now confront.

Among the new threats to the environment, perhaps none is as troubling as the problem of global warming. By now, there is a flood of scientific evidence that global warming is a very real problem, that it is heavily caused by human activity—especially the burning of fossil fuels—and that it carries the potential for enormous and costly changes both to the earth's environment and to the world economy. But so far our response hasn't come close to matching the urgency of the threat.

Part of the reason for the halting response to global warming is that the steps we could take to reduce it—especially cutting back our reliance on fossil fuels—have been fiercely resisted by some of the most powerful corporations in America. That resistance has included spending large amounts of money to promote the idea that the threat of global warming has been greatly exaggerated. The report "Smoke, Mirrors, and Hot Air," by the Union of Concerned Scientists, details the efforts of one corporation in particular—ExxonMobil, at the time the largest publicly traded corporation in the world—to counter the growing scientific consensus on the problem. Using tactics borrowed from the earlier campaign by the tobacco industry to deny that smoking was harmful to health, ExxonMobil funded a variety of ostensibly "scientific" organizations whose sole purpose was to "manufacture uncertainly" about the danger of global warming and the role of human activity in creating it. That effort was arguably unsuccessful in the long run: as the report points out, legitimate scientists increasingly agree on the reality of the threat of global warming, as does most of the American public. But efforts like these surely helped to hold back a more effective national response to this critical problem.

The adverse environmental trends described in these articles affect everyone on the planet, but it remains true that some people are affected more harshly, and more immediately, than others. Indeed, the concentration of some of the worst environmental problems among America's most disadvantaged people is one of the most troubling aspects of the growing inequality we've charted in previous sections of this book. Blacks, Hispanics, and Native Americans now carry much more than their share of the burden of environmental pollution. They are more likely to live near toxic waste dumps and other hazardous facilities, they breathe the most polluted air, and they suffer more often from lead poisoning and contaminated water supplies. Moreover, violations of pollution regulations are likely to be prosecuted much more zealously in white than in minority communities. In other words, the benefits of economic growth—jobs and income—go disproportionately to the affluent, while the toxic *costs* of growth are allotted to the poor, turning some poor communities into what the sociologist Robert Bullard[3] has called "sacrifice zones." Steve Lerner's harrowing description of the plight of the African American residents of Diamond, a small, poor community hard up against the "fenceline" of a massive Shell petrochemical complex in Louisiana, provides a compelling look at the human face of this widespread environmental injustice.

ENDNOTES

1. "More than half of Americans living with dirty air," http://www.nim.nth.gov/medlineplus/news/fullstory_83560.html.

2. John Heilprin, "Report Paints Gloomy U.S. Ecological Picture," Associated Press, September 25, 2002.

3. Robert Bullard, "Environmental Racism," in Jerome H. Skolnick and Elliott Currie, eds., *Crisis in American Institutions,* 12th edition, Boston, Allyn and Bacon, 2004, p. 241.

Crisis...

CHAPTER 23

A World of Wounds

James Gustave Speth

crisis *1*. Med. *That change in a disease that indicates whether the result is to be recovery or death. 2. The decisive moment; turning point. 3. crucial time.*

We live in the twenty-first century, but we live with the twentieth century. The expansion of the human enterprise in the twentieth century, and especially after World War II, was phenomenal. It was in this century that human society truly left the moorings of its past and launched itself upon the planet in an unprecedented way.

Most familiar is the population explosion. It took all of human history for global population to expand by 1900 to a billion and a half people. But over the past century that many more people were added, on average, every thirty-three years. In the past twenty-five years, global population increased by 50 percent from four to six billion, with virtually all of this growth occurring in the developing world.[1]

Population may have increased fourfold in the past century, but world economic output increased twentyfold. From the dawn of history to 1950 the world economy grew to seven trillion dollars. It now grows by this amount every five to ten years. Since 1960 the size of the world economy has doubled and then doubled again.[2] Energy use moved in close step with economic expansion, rising at least sixteenfold in the twentieth century. One calculation suggests that more energy was consumed in those hundred years than in all of previous history.[3]

The twentieth century was thus a remarkable period of prodigious expansion in human populations and their production and consumption. Four consequences of these developments are important to note. *First*, while twentieth-century growth has brought enormous benefits in terms of health, education, and overall standards of living, these gains have been purchased at a huge cost to the environment. The enormous environmental deterioration is partly due to the greater scale of established insults: traditional pollution like soot, sulfur oxides, and sewage grew from modest quantities to huge ones. What were once strictly local impacts not only intensified locally but became regional and even global in scope.

Many previously unknown environmental risks also surfaced in the twentieth century. After World War II, the chemical and nuclear industries emerged, giving rise to a vast armada of new chemicals and radioactive substances, many highly biocidal in even the most minute quantities and some with the potential to accumulate in biological systems or in the atmosphere. Between 1950 and 1985 the U.S. chemical industry expanded its output tenfold. By 1985 the number of hazardous waste sites in the United States requiring clean-up was estimated to be between two thousand and ten thousand. The use of pesticides also skyrocketed during this period.[4] Today about six hundred pesticides are registered for use around the world, and five to six billion pounds of pesticides are released into the global environment each year.[5]

Turning from pollution to the world's natural resource base we find severe losses. From a third to a half of the world's forests are now gone, as are about half the mangroves and other wetlands.[6] Agricultural productivity of a fourth of allusable land has been significantly degraded due to overuse and mismanagement.[7] In 1960, 5 percent of marine fisheries were either fished to capacity or overfished; today 75 percent of marine fisheries are in this condition.[8] A crisis in the loss of biodiversity is fast upon us. A fourth of bird species are extinct, and another 12 percent are listed as threatened. Also threatened are 24 percent of mammals, 25 percent of reptiles, and 30 percent of fish species.[9] The rate of species extinction today is estimated to be a hundred to a thousand times the normal rate at which species disappear.[10]

Environmentalist Aldo Leopold wrote that "one of the penalties of an ecological education is that one lives alone in a world of wounds."[11] As is clear, there is a lot of bad news in the world of environmental affairs. Since Leopold wrote those words, alas, scientists have begun to study damage that he could not. Our world now suffers wounds beyond imagining at his death in 1948.

That said, in recent decades industrial countries have invested heavily in reducing a variety of well-known pollutants and in banning a number of severely risky substances such as leaded gasoline, DDT, and PCBs. Similarly, advances in agricultural productivity have reduced pressures to expand crop and grazing land into additional natural areas.

Second, the twentieth-century expansion is significant because it has pushed the human enterprise and its effects to planetary scale. This is the globalization of environmental impacts as well as economic activity. Human influences in the environment are everywhere, affecting all natural systems and cycles. Environmental writer Bill McKibben wrote in 1989 about what he called "the end of nature," by which he meant the end of the millennia in which humanity could view nature as a force independent of human beings.[12] Previously it was possible to think of nature as a place free of human control, an external and complex system sustaining life on earth, but the twentieth century brought us across a threshold to a new reality.

There are many measures of this new reality. Human activities have significantly depleted the earth's stratospheric ozone layer, thereby increasing the ultraviolet radiation that reaches the earth's surface and damaging both human health and ecosystems. Our use of fossil fuels—coal, oil, and natural gas—together with deforestation have increased the concentration of atmospheric carbon dioxide, a heat-trapping "greenhouse" gas, by about 32 percent and thus begun the process of man-made climate change.[13] Spring is arriving earlier, and species' ranges are shifting toward the poles.[14] Industrial processes such as the manufacture of fertilizers and other human activities now double the amount of nitrogen transferred from the atmosphere into biologically active forms,[15] with consequences that include the creation of at least fifty dead zones in the oceans, one the size of New Jersey in the Gulf of Mexico.[16] Each year human societies are appropriating, wasting, or destroying about 40 percent of nature's net photosynthetic product.[17] This output is the basic food supply for all organisms, so we are not leaving much for other species. Appropriation of freshwater supplies is similarly extensive, with widespread devastation of freshwater habitats.[18] More than 40 percent of the world's people live in river basins that suffer water stress.[19] By the mid-1990s, eighty countries with 40 percent of the world's population were experiencing serious water shortages.[20]

In terms of humans commandeering natural systems, our impact on the global climate machine is the most risky. In part because of fossil fuel use in the twentieth century, carbon dioxide in the atmosphere is now at its highest level in 420,000 years. While the public in the United States and especially abroad is increasingly aware of this issue, few Americans appreciate how close at hand is the widespread loss of the American landscape. The best current estimate is that, unless there is a major world correction, climate change projected for late this century will make it impossible for about half the American land to sustain the types of plants and animals now on that land.[21] A huge portion of America's protected areas—everything from wooded lands held by community conservancies to our national parks, forests, and wilderness—is threatened. In one projection, the much-loved maple-beech-birch forests of New England simply disappear off the U.S. map.[22] In another, the Southeast becomes a huge grassland savanna unable to support forests because it is too hot and dry.[23]

Ecologist Jane Lubchenco, in her 1998 address as president of the American Association for the Advancement of Science, made the following observation: "The conclusions . . . are inescapable: during the last few decades, humans have emerged as a new force of nature. We are modifying physical, chemical, and biological systems in new ways, at faster rates, and over larger spatial scales than ever recorded on Earth. Humans have unwittingly embarked upon a grand experiment with our planet. The outcome of this experiment is unknown, but has profound implications for all of life on Earth."[24]

A similar point was made in an eloquent plea released a decade ago by fifteen hundred of the world's top scientists, including a majority of Nobel scientists: "The earth is finite. Its ability to absorb wastes and destructive effluents is finite. Its ability to provide food and energy is finite. Its ability to provide for growing numbers of people is finite. And we are fast approaching many of the earth's limits. Current economic practices which damage the environment, in both developed and underdeveloped nations, cannot be continued without the risk that vital global systems will be damaged beyond repair.

"We must recognize the earth's limited capacity to provide, for us. We must recognize its fragility. We must no longer allow it to be ravaged. This ethic must motivate a great movement, convincing reluctant leaders and reluctant governments and reluctant peoples themselves to effect the needed changes."[25]

Third, the world economy's forward momentum is large. Economic growth will continue to expand dramatically in this century. With population poised to grow by 25 percent over the next twenty years, with people everywhere striving to better themselves, and with governments willing to go to extraordinary measures to sustain high levels of economic expansion, there is no reason to think that the world economy will not double and perhaps double again within the lifetimes of today's young people.

The next doubling of world economic activity will surely differ in some respects from the growth of the past. But there are good reasons to believe that that doubling could, from an environmental perspective, look a lot like the last. The pressures to persist with environmentally problematic technologies and practices are enormous. The U.S. Energy Information Agency projects that global emissions of carbon dioxide, the principal climate-altering gas, will increase by 60 percent between 2001 and 2025.[26] The Paris-based Organization for Economic Cooperation and Development estimates that its members' carbon dioxide emissions will go up by roughly a third between 1995 and 2020 if there is not major policy intervention,[27] while OECD motor vehicle use could rise by almost 40 percent.[28] During this same period, emissions of carbon dioxide outside the OECD are projected to go up 100 percent. Growing food demand is expected to increase the area under cultivation in Africa and Latin America, extending agriculture further into once-forested areas and onto fragile lands in semiarid zones. For this reason and others, countries outside the OECD are projected to lose another 15 percent of their forests by 2020.[29]

One area where growing populations and growing demands will come together to challenge us enormously is water—the supply of clean, fresh water. The United Nations' 2003 *World Water Development Report* concludes that twenty-five years of international conferences have yielded few solutions. A fifth of the world's people lack clean drinking water; 40 percent lack sanitary services. Between 1970 and 1990 water supplies per person decreased by a third globally and are likely to drop by a further third over the next twenty years absent a concerted international response.[30] Peter Aldhous, the chief news editor at *Nature,* puts the situation with water in perspective: "The water crisis is real. If action isn't taken, millions of people will be condemned to a premature death. . . . [P]opulation growth, pollution and climate change are conspiring to exacerbate the situation. Over the next two decades, the average supply of water per person will drop by a third. Heightened hunger and disease will follow. Humanity's demands for water also threaten natural ecosystems, and may bring nations into conflicts that—although they may not lead to war—will test diplomats' skills to the limit."[31] The U.N. report notes that to meet internationally agreed water supply and sanitation targets, 342,000 additional people will have to be provided with sanitation every day until 2015.[32]

Of course, economic growth can generate benefits for the environment, and has done so in many contexts. As people become wealthier, public support for a healthy environment and leisure activities based on nature increases. The press of the poor on the resource base can diminish as people live less close to the land.

Governments of well-to-do countries tend to be more capable regulators and managers and can have more revenue for environmental, family planning, and other programs. There is no doubt that some important environmental indicators, such as sanitation, improve with rising incomes. But it is extraordinarily misguided to conclude from such considerations, as some do, that the world can simply grow out of its environmental problems. Were that true, the rich countries would have long ago solved their environmental challenges, and we would not have projections such as those just cited from the OECD and the United Nations. In developing countries undergoing rapid industrialization, new environmental problems (such as truly terrible urban air pollution and acid rain and smog over large regions) are replacing old ones. Collectively the environmental impacts of rich and poor have mounted as the world economy has grown, and we have not yet deployed the means to reduce the human footprint on the planet faster than the economy expands.[33]

The *fourth* and final observation about the economic expansion of the twentieth century follows from the preceding three: human society is in a radically new ethical position because it is now at the planetary controls. Scientist Peter Vitousek and his coauthors stated the matter forcefully in a 1997 article in *Science:* "Humanity's dominance of Earth means that we cannot escape responsibility for managing the planet. Our activities are causing rapid, novel, and substantial changes to Earth's ecosystems. Maintaining populations, species, and ecosystems in the face of those changes, and maintaining the flow of goods and services they provide humanity, will require active management for the foreseeable future."[34]

Scientists are a cautious lot, by and large, so when the most respected issue a plea for "active management of the planet," we should take careful notice. I do not think Vitousek and others who call for "planetary management" are suggesting that the uncontrolled planetary experiment we are now running can be made safe through flawless planning, more sophisticated human interventions, or large-scale engineering feats such as seeding the oceans with iron to draw more carbon dioxide out of the air. Rather, our responsibility is to manage ourselves and our impacts on nature in a way that minimizes our interference with the great life-support systems of the planet.

We know what is driving these global trends. The much-used "IPAT equation" sees environmental *Impact* as a product of the size of human *Populations,* our *Affluence* and consumption patterns, and the *Technology* we deploy to meet our perceived needs.[35] Each of these is an important driver of deterioration. However, what this useful IPAT formulation can obscure, in addition to the effects of poverty, is the vast and rapidly growing scale of the human enterprise.

Regarding this growth, here is what happened in just the past twenty years:[36]

Global population	up 35 percent.
World economic output	up 75 percent.
Global energy use	up 40 percent.
Global meat consumption	up 70 percent.
World auto production	up 45 percent.
Global paper use	up 90 percent.
Advertising globally	up 100 percent.

Today, the world economy is poised to quadruple in size again by midcentury, just as it did in the last half-century, perhaps reaching a staggering $180 trillion in annual global output. We probably could not stop this growth if we wanted to, and most of us would not stop it if we could. Close to half the world's people live on less than two dollars per day. They both need and deserve something better. Economic expansion at least offers the potential for better lives, though its benefits in recent decades have disproportionately favored the already well-to-do. Remember also that while growth is a serious complicating factor, even if we immediately stopped all growth in both population and economic activity, we would still bring about an appalling deterioration of our planetary habitat merely by continuing to do exactly what we are doing today.

The implications of all this are profound. We have entered the endgame in our traditional, historical relationship with the natural world. The current Nature Conservancy campaign has an appropriate name: they are seeking to protect the Last Great Places. We are in a race to the finish. Soon, metaphorically speaking, whatever is not protected will be paved. For biologists Pimm and Raven, the past loss of half the tropical forests will likely cost us 15 percent of the species there. Comparable rates of deforestation in the future would lead to much greater loss.[37] More generally, attacks on the environment of many types will likely be increasingly consequential. Whatever slack nature once cut us is gone.

Humans dominate the planet today as never before. We now live in a full world. An unprecedented responsibility for planetary management is now thrust upon us, whether we like it or not. This huge new burden, for which there is no precedent and little preparation, is the price of our economic success. We brought it upon ourselves, and we must turn to it with urgency and with even greater determination and political attention than has been brought to liberalizing trade and making the world safe for market capitalism. The risks of inaction extend beyond unprecedented environmental deterioration. Following closely in its wake would be widespread loss of livelihoods, social tensions and conflict, and huge economic costs.

Editors' Note: *Notes for this reading can be found in the original source.*

CHAPTER 24

Diamond
A Struggle for Environmental Justice in Louisiana's Chemical Corridor

Steve Lerner

Josephine Bering, 87 years old,[1] can be found most days in her living room, sitting in a comfortable armchair next to her fish tank. She lives in Diamond, an African-American community 25 miles west of New Orleans on the banks of the Mississippi. Her house is located three streets from the fenceline with a Shell Chemical plant. The day I met her, she was wearing a white and green plaid dress and white socks. One of her many grandchildren slept on the couch while two others played in a back room. Outside and inside her home, the air was permeated with a smell that one would expect to encounter in a closed storage closet filled with industrial-strength cleansers.

Bering lived on the fenceline with the chemical plant for more than 60 years. Her late father polished floors and cut grass at the plant. A few years ago, in recognition of her father's long service, Shell officials helped Bering fix up her house. But when she suggested that it would be better to move her away from the fenceline and the health problems she associated with the fumes from their plants, Don Baker, a Shell official, replied "Repair is one thing; relocation is another."

That was not good enough for Bering. "I want to get out of here for the sake of my health," she said. Her sister, also a resident of Diamond, died at 43 of what Bering describes as "phlegm on her lungs." The doctors told her that it came from living near the chemical plant and the refinery. "She suffered with that a long time," Bering remembered. Like her sister, Bering had respiratory problems and was "short-winded." Her asthma improved only when she left the area. She described the air around Diamond as smelling like ammonia or bleach. "It works on me terrible," she said. Asthma also afflicted one of her grandsons; when he stayed with her, she had to hook him up to "a breathing machine."

Then there were the unexplained allergies and skin problems that ran in the family. Bering attributed the cracked and discolored skin on her wrists to the chemicals coming from the adjacent Shell plant. To underscore the severity of this problem, she called in one of her granddaughters from the bedroom and told the gangly adolescent "Show the man your arms." Reluctantly, the 14-year-old girl stretched out her arms. "It is like that all over her body," volunteered Bering, whose sister was similarly afflicted.

"I don't have enough money to get out of here, so I have to just stay and suffer with it," Bering said. "All Shell has to do is buy people out and let them go. Just give us enough to get out of here. If they would move me out of here and relocate me, I would surely be happy." . . .

Diamond is not a place where most people would choose to live. Located in the heart of the "chemical corridor" between the mouth of the Mississippi River and Baton Rouge, the four streets of this subdivision are hard up against fencelines with a Shell Chemical plant and the huge Shell/Motiva oil refinery.[1] Residents here have long breathed the fumes from these two plants, suffered illnesses they attributed to toxic exposures, and mourned neighbors and friends killed by explosions at these facilities.

The view from the homes in Diamond is of heavy industry at work. There are catalytic cracking towers, stacks topped by flares burning off excess gas, huge oil and gasoline storage tanks, giant processing units where oil and its derivatives are turned into a wide variety of useful chemicals, and a Rube Goldberg maze of oversized pipes. The clanking and crashing of railroad cars coupling and uncoupling can be deafening, and the eerie sight of the superstructures of gargantuan oil tankers soundlessly moving up the Mississippi to dock and unload their crude oil completes the industrial landscape.

The streams of chemicals pouring out of the plants in the vast, sprawling Shell/Motiva Norco Complex are used in factories around the United States. Truly, these two mammoth plants are part of the front end of the system that has forged the American lifestyle by making products cheap and convenient. One cannot help but be in awe of the ingenuity, tenacity, and hard work that built these technological behemoths.

What seemed an incongruous sight, however, was a small residential community sandwiched between these two giant plants. The terrible cost of introducing heavy industry into a residential neighborhood soon became apparent. In the homes of Diamond residents there were many signs that this was not a healthy place to live. On many days the plant stank. Shell officials said that the smell was not dangerous and was caused by an organic digester unit that became backed up and gave off a rotten odor as millions of micro-organisms died. They were working on a solution to the problem, they said. But on some days the smell emanating from the plants had a toxic bouquet. Not infrequently, there was an acrid, metallic odor that caused headaches, sinus problems, and stinging eyes. There were even days, residents and visitors reported, when they could actually see a chemical fog swirling around their legs and seeping through the cracks into the houses.

And while it was notoriously difficult to prove that there existed a causal link between the toxic chemical released from the plant and the health of neighboring residents, inside the homes of Diamond residents were a disturbing number of children with asthma; young adults with severe respiratory, allergic, and unusual skin problems; and older people whose breathing had to be aided with oxygen tanks.

Then there was the history of periodic explosions. A 1973 explosion took the lives of two Diamond residents. A 1988 explosion that killed seven Shell workers blew out windows and doors and brought down sheetrock ceilings in many homes. Diamond was evacuated in the middle of the night. Many homes required extensive reconstruction.

If it was so poisonous and dangerous to live there, why didn't the residents of Diamond just move? The answer was that few of those who lived in Diamond stayed because they wanted to. Given an opportunity to sell their homes and move they would do so, but without getting decent prices for their homes they could not afford to leave. Living next to the Shell plants had not only been bad for their health, they said; it also had been lethal to property values. As the chemical and oil plants expanded to an area just across the street, residents who wanted to sell their homes and relocate could not find buyers who were foolish enough to want to purchase their homes. In other words, they were stuck: they could not bear living where they were because of the bad air, but they could not afford to move elsewhere. . . .

On a beautiful summer day in 1973, a Shell Chemical pipeline sprang a leak, eyewitnesses report. The pipe ran parallel to Washington Street in Diamond, which forms the fenceline between the industrial facility and the residential community. Diamond residents saw a white cloud of gas snake down the street. Dorothy Pedescleaux recalled telling some young men "You see that white stuff coming down the street? I bet it's going to be a fire." Just down the street, Leroy Jones, 16, was cutting grass at the home of Helen Washington, an elderly woman, who was indoors taking a nap. Jones had taken a break from his chore and was chatting with some friends who had stopped on their bike rounds of the neighborhood. After they left, Jones pulled the cord to start the lawnmower. A spark from the engine ignited the gas that had leaked out of the Shell pipeline, residents conjectured. The ensuing explosion scorched Leroy Jones and burned Helen Washington's house down. Badly burned, Jones stumbled around in shock, clutching his eyes. "When emergency workers arrived they wrapped (Jones's) blistered body in a baby quilt that a neighbor had hung out to dry," neighbors reported.[1] Jones died a few days later in the hospital. Helen Washington died immediately, burned up in her own home.

Larry Brown described the day Helen Washington and Leroy Jones died as one of the most traumatic in his life. He recalled a fog-like gas escaping from the Shell pipe and said he called out a warning to Leroy Jones not to start the lawnmower. "When he cranked it there was a big BOOM . . . a big flame . . . and I saw him crumple and claw his eyes," Brown recalled. Then one of the grandsons of Helen Washington ran into the burning house and pulled his grandmother out. "She was burned," Brown said. "I couldn't look at it. I just left. I'm trying to think how to put it: seeing someone burn . . . that is a horrible feeling to watch . . . another human being. I saw it, I smelled it, I still feel the stink of that flesh. . . . I ran for my life. I feel bad that I ran and didn't try to help. I didn't know what was going to happen [blow up] next."

Delwyn Smith, 51, remembered the bodies of Washington and Jones being carried to her mother's property: "They brought them over there and set them under mamma's oak tree right in the front yard."

Two boys on motorbikes had just passed when the explosion erupted. One of them was Devaliant Christopher Cole, 13 at the time. Cole remembered riding with a friend that day past a young man messing with a lawn-mower. When they were about two blocks past him there was a loud explosion. "I looked back and WHOOF . . . just like a big old fireball . . . and it kept burning for awhile," Cole recalled. "It looked like a flame-thrower. A big flame just shot across the street. It tore the house down . . . everything all at one time. . . . I never saw anything like that in my life."

The horror of death by fire rippled through the close-knit community. "I'm sorry in a way that I went over to see because it is forever etched in my memory. The fireball was like a rolling ball of fire through the street, and that lady and that little boy burned," said Audrey Eugene. Later Shell put a little sign up near the pipes saying that they were hazardous.

Ernestine Roberts, 52, was watching TV when the explosion occurred. She recalls: "We just started running. When we got there . . . the whole house was just flat. There was a lot of hollering and screaming going on because in a small town everyone knows everyone."

The fatal accident changed the way residents of Diamond viewed living next to Shell's facilities. "That [explosion] made quite a difference," recalled Lois Gales, who was in Diamond that day, pregnant with her first son. Suddenly she realized that accidents from the plant could reach out across the fenceline and take lives. It was at that moment that Gales realized "it was kind of dangerous living here."

Part of the fear this accident engendered had to do with the fact that no one was sure what was going to blow up next. "I just couldn't stop screaming," said Lois Parquet, who was afraid at the time that a pipeline near her house would burst next. "Who is to say what is under my property? . . . You don't know the danger that lies underground. . . . It was their time then, but it could be our time next. . . ."

Fear that there would be additional explosions continued to trouble some residents for years. "When the explosion happened I was under the line hanging up clothes," recalled 72-year-old Deloris Brown. "My nerves were just shattered when those people died. I went out in the street and looked at the flames and everything. . . . I was shook up. Other people got over it [the accident] right quick but I will never get over it." Jenny Taylor, 61, has the same problem: "After that fast big explosion you really haven't been yourself since because if trains hit too hard [coupling and uncoupling] you think one of them plants blowed up."

When asked how much the victims' families were paid in compensation, Shell officials say they have no record of it. But Diamond residents are unanimous in recalling that the relatives of Helen Washington were paid $3,000 for her burned house and land, and that Ruth Jones, Leroy's mother, was paid $500.[2] This compares poorly with a multi-million-dollar settlement Shell made with the families of two boys who were killed in a pipeline explosion in Canada.

Not only are there no records of the two fatalities that occurred in Diamond in 1973; there is also no mention of the event in Shell's Norco Museum. When questioned about the incident, curator Clarisse Webb did not know the details. Indeed, she asked if it had anything to do with Shell. Residents of Diamond, however, recall the incident well. "I think I heard they gave [Ruth Jones] $500, but, being elderly, she didn't know [that she deserved more], poor thing," Wendy Mashia said, adding that Shell had been "messing over people" for years. Gaynel Johnson also finds the minimal compensation for the deaths on Washington Street troubling: "You [Shell] could have given her [Ruth Jones] a check every month, and you could have bought her a home. But [instead] this lady was on rent until she died." Margie Richard goes even further, arguing that Shell should have offered to relocate the whole neighborhood after the explosion in 1973, when it became clear that living there was unsafe.

Monique Harden, formerly an attorney for the EarthJustice Legal Defense Fund, is also incensed about how Shell handled the deaths of Jones and Washington. "This horrendous tragedy in 1973 shows how little the lives of African-American residents in the Diamond community meant to Shell at the time. It is beyond an insult. The company doesn't feel sorry for what happened. It doesn't feel sorry for the loss of lives. It doesn't value the people and what they meant to the community or their families or survivors."

Providing some historical context for how it could have happened that the families of Leroy Jones and Helen Washington were compensated so minimally by Shell, Beverly Wright said: "It speaks, in the deep South, to the race issue and the extent to which African-Americans have been disenfranchised and have had no political power or support. That made it possible for people to devalue them and know that they were not going to be challenged."

While noting that there are no company records about what compensation was provided to victims of the accident in 1973, Shell spokesman David Brignac said he understands that the minimal compensation residents say was provided by Shell spoke powerfully to them about how their lives were valued by the company at the time. "We would do vastly differently today than what you describe people say we did back in 1973," he continued. "If [the minimal compensation] is a sore point and it is something that people are hanging onto, I agree that it is something we should do something about."

THE BIG BANG

The "big bang" in Diamond was not a cosmic event that occurred light years away; it was right next door. At 3:40 A.M. on May 4, 1988, a catalytic cracking unit at the Shell refinery blew up, killing seven Shell workers and injuring 48 other people (some workers, some residents). The explosion spewed 159 million pounds of toxic chemicals into the air, caused widespread property damage, and required the evacuation of 4,500 people.

Corrosion in a pipeline eight inches in diameter permitted 20,000 pounds of C-3 hydrocarbons to escape. A vapor cloud formed and then ignited. The explosion toppled a 16-story-tall fractionator. Debris from the explosion was found 5 miles away, and structural damage to homes and businesses radiated out a mile from the point of the explosion. The blast could be heard 25 miles away in New Orleans, where it set off burglar alarms. The east wall of the Norco Coop Supermarket on Fourth Street was blown off, and the ceiling of Bill's Dollar Store partially collapsed.

After the explosion, a fire burned for 8 hours at the refinery before it was brought under control. A black film covered homes and cars in surrounding towns. The governor declared a state of emergency in Norco and St. Charles Parish.[3]

"The night the explosion happened. . . . I actually thought it was a nuclear bomb that had hit our area . . . that we were being invaded by another country," said Larry Brown, 51, as he sat in his house next to his parents' burned-out tavern. "At that particular time I was here with my parents. The explosion knocked me out of bed, and it scared the hell out of me because all I saw was flashes and everything falling down. . . . I ran outside, which was stupid, and I saw fire shooting 150 feet in the air. So I told my parents that it was time for us to go. At that time my father had both of his legs amputated because of poor circulation, so I got him and my mother together in the car and we got out. The police were in town with the mikes on their cars open telling everyone to evacuate. We went out through the spillway. . . . If the spillway had been full I hate to even think what would have happened, because it was real crowded on the road. It was a [traffic] jam with everyone trying to get out."

Brown had been a member of the crew Shell had hired to clean up after the explosion. One of the Shell workers killed was a friend of Brown's, and they found his foot about eight blocks away from the site of the explosion, Brown said. Brown quit the cleanup job when he was instructed to pick up material covered in asbestos. Told that there was no reason to believe the material was dangerous since it had not been tested, Brown said, "I don't care if you tested it or not. I'm not going to be here." And he left. "They didn't have proper equipment to work with asbestos," he observed. Brown suspects that many residents were exposed to airborne asbestos when they returned home from the evacuation. "We later came to find that there was enough asbestos in the air that we shouldn't have been let back in for a week. . . . But you won't find that in their [Shell's] files," he charged.

Just as most people who were alive at the time remember where they were when Martin Luther King Jr. and John F. Kennedy were assassinated, everyone in Diamond remembers where he or she was when the catalytic cracking unit at the Shell refinery blew up. And each of them has a very personal way of describing the noise it made.

Delwyn Smith recalled that she had just gotten out of bed to get a glass of water and had returned to bed when the explosion hit. "BAAATUNG. . . . I thought it was a plane had crashed," recalled Smith, who noted that Diamond was in the flight path of nearby New Orleans Airport. All the windows in Smith's house were blown out, and the door was broken and hanging from the top hinge. Smith needed to buy gas to get out of town. "It was like chaos. . . . People were out there crying . . . like my aunt whose husband had just had open-heart surgery." The explosion made Smith realize that "it was not really safe here [in Diamond] at all."

Just how terrifying this explosion was to small children is best described by Ernestine Roberts, 52, who recalled lying in bed listening to Shell's industrial cacophony that night: "Shell had been roaring all night, but it was a different kind of roar. I could hear the difference and you knew something was going to happen. You could feel that something was going to happen. So I lay in bed and it was making this sound, making this sound, making this sound . . . and you get to know the sounds . . . but this was a different sound. I got up bedroom [sic] and headed for the kitchen and then all of a sudden BOOOOOM. It knocked me off my feet. I went running to the door, and all I could see was fire. I ran back in here to get my son. I was calling for him and he is not answering me. And all I could see was fire through the windows. And I am calling for him, I can't find him, I am looking in all the closets, I can't find him. . . . Now I am panicking. . . . I can't find him. Finally when I did find him he was under the bed. And I couldn't get him out because he was holding on to the box springs so I am telling him 'Come out, come out.' And he is not crying. He is just holding on and I cannot get him out. And I am pulling and trying to get him out. . . . And finally I pull him out and grab him up in a blanket. . . . And we just run. . . ."

Others were also terrified by the explosion. "That was just scary, scary, scary," say Deloris Brown, 72. "I just ran out through the back. . . . I just prayed I wouldn't cut my feet [on all the broken glass] . . . but I was running the wrong way. . . . The explosions worry me the most . . . and the odor. You hear a noise and you think: I wonder what is happening in Norco. I am afraid of the explosion and that anytime it might be something."

Many residents have not slept well since the explosion. "We slept in our clothes for a long time," said Jenny Taylor. "Tell you the truth I still have my clothes laid out on a chair so I can jump into them. . . . We don't know what they [the plants] are going to do, so you can't ever really be relaxed."

Many people decided to move out of Diamond. "It tore up the neighborhood so bad. You had people that rebuilt their house but you had a lot of people who didn't," recalled Devaliant Christopher Cole. Some just left. Boarded-up homes gave the community a damaged and bedraggled look and brought real estate values down.

Ever since 1988, Devaliant Cole has been waiting for the next accident. "Even now, with the train nearby and the train cars pushing and slamming, I jump up," he said. And when he drives home in the evening and sees smoke rising over Norco, he wonders what has happened.

After the explosion, some Diamond residents just wanted to get out of town. Audrey Eugene spoke with Shell officials about selling her home. "I was ready to leave. . . . You know when something like that happens you don't rest well. It is just too much. You sleep with your shoes right there by your bed, so while it happened in 1988 it didn't go away. . . . I don't have the means to just leave here without selling. . . . I didn't cause this problem. . . . If the land is important to them, let them have it as long as they compensate me what is fair," said Eugene.

Commenting on the safety record of the Shell/Motiva complex, Shell spokesman David Brignac said he was "confident that our safety record is going to improve and continue to improve." Shell had a strong safety program in place, not only for the benefit of the community but also for its own workers, he noted. Shell officials took the attitude that accidents don't just happen but rather have a preventable cause. A lot of time and money was spent on safety, he added. "Regrettably, we have had significant incidents," Brignac conceded, referring to the explosions in 1973 and 1988. The 1988 explosion was last major incident, and since then there have been improvements in safety procedures. Despite these improvements,

Brignac is careful not to overpromise. "I can't tell residents that we will never have a big event [again]," he said. "So I don't know how to deal with that fear. I don't have a good answer."

"I FEEL LIKE I'M IN A HOLE"

"I made 80," said Janie Campbell when asked her age. She said it with no small amount of pride. Many of her friends who lived in the same heavily polluted neighborhood in Diamond died prematurely, she claimed. And, while she cannot prove it, Campbell attributes their early illnesses and deaths to fumes from the adjacent Shell petrochemical plants located just three short blocks from her front door. "Everybody that I knew they died of the cancer. And they all have their breathing machine. A lady died day before yesterday, and she had a big old breathing tank she had to travel with all the time because she couldn't breathe. Another young girl she died also," she said. Giving substance to Campbell's suspicions was a long history of air pollution violations by the neighboring refinery and chemical plant. The air in and outside her home had a biting metallic taste.

Forty years ago, Campbell moved to her home in Diamond, arriving in St. Charles Parish with a sick husband and seven children. She chose Diamond because she found a house there that cost $4,500 and buying it meant that she could own her own home instead of paying rent. The house was cheap because it was located right on the fenceline with Shell's chemical plant and refinery. Shortly after she arrived, her husband, a laborer for Louisiana Power and Gas, died from a stroke. To feed her family, Campbell took a job first as a janitor at Shell's refinery and later as a maid working in the home of a white family in Norco until age 70, when chronic health problems forced her to retire.

Born with poor eyesight, Campbell subsequently developed diabetes, an irregular heartbeat, and a cyst on her spine. She also has arthritis and is often short of breath. "Sometimes I can make do for myself and sometimes I can't," she explained. Though most of her children had left Diamond, one daughter, Mary, lived a few blocks away, that daughter checked on her mother, prepared her meals, did her shopping, and drove her to the doctor.

Explosions at the Shell plants in 1973 and 1988 left Campbell with a bad case of what she called "nerves." During the earlier incident she was sitting on her porch when, as she described it, "something blowed up at the chemical plant and it killed the old lady [Helen Washington] and the little boy [Leroy Jones] who was in the yard. It was like the fire [from the explosion] was coming over my house." Campbell became hysterical. "The funniest part is that every time the kids would start yelling and screaming I would tell them to shut up but then I would start screaming. But it wasn't really funny," she allowed. Hearing about the explosion, one of her sons-in-law came with a dump truck to evacuate her and the kids. The bed of the dump truck was so high that normally Campbell would have been unable to climb into it, but not this time. "I was so frightened that nothing was too high for me to get in," she said.

Campbell found that she did not get over her fright. The home she was working in as a maid had a squeaky faucet, and when the owner of the house turned it on Campbell thought there was another explosion: "I went running down the hall hollering and screaming that [the plant] blowed up again." It got so bad that her employer told her she had to see a doctor. Sent to a mental health clinic, Campbell told the doctor "My nerves are bad, but I don't think I'm crazy." "Janie," he said, "you aren't crazy. You just need some pills."

The 1988 explosion "picked my house off the pillars and dropped it back down," Janie Campbell recalled. "It was . . . just like going through hell. And since that time I don't sleep, I sleep light and if the house creaks I wake and if the trains hit connecting with each other I sit up in bed and say to myself 'Well, that is just the train.' So it is just scary and I have to live on nerve pills and I think that is just horrible to have to live on nerve pills to keep together at night. I just shake because there is too much pressure. I'm frightened."

Campbell is still worried that the refinery or the chemical plant might blow up again, and that she would be left behind in the confusion or the evacuation routes might be cut. She counts it a blessing that during the last big explosion the spillway was not full and Diamond residents were able to escape across it. But if the spillway is full during the next explosion she does not know how she will get out. She cannot drive or swim. "I feel like I am in a hole," she said. "Have you ever seen a hole way down and there is no way for you to come out? Well, I feel like I am in a hole. I'm in a hole with nowhere to go. I'm surrounded. The [railroad] track is there, the river is there, you don't know when an accident is going to happen and the spillway could be full of water. And I can't swim it and I can't walk it, and I can't go through it in a car because it [the water] is so high. . . . Where am I going to go? I just wish I could get away from here before I die so I could have peace of mind and sleep one night in peace without being afraid that the plant is going to blow up." Campbell was acutely aware of how close the plants are to her: "It is not like they are ten miles away. They are right here. And the odors. . . . It is just horrible. And now and then [the plants make loud noises like] VROOM, VROOM, like something they are trying to keep from blowing up. It [the gas] wants to blow up, and it is trying to escape from something. And when they have the flares coming out of the top, it makes a noise like something that is too full and it is trying to escape . . . the pressure. And you don't know if it is going to explode. You don't know what it is going to do. Nobody knows but the good Lord." Shell officials told her the plant was not going to blow up but, as she pointed out, they had not anticipated that the catalytic cracking plant would blow up in 1988. In fact, after the 1990 Clean Air Act required chemical companies to prepare a "worst-case scenario" map of vulnerable areas around their plants it became clear that Diamond was within three overlapping vulnerable zones.

Campbell prays to God that Shell officials will move her so she can have a few years of peace. "My [government] check is $525 a month," she noted. "You can't move on that, and nobody ain't going to buy here in Norco because everybody is afraid [of living near the plants]. I can't sell my house to nobody. Nobody don't want it."

Like many of her neighbors, Campbell would prefer to leave town rather than fight Shell. "I would go," she insisted, as long as Shell paid enough for her house that she could relocate in a safe area. "I'm not particular as long as it is a decent place. . . . I am not a picky person. . . . I just want to get away from here. I am looking just to get away. I just want to be gone. . . . People want to get away from here so bad. They are desperate because they know what they have been going through here and they don't want to raise up children here in this mess."

Editors' Note: *Notes for this reading can be found in the original source.*

CHAPTER 25

Smoke, Mirrors & Hot Air

How ExxonMobil Uses Big Tobacco's Tactics to Manufacture Uncertainty on Climate Science

Union of Concerned Scientists

The Facts About ExxonMobil

Background

ExxonMobil is a powerful player on the world stage. It is the world's largest publicly traded company: at $339 billion,[1] its 2005 revenues exceeded the gross domestic products of most of the world's nations.[2] It is the most profitable corporation in history. In 2005, the company netted $36 billion[3]—nearly $100 million in profit *each day*.

As the biggest player in the world's gas and oil business, ExxonMobil is also one of the world's largest producers of global warming pollution. Company operations alone pumped the equivalent of 138 million metric tons of carbon dioxide into the atmosphere in 2004[4] and roughly the same level of emissions in 2005, according to company reporting.[5] In 2005, the end use combustion of ExxonMobil's products—gasoline, heating oil, kerosene, diesel products, aviation fuels, and heavy fuels—resulted in 1,047 million metric tons of carbon dioxide–equivalent emissions.[6] If it was a country, ExxonMobil would rank sixth in emissions.

While some oil companies like BP, Occidental Petroleum, and Shell have begun to invest in clean energy technologies and publicly committed to reduce their heat-trapping emissions, ExxonMobil has made no such commitment.

Lee Raymond, ExxonMobil's chief executive officer (CEO) until 2006, set a brazenly unapologetic corporate tone on global warming. During his nearly 13 years as ExxonMobil's leader, Raymond unabashedly opposed caps on carbon dioxide emissions and refused to acknowledge the scientific consensus on global

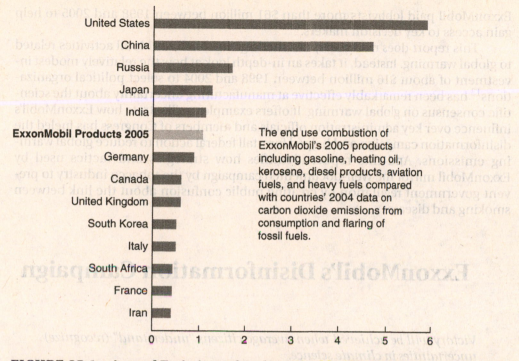

The end use combustion of ExxonMobil's 2005 products including gasoline, heating oil, kerosene, diesel products, aviation fuels, and heavy fuels compared with countries' 2004 data on carbon dioxide emissions from consumption and flaring of fossil fuels.

FIGURE 25.1   Annual Emissions of Carbon Dioxide (Gigatons)

*Country data available at *http://www.eia.doe.gov/iea/carbon.html*

warming. Under Raymond's direction, ExxonMobil positioned itself, as Paul Krugman of the *New York Times* recently put it, as "an enemy of the planet."[7] Not only did he do nothing to curb his company's global warming emissions, during his tenure Raymond divested the company of nearly all its alternative energy holdings.[8] During his time as CEO, ExxonMobil's board lavishly rewarded him with compensation amounting to more than $686 million.[9] When Raymond retired at the end of 2005, he received an exorbitant retirement package worth nearly $400 million, prompting sharp criticism from shareholders.[10] ExxonMobil is now headed by CEO Rex Tillerson, but the corporate policies Raymond forged so far remain largely intact.

ExxonMobil has played the world's most active corporate role in underwriting efforts to thwart and undermine climate change regulation. For instance, according to the Center for Responsive Politics, ExxonMobil's PAC—its political action committee—and individuals affiliated with the company made more than $4 million in political contributions throughout the 2000 to 2006 election cycles. It was consistently among the top four energy sector contributors. In the 2004 election cycle alone, ExxonMobil's PAC and individuals affiliated with the company gave $935,000 in political contributions, more than any other energy company. Much of that money went in turn to President Bush's election campaign.[11] In addition,

ExxonMobil paid lobbyists more than $61 million between 1998 and 2005 to help gain access to key decision makers.[12]

This report does not attempt to shed light on all ExxonMobil activities related to global warming. Instead, it takes an in-depth look at how the relatively modest investment of about $16 million between 1998 and 2004 to select political organizations[13] has been remarkably effective at manufacturing uncertainty about the scientific consensus on global warming. It offers examples to illustrate how ExxonMobil's influence over key administration officials and members of Congress has fueled the disinformation campaign and helped forestall federal action to reduce global warming emissions. And this report identifies how strategies and tactics used by ExxonMobil mirror the well-documented campaign by the tobacco industry to prevent government regulation by creating public confusion about the link between smoking and disease . . . .

ExxonMobil's Disinformation Campaign

Victory will be achieved when average citizens "understand" (recognize) uncertainties in climate science.

—Internal Memo by the American Petroleum Institute, 1998

In the late 1980s, when the public first began to hear about global warming, scientists had already conducted more than a century of research on the impact of carbon dioxide on earth's climate (see Appendix A for more information). As the science matured in the late 1980s, debate, a key component of the scientific process, surfaced among reputable scientists about the scope of the problem and the extent to which human activity was responsible. Much like the status of scientific knowledge about the health effects of smoking in the early 1950s, emerging studies suggested cause for concern but many scientists justifiably argued that more research needed to be done.[14]

Exxon (and later ExxonMobil), concerned about potential repercussions for its business, argued from the start that no global warming trend existed and that a link between human activity and climate change could not be established.[15] Just as the tobacco companies initially responded with a coalition to address the health effects of smoking, Exxon and the American Petroleum Institute (an organization twice chaired by former Exxon CEO Lee Raymond) joined with other energy, automotive, and industrial companies in 1989 to form the Global Climate Coalition.[16] The coalition responded aggressively to the emerging scientific studies about global warming by opposing governmental action designed to address the problem.

Drawing on a handful of scientific spokespeople during the early and mid-1990s, the Global Climate Coalition emphasized the remaining uncertainties in climate science.[17] Exxon and other members of the coalition challenged the need for action on global warming by denying its existence as well as characterizing global warming as a natural phenomenon.[18] As Exxon and its proxies mobilized forces to cast doubt on global warming, however, a scientific consensus was emerging that put their arguments on exceptionally shaky scientific ground (see Appendix A).

MANUFACTURING UNCERTAINTY

By 1997, scientific understanding that human-caused emissions of heat-trapping gases were causing global warming led to the Kyoto Protocol, in which the majority of the world's industrialized nations committed to begin reducing their global warming emissions on a specified timetable. In response to both the strength of the scientific evidence on global warming and the governmental action pledged to address it, leading oil companies such as British Petroleum, Shell, and Texaco changed their stance on climate science and abandoned the Global Climate Coalition.[19]

ExxonMobil chose a different path.

In 1998, ExxonMobil helped create a small task force calling itself the "Global Climate Science Team" (GCST). Members included Randy Randol, ExxonMobil's senior environmental lobbyist at the time, and Joe Walker, the public relations representative of the American Petroleum Institute.[20] One member of the GCST task force, Steven Milloy, headed a nonprofit organization called the Advancement of Sound Science Coalition, which had been covertly created by the tobacco company Philip Morris in 1993 to manufacture uncertainty about the health hazards posed by secondhand smoke.[21]

A 1998 GCST task force memo outlined an explicit strategy to invest millions of dollars to manufacture uncertainty on the issue of global warming[22]—a strategy that directly emulated Big Tobacco's disinformation campaign. Despite mounting scientific evidence of the changing climate, the goal the team outlined was simple and familiar. As the memo put it, "Victory will be achieved when average citizens understand (recognize) uncertainties in climate science" and when public "recognition of uncertainty becomes part of the 'conventional wisdom.'"[23]

Regardless of the mounting scientific evidence, the 1998 GCST memo contended that "if we can show that science does not support the Kyoto treaty . . . this puts the United States in a stronger moral position and frees its negotiators from the need to make concessions as a defense against perceived selfish economic concerns."[24]

ExxonMobil and its partners no doubt understood that, with the scientific evidence against them, they would not be able to influence reputable scientists. The 1998 memo proposed that ExxonMobil and its public relations partners "develop and implement a national media relations program to inform the media about uncertainties in climate science."[25] In the years that followed,

ExxonMobil executed the strategy as planned underwriting a wide array of front organizations to publish in-house articles by select scientists and other like-minded individuals to raise objections about legitimate climate science research that has withstood rigorous peer review and has been replicated in multiple independent peer-reviewed studies—in other words, to attack research findings that were well established in the scientific community. The network ExxonMobil created masqueraded as a credible scientific alternative, but it publicized discredited studies and cherry-picked information to present misleading conclusions.

INFORMATION LAUNDERING

A close review reveals the company's effort at what some have called "information laundering": projecting the company's desired message through ostensibly independent nonprofit organizations. First, ExxonMobil underwrites well-established groups such as the American Enterprise Institute, the Competitive Enterprise Institute, and the Cato Institute that actively oppose mandatory action on global warming as well as many other environmental standards. But the funding doesn't stop there. ExxonMobil also supports a number of lesser-known organizations that help to market and distribute global warming disinformation. Few of these are household names. For instance, most people are probably not familiar with the American Council for Capital Formation, Center for Policy Research, the American Legislative Exchange Council, the Committee for a Constructive Tomorrow, or the International Policy Network, to name just a few. Yet these organizations—and many others like them—have received sizable donations from ExxonMobil for their climate change activities.[26]

Between 1998 and 2005 (the most recent year for which company figures are publicly available), ExxonMobil has funneled approximately $16 million to carefully chosen organizations that promote disinformation on global warming.[27] As the *New York Times* has reported, ExxonMobil is often the single largest corporate donor to many of these nonprofit organizations, frequently accounting for more than 10 percent of their annual budgets.[28]

A close look at the work of these organizations exposes ExxonMobil's strategy. Virtually all of them publish and publicize the work of a nearly identical group of spokespeople, including scientists who misrepresent peer-reviewed climate findings and confuse the public's understanding of global warming. Most of these organizations also include these same individuals as board members or scientific advisers.

Why would ExxonMobil opt to fund so many groups with overlapping spokespeople and programs? By generously funding a web of organizations with redundant personnel, advisors, or spokespeople, ExxonMobil can quietly and effectively provide the appearance of a broad platform for a tight-knit group of vocal climate science contrarians. The seeming diversity of the organizations creates an "echo chamber" that amplifies and sustains scientific disinformation even though many of the assertions have been repeatedly debunked by the scientific community.

Take, for example, ExxonMobil's funding of a Washington, DC-based organization called Frontiers of Freedom.[29] Begun in 1996 by former Senator Malcolm Wallop, Frontiers of Freedom was founded to promote property rights and critique environmental regulations like the Endangered Species Act.[30] One of the group's staff members, an economist named Myron Ebell, later served as a member of the Global Climate Science Team, the small task force that laid out ExxonMobil's 1998 message strategy on global warming. Following the outline of the task force's plan in 1998, ExxonMobil began funding Frontiers of Freedom—a group that Vice President Dick Cheney recently called "an active, intelligent, and needed presence in the national debate."[31]

Since 1998, ExxonMobil has spent $857,000 to underwrite the Frontiers of Freedom's climate change efforts.[32] In 2002, for example, ExxonMobil made a grant to Frontiers of Freedom of $232,000[33] (nearly a third of the organization's annual budget) to help launch a new branch of the organization called the Center for Science and Public Policy, which would focus primarily on climate change.

A recent visit to the organization's website finds little information about the background or work of the Center for Science and Public Policy.[34] The website offers no mention of its staff or board members other than its current executive director Robert Ferguson, for whom it offers no biographical information. As of September 2006, however, the website did prominently feature a 38-page non-peer-reviewed report by Ferguson on climate science, heavily laden with maps, graphs, and charts, entitled "Issues in the Current State of Climate Science: A Guide for Policy Makers and Opinion Leaders."[35] The document offers a hodgepodge of distortions and distractions posing as a serious scientific review. Ferguson questions the clear data showing that the majority of the globe's glaciers are in retreat by feebly arguing that not all glaciers have been inventoried, despite the monitoring of thousands of glaciers worldwide.[36] And, in an attempt to dispute solid scientific evidence that climate change is causing extinctions of animal species, Ferguson offers the non sequitur that several new butterfly and frog species were recently discovered in New Guinea.[37]

Perhaps most notable are Ferguson's references, citing a familiar collection of climate science contrarians such as Willie Soon. In fact, although his title is not listed on the organization's website, Soon is the Center for Science and Public Policy's "chief science researcher," according to a biographical note accompanying a 2005 *Wall Street Journal* op-ed co-authored by Ferguson and Soon.[38] Ferguson's report was not subject to peer review, but it is nonetheless presented under the auspices of the authoritative-sounding Center for Science and Public Policy.

Another organization used to launder information is the George C. Marshall Institute. During the 1990s, the Marshall Institute had been known primarily for its work advocating a "Star Wars" missile defense program. However, it soon became an important home for industry-financed "climate contrarians," thanks in part to

ExxonMobil's financial backing. Since 1998, ExxonMobil has paid $630,000 primarily to underwrite the Marshall Institute's climate change effort.[39] William O'Keefe, CEO of the Marshall Institute, formerly worked as executive vice president and chief operating officer of the American Petroleum Institute, served on the board of directors of the Competitive Enterprise Institute, and is chairman emeritus of the Global Climate Coalition.[40]

Since ExxonMobil began to support its efforts, the Marshall Institute has served as a clearinghouse for global warming contrarians, conducting round-table events and producing frequent publications. Most recently, the Marshall Institute has been touting its new book, *Shattered Consensus: The True State of Global Warming*, edited by long-time climate contrarian Patrick Michaels (a meteorologist). Michaels has, over the past several years, been affiliated with at least ten organizations funded by ExxonMobil.[41] Contributors to the book include others with similar affiliations with Exxon-funded groups: Sallie Baliunas, Robert Balling, John Christy, Ross McKitrick, and Willie Soon.[42]

The pattern of information laundering is repeated at virtually all the private, nonprofit climate change programs ExxonMobil funds. The website of the Chicago-based Heartland Institute, which received $119,000 from ExxonMobil in 2005,[43] offers recent articles by the same set of scientists. A visit to the climate section of the website of the American Legislative Exchange Council, which received $241,500 from ExxonMobil in 2005,[44] turns up yet another non-peer-reviewed paper by Patrick Michaels.[45] The Committee for a Constructive Tomorrow, which received $215,000 from ExxonMobil over the past two funding cycles of 2004 and 2005,[46] boasts a similar lineup of articles and a scientific advisory panel that includes Sallie Baliunas, Robert Balling, Roger Bate, Sherwood Idso, Patrick Michaels, and Frederick Seitz—all affiliated with other ExxonMobil-funded organizations.[47]

A more prominent organization funded by ExxonMobil is the Washington, DC-based Competitive Enterprise Institute (CEI). Founded in 1984 to fight government regulation on business, CEI started to attract significant ExxonMobil funding when Myron Ebell moved there from Frontiers of Freedom in 1999. Since then, CEI has not only produced a steady flow of vituperative articles and commentaries attacking global warming science, often using the same set of global warming contrarians; it has also sued the federal government to stop the dissemination of a National Assessment Synthesis Team report extensively documenting the region-by-region impacts of climate change in the United States.[48] For its efforts, CEI has received more than $2 million in funding from ExxonMobil from 1998 through 2005.[49]

The irony of all these efforts is that ExxonMobil, a company that claims it is dedicated to supporting organizations favoring "free market solutions to public policy problems,"[50] is actively propping up discredited studies and misleading information that would otherwise never thrive in the scientific marketplace of ideas.

APPENDIX A

The Scientific Consensus on Global Warming

The scientific understanding of climate change is now sufficiently clear to justify nations taking prompt action. It is vital that all nations identify cost-effective steps that they can take now, to contribute to substantial and long-term reduction in net global greenhouse gas emissions.

—*Joint Statement by the Science Academies of 11 Nations, June 7, 2005*

Ever since Svante Arrhenius published "On the influence of carbonic acid in the air upon the temperature of the ground" in 1896, scientists have appreciated the fundamental principle regarding heat-trapping emissions and their influence on Earth's temperature. The burning of fossil fuels in power plants and vehicles releases heat-trapping emissions, principally carbon dioxide, which accumulates in the atmosphere. These emissions function much like a blanket, trapping heat and warming the planet. The concentration of carbon dioxide in the atmosphere has already increased nearly 40 percent since the dawn of the industrial era and average global temperature is around 1 degree Fahrenheit higher then a century ago.

If global warming emissions grow unabated, climate scientists expect mean temperatures around the world will rise dramatically this century.[51] Without concerted human intervention to try to correct or at least stabilize this trend, researchers have identified a host of disruptive and possibly irreversible consequences, including coastal flooding caused by rising sea levels, an increase in powerful tropical storms, extreme heat waves in summer, and reduced productivity of farms, forests, and fisheries worldwide.[52]

This unprecedented rate of recent warming is caused primarily by human activity. That, in a nutshell, is the overwhelming scientific consensus about global climate change, ever since the publication of a landmark review in 2001 by an international panel of leading climate experts under the auspices of the United Nations, called the Intergovernmental Panel on Climate Change (IPCC).[53] The 2001 IPCC assessment drew upon more than 1,200 scientists and approximately 120 countries. It quickly became a standard reference and solidified the scientific consensus about global warming internationally. Released just days after the inauguration of President George W. Bush, the IPCC report laid out the mounting and consistent scientific evidence of global warming. In May 2001, the White House officially asked the U.S. National Academy of Sciences (NAS) to conduct its own review of the IPCC assessment.[54] Within a month, in June 2001, the NAS confirmed the conclusions of the IPCC that global warming is occurring and that it is caused primarily by human activity.[55] More recently, 11 of the world's major national scientific academies including those from the leading industrialized nations issued a joint statement that declared. "The scientific understanding of climate change is now sufficiently clear to justify nations taking prompt action. It is vital that all nations identify cost-effective steps that they can take now to contribute to substantial and long-term reduction in net global greenhouse gas emissions."[56]

One of the reasons scientists consider the evidence so compelling is that it draws on such a broad range of sources. In addition to climate specialists who use sophisticated computer models to study climatic trends, researchers from an array of disciplines, including atmospheric scientists, paleoclimatologists, oceanographers, meteorologists, geologists, chemists, biologists, physicists, and ecologists have all corroborated global warming by studying everything from animal migration to the melting of glaciers. Evidence of a dramatic global warming trend has been found in ice cores pulled from the both polar regions, satellite imagery of the shrinking polar ice masses, tree rings, ocean temperature monitoring, and so on.

Ralph Cicerone, President of the National Academy of Sciences stated during a U.S. House of Representatives hearing for the Committee on Energy and Commerce on July 27, 2006: "I think we understand the mechanisms of CO_2 and climate better than we do of what causes lung cancer . . . In fact, it is fair to say that global warming may be the most carefully and fully studied scientific topic in human history."[57] Similarly, Donald Kennedy, the editor of *Science,* has noted, "Consensus as strong as the one that has developed around [global warming] is rare in science."[58]

To get a sense of just how powerful the scientific consensus about global warming is, consider this: in a December 2004 article published in the journal *Science,* Naomi Oreskes, a historian of science at the University of California, San Diego, reviewed the peer-reviewed scientific literature for papers on global climate change published between 1993 and 2003. Oreskes reviewed a random sample of approximately 10 percent of the literature; of the 928 studies, *not one* disagreed with the consensus view that humans are contributing to global warming.[59]

Despite what ExxonMobil might try to tell you, today, in 2006, there is widespread agreement among credentialed climate scientists around the world that human-caused global warming is well under way. Without a concerted effort to curb heat-trapping emissions, it spells trouble for the health and well-being of our planet.

PART EIGHT

Work and Welfare

Americans pride themselves on their commitment to the "work ethic." And despite predictions in the 1950s and 1960s that we were on the verge of becoming a "leisure" society, work remains central to the lives of most of us. It is how, as adults, we make a living, define our identities, and find our place in the scheme of things. Ideally, work is one of the most important ways in which we are enabled to participate in a larger human community.

But the reality of work, for all too many people, has always fallen short of the ideal. In the nineteenth century, many social theorists and social critics argued that for the great bulk of people in the emerging industrial societies, work had become a source of torment and exploitation rather than fulfillment. Karl Marx, one of the most influential of those critics, put it this way:

> What constitutes the alienation of labour? First, that the work is *external* to the worker, that it is not part of his nature; and that, consequently, he does not fulfill himself in his work but denies himself, has a feeling of misery rather than well-being, does not develop freely his mental and physical energies but is physically exhausted and mentally debased. The worker, therefore, feels himself at home only during his leisure time, whereas at work he feels homeless. His work is not voluntary but imposed, *forced labour.* It is not satisfaction of a need, but only a *means* for satisfying other needs. Its alien character is clearly shown by the fact that as soon as there is no physical or other compulsion it is avoided like the plague.[1]

Today, in the twenty-first century, the concerns of the nineteenth-century critics have become, if anything, more urgent. An array of rapid economic and technological changes has made the link between work and well-being more and more problematic. The increasingly competitive global economy has put new strains on the institution of work—radically reshaping the workplace, eliminating jobs, and lowering incomes and benefits for many of those who do work steadily. While these changes have affected workers around the world, they have had an unusually destructive impact on *American* workers, who were once widely considered to be better off than their counterparts in Europe. Today the opposite is true. European workers are typically paid more, have longer vacations and shorter work-weeks, and enjoy a much more generous set of social benefits.

That helps explain why, as we've seen earlier, poverty is both broader and deeper in America than in most European countries. We are often told that the United States has become a high-tech economy in which most jobs require considerable education and skill and are rewarded accordingly. But the reality is less bright. Our economy has indeed produced many high-skill, high-wage jobs in recent years, but it has also produced a far greater number of low-level ones, paying only the minimum wage or a little above it. This means increased stress and hardship for growing numbers of American workers and their families; beyond that, it has undercut one of the basic tenets of the American ethos: the conviction that hard work will lead to economic security and personal fulfillment. For more and more Americans, that is only a dream.

Nowhere is this more true than for many of the immigrant workers who make up a growing part of the American labor force—often doing the least attractive, but crucial jobs on which the rest of the economy depends. We have exported many low-level (and increasingly some higher-level) jobs to the developing world, but we have also kept many of those jobs here at home, and "imported" many Third World workers to take them on. Some of those workers will surely move upward out of those jobs, as many did in the past. But many will not, because—as we've seen— upward mobility has become more difficult and less certain in today's economy. Meanwhile, along with their counterparts in other countries, they provide the steady flow of inexpensive goods and services that most Americans have come to expect, but at the cost of long hours and sharply limited opportunities. Pierette Hondagneu-Sotelo, in "Doméstica," illuminates the situation of one group of the working poor—the largely immigrant women working as domestic servants in private homes, who face a dispiriting combination of long hours, low pay, social isolation, and, all too frequently, poor treatment from the people who hire them.

If succeeding through work has become increasingly problematic for many of the "working poor," it is even more so for those with no work at all. As far back as the 1950s, many observers warned that the looming decline in manufacturing employment would have devastating consequences for the inner cities—already wracked by crime, drugs, and family disruption—if we failed to develop alternative ways to put people to work. For the most part, however, we didn't heed those warnings. The results are exactly what was predicted. Deindustrialization has laid waste to job prospects in the inner cities, bringing a corresponding—but hardly surprising— deepening of social problems in its wake.

The impact has been especially destructive for young minority men, as Peter Edelman, Harry Holzer, and Paul Offner show. Stunning proportions of those youth are neither in school nor at work, and their "disconnection" from the legitimate economy has persisted stubbornly in good times as well as bad. The raw figures on the numbers of disconnected youth are cold and abstract, but they translate into very real human consequences—hopelessness, crime, ill health, drug use, and incarceration. The cost of our failure to seriously address the plight of these young people is measured in stunted opportunities and shortened lives.

It might seem logical that we would have responded to this massive loss of jobs by creating new ones to take their place. For the most part, however, that is not what we did. One reason for our reluctance to invest directly in new jobs was the widespread belief that the lack of jobs wasn't the real problem; that, as it was often said, anybody could get a job if they really wanted one. Instead, many people blamed the stubborn unemployment, poverty, and related ills of the cities on the personal or cultural deficiencies of what has come to be called the "underclass." As Herbert Gans argues, labeling many of the poor—especially the jobless poor—as an intractable "underclass" serves to absolve the better-off from responsibility for their condition while emphasizing the moral and psychological failings of the poor themselves. Such labels, Gans suggests, may allow mainstream Americans to vent their anger and frustration at the poor, but they do not help us develop realistic ways of tackling the roots of poverty or joblessness.

The tendency to regard the problems of the jobless poor as, in effect, mainly their own fault has powerfully influenced our approach to providing support for the unemployed and marginally employed. Not only have we shied away from making a serious commitment to a strategy of full employment, but we have also been remarkably tightfisted in offering income benefits to those who cannot make a living through legitimate work. Indeed, by the 1980s it had become common to hear that the system we had established to help the casualties of economic insecurity—the welfare system—was itself the problem. Welfare, it was argued, caused joblessness and poverty by undermining the work ethic and encouraging people to become dependent on the "state" for survival. In fact, the provision of welfare in the United States had always been minimal by comparison with most other advanced industrial nations. But the belief that the welfare system was self-defeatingly generous has nevertheless prevailed in American social policy. In the 1990s, the nation embarked on a controversial welfare "reform" designed to get people off the welfare rolls and into jobs—without much concern about whether there were enough jobs available to accommodate them, at wages that could realistically support a family. But was the welfare system itself really the problem? Recent evidence on the effects of welfare reform suggests that though this policy did manage to move many people off of the welfare rolls, it was far less successful in moving them out of *poverty.*

Sharon Hays, in "Flat Broke with Children," dissects the limits of welfare reform as a strategy for ending poverty and shows compellingly that this policy has been nowhere near as successful as many people believe. And with the current economic downturn, the prospects for economic opportunity and security for low-income women with children have receded even further.

ENDNOTE

1. Quoted in Shlomo Avineri, *The Social and Political Thought of Karl Marx* (Cambridge, Eng.: Cambridge University Press, 1971), p. 106.

CHAPTER 26

Doméstica

Pierrette Hondagneu-Sotelo

I magine that you are a young woman, newly arrived in the United States. You are penniless—no, hugely in debt from making the trip—you do not speak English, and you are without a passport or any other legitimizing documents. Vilified in political campaigns as an "illegal," or simply scorned as a "Mexican," you live as a fugitive. You know only a distant cousin, a childhood friend, or perhaps an older brother whose wife is determined to cut your stay in their already-crowded apartment to a minimum. What do you do? You take a live-in job; or as the women say, *te encierras.* You lock yourself up. . . .

Who are these women who come to the United States in search of jobs, and what are those jobs like? Domestic work is organized in different ways, and in this chapter I describe live-in, live-out, and housecleaning jobs and profile some of the Latina immigrants who do them and how they feel about their work. . . .

LIVE-IN NANNY/HOUSEKEEPER JOBS

For Maribel Centeno, newly arrived from Guatemala City in 1989 at age twenty-two and without supportive family and friends with whom to stay, taking a live-in job made a lot of sense. She knew that she wouldn't have to spend money on room and board, and that she could soon begin saving to pay off her debts. Getting a live-in job through an agency was easy. The *señora,* in her rudimentary Spanish, only asked where she was from, and if she had a husband and children. Chuckling, Maribel recalled her initial misunderstanding when the *señora,* using her index forger, had drawn an imaginary "2" and "3" in the palm of her hand. "I thought to myself, well, she must have two or three bedrooms, so I said, fine. 'No,' she said. 'Really, really big.' She started counting, 'One, two, three, four . . . two-three rooms.' It was twenty-three rooms! I thought, *huy!* On a piece of paper, she wrote '$80 a week,' and she said, 'You, child, and entire house.' So I thought, well, I have to do what I have to do, and I happily said, 'Yes.'"

"I arrived on Monday at dawn," she recalled, "and I went to the job on Wednesday evening." When the *señora* and the child spoke to her, Maribel remembered "just laughing and feeling useless. I couldn't understand anything." On that first evening, the *señora* put on classical music, which Maribel quickly identified. "I said, 'Beethoven.' She said, 'Yeah,' and began asking me in English, 'You like it?' I said 'Yes,' or perhaps I said, '*Sí*,' and she began playing other cassettes, CDs. They had Richard Clayderman and I recognized it, and when I said that, she stopped in her tracks, her jaw fell open, and she just stared at me. She must have been thinking, 'No schooling, no preparation, no English, how does she know this music?' " But the *señora*, perhaps because of the language difficulty, or perhaps because she felt upstaged by her live-in's knowledge of classical music, never did ask. Maribel desperately wanted the *señora* to respect her, to recognize that she was smart, educated, and cultivated in the arts. In spite of her best status-signaling efforts, "They treated me," she said, "the same as any other girl from the countryside." She never got the verbal recognition that she desired from the *señora*.

Maribel summed up her experiences with her first live-in job this way: "The pay was bad. The treatment was, how shall I say? It was cordial, a little, uh, not racist, but with very little consideration, very little respect." She liked caring for the little seven-year-old boy, but keeping after the cleaning of the twenty-three-room house, filled with marble floors and glass tables, proved physically impossible. She eventually quit not because of the polishing and scrubbing, but because being ignored devastated her socially.

Compared to many other Latina immigrants' first live-in jobs, Maribel Centeno's was relatively good. She was not on call during all her waking hours and throughout the night, the parents were engaged with the child, and she was not required to sleep in a child's bedroom or on a cot tucked away in the laundry room. But having a private room filled with amenities did not mean she had privacy or the ability to do simple things one might take for granted. "I had my own room, with my own television, VCR, my private bath, and closet, and a kind of sitting room—but everything in miniature, Thumbelina style," she said. "I had privacy in that respect. But I couldn't do many things. If I wanted to walk around in a T-shirt, or just feel like I was home, I couldn't do that. If I was hungry in the evening, I wouldn't come out to grab a banana because I'd have to walk through the family room, and then everybody's watching and having to smell the banana. I could never feel at home, never. Never, never, never! There's always something invisible that tells you this is not your house, you just work here."

It is the rare California home that offers separate maid's quarters, but that doesn't stop families from hiring live-ins; nor does it stop newly arrived Latina migrant workers from taking jobs they urgently need. When live-ins cannot even retreat to their own rooms, work seeps into their sleep and their dreams. There is no time off from the job, and they say they feel confined, trapped, imprisoned.

"I lose a lot of sleep," said Margarita Gutiérrez, a twenty-four-year-old Mexicana who worked as a live-in nanny/housekeeper. At her job in a modest-sized condominium in Pasadena, she slept in a corner of a three-year-old child's bedroom. Consequently, she found herself on call day and night with the child, who sometimes went several days without seeing her mother because of the latter's schedule at an insurance company. Margarita was obliged to be on her job twenty-four hours a day; and like other live-in nanny/housekeepers I interviewed, she claimed that she could scarcely find time to shower or brush her teeth. "I go to bed fine," she reported, "and then I wake up at two or three in the morning with the girl asking for water, or food." After the child went back to sleep, Margarita would lie awake, thinking about how to leave her job but finding it hard to even walk out into the kitchen. Live-in employees like Margarita literally have no space and no time they can claim as their own.

Working in a larger home or staying in plush, private quarters is no guarantee of privacy or refuge from the job. Forty-four-year-old Elvia Lucero worked as a live-in at a sprawling, canyon-side residence, where she was in charge of looking after twins, two five-year-old girls. On numerous occasions when I visited her there, I saw that she occupied her own bedroom, a beautifully decorated one outfitted with delicate antiques, plush white carpet, and a stenciled border of pink roses painstakingly painted on the wall by the employer. It looked serene and inviting, but it was only three steps away from the twins' room. Every night one of the twins crawled into bed with Elvia. Elvia disliked this, but said she couldn't break the girl of the habit. And the parents' room lay tucked away at the opposite end of the large (more than 3,000 square feet), L-shaped house.

Regardless of the size of the home and the splendor of the accommodations, the boundaries that we might normally take for granted disappear in live-in jobs. They have, as Evelyn Nakano Glenn has noted, "no clear line between work and non-work time," and the line between job space and private space is similarly blurred.[1] Live-in nanny/housekeepers are at once socially isolated and surrounded by other people's territory; during the hours they remain on the employers' premises, their space, like their time, belongs to another. The sensation of being among others while remaining invisible, unknown and apart, of never being able to leave the margins, makes many live-in employees sad, lonely, and depressed. Melancholy sets in and doesn't necessarily lift on the weekends.

Rules and regulations may extend around the clock. Some employers restrict the ability of their live-in employees to receive telephone calls, entertain friends, attend evening ESL classes, or see boyfriends during the workweek. Other employers do not impose these sorts of restrictions, but because their homes are located on remote hillsides, in suburban enclaves, or in gated communities, their live-in nanny/housekeepers are effectively kept away from anything resembling social life or public culture. A Spanish-language radio station, or maybe a *telenovela*, may serve as their only link to the outside world.

Food—the way some employers hoard it, waste it, deny it, or just simply do not even have any of it in their kitchens—is a frequent topic of discussion among Latina live-in nanny/housekeepers. These women are talking not about counting calories but about the social meaning of food on the job. Almost no one works with a written contract, but anyone taking a live-in job that includes "room and board" would assume that adequate meals will be included. But what constitutes an adequate meal? Everyone has a different idea, and using the subject like a secret handshake, Latina domestic workers often greet one another by talking about the problems of managing food and meals on the job. Inevitably, food enters their conversations.

No one feels the indignities of food more deeply than do live-in employees, who may not leave the job for up to six days at a time. For them, the workplace necessarily becomes the place of daily sustenance. In some of the homes where they work, the employers are out all day. When these adults return home, they may only snack, keeping on hand little besides hot dogs, packets of macaroni and cheese, cereal, and peanut butter for the children. Such foods are considered neither nutritious nor appetizing by Latina immigrants, many of whom are accustomed to sitting down to meals prepared with fresh vegetables, rice, beans, and meat. In some employers' homes, the cupboards are literally bare. Gladys Villedas recalled that at one of her live-in jobs, the *señora* had graciously said, " 'Go ahead, help yourself to anything in the kitchen.' But at times," she recalled, "there was nothing, nothing in the refrigerator! There was nothing to eat!" Even in lavish kitchens outfitted with Subzero refrigerators and imported cabinetry, food may be scarce. A celebrity photographer of luxury homes that appear in posh magazines described to a reporter what he sees when he opens the doors of some of Beverly Hills' refrigerators: "Rows of cans of Diet Coke, and maybe a few remains of pizza."[2]

Further down the class ladder, some employers go to great lengths to economize on food bills. Margarita Gutiérrez claimed that at her live-in job, the husband did the weekly grocery shopping, but he bought things in small quantities—say, two potatoes that would be served in half portions, or a quarter of a watermelon to last a household of five all week. He rationed out the bottled water and warned her that milk would make her fat. Lately, she said, he was taking both her and the children to an upscale grocery market where they gave free samples of gourmet cheeses, breads, and dips, urging them all to fill up on the freebies. "I never thought," exclaimed Margarita, formerly a secretary in Mexico City, "that I would come to this country to experience hunger!"

Many women who work as live-ins are keenly aware of how food and meals underline the boundaries between them and the families for whom they work. "I never ate with them," recalled Maribel Centeno of her first live-in job. "First of all, she never said, 'Come and join us,' and secondly, I just avoided being around when they were about to eat." Why did she avoid mealtime? "I didn't feel I was part of that family. I knew they liked me, but only because of the good work I did, and because of the affection I showered on the boy; but apart from that, I was just like the gardener, like the pool man, just one more of their staff." Sitting down to share a meal symbolizes membership in a family, and Latina employees, for the most part, know they are not just like one of the family.

Food scarcity is not endemic to all of the households where these women work. In some homes, ample quantities of fresh fruits, cheeses, and chicken stock the kitchens. Some employer families readily share all of their food, but in other households, certain higher-quality, expensive food items may remain off-limits to the live-in employees, who are instructed to eat hot dogs with the children. One Latina live-in nanny/housekeeper told me that in her employers' substantial pantry, little "DO NOT TOUCH" signs signaled which food items were not available to her; and another said that her employer was always defrosting freezer-burned leftovers for her to eat, some of it dating back nearly a decade.

Other women felt subtle pressure to remain unobtrusive, humble, and self-effacing, so they held back from eating even when they were hungry. They talked a lot about how these unspoken rules apply to fruit. "Look, if they [the employers] buy fruit, they buy three bananas, two apples, two pears. So if I eat one, who took it? It's me," one woman said, "they'll know it's me." Another nanny/housekeeper recalled: "They would bring home fruit, but without them having to say it, you just knew these were not intended for you. You understand this right away, you get it." Or as another put it, "*Las Americanas* have their apples counted out, one for each day of the week." Even fruits growing in the garden are sometimes contested. In Southern California's agriculture-friendly climate, many a residential home boasts fruit trees that hang heavy with oranges, plums, and peaches, and when the Latina women who work in these homes pick the fruit, they sometimes get in trouble.[3] Eventually, many of the women solve the food problem by buying and bringing in their own food; early on Monday mornings, you see them walking with their plastic grocery bags, carting, say, a sack of apples, some chicken, and maybe some prepared food in plastic containers.

The issue of food captures the essence of how Latina live-in domestic workers feel about their jobs. It symbolizes the extent to which the families they work for draw the boundaries of exclusion or inclusion, and it marks the degree to which those families recognize the live-in nanny/housekeepers as human beings who have basic human needs. When they first take their jobs, most live-in nanny/housekeepers do not anticipate spending any of their meager wages on food to eat while on the job, but in the end, most do—and sometimes the food they buy is eaten by members of the family for whom they work.

Although there is a wide range of pay, many Latina domestic workers in live-in jobs earn less than minimum wage for marathon hours: 93 percent of the live-in workers I surveyed in the mid-1990s were earning less than $5 an hour (79 percent of them below minimum wage, which was then $4.25), and they reported working an average of sixty-four hours a week.[4] Some of the most astounding low rates were paid for live-in jobs in the households of other working-class Latino immigrants, which provide some women their first job when they arrive in Los Angeles. Carmen Vasquez, for example, had spent several years working as a live-in for two Mexican families, earning only $50 a week. By comparison, her current salary of $170 a week, which she was earning as a live-in nanny/housekeeper in the hillside home of an attorney and a teacher, seemed a princely sum.

Many people assume that the rich pay more than do families of modest means, but working as a live-in in an exclusive, wealthy neighborhood, or in a twenty-three-room house, provides no guarantee of a high salary. Early one Monday morning in the fall of 1995, I was standing with a group of live-in nanny/housekeepers on a corner across the street from the Beverly Hills Hotel.

As they were waiting to be picked up by their employers, a large Mercedes sedan with two women (a daughter and mother or mother-in-law?) approached, rolled down the windows, and asked if anyone was interested in a $150-a-week live-in job. A few women jotted down the phone number, and no one was shocked by the offer. Gore Vidal once commented that no one is allowed to fail within a two-mile radius of the Beverly Hills Hotel, but it turns out that plenty of women in that vicinity are failing in the salary department. In some of the most affluent Westside areas of Los Angeles—in Malibu, Pacific Palisades, and Bel Air—there are live-in nanny/housekeepers earning $150 a week. And in 1999, the *Los Angeles Times* Sunday classified ads still listed live-in nanny/housekeeper jobs with pay as low as $100 and $125.[5] Salaries for live-in jobs, however, do go considerably higher. The best-paid live-in employee whom I interviewed was Patricia Paredes, a Mexicana who spoke impeccable English and who had legal status, substantial experience, and references. She told me that she currently earned $450 a week at her live-in job. She had been promised a raise to $550, after a room remodel was finished, when she would assume weekend housecleaning in that same home. With such a relatively high weekly salary she felt compelled to stay in a live-in job during the week, away from her husband and three young daughters who remained on the east side of Los Angeles. The salary level required that sacrifice.

But once they experience it, most women are repelled by live-in jobs. The lack of privacy, the mandated separation from family and friends, the round-the-clock hours, the food issues, the low pay, and especially the constant loneliness prompt most Latina immigrants to seek other job arrangements. Some young, single women who learn to speak English fluently try to move up the ranks into higher-paying live-in jobs. As soon as they can, however, the majority attempt to leave live-in work altogether. Most live-in nanny/housekeepers have been in the United States for five years or less; among the live-in nanny/housekeepers I interviewed, only two (Carmen Vasquez and the relatively high-earning Patricia Paredes) had been in the United States for longer than that. Like African American women earlier in the century, who tired of what the historian Elizabeth Clark-Lewis has called "the soul-destroying hollowness of live-in domestic work,"[6] most Latina immigrants try to find other options.

Until the early 1900s, live-in jobs were the most common form of paid domestic work in the United States, but through the first half of the twentieth century they were gradually supplanted by domestic "day work."[7] Live-in work never completely disappeared, however, and in the last decades of the twentieth century, it revived with vigor, given new life by the needs of American families with working parents and young children—and, as we have seen, by the needs of newly arrived Latina immigrants, many of them unmarried and unattached to families. When these women try to move up from live-in domestic work, they see few job alternatives. Often, the best they can do is switch to another form of paid domestic work, either as a live-out nanny/housekeeper or as a weekly housecleaner. When they do such day work, they are better able to circumscribe their work hours, and they earn more money in less time.[8] . . .

JOB STRUCTURES

Live-in and live-out nanny/housekeepers find that the spatial and social isolation of the job intensifies their craving for personal contact. Typically they work for only one employer, and spend each day at the home of the same family. With the exception of those hired by very high income families who simultaneously employ several domestic workers, they generally have no co-workers with whom to speak. The job is, as one employer conceded, "a lonesome one." Nanny/housekeepers may be alone for most of the day, or they may spend the entire day with infants. If they are lucky, they may meet up for an hour or two with a group of nannies at a public park, or on arranged play dates.

Nanny/housekeepers with live-in jobs are the most isolated. They work long hours—on average, more than sixty hours a week—leaving the employer's home only on Saturday afternoons, when they retreat to a shared apartment or a rented room until Monday morning. During the rest of the week, they remain confined to their work site. Without anyone to speak with day after day, many of them become emotionally distraught and depressed. It is little wonder that they often seek more personalistic relations with the only adults they see, their employers.

Erlinda Castro, a middle-aged Guatemalan woman and mother of five, had spent three years working as a live-in housekeeper in three different households before finally establishing her route of weekly housecleaning jobs. In the first of her live-in jobs, she worked for a family whom she described as good employers, because they paid her what she had expected to earn and because they did not pile on an unreasonable number of duties. The school-age children were gone for most of the day, and her job tasks seemed fair and physically manageable. The employers did not criticize her work, and they never insulted or yelled at her. Unlike many other live-ins, she had her own room and there was food for her to eat. Yet Erlinda found her employers cold and impersonal, unresponsive to her attempts to engage them in conversation; and she told me that their aloofness drove her out of the job.

"I would greet the *señora*, 'Good morning, *señora* Judy,' " she recalled. "They spoke a little Spanish, but the *señor* never spoke. If I greeted him, maybe in between his teeth he would mutter, 'Heh,' just like that. That's how one is often treated, and it feels cruel. You leave your own home, leaving everything behind only to find hostility. You're useful to them only because you clean, wash, iron, cook—that's the only reason. There is no affection. There is nothing." She expected some warmth and affection, but instead she found a void. Erlinda Castro entered the home of these employers directly after leaving her home and five children in Guatemala. On weekends she visited with her husband, whom she had joined in Los Angeles. It was her first experience with paid domestic work, and although she was not put off by the pay, the job tasks, or the low status of the job, the impersonal treatment became intolerable. "I felt bad, really bad. I couldn't go on with that, with nothing more than, 'Good morning, *señora*' and, 'Good night, *señora*.' Nothing else. They would say nothing, nothing, absolutely nothing to me! They would only speak to me to give me orders." Erlinda stayed on that job for approximately one year, leaving it for another live-in job that a friend had told her about.

Being treated as though one is invisible is a complaint commonly voiced by domestic workers of color working for white employers. As the historian David Katzman has noted in his study of the occupation in the South, "One peculiar and most degrading aspect of domestic service was the requisite of invisibility. The ideal servant . . . would be invisible and silent[,] . . . sensitive to the moods and whims of those around them, but undemanding of family warmth, love or security."[9] In her early 1980s ethnographic research, for which she posed as a housecleaner, Judith Rollins revealed a telling moment: an employer and her teenage son conducted an entire conversation about personal issues in her presence. "This situation was," Rollins wrote in her field notes, "the most peculiar feeling of the day: being there and not being there."[10] At different times, African American, Japanese American, and Chicana domestic workers in the United States have had the same disturbing experience.[11]

Some domestic workers see personalism as the antidote to these indignities and humiliations. Verbal interaction affords them respect and recognition on the job. Elvira Areola, a Mexicana, had worked for eleven years for one family. I interviewed her several days after an acrimonious fight with her employer—a disagreement that became physical—had left her jobless and without an income. As a single mother, she found herself in a frightening position. Still, she expressed no regrets, partly because the almost completely nonverbal relationship that she had maintained for several years with the *patrona* had been so strained. Her female employer had not worked and was physically present in the home, yet they hardly interacted. "I would arrive [in the morning] and sometimes she wouldn't greet me until two in the afternoon. . . . I'd be in the kitchen, and she'd walk in but wouldn't say anything. She would ignore me, as if to say, 'I'm alone in my house and there's no one else here.' Sometimes she wouldn't speak to me the whole day . . . she'd act as if I was a chair, a table, as if her house was supposedly all clean without me being there." Her dissatisfaction with the lack of appreciation and verbal recognition was echoed in the accounts of many other women.

ENDNOTES

1. Glenn 1986:141.
2. Lacher 1997:E1.
3. One nanny/housekeeper told me that a *señora* had admonished her for picking a bag of fruit, and wanted to charge her for it; another claimed that her employer had said she would rather watch the fruit fall off the branches and rot than see her eat it.
4. Many Latina domestic workers do not know the amount of their hourly wages; and because the lines between their work and nonwork tend to blur, live-in nanny/housekeepers have particular difficulty calculating them. In the survey questionnaire I asked live-in nanny/housekeepers how many days a week they worked, what time they began their job, and what time they ended, and I asked them to estimate how many hours off they had during an average workday (39 percent said they had no time off, but 32 percent said they had a break of between one and three hours). Forty-seven percent of the women said they began their workday at 7 A.M. or earlier, with 62 percent ending their workday at 7 P.M. or later. With

the majority of them (71 percent) working five days a week, their average workweek was sixty-four hours. This estimate may at first glance appear inflated; but consider a prototypical live-in nanny/housekeeper who works, say, five days a week, from 7 A.M. until 9 P.M., with one and a half hours off during the children's nap time (when she might take a break to lie down or watch television). Her on-duty work hours would total sixty-four and a half hours per week. The weekly pay of live-in nanny/housekeepers surveyed ranged from $130 to $400, averaging $242. Dividing this figure by sixty-four yields an hourly wage of $3.80. None of the live-in nanny/housekeepers were charged for room and board—this practice is regulated by law—but 86 percent said they brought food with them to their jobs. The majority reported being paid in cash.

5. See, e.g., Employment Classified Section 2, *Los Angeles Times,* June 6, 1999, G9.

6. Clark-Lewis 1994:123. "After an average of seven years," she notes in her analysis of African American women who had migrated from the South to Washington, D.C., in the early twentieth century, "all of the migrant women grew to dread their live-in situation. They saw their occupation as harming all aspects of their life" (124). Nearly all of these women transitioned into day work in private homes. This pattern is being repeated by Latina immigrants in Los Angeles today, and it reflects local labor market opportunities and constraints. In Houston, Texas, where many Mayan Guatemalan immigrant women today work as live-ins, research by Jacqueline Maria Hagan (1998) points to the tremendous obstacles they face in leaving live-in work. In Houston, housecleaning is dominated by better-established immigrant women, by Chicanas and, more recently, by the commercial cleaning companies—so it is hard for the Maya to secure those jobs. Moreover, Hagan finds that over time, the Mayan women who take live-in jobs see their own social networks contract, further reducing their internal job mobility.

7. Several factors explain the shift to day work, including urbanization, interurban transportation systems, and smaller private residences. Historians have also credited the job preferences of African American domestic workers, who rejected the constraints of live-in work and chose to live with their own families and communities, with helping to promote this shift in the urban North after 1900 (Katzman 1981; Clark-Lewis 1994:129–35). In many urban regions of the United States, the shift to day work accelerated during World War I, so that live-out arrangements eventually became more prevalent (Katzman 1981; Palmer 1989). Elsewhere, and for different groups of domestic workers, these transitions happened later in the twentieth century. Evelyn Nakano Glenn (1986:143) notes that Japanese immigrant and Japanese American women employed in domestic work in the San Francisco Bay Area moved out of live-in jobs and into modernized day work in the years after World War II.

8. Katzman 1981; Glenn 1986.

9. Katzman 1981:188.

10. Rollins 1985:208.

11. Rollins 1985; Glenn 1986; Romero 1992; Dill 1994.

CHAPTER 27

Reconnecting Disadvantaged Young Men

Peter Edelman
Harry J. Holzer
Paul Offner

By several recent counts, the United States is home to 2 to 3 million youth age 16 through 24 who are without postsecondary education and "disconnected" from the worlds of school and work (Wald and Martinez 2003). By "disconnected," we mean young people who are not in school and have been out of work for a substantial period, roughly a year or more.[1] Among young minority men, and especially African-American men, the facts are particularly disturbing. For instance,

- as few as 20 percent of black teens are employed at any time;
- among young black men age 16 through 24 not enrolled in school, only about half are working; and
- roughly one-third of all young black men are involved with the criminal justice system at any time (awaiting trial, in prison or jail, or on probation or parole), and a similar percentage will spend some time in prison or jail during the course of their lives.[2]

Why are so many young people "disconnected" from the worlds of school and work, and what can public policy do about it? . . .

SOME STATISTICS ABOUT YOUTH IDLENESS

We begin with evidence on enrollment, employment, and idleness. Several authors have recently provided detailed accounts of the youth population's characteristics (e.g., Sum 2003; Wald and Martinez 2003). Rather than reproducing their results, we highlight some facts that shed light on particular dimensions of the youth problem and what we (as a society) might do about it.

We define youth as those age 16 through 24.[3] We present data from the Current Population Survey (CPS), the monthly household survey administered by

TABLE 27.1   School Enrollment and Employment Rates for Youth Age 16 to 24, 1999

	Men (%)			Women (%)		
	White	*Black*	*Hispanic*	*White*	*Black*	*Hispanic*
Civilian noninstitutional population						
Enrolled	49.0	47.6	36.6	50.8	46.5	38.6
Secondary school	25.3	28.1	23.8	23.4	25.0	22.2
Postsecondary or other school	23.7	19.6	12.8	27.4	21.5	16.4
Employed and not enrolled in school	42.3	29.6	50.6	35.9	31.9	32.6
Idle	8.7	22.8	12.8	13.3	21.6	28.8
Civilian noninstitutional population and incarcerated population[a]						
Enrolled	48.5	44.1	35.6	50.8	46.1	38.6
Secondary school	25.1	26.0	23.1	23.4	24.8	22.2
Postsecondary or other school	23.4	18.1	12.5	27.4	21.3	16.4
Employed and not enrolled in school	41.8	27.4	49.1	35.9	31.6	32.6
Idle	9.6	28.5	15.3	13.3	22.4	28.8

a. CPS calculations were supplemented with summary data on youth incarceration rates available from the Bureau of Justice Statistics at the U.S. Department of Justice.

Source: Bureau of the Census, Current Population Survey (1999).

the federal government to 60,000 households and used to compute unemployment rates and other statistics.[4] As a survey of households, the CPS focuses on those not in the institutional population—it omits those who are incarcerated or enlisted in the military. As the former have become a growing segment of the youth population, we adjust some of our numbers below to account for differences across groups in incarceration rates.[5]

In Table 27.1, we present data on youths' school enrollment and employment in 1999, one of the last years of the 1990s economic boom.[6] We present the fractions of all youth who are enrolled in school (secondary versus postsecondary education), employed but not enrolled, and "idle." We do so separately by race/ethnicity and gender.

- *Employment rates among young African-American men lag dramatically behind those of white and even Hispanic men. Their rates of idleness are dramatically higher as well, especially when we account for those who are incarcerated.*
- *Postsecondary enrollment rates are now higher among women than men in each racial/ethnic group. A "gender gap" has thus developed in educational attainment that favors young women over young men. Employment rates among*

*young black women also exceed those observed among young black men—even
though many of these young women have childrearing responsibilities.*
- *Hispanic youth are enrolled in school, especially postsecondary school, at much
  lower rates than white or black youth. And postsecondary enrollments among
  African Americans lag behind those of whites (as do high school graduations,
  though the data in the table do not indicate the latter).[7]*

In Table 27.2, we present idleness rates, once again for 1999, but this time we
focus on youth who, at the time of the survey, had been idle for at least the entire
previous year. These are the youth we define as "disconnected" for this book. This
distinction is important, since temporary idleness is frequently observed among
youth and has far less negative longer-term consequences than does long-term
idleness. In addition, we consider the marital status and childrearing behavior of
those who are idle for a longer period; parenting might account for a lack of
schooling and employment among some, especially young single mothers. We
also present separate rates of long-term idleness for the civilian noninstitutional
population—the group on which most published statistics for education and employment are based—and for a broader group that also includes those who are
incarcerated.

The results show that full-year idleness, or disconnectedness, rates are somewhat lower than those shown in table Table 27.1. Still, 10 percent of young black
men and 9 percent of young Hispanic men in the civilian noninstitutional population are idle each year by this measure. These idleness rates for young black and
Hispanic men rise substantially—to 17 percent and 12 percent, respectively—when
we include those who are incarcerated in the population. Furthermore, in this category, long-term idleness rates are lower for young women—around 10 percent for
both blacks and Hispanics—than for men in both minority groups. Also, among the

TABLE 27.2   Idleness Rates for Youth Age 16 to 24, 1999

	Men (%)			Women (%)		
	White	*Black*	*Hispanic*	*White*	*Black*	*Hispanic*
Civilian noninstitutional population						
Disconnected (idle for						
at least one year)	3.2	10.5	9.3	7.1	9.0	10.4
Married parent	0.2	...	0.3	3.1	0.3	3.1
Single parent	...	...	...	1.3	3.2	0.6
Not married, no children	3.0	10.5	9.0	2.8	5.4	6.8
Civilian noninstitutional and incarcerated population						
Disconnected (idle for						
at least one year)	4.2	17.1	11.9	7.1	9.9	10.4

Source: Bureau of the Census, March Current Population Survey (2000).

noninstitutional population of continuingly idle young women, more than one-third of blacks and Hispanics are parents. In contrast, virtually none of the idle men in any racial or ethnic group are married or has custody of a child.

In other words, *more than one out of six young black men, and nearly one out of eight young Hispanic men, experience long-term idleness without any major child-rearing responsibilities*. No doubt many of these young men are active in the casual or "underground" economy, engaged in either legal or illegal pursuits for income. But, if we define productive work as officially reported, steady employment, large fractions of young minority men are forgoing productive work as well as schooling. And the idleness rates have surely been even higher during the labor market downturn of 2001 to 2004.[8]

Although young whites experience much lower rates of long-term idleness than do minorities (at 4 percent of their total populations for men and 7 percent for women), whites also account for a much larger percentage of the overall population. Thus, though the incidence of long-term idleness within the white youth community is much lower than among minorities, *young whites also account for a significant percentage of the overall total.*[9]

How have school enrollment and employment rates among different groups of youth changed over time? In Table 27.3, the data show that

- employment rates stayed constant for less-educated young white and Hispanic men, but declined precipitously for young black men in the 1990s;
- employment rates rose for less-educated young women, especially black women; and
- enrollment rates have been rising for all groups of youth, but especially white and black women.[10]

TABLE 27.3   School Enrollment and Employment Rates for Less-Educated Youth Age 16 to 24, 1989 and 1999

	Men (%)			Women (%)		
	White	*Black*	*Hispanic*	*White*	*Black*	*Hispanic*
1989						
Enrolled in school	35.6	38.3	25.9	32.9	32.2	26.6
Employed among those						
not enrolled in school	80.2	59.3	77.7	64.1	40.4	44.1
1999						
Enrolled in school	47.3	46.0	34.3	50.1	44.2	34.6
Employed among those						
not enrolled in school	80.0	50.0	78.4	64.8	52.3	47.4

Source: Bureau of the Census, Current Population Survey (1989, 1990).

Note: Sample includes all youth age 16 to 24 who have at most a high school diploma.

The decline in employment among young African-American men is particularly troubling, given that their rates of employment already lagged behind those of white and Hispanic men by about 20 percentage points at the end of the 1980s. By the end of the 1990s, this gap had grown to about 30 percentage points. As noted earlier, employment rates among less-educated young black men now lag behind those of black women, even though the latter more often have significant custodial responsibilities. The gap would be considerably wider if the incarcerated were included in these calculations.

And, perhaps most troubling, the declining employment rates of young black men occurred despite the stunning boom in the U.S. economy in the latter half of the 1990s. Indeed, labor markets were considerably tighter in 1999 than they had been in 1989, even though both years were business cycle peaks.

These results seem to suggest that less-educated African Americans are now unaffected by the business cycle, but this is not the case. Historically, blacks have been more severely impacted by economic downturns and more positively affected by recoveries than any other major group. In fact, both Sum (2003) and Holzer and Offner (2002) find that this continues to be the case. Furthermore, Holzer and Offner (2002) find that every percentage-point increase in the local unemployment rate reduces the employment rates of young black men by nearly 3 percentage points. Unfortunately for young black men, the positive effects of the business cycle in the 1990s were swamped by a downward trend in employment that has been ongoing for several decades but seemed to accelerate in the 1980s. Had it not been for the strong economy at the end of the 1990s, young black men's observed employment rates would simply have been that much worse.[11]

The growing gap in employment rates between young black and Hispanic men is quite noteworthy, especially given the lower school enrollment (and presumably completion) rates we find among the latter. But Hispanics in the U.S. are an extremely heterogeneous group that includes the foreign-born as well as natives and also encompasses a wide range of national origins. In Table 27.4 we present enrollment and employment rates among less-educated young Hispanics (again, with a high school diploma or less) according to whether they are foreign- or native-born and country of origin among the former.

The results show that foreign-born Hispanics' school enrollment and employment are different from those of their native-born counterparts. The foreign-born are much less likely to be enrolled in school; and the men are more likely to be employed, while the women are less likely to be employed than their native-born counterparts. This is consistent with traditional family patterns among immigrants in which men work at high rates while women rear children exclusively.

But, even among the foreign-born, wide variations exist in enrollment and employment rates. For instance, rates of employment are highest among men from Mexico and lowest among men from Puerto Rico. Indeed, it has been noted elsewhere (e.g., Borjas 1996) that employment rates among the latter group are not dramatically higher than those of blacks, while Mexican-American employment rates are considerably higher. Differing outcomes among Hispanic men by nativity and

TABLE 27.4   School Enrollment and Employment Rates for Less-Educated Hispanic Youth Age 16 to 24, 1999

	Foreign-born (%)					Native-born (%)
	Puerto Rican	*Mexican*	*Cuban*	*Other*	*All*	*All*
Enrolled in school						
Men	18.7	16.1	31.7	23.6	18.2	38.2
Women	14.3	14.6	—	17.4	15.3	37.4
Employed among those not enrolled in school						
Men	49.7	75.4	—	66.0	71.6	60.3
Women	16.9	29.6	52.9	51.3	35.8	44.3

Source: Bureau of the Census, March Current Population Survey (2002).

national origin must be kept in mind as we consider policies aimed at youth who are not enrolled in school or employed.

Finally, what do these varying enrollment rates imply about differences in overall educational attainment and associated labor market outcomes? In Table 27.5, we present employment rates and real hourly wages for young white, black, and Hispanic young men not enrolled in school, separately by educational attainment for each group.

The results show quite dramatic differences in employment and earnings outcomes between educational groups, and, with some exceptions, a strong positive correlation between employment and earnings. Employment rates of young black men lag behind those of both whites and Hispanics at every educational level, but the results among high school dropouts are quite stunning. Indeed, *just over a third of young black male dropouts are employed*—a figure that falls below one-third when the incarcerated are included.[12] Real wages of young black men, as well, are less than those of Hispanics and whites within each group, except among college graduates.

The data in Table 27.5 also indicate the real cost to young Hispanic men of their relatively low rates of school enrollment and completion. Clearly, Hispanics work at much higher rates than do young blacks; the exact reasons are explored below. They also earn wages fairly comparable to those of young whites *within* each educational category. But young Hispanics' overall labor market outcomes suffer as a result of their much greater concentration in the categories of low educational attainment. The earnings gaps between Hispanics and whites will also grow over time, considering college graduates' earnings grow with experience more than high school graduates' or dropouts' do (e.g., Filer, Hamermesh, and Rees 1996).

TABLE 27.5   Employment Rates and Wages for Young Men Age 16 to 24 Not Enrolled in School, 1999

	White	Black	Hispanic
Employed (%)			
Less than high school	58.2	36.2	55.9
High school	80.0	65.2	75.0
Some college	83.5	81.1	82.7
College degree or more	92.3	77.8	95.9
Real hourly wages ($)			
Less than high school	7.29	6.58	7.03
High school	8.23	7.54	8.66
Some college	8.56	7.11	8.49
College degree or more	10.51	11.37	10.09

Source: Bureau of the Census, March Current Population Survey (2000).

Note: Hourly wages are in 1999 dollars.

Overall, what do these statistics tell us about idle, less-educated youth? We find that the trends for young women are quite positive—their rates of school enrollment and employment are rising. In fact, their rates of enrollment in postsecondary schools now exceed those of young men in each racial or ethnic group, especially among blacks and Hispanics. Of course, at least part of the traditional male-female gaps in employment and earnings remain, but they have narrowed for all groups; however, employment rates are actually higher, and idleness rates lower, among young African-American women than among young African-American men, even though substantial fractions of the women have childrearing responsibilities.

In contrast, employment rates among young African-American men are falling further behind those of white and Hispanic men (as well as black women), especially when we account for trends in incarceration. Young Hispanic men also have somewhat high rates of long-term idleness; and, though employment rates for less-educated young Hispanic men are fairly high relative to other less-educated men, their low rates of educational attainment imply low earnings over their lifetimes. And even young white men have small but significant rates of idleness, which account for considerable fractions of idle youth nationwide. . . .

THE MANY COSTS OF YOUNG MEN'S DISCONNECTION

For young men who disconnect from school and work, the price they pay over the course of their lives, in terms of lost employment and earnings, will be very large. A lack of education will diminish their earnings, while a lack of early work experience will feed into future wage and employment losses.[33]

But young men's disconnection also imposes large costs on others. Those who engage in crime and are incarcerated impose large public safety costs on their communities. State corrections budgets have grown dramatically since the 1990s, while the absence of employment for ex-offenders imposes an economic cost on the nation. Indeed, Freeman (1996) has estimated that these two components of crime together cost the U.S. up to 4 percent of gross domestic product, which would now amount to over $400 billion annually.

The cost to families and children of fathers who are uninvolved and contribute little financially to their families is also high. Poor employment prospects among young men help account for their low marriage rates (Blau, Kahn, and Waidfogel 2000; Ellwood and Jencks 2004; Wilson 1996), which in turn contribute to the high poverty rates of children in single-parent families (McLanahan and Sandefur 1994). Poor work incentives for low-income noncustodial fathers also reduce their ability to provide financial support, and perhaps emotional support and involvement as well (Mincy 2002).

Finally, the loss of employment among disconnected young men—both today and over the course of their lives—will reduce the nation's labor force and ultimately its economic output and income. This will be particularly true when labor markets are tight and employers have difficulty finding workers, which will occur more frequently after baby boomers begin retiring in a few years.

Editors' Note: *Notes for this reading can be found in the original source.*

CHAPTER 28

The Underclass Label

Herbert J. Gans

One of America's popular pejorative labels is "slum," which characterizes low-income dwellings and neighborhoods as harmful to their poor occupants and the rest of the community. In the nineteenth century, slums were openly faulted for turning the deserving poor into the undeserving poor, but in the twentieth century the causality was sometimes reversed, so that poor people with "slum-dweller hearts" were accused of destroying viable buildings and neighborhoods.

After World War II, "slum" and "slum dweller" as well as "blight" all became more or less official labels when the federal government, egged on by a variety of builder and realty pressure groups, started handing out sizeable sums for the "clearance" of low-income neighborhoods unfortunate enough to fit these terms as they were defined in the 1949 U.S. Housing Act. Although by and large only slums located in areas where private enterprise could build luxury and other profitable housing were torn down, more than a million poor households lost their homes in the next twenty years, with almost nothing done for the people displaced from them.

This chapter is written with that much-told history in mind, in order to suggest that the underclass label—as well as all but the most neutrally formulated behavioral term—can have dangerous effects for the poor and for antipoverty policy. While the emphasis will be on "underclass," the dangers of related labels will be discussed as well.

Labels may be only words, but they are judgmental or normative words, which can stir institutions and individuals to punitive actions. The dangers from such labels are many, but the danger common to all behavioral labels and terms is that they focus on behavior that hides the poverty causing it, and substitutes as its cause moral or cultural or genetic failures.

"THE UNDERCLASS" AS CODE WORD

The term "underclass" has developed an attention-getting power that constitutes its first danger. The word has a technical aura that enables it to serve as a euphemism or code word to be used for labeling. Users of the label can thus hide their disapproval of the poor behind an impressively academic term. "Underclass" has also become morally ambiguous, and as it is often left undefined, people can understand it in any way they choose, including as a label.

Because "underclass" is a code word that places some of the poor *under* society and implies that they are not or should not be *in* society, users of the term can therefore favor excluding them from the rest of society without saying so. Once whites thought of slaves, "primitives," and wartime enemies as the inhuman "other," but placing some people under society may not be altogether different.

A subtler yet in some ways more insidious version of the exclusionary mechanism is the use of "underclass" as a synonym for the poor, deserving and undeserving. While not excluding anyone from society, it increases the social distance of the poor from everyone else. This distance is increased further by the contemporary tendency of elected officials and journalists to rename and upgrade the working class as the lower middle class—or even the middle class.

Because "underclass" is also used as a racial and even ethnic code word, it is a convenient device for hiding antiblack or anti-Latino feelings. As such a code word, "underclass" accommodates contemporary taboos against overt prejudice, not to mention hate speech. Such taboos sometimes paper over—and even repress—racial antagonisms that people do not want to express openly.

Ironically, the racial code word also hides the existence of very poor whites who suffer from many of the same problems as poor blacks. When used as a racial term, "underclass" blurs the extent to which the troubles of whites and blacks alike are generated by the economy and by classism or class discrimination and require class-based as well as race-based solutions.

Like other code words, "underclass" may interfere with public discussion. Disapproval of the actions of others is part of democracy, but code words make covert what needs to be overt in order for the disapproval to be questioned and debated. If openly critical terms such as "bums" and "pauper" were still in use, and if umbrella terms such as "underclass" were replaced with specific ones such as "beggars" or "welfare dependents," upset citizens could indicate clearly the faults of which they want to accuse poor people. In that case, public discussion might be able to deal more openly with the feelings the more fortunate classes hold about the poor, the actual facts about the poor, and the policy issues having to do with poverty and poverty-related behavior.

THE FLEXIBILITY OF THE LABEL

Terms and labels undergo broadening in order to adapt them for use in varying conditions. Broadening also makes labels flexible so that they can be used to stigmatize new populations, or accuse already targeted ones of new failures.

One source of harm to such populations is flexible *meaning*, which stems from the vagueness of a new word, the lack of an agreed-upon definition for it. Since Oscar Lewis once identified nearly sixty-five "traits" for his culture of poverty, there is apt precedent for the flexibility of the underclass label that replaced Lewis's term. Flexibility becomes more harmful when pejorative prefixes can be added to otherwise descriptively used terms; for example, a female welfare recipient can also be described as a member of a permanent underclass, which suggests that she is incapable of ever escaping welfare. An underclass of young people becomes considerably more threatening when it is called "feral," and even worse is the idea of a biological underclass, which implies a genetic and thus permanent inferiority of a group of people whom public policy can render harmless only by sterilizing, imprisoning, or killing them.

Another serious danger follows from the flexibility of *subjects:* the freedom of anyone with labeling power to add further populations to the underclass, and to do so without being accountable to anyone. The poor cannot, after all, afford to bring libel and slander suits. If tenants of public housing are also assigned to the underclass, they are even more stigmatized than when they are coming from "the projects." Illegal immigrants who are refugees from a country not favored by the State Department or the Immigration and Naturalization Service are more likely candidates for public harassment or deportation if their native-born neighbors decide that their behavior marks them as members of the underclass. That they may be doing work that no one else will do or collecting entitlements for which they have paid their share of taxes becomes irrelevant once they have been assigned the label.

THE REIFICATION OF THE LABEL

A further source of danger is the reification of the label, which takes place when a definition is awarded the gift of life and label users believe there to be an actually existing and homogeneous underclass that is composed of whatever poor people are currently defined as underclass. Reification, which turns a definition into an actual set of people, hides the reality that the underclass is an imagined group that has been constructed in the minds of its definers. Once a stigmatized label is reified, however, visible signs to identify it are sure to be demanded sooner or later, and then invented, so that people bearing the signs can be harassed more easily.

Furthermore, once the signs are in place so that imagined groups can be made actual, the labels run the danger of being treated as causal mechanisms. As a result, the better-off classes may decide that being in the underclass is a cause of becoming homeless or turning to street crime. Homelessness then becomes a symptom of underclass membership, with the additional danger of the hidden policy implication: that the elimination of the underclass would end homelessness, thereby avoiding the need for affordable housing or for jobs and income grants for the homeless.

Even purely descriptive terms referring to actual people, such as "welfare recipients," can be reified and turned into causal labels. People may thus persuade themselves to believe that being on welfare is a cause of poverty, or of single-parent families. Once so persuaded, they can propose to eliminate both effects by ending welfare, and without appearing to be inhumane—which is what conservative politicians running for office, and the intellectuals supporting them, have been doing since the early 1990s. They ignore the fact that in the real world the causal arrow goes in the other direction, but they achieve their political aim, even if they also harm poor mothers and their children.

Since popular causal thinking is almost always moral as well as empirical, the reification of a label like "the underclass" usually leads to the assignment of *moral* causality. If the underclass is the cause of behavior that deviates from mainstream norms, the solution is moral condemnation, behavioral modification, or punishment by the elimination of financial aid. Thus people are blamed who are more often than not victims instead of perpetrators, which ignores the empirical causes, say, of street crime, and interferes with the development of effective anticrime policy. Blaming people may allow blamers to feel better by blowing off the steam of righteous (and in the case of crime, perfectly justified) indignation, but even justified blaming does not constitute or lead to policy for ending street crime.

A scholarly form of reification can be carried out with labels that are also scientific terms, so that the former are confused with the latter and thus obtain the legitimacy that accompanies scientific concepts. Conversely, the moral opprobrium placed on the labeled allows social scientists either to incorporate overt biases in their concepts or to relax their detachment and in the process turn scientific concepts into little more than operationalized labels.

A case in point is the operational definition of "the underclass" by Erol Ricketts and Isabel Sawhill, which has been widely used by government, scholars, and in simplified form even by popular writers. The two social scientists argue that the underclass consists of four populations: "high school dropouts," "prime-age males not regularly attached to the labor force," welfare recipients, and "female heads." Ricketts and Sawhill identify these populations as manifesting "underclass behaviors," or "dysfunctional behaviors," which they believe to be "at variance with those of mainstream populations."

The two authors indicate that they can "remain agnostic about the fundamental causes of these behaviors." Nonetheless, they actually adopt an implicit moral causality, because in defining the underclass as "people whose behavior departs from (mainstream) norms" and remaining silent about causality, they imply that the behaviors result from the violations of these values.

Ricketts and Sawhill provide no evidence, however, that the four behaviors in question are actually the result of norm violation. More important, their operational definition does not consider other causal explanations of the same behavior. No doubt some poor young people drop out of school because they reject mainstream norms for education, but Ricketts and Sawhill omit those who drop out because they have to go to work to support their families, or because they feel that their future in the job market is nil, as well as the youngsters who are forced out by school administrators and who should be called "pushouts."

Likewise, in addition to the "prime-age males" Ricketts and Sawhill believe to be jobless because they do not want to work, some of these men reject being targeted for a career of dead-end jobs, and others, most in fact, are jobless because there are no jobs for them. Indeed, the irony of the Ricketts-Sawhill definition is that when an employer goes out of business, workers who may previously have been praised as working poor but now cannot find other jobs are then banished to the underclass.

Poor mothers go on welfare for a variety of reasons. Some are working mothers who need Medicaid for their children and cannot get health benefits from their employers. Female family heads are often single because jobless men make poor breadwinners, not because they question the desirability of mainstream marriage norms.

If I read the two authors correctly, they are conducting essentially normative analyses of the four types of underclass people they have defined, even if they may not have intended to be normative. Thus, the measures they have chosen to operationalize their definitions bear some resemblance to popular pejorative labels that condemn rather than understand behavior. Conversely, Ricketts and Sawhill do not appear to consider the possibility that the failure of the mainstream economy is what prevents people from achieving the norms they are setting for the poor.

As a result, the two authors make no provision for data that measure the failures of the mainstream economy, and they do not include—or operationalize—a good deal of other information. For example, they could count home, school, and neighborhood conditions that interfere with or discourage learning, and the economic conditions that cause the disappearance of jobs and frustrate the desire for work. In addition, they might obtain information on job availability for jobless prime-age males, as well as for women on welfare—just to mention some of the relevant data that are publicly available. Until they include such data, their definition and operationalization of "underclass" are scientific only because and to the extent that their counting procedures observe the rules of science.

A different approach to the indiscriminate mixing of science and labeling, and to the reification of stereotypes, emerged in some proposals in the late 1980s to measure underclass status by poor people's answers to attitude questions: on their willingness to plan ahead, for example. Such attitude data could be found in the widely used Panel Survey of Income Dynamics. This type of question assumes not only that people should plan ahead, but that their failure to do so reflects their unwillingness, rather than their inability, to plan ahead, which has been documented in many empirical studies. Nonetheless, people whose poverty prevented them from planning ahead and who answered honestly that they did not so plan, would have been assigned a stigmatizing label—merely on the basis of their response to superficial and general questions. Fortunately this approach to "measuring" the underclass appears not to have been used so far by anyone in an influential position.

A final reification is spatial, an approach in which behavioral labels are applied to census tracts to produce "underclass areas." Such areas derive from statistical artifacts invented by the U.S. Bureau of the Census. The bureau developed the concept of "extreme poverty areas" for those places in which at least 40 percent of the people were poor. While this is inaccurate enough—especially for the 60 percent not poor—Ricketts and Sawhill subsequently identified "underclass areas," in which the proportion of people exhibiting all four of their behavioral indicators for being in the underclass was "one standard deviation above the mean *for the country as a whole*." The two authors did not explain why they chose this measure, even though poverty is not dispersed through the country as a whole but is concentrated in the cities of the northeast, midwest, and south, the latter being also the location of the most severe rural poverty.

Most people lack the methodological skills of social scientists, and do not see the assumptions that underlie the approaches to underclass counting. Once word gets out that social scientists have identified some areas as underclass areas, however, these neighborhoods can easily be stigmatized, the population labeled accordingly and accused of whatever local meanings the term "underclass" may have acquired.

When areas become known as underclass areas, local governments and commercial enterprises obtain legitimation to withdraw or not provide facilities and services that could ameliorate the poverty of the area's inhabitants. Labeling areas as underclass can also encourage governments to choose them as locations for excess numbers of homeless shelters, drug treatment centers, and other facilities that serve the very poor and that are therefore rejected by other neighborhoods.

In fact, "underclass areas" is basically a current version of the old label "slum," which also treated indicators of poverty as behavioral failures. In the affluent economy of the post–World War II era, similar defining and subsequent counting activities were used to justify "slum clearance," and the displacement of poor people for subsidized housing for the affluent. And as in all labeling, the poor people who are labeled are left to fend for themselves.

THE DANGERS OF THE UMBRELLA EFFECT

Since "underclass" is an umbrella label that can include in its definition all the various behavioral and moral faults that label-makers and users choose to associate with it, two further dangers accrue to those it labels.

The sheer breadth of the umbrella label seems to attract alarmist writers who magnify the many kinds of moral and behavioral harmfulness attributed to people it names. A correlate of the umbrella effect is amnesia on the part of writers about the extreme and usually persistent poverty of the labeled. Thus, the more widely people believe in the validity of the underclass label, and the broader its umbrella becomes, the more likely it is that political conditions will not allow for reinstituting effective antipoverty policy. If the underclass is dangerous, and dangerous in so many different ways, it follows that the government's responsibility is to beef up the police, increase the punishments courts can demand, and create other punitive agencies that try to protect the rest of society from this dangerous class.

Umbrella labels also do harm when they lump into a single term a variety of diverse people with different problems. This ignores the reality that the people who are assigned the underclass label have in common only that their actual or imagined behaviors upset the mainstream population, or the politicians who claim to speak in its name. Using this single characteristic to classify people under one label can be disastrous, especially if politicians and voters should ever start talking about comprehensive "underclass policies," or what Christopher Jencks has called "meta solutions." For one thing, many of the people who are tagged with the label have not even deviated from mainstream norms, and yet others have done nothing illegal. An underclass policy would thus be a drastic violation of civil rights and civil liberties.

At this writing, electioneering politicians as well as angry voters still remain content with policies that harm the people who bear specific labels, such as welfare recipients, illegal immigrants, and the homeless. In the past, however, the makers of earlier umbrella labels have proposed extremely drastic policies. In 1912, Henry Goddard suggested dealing with the feebleminded by "unsexing . . . removing, from the male and female, the necessary organs for procreation." Realizing that there would be strong popular opposition both to castration and ovariectomies, he proposed instead that the next best solution was "segregation and colonization" of the feebleminded. A few decades earlier, Charles Booth had offered the same solution for an equivalent category of poor people, and not long before he was forced to resign as vice president of the United States in 1974, Spiro Agnew suggested that poor people accused of behavioral shortcomings should be rehoused in rural new towns built far away from existing cities and suburbs.

Even a thoughtful underclass policy would be dangerous, because the people forced under the underclass umbrella suffer from different kinds of poverty and, in some cases, poverty-related problems, which may require different solutions. Reducing poverty for able-bodied workers requires labor market policy change; reducing it for people who cannot work calls for a humane income grant program. Enabling and encouraging young people to stay in school requires different policies than the elimination of homelessness, and ending substance abuse or street crime demands yet others. Labelers or experts who claim one policy can do it all are simply wrong.

THE HUMAN DANGERS OF LABELING

Most immediately, the underclass label poses a danger for poor people in that the agencies with which they must deal can hurt clients who are so labeled. For one thing, agencies for the poor sometimes build labels into their operating procedures and apply them to all of their clients. As a result, either evidence about actual clients is not collected, or the label is assumed to fit regardless of evidence to the contrary. Agencies responsible for public safety typically resort to this procedure as a crime prevention or deterrence measure, especially when those labeled have little legal or political power. For example, in 1993, the Denver police department compiled a roster of suspected gang members based on "clothing choices," "flashing of gang signals," or associating with known gang members. The list included two-thirds of the city's young black men, of whom only a small percentage were actual gang members.

Labeling also creates direct punitive effects of several kinds. Bruce Link's studies of people labeled as mentally ill have found that the labeling act itself can lead to depression and demoralization, which prevent those labeled from being at their best in job interviews and other competitive situations. Likewise, when poor youngsters who hang out on street corners are treated as "loiterers," they may end up with an arrest record that hurts them in later life—which is probably why middle-class teenagers who also hang out are rarely accused of loitering.

Some effects of labels are felt even earlier in children's lives. Teachers treat students differently if they think they come from broken homes. A long-term study of working-class London has found that labeling effects may even be intergenerational. Labeling of parents as delinquent makes it more likely that their children will also be labeled, adding to the numbers in both generations who are accused of delinquent or criminal behavior.

Sometimes the effect of labeling is more indirect: agencies cut off opportunities and the label turns into a self-fulfilling prophecy. When teachers label low-income or very dark-skinned students as unable to learn, they may reduce their efforts to teach them—often unintentionally, but even so students then become less able to learn. If poor youngsters accused of loitering are assumed to have grown up without the self-control thought to be supplied by male supervision, they may be harassed—sometimes to tease and entrap them into an angry response. The arrests and arrest records that inevitably follow may deprive youngsters from fatherless families of legal job opportunities, and help force them into delinquent ones. In all these cases, the self-fulfilling prophecy is used to declare the labeled guilty without evidence of misconduct.

Another variation of the entrapment process takes place in jails. John Irwin's study of San Francisco courts and jails reports that these sometimes punished defendants whether they were guilty or not, and adds that "the experience of harsh and unfairly delivered punishment frequently enrages or embitters defendants and makes it easier for them to reject the values of those who have dealt with them in this way." In this instance, as in many of the other instances when the labels are applied by penal institutions, the labeled are not necessarily "passive innocents," as Hagan and Palloni put it. Instead, labeling sometimes generates reactions, both on the part of the police and of those they arrest, that push both sides over the edge.

The direct and indirect effects of labeling even hurt the poor in seeking help, because when they evoke labels in the minds of service suppliers they may be given inferior service, the wrong service, or none at all. Services for the labeled are normally underfunded to begin with and service suppliers are frequently overworked, so that the agencies from which the poor seek help must operate under more or less permanent triage conditions. One way of deciding who will be sacrificed in triage decisions is to assume that most clients cheat, use every contact with them to determine whether they are cheating, and exclude those who can be suspected of cheating. Since clients are of lower status than service suppliers and lack any power or influence over them, the suppliers can also vent their own status frustrations on clients. An arbitrary denial of services to clients not only relieves such frustrations but also enables suppliers to make the needed triage choices. For that reason alone, poor clients who object to being mistreated are usually the first to be declared ineligible for help.

Labeling clients as cheaters encourages service suppliers to distrust them, and that distrust is increased if the suppliers fear revenge, particularly violent revenge, from these clients. Consequently, suppliers hug the rules more tightly, making no leeway in individual cases, and even punishing colleagues who bend the rules in trying to help clients. When clients, who presumably come with prejudices of their own about agency staffs, develop distrust of the staff, a spiraling effect of mutual distrust and fear is set up. This creates data to justify labeling on both sides. The mutual distrust also encourages the exchange of violence, or the preemptive strikes of staff members who fear violence from angry clients.

Admittedly, labeling of clients is only a small part of staff–client misunderstandings and client mistreatment. The previously noted lack of funds and staff, the stresses of operating in stigmatized agencies and with stigmatized clients, normal bureaucratic rules that always put the demands of the agency and its staff ahead of the needs of clients, as well as differences of class and race between staff and clients, wreak their own cumulative havoc.

The added role of labeling in reducing services is particularly serious for poor people who live at the edge of homelessness or starvation or ill health. Yet another cause for the reduction or ending of already minimal services may push them over the edge, into the streets or an emergency clinic, into chronic illness or permanent disability, or into street crime.

Nevertheless, agencies sometimes actively discourage labeled people from escaping their stigmatized status. Liebow reports a dramatic but typical incident from a women's shelter: two women were trying to escape homelessness by taking second jobs, which they were forced to give up in order to attend obligatory but aimless night meetings so as to retain their beds in the shelter. In unlabeled populations, taking second jobs would have been rewarded as upward mobility; among labeled ones it is identified as evasion of agency rules or flouting of service supplier authority, as well as evidence of the client troublemaking that is often associated with the label.

Consequently, one major ingredient in successful efforts to help the labeled poor is to remove the label. For example, scattered site housing studies suggest that such housing is successful in changing the lives of the rehoused when their origins and backgrounds are kept from their new neighbors, so that these cannot react to pejorative labels about slum dwellers.

The labels that have produced these effects are not created solely from overheated mainstream fears or imaginations. Like all stereotypes, such labels are built around a small core of truth, or apply "to a few bad apples," as lay psychology puts it. Labeling, however, punishes not only the bad apples but everybody in the population to whom the label is applied. By labeling poor young black males as potential street criminals, for example, the white and black populations fearful of being attacked may feel that they protect themselves, but at the cost of hurting and antagonizing the large majority of poor young black males who are innocent. Inevitably, however, a proportion of the innocent will react angrily to the label, and find ways of getting even with those who have labeled them. In the end, then, everyone loses, the label users as well as the labeled.

Nonetheless, labeling is only a by-product of a larger structural process that cannot be ignored. In any population that lacks enough legitimate opportunities, illegitimate ones will be created and someone will take them. When the jobs for which the poor are eligible pay such a low wage that even some of the employed will turn to drug selling or other crime to increase their incomes, the labeling process is set in motion that finally hurts many more people, poor and nonpoor, whether or not they are guilty or innocent. Still, the real guilt has to be laid at the door of the employers that pay insufficient wages and the market conditions that may give some of them little other choice.

THE INACCURACIES OF LABELS

Last but not least, labels are dangerous simply because they are inaccurate. "Underclass" is inaccurate if interpreted literally, because there can be no class that exists *under* society, as the class hierarchy extends from the top of society to its very bottom. Indeed, "underclass" is like "underworld," which is also part of society, and in fact could not long exist if it were not supplying demanded goods or services to an "overworld."

"Underclass" is also an inaccurate label because it so vague that there is no agreement on a single or simple definition. Several other labels, however, which have evolved from descriptive terms about which there is widespread consensus, offer good illustrations of how much the portraits of the labeled vary from data on actual people.

"Welfare dependent," "single-parent family," "teenage mother," and "the homeless" are relevant examples. "Welfare dependent" is a corruption of "welfare recipient," which assumes that recipients become dependent on the government by virtue of obtaining welfare. In fact, however, only 30 percent of all recipients who begin a period on welfare will stay on for more than two years, and only 7 percent will be on more than eight years, although some of those who leave it also return to it later. Further, about 20 percent of all welfare recipients report non-AFDC income, although if off-the-books employment is counted, nearly half of all recipients are working.

Some recipients would leave welfare and take their chances in the labor market if they could obtain medical insurance for their children. Still, many poor women clearly rely on AFDC and are thus dependent on the government program; what is noted less often is that often they are even more dependent on staying in the good graces of their welfare agency, which can decide to cut them off arbitrarily without a great deal of accountability.

Ironically enough, only welfare recipients are accused of being dependents; others who are subsidized by government without adding something to the economy in exchange for their subsidy are not so labeled. Students with government fellow-ships, home owners who receive federal tax and mortgage interest deductions, cor-porations that receive subsidies to stay in existence, as well as unproductive civil ser-vants and the workers on superfluous military bases kept open to prevent the elimination of jobs, are not thought of as being dependent. Thus the economic de-pendency of welfare recipients is not the real issue, and the label is misnamed as well as partly inaccurate.

"Single-parent family," or at least the label, is also partly or wholly incorrect. For one thing, some families have a man in or near the household de facto if not de jure; more are embedded in an extended family in which mothers, grandmothers, and others share the parenting.

The notion that the children of such families are subject to undue school leav-ing, joblessness, and poverty, as well as crime and various pathologies, because they did not grow up in two-parent households is similarly incorrect. Since the modern family is not an economically productive institution, single-parenthood per se cannot logically cause poverty in the next generation, any more than growing up in a two-parent family can cause affluence. This helps to explain why well-off single parents are rarely accused of raising children who will grow up with eco-nomic or other problems. And since single-parent households are almost always poorer than other poor households, at least when their economic condition is mea-sured properly, whatever economic effects children from such households suffer can be traced to their more extreme poverty or greater economic insecurity.

In addition, while the children of happy two-parent families are best off, all other things being equal, the children of single parents are sometimes emotionally and otherwise better off than the children of two parents who are in constant con-flict. If parental conflict is more detrimental to children's well-being and perfor-mance than is single parenthood, it would explain the results of studies concluding that children of divorced parents are not uniformly worse off than those from intact families. Since the scarcity of money is a major cause of conflict—and spouse battering—among poor parents, this also helps to explain further the unwillingness of pregnant young women to marry their partners if they are jobless. None of this argues that poor single-parent families are desirable and should be encouraged, because if there is only one parent, the economic and other burdens on her and the children are often too great, and all may suffer. But the single-parent family struc-ture and the burdens that come with it are usually the result of poverty.

The same conclusions apply to teenage pregnancy. Unmarried adolescents who bear children constitute about half of all adolescent mothers and 8 percent of all welfare recipients, although some adult welfare recipients also became mothers in adolescence. The younger among them may be reacting to school failures as well as family conflict, which can increase the urgency of the normal desire to feel use-ful to and loved by someone. More to the economic point, many scholars, begin-ning with Frank Furstenberg, Jr., have pointed out that the babies of such mothers will be in school when their occupational chances are better.

These observations are no argument for adolescent motherhood, especially since many of the babies are actually unwanted at time of conception, and may even be the product of a young woman's defeat by her sexual partner in a power struggle over wearing a condom, or over having sex at all. Unwanted fetuses, however, seem to turn into wanted babies, partly because of lack of access to abortion facilities but perhaps also because low-income families have traditionally welcomed new arrivals. Given the limited chances for upward mobility among the poor, additional babies do not represent the same obstacle to higher status that they sometimes do among the more affluent classes.

There is not even reliable evidence that poor women in their twenties are automatically better mothers than poor girls in their teens, especially if the teenagers have already been responsible for taking care of their younger siblings. Older mothers are probably more mature, but if adolescent mothers receive more help from their mothers and grandmothers than they would if they were older, then adolescence may sometimes be an advantage. It could also be an advantage on health grounds, if the hypothesis that poor mothers are healthier as teenagers than as adults turns out to be supported by sufficient evidence. Conversely, today's poor teenagers are in the unfortunate position of becoming mothers when America's culturally dominant female role models—upper-middle-class professional women—postpone motherhood as long as possible in order to put their careers on a secure footing. Thus what may be rational behavior for poor young women is decidedly irrational according to cultural norms these days. Teenage motherhood does not thereby become desirable, but once more, the fundamental problem is the poverty that helps to make it happen.

Finally, even the homeless label can be incorrect. For one thing, label users tend to combine panhandlers with the homeless, even though the former are frequently housed. Furthermore, homeless populations differ from community to community depending on the nature of the low-income labor and housing markets, and particularly of housing vacancy rates for poor nonwhites in these communities. Even the rates of mental illness and substance abuse vary.

More important, since the mentally ill and addicted homeless were poor to begin with, curing them would not by itself significantly increase their ability to find affordable housing, or jobs that would enable them to afford such housing. Most lack occupational skills and skin colors that are needed on the job market these days, the obvious virtues of mental health and freedom from addiction notwithstanding. Jencks argues that money spent on substance abuse could be used instead for shelter, but in most communities, it is both easier and cheaper to get hard drugs and alcohol than low-income housing. It is not yet even known how many homeless people turned to alcohol or drugs because of economic problems or familial ones—or just lack of family—and then became homeless, and how many became homeless first and addicts subsequently.

While dealing with mental illness and addiction are vital, homelessness is a disease of the housing market, just as being on welfare is a disease of the job market. The mentally ill and the addicted are the most vulnerable to both of these economic diseases, but as long as there are not enough dwelling units and jobs for the poor, someone will have to be homeless and on welfare. Whether intentionally or not, the most vulnerable are almost always "selected" for most deprivations, among other reasons because they are the least able to protest or to defend themselves.

Labels, whether applied to welfare recipients, the homeless, and other poor people, cannot ever describe the labeled, because labels mainly describe their imagined behavioral and moral deviations from an assumed mainstream. Justified or not, labels express the discontents of the mainstream and those speaking for it, not the characteristics and conditions of the labeled themselves. When label users are discontented and seek people on whom they can project their frustrations, the accuracy of the resultant labels is not a major consideration. In fact, accuracy may get in the way if frustrated people want to be enraged by poor people and thus able to blame them.

Ultimately, however, even accurate labels for the poor are dangerous because the labels cannot end poverty or the criminal and offending poverty-related behavior of some of the poor, or the fear, anger, and unhappiness of the labelers. In the long run, these latter may be the most dangerous effects of labels.

CHAPTER **29**

Flat Broke with Children
Women in the Age of Welfare Reform

Sharon Hays

A NATION'S LAWS REFLECT
A NATION'S VALUES

The 1996 federal law reforming welfare offered not just a statement of values to the thousands of local welfare offices across the nation, it also backed this up with something much more tangible. Welfare reform came with money. Lots of it. Every client and caseworker in the welfare office experienced this. New social workers and employment counselors were hired. New signs were posted. New workshops were set up. In Arbordale and Sunbelt City, the two welfare offices I studied to write this book, every caseworker found a new computer on her desk.* In small-town Arbordale, the whole office got a facelift: new carpets, new paint, a new conference room, new office chairs, and plush new office dividers. The reception area, completely remodeled with plants and posters and a children's play area, came to resemble the waiting room of an elite pediatrician's office more than the entrance to a state bureaucracy. Sunbelt City acquired new carpets, a new paint job, and new furniture as well. And all the public areas in that welfare office were newly decorated with images of nature's magnificence—glistening raindrops, majestic mountains, crashing waves, setting sun—captioned with inspirational phrases like "perseverance," "seizing opportunities," "determination," "success."

As I walked the halls of the Sunbelt City welfare office back in 1998, situated in one of the poorest and most dangerous neighborhoods of a western boom town, those scenes of nature's magnificence struck me as clearly out of place. But the inspirational messages they carried nonetheless seemed an apt symbolic representation of the new legislative strategy to train poor families in "mainstream" American

---

*Arbordale and Sunbelt City are pseudonyms for the two towns where I studied the effects of welfare reform. I gave them these ficticious names to protect all the clients and caseworkers who shared with me their experiences of reform.

values. Welfare reform, Congress had decreed, would "end the dependence of needy parents on government benefits by promoting job preparation, work, and marriage."[1] Welfare mothers, those Sunbelt signs implied, simply needed a *push*—to get them out to work, to keep them from having children they couldn't afford to raise, to get them married and safely embedded in family life. Seizing opportunities.

States were awash in federal funds. And the economy was booming in those early years of reform. Everyone was feeling it. There was change in the air. A sense of possibilities—with just a tinge of foreboding.

The Personal Responsibility and Work Opportunity Reconciliation Act of 1996, the law that ended 61 years of poor families' entitlement to federal welfare benefits—the law that asserted and enforced a newly reformulated vision of the appropriate values of work and family life—provided all that additional funding as a way of demonstrating the depth of the nation's commitment to change in the welfare system. It provided state welfare programs with federal grants in amounts matching the peak years of national welfare caseloads (1992 to 1995)—even though those caseloads had everywhere since declined. This meant an average budget increase of 10 percent, before counting the tremendous amount of additional federal funding coming in for new childcare and welfare-to-work programs. Even though there was lots more money, most states did not pass it on to poor mothers in the form of larger welfare checks. In fact, only two states raised their benefit amounts, while two others lowered theirs at the inception of reform.[2] . . .

By the time I was completing my research, the Personal Responsibility Act along with the strong economy of the previous decade had resulted in a dramatic decline in the welfare rolls—from 12.2 million recipients in 1996, to 5.3 million in 2001. The rolls had thus been cut by more than half; yet during that same period, the number of people living in dire poverty had declined by only 15 percent. Although nearly two-thirds of former welfare clients had found some kind of work, half of those were not making wages sufficient to raise them out of poverty. The fate of those who were without jobs or welfare—over one-third of former recipients—remained largely unknown.[6]

As the economy stalled in 2001, it was evident that welfare reform had impacted poor families' willingness to seek help as well as the government's willingness to provide it.[7] While 84 percent of desperately poor (welfare-eligible) families had received benefits prior to the passage of the Personal Responsibility Act, by 2001 less than half of them did. This meant that millions of parents and children in America were living on incomes lower than half the poverty level and not receiving the benefits for which they were technically eligible. No one was certain how all those families were surviving but food banks, homeless shelters, and local charitable organizations were all reporting an increasing number of customers, and welfare offices were seeing some of the families who had left earlier, coming back again.[8] . . .

READING THE GOOD NEWS

In the months and years following welfare reform, newspaper headlines offered a seemingly unequivocal vision of success: "10,000 Welfare Recipients Hired by Federal Agencies." "Number on Welfare Dips Below 10 Million." "White House

Releases Glowing Data on Welfare." "Businesses Find Success in Welfare-to-Work Program." "The Welfare Alarm That Didn't Go Off." "Most Get Work after Welfare."[5] The message was clearly upbeat, congratulatory. It seemed that one could almost hear the clucking sounds emanating from Capitol Hill.

Yet the newspapers also followed a second story, one more cautious and disturbing: "Most Dropped from Welfare Don't Get Jobs." "New York City Admits Turning away Poor." "Penalties Pushing Many Off Welfare." "Mothers Pressed into Battle for Child Support." "As Welfare Rolls Shrink, Load on Relatives Grows." "Welfare Policies Alter the Face of Food Lines."[6] The bigger picture, the one that could put a damper on all the celebrations, was carried in the stories behind these headlines. But overall, this reality seemed drowned out by the first story, the good news.

Given the inadequacies of the Personal Responsibility Act—the relentless bureaucracy, the sanctions, the unpaid work placements, the grossly insufficient childcare subsidies, the policies that operate at cross purposes, and the genuine hardship suffered by current and former welfare recipients—why has welfare reform been deemed such a success? Part of the reason, as I've argued, is that the cultural message of reform has always been more important than its practical efficacy. A simpler answer is that the success of welfare reform has been measured by the decline of the welfare rolls. The trimming of the rolls from 12.2 million recipients at the start of reform to 5.3 million in 2001 is read as a sign that all those former welfare recipients are going to work, getting married, or otherwise taking care of themselves in the same (mysterious) way the poor have always taken care of themselves. But what, exactly, is behind the decline of the welfare rolls?

Financial success is clearly not the central reason that so many have left welfare. Although the booming economy of the 1990s had a crucial impact on welfare mothers' ability to get off the rolls and find some kind of work (see Chapter 2), even in that prosperous decade, the majority of former welfare recipients were not faring well. Between 1996 and 2000, the number of families living in desperate (welfare-level) poverty declined by only 15 percent, yet the number of welfare recipients declined by over half.[7] Although all the answers are not yet in, from the work of policy institutes, scholars, journalists and my own research, I can piece together the following portrait. In the context of a highly favorable economy, the welfare rolls were cut in half for four central reasons:

1. More welfare clients were getting jobs more quickly than they did under the old system.
2. More poor families were being discouraged from using welfare than was true under AFDC.
3. More were leaving welfare faster and returning more slowly than they did in the past.
4. More welfare mothers were being sanctioned or otherwise punished off the welfare rolls.

The best news in all this is the number of welfare mothers who have gotten jobs. Nationwide, as I've noted, researchers estimate that approximately 60 percent of all the adults who left welfare since reform were working, at least part of the time, in 2002. This reality not only offered good news to the proponents of reform; it also offered, for a time at least, a real sense of hope to many welfare mothers. On the other hand, only half of the former welfare recipients who found work were actually making sufficient money to raise their families out of poverty. Only one-third were able to remain employed continuously for a full year. A good number would thus end up, at one time or another, among the 40 percent of former welfare recipients who had neither work nor welfare. Some of those would go back to the welfare office again and start the process anew: policy analysts suggest that over one-third of those who left since reform had already returned to welfare at least once by 2002. In any case, even among those who were employed during that prosperous decade, according to federal statistics their earnings averaged only $598 a month for the support of themselves and their children. Other researchers have estimated average hourly wages at $7.00 an hour and average annual earnings at between $8,000 and $10,800.[8]

With the economy no longer booming, there is reason to worry that many will be unable to sustain even these levels of work and income over time. No matter how you look at it, such facts indicate very difficult living conditions for families. And most of the low-wage jobs acquired by former welfare recipients, as I've pointed out, are without health insurance, many are without sick and vacation leave, a good proportion are at odd or fluctuating hours, and many are only part time.[9] When the problems implied by these facts are coupled with the hardship of trying to find and keep affordable childcare and housing, worries about family health, how to pay the utility bills, and the everyday distress that comes with managing life in the debit column, then one can understand why Barabara Ehrenreich, in *Nickel and Dimed*, referred to the lives of low-wage workers as not just a situation of chronic distress and insecurity but as a "state of emergency."[10]

The second group contributing to the decline of the welfare rolls is even less upbeat. This is the relatively invisible group of discouraged welfare clients—those poor mothers who have left or avoided welfare rather than face the increased stigma and the demanding "rigmarole" of rules and regulations that came with reform. This includes, first, all those mothers and children who never show up on any paperwork but have nonetheless been deeply affected by the law. These are the mothers who went to Sunbelt City's "diversionary workshop" and just headed back home without ever filling out an application. These are all the potential applicants in New York City and elsewhere who by state rules, were not allowed to apply until they had completed their job search, many of whom simply never went back to the welfare office. These are also all those very poor families who have heard the stories on the streets and on the news and are now more reluctant to go to the welfare office than they were in the past. Finally, this group includes all the welfare clients who have filled out the forms, begun their job search, started the workshops, or taken a workfare placement, but then just stopped showing up—depressed, ill, angry, without childcare, without hope, unable or unwilling to meet the new standards. Some proportion of these women will eventually find jobs, and if they made it through the application process and if researchers are able to track them, they will be counted in the first category of "successes," working somewhere, for some period of time, for that $598 a month, no benefits. For those who go long stretches without work or welfare, it is difficult to determine precisely how they and their children will survive (although I will speculate on their fate in a moment).

Once it becomes clear that welfare reform has resulted in both encouragement and discouragement, the third reason behind the decline of the rolls can be surmised. The Personal Responsibility Act has effectively transformed the process of "cycling." As I've noted, long before reform, most welfare clients cycled on and off the welfare rolls, moving between jobs and welfare. Now that welfare reform has instituted the "carrots" of supportive services and the "sticks" of time limits, sanctions, and work rules, the process of cycling has been altered—speeded up at the exiting end and slowed down at the return end. That is, poor mothers are now getting jobs or getting off welfare faster than they would have in the past, and they are also entering or returning to the welfare office more slowly and reluctantly. Given that welfare rolls are counted from moment to moment, on paper this speed up/slow down appears as an absolute decline in the welfare rolls.[12] It says nothing, however, about the health and well-being of poor mothers and their kids.

Finally, about one-quarter of welfare recipients are now sanctioned or denied benefits for failure to comply with welfare rules. A 50-state Associated Press survey in 1999 found wide variations by state, with 5 to 60 percent of welfare recipients sanctioned (or procedurally penalized) at any given time in any given state—with rates twice as high as they were prior to reform. In one careful study of three major U.S. cities, 17 percent of clients had their benefits stopped or reduced as a result of sanctions or procedural penalties. In Wisconsin, the most carefully analyzed welfare program in the nation, 31 percent of the caseload was sanctioned in 1999, 21 percent in 2000. (Of those Wisconsin clients who had the wherewithal to appeal their cases, 70 percent of appeals were resolved in favor of clients, suggesting that many of these penalties were unfounded or improperly administered). Federal statistics find just 5 percent of clients under sanction but also note that 23 percent of cases are "procedural closures" (many of which could be penalties for noncompliance).[13]

These sanctioning practices, along with discouragement, faster cycling, and below-poverty wages explain why the number of welfare-eligible families who actually receive welfare benefits has fallen at a much faster pace than the rate of dire poverty. It is clear, in other words, that a substantial portion of desperately poor mothers and children are being punished, worn down, or frightened off the welfare rolls.

Putting it all together, in the context of a booming economy *more than two-thirds of the mothers and children who left welfare have either disappeared or are working for wages that do not meet federal standards for poverty.* At best, only 30 percent of the decline of the welfare rolls represents a "successful" escape from poverty—and many of those successes are only temporary, and many would have occurred with or without reform. The state of Wisconsin, marked as the most outstanding welfare program in the nation, matches these proportions precisely.[14]

In the meantime, there are still millions of poor women and children on welfare and hundreds of thousands coming in anew—or coming back again, unable to find or keep work or to establish some other means of survival under the terms of welfare reform. All of them are desperately poor.

That all this information on the declining welfare rolls still leaves many questions unanswered is one indication that it will take many, many years before we can comprehend the full impact of reform. And almost all of what we now know pertains only to the period of economic boom and only to welfare mothers who had not yet faced the time limits on welfare receipt. Given that time limits do not result in a massive exodus from the rolls but rather a (relatively) slow trickle, it will take a very long time before all the consequences of "the end of entitlement" are surmised.[15]

One final related note is in order.[16] For those who were worried about the consequences of reform from the start, one source of protection against hardship appeared to be the federal rule allowing states to "exempt" up to 20 percent of their caseloads from the time limits. These exemptions, however, have proven severely inadequate, as I have argued. Some states have made the rules so complex and demanding that few clients can qualify. Other states have used all the exemptions available and still cannot fully protect all those recipients with serious physical disabilities and mental health problems, let alone all those who are at risk for domestic violence or who cannot find or afford childcare.[17] The number of families protected over the long haul will vary greatly depending on the rigidity or generosity of state and federal policies. But given what we know about those who have left already, it is clear that the exemptions available in 2002 are not enough to spare all the women and children faced with extreme poverty.

Looking on the brighter side, welfare reform, and the money that came with it—the income supplements, childcare subsidies, bus vouchers, work clothing, and for the lucky ones, the new eyeglasses, the help in buying used cars or making a down payment on an apartment—has been truly helpful, improving the lives of many poor mothers and children, at least for a time. Further, in some cases reform has meant that mothers are getting *better* jobs than they would have in the past, thanks to the education and mentoring offered by some state welfare programs. As I've suggested, as many as 10 to 15 percent of welfare mothers are in a better position now than they would have been had this law not been passed. Perhaps equally important, though harder to quantify, is the positive sense of hope and social inclusion that many recipients experienced (in the short term at least) as a result of the supportive side of welfare reform.

The number of families that have been genuinely helped by reform is neither insignificant nor superfluous. At a practical as well as moral level, the services and income supports offered by the Personal Responsibility Act have clearly been positive. Yet in the long run and in the aggregate, poor mothers and children are worse off now than they were prior to reform. Among those who are working and still poor, among those without work or welfare, and among those who are still facing constant and intense pressure to find work and figure out some way to care for their children, we can only guess what impact this law will have on their ability to retain hope over the long term. Even the U.S. Census Bureau (not anyone's idea of a bleeding heart organization) has found itself answering the question, "Is work better than welfare?" in the negative, at least for those without substantial prior education and work experience.[18] With a slower economy and increasing numbers of poor families due to hit their time limits in coming years, there are reasons to expect that conditions will become increasingly difficult.

Empathy for the downtrodden is one reason to worry about these results. As the following sections will emphasize, enlightened self-interest, a concern with financial costs, and a commitment to our collective future are also very good reasons to be troubled by the consequences of welfare reform.

WINNERS AND LOSERS

The extent to which the facts about the declining welfare rolls are read as a success ultimately depends on one's primary goals. If the goal of reform was solely to trim the rolls, then it has surely succeeded. If the goal was to place more single mothers in jobs regardless of wages, that goal has been met. If we sought to ensure that more welfare mothers would face a double shift of paid work and childcare, placing them on an "equal" footing with their middle-class counterparts, then some celebrations are in order. If the aim was to ensure that poor men are prosecuted for failure to pay child support, then welfare reform has been relatively effective. If the goal was to make low-income single mothers more likely to seek out the help of men, no matter what the costs, there is some (inconclusive) evidence that this strategy may be working.[19] If the goal was to decrease poverty overall, there is no indication that anything but the cycle of the economy has had an impact. Beyond this, the answers are more complicated.

Thinking about losers, one can start with the families who have left welfare. One-half are sometimes without enough money to buy food. One-third have to cut the size of meals. Almost half find themselves unable to pay their rent or utility bills. Many more families are turning to locally funded services, food banks, churches, and other charities for aid. Many of those charities are already overburdened. In some locales, homeless shelters and housing assistance programs are closing their doors to new customers, food banks are running out of food, and other charities are being forced to tighten their eligibility requirements.[20]

Among the former welfare families who are now living with little or no measurable income, will those charities be enough? At ground level, Nancy, the supervisor in Arbordale's welfare office, told me more than once that she was deeply concerned about these families, particularly the children. Melissa, the supervisor in Sunbelt City, on the other hand, repeatedly responded to my questions regarding the fate of former welfare recipients with the simple statement, "They have other resources." Melissa was referring not only to all those (overloaded) charities, but also to all the boyfriends and family members who could help in paying the bills, and to all those unreported or underreported side jobs (doing hair, cleaning houses, caring for other people's children, selling sex or drugs).[21] Between these two welfare supervisors, both of whom have spent many years working with poor mothers, who is right? And what about Denise, who both agreed with Melissa that many welfare mothers didn't *really* need the help, and who predicted that welfare reform would result in frightening hardship, including a rise in crime?

Consider the "other resources" available to the women I have introduced in this book. In the case of Sheila, the Sunbelt mother who was caring for her seven-year-old daughter and her terminally ill mother, the three of them might be able to survive somehow on her mom's disability check (about $550 per month) with the help of food stamps and local charities. If worse came to worst, she might be able to find some work on the graveyard shift so that she wouldn't have to leave her mom and daughter alone during the day (but she would be faced with leaving them alone at night in that very dangerous housing project). Diane, the Sunbelt mother with a three-year-old son and a long history of severe depression and domestic violence, could go back to operating that illegal flophouse and taking under-the-table housecleaning work (though it is not clear what impact this would have on her son, not to mention Diane). Nadia, the Arbordale mother with four children and no work experience, might rejoin her old friends in petty thievery and prostitution, or she could put further pressure on her employed aunt or the two unemployed fathers of her children, or she might consider turning her children over to relatives or to the foster care system (a worst case scenario recognized by many of the mothers I talked to). Monique, the second-generation Arbordale recipient who'd had her first child at 17, could probably manage on her current job, though one might be a little concerned that her abusive ex-husband would return, force her to move, and throw the fragile balance of her life into chaos. Of course, there are also women like Sonya, the compulsive house rearranger (and incest survivor), who have no family, no work experience, no marketable skills, and no idea about how to make use of local charitable institutions. Someone would surely notice such women eventually, if only because their children missed school or appeared too ill-kept or malnourished.

Most welfare mothers *do* have other resources. Yet many of those resources are only temporary, and many are, at best, inadequate. Most will likely add greater instability and uncertainty to the lives of these families. And nearly all these resources have their own price tags—practical, emotional, moral, and social.

As these negative effects begin to overburden ever-larger numbers of women, we can expect to see more crime, drug abuse, prostitution, domestic violence, mental health disorders, and homelessness. More children will end up in foster care, residing with relatives other than their parents, or living on the streets. These children will also be at greater risk for malnutrition, illness, and delinquency. At the same time, more sick and disabled relatives who once relied on the care of welfare mothers will find their way into state-supported facilities or be left to fend for themselves. Caseworkers in Arbordale told me that they were already noticing the rise in foster care cases and in child-only welfare cases (where mothers had relinquished their children to relatives—making those children eligible for welfare benefits until age 18).* In Sunbelt City, welfare clients told me they were already witnessing rising rates of hunger, drug abuse, prostitution, and crime among sanctioned or discouraged former welfare mothers they knew.

All this hardship will affect poor men as well as women. Not only are these men faced with a more rigid and unforgiving child support system, but they are also very likely to face pressure from the mothers of their children and from the recognition that their children may go hungry or become homeless.[22] The desperation of some of these men could result in a greater incidence of violence, crime, and drug abuse among a low-wage, chronically underemployed male population that is already suffering from severe hardship.

The long-term consequences of welfare reform will also place a tremendous burden on other working-poor and working-class families. The upper classes can rest (fairly) assured that most desperately poor mothers won't come knocking on their doors, asking for cash, a meal, a place to stay, or the loan of a car. But many poor mothers will (reluctantly) knock on the doors of the working-poor and working-class people who are their friends and relatives. It is these people who will share their homes, their food, and their incomes and provide practical help with childcare and transportation. These good deeds won't appear on any income tax forms, welfare case reports, or analyses of charitable spending. But this burden on low-income working people will be one of the very real, and largely invisible, costs of welfare reform. And it will surely exacerbate existing income inequalities.

In the end, it is simultaneously true that most welfare mothers have other resources, many will face frightening hardship, and some proportion will turn to desperate measures. If nothing changes and welfare reform isn't itself reformed, by the close of the first decade of the twenty-first century, we will see the beginnings of measurable impacts on prison populations, mental health facilities, domestic violence shelters, children's protective services, and the foster care system.

This brings us to the goal of saving taxpayers' money. Given drastic cuts in food stamps and aid to legal immigrants as well as the declining number of welfare recipients, taxpayers are paying somewhat less in aid to the disadvantaged overall, though relative to the size of the welfare rolls, the 2002 per client costs are higher than they were in 1996.[23] Over the long haul, welfare reform is likely to become increasingly costly. Savings in welfare benefits will eventually be more than offset by the expenses associated with the social problems made worse as a result of reform. The average individual welfare recipient received approximately $1680 in cash and services annually in 1996; that same year, the annual cost of keeping

---

*According to the rules of reform, there are no time limits on welfare benefits to children who live with relatives (or other adults) who are not themselves receiving welfare. This policy thereby offers welfare mothers an *incentive* to give up their children to other family members, since it means continued financial assistance for those children. Among "streetwise" welfare recipients, this is already a well-known rule. And the number of child-only welfare cases has, in fact, been on the rise since reform (U.S. House of Representatives 2000, see also Bernstein 2002).

one child in foster care was $6,000, and the cost of keeping one person in prison was $20,100.[24]

From this angle, the real winners in the story of welfare reform are all the restaurant, hotel, retail, and food service chains, and all the corporations, manufacturers, and small business owners across America who employ low-wage workers. These owners (and their stockholders) benefit not just from the availability of millions of poor women desperate to find work and willing to accept the lowest wages and the worst working conditions, they benefit not just from the additional availability of all those now more-desperate poor men, they also benefit because all this desperation creates more profitable labor market conditions overall. Welfare reform helps to convince all low-wage workers that they can be easily displaced by former welfare recipients and therefore makes them less likely to complain, change jobs, join unions, or demand higher wages. The logic of reform also means that low-wage employers can rest assured, for the moment at least, that no one will be calling into question the fact that their policies are less than family friendly and their workers are unable to support their children on the wages they take home.[25]

On a superficial level, the "end of welfare" appears to hold in place the symbolic messages that work is better than welfare and marriage is better than single parenthood. But by no stretch of the imagination could one argue that welfare reform brings with it anything resembling the triumph of "family values." And the practical reality of most low-wage employment no more offers "independence" and self-sufficiency to former welfare recipients than it does to all the middle-class teenagers who spend their summers working in fast-food restaurants and retail chains.

Although the negative results of welfare reform are dramatic, it is nonetheless quite possible that a substantial number of former welfare recipients will simply be "absorbed" into the society without a great deal of fanfare. In the larger scheme of things, after all, 12 million or so desperately poor people in a nation of 285 million are not that many. On the other hand, it's important to remember that those figures include the many millions of American children who were once supported by welfare checks. Further, such figures are inadequate to capture the reality that welfare poverty covers an ever-changing group of citizens: in coming decades, tens of millions will be affected by changes to the welfare system. But given class and race segregation in housing, work, and services, many middle-class Americans will not actually witness the daily hardships of poor families, at least not in a direct and immediate way.[26]

Of course, as I've suggested, there is also a real possibility that as conditions worsen, the nation will see higher levels of civil disobedience, especially in those locales with high concentrations of the poor—including New York City, Los Angeles, Baltimore, St. Louis, Philadelphia, Washington, D.C., and elsewhere. In any case, over the long haul the reform of welfare will be costly—in its human toll, its fiscal toll, and its moral and political toll.

Editor's Note: *Notes for this reading can be found in the original source.*

PART NINE

Health and Medical Care

The social stratification of health and illness is one of the most devastating inequalities in American society. Despite our enormous wealth and technological potential, the United States still lags behind most other advanced industrial societies on many measures of health and access to health care. Americans have lower life expectancies and higher rates of infant death than citizens of many other developed countries; and some groups—including the urban and rural poor—still suffer shockingly high levels of preventable diseases and inadequate health care services. These problems are hardly new ones. In 1967, a National Advisory Commission on Health Manpower noted that the health statistics of the American poor "occasionally resemble the health statistics of a developing country."[1] Unfortunately, despite several decades of economic growth and stunning advances in medical technology, the same statement could still be made.

To be sure, for those who can afford it, the United States offers some of the best medical care in the world. Yet most Americans are less fortunate. One of the most striking differences between the United States and almost every other advanced society is our lack of any comprehensive system of national health insurance that makes adequate health care available to all citizens as a matter of right. Forty-three million Americans under 65—over 16 percent of the population—had no insurance coverage in 2007. A recent study estimates that a much larger number—almost one out of three nonelderly Americans—go without health insurance at some point over the course of two years.[2] The proportions are even higher among some groups—notably the young, minorities, and the working poor. Many studies have shown that providing health insurance for everyone would not be hugely expensive, measured against the more than $2 trillion the United States now spends on health care. But we have not moved to make health care for all a reality, and in some respects have gone backwards in recent years, as health care "reforms" have led to ever more intensive efforts to cut costs and as pinched budgets have decimated the ability of states and counties to supply adequate care.[3]

The human impact of the lack of accessible health care for all is compellingly illustrated in Susan Starr Sered and Rushika Fernandopulle's article on the health troubles of the uninsured. Health insurance, the authors point out, was once part of the package of benefits American workers could expect from their employers, like generous retirement plans. But as fewer and fewer jobs now provide insurance, increasing numbers of workers are left to fend with health problems without support. The result is a downward spiral in which workers who can't afford health care are forced to put off getting needed medical attention, which makes them sicker, which in turn makes them less able to get the kinds of jobs that could provide them with reliable health care—and the cycle continues, at great cost not only to the uninsured themselves but, ultimately, to the economy as a whole.

Lack of health insurance, however, is only one part of a more general crisis of medical care in the United States, as the next selection makes clear. The nonprofit Commonwealth Fund's periodic Scorecard on the American health care system finds it falling down on many fronts—especially as compared to its counterparts in other developed countries. We spend far more on health care, proportionately, than comparable countries (more than 16 percent of our Gross Domestic Product), and those costs have risen inexorably. But what we get for all that money is disappointing. The quality of care most Americans receive, even when they do get it, is "uneven and often suboptimal" Patients face a fragmented and often unresponsive medical system—and, unsurprisingly, are increasingly dissatisfied with it. Taken together, the lack of coverage and the spotty quality of care mean that the U.S. medical care system is uniquely failing in its central mission of contributing to "healthy, long and productive lives for everyone." Shockingly, we stand in last place among 19 countries when it comes to deaths that could potentially been prevented by adequate health care. If we achieved the same success in preventing premature deaths as the best-performing countries— including Japan, France and Australia—we could save over 100,000 American lives a year.

Why don't we have a system that provides health care to everyone? One reason is the American mistrust of government we've encountered already. We have, accordingly, left it up to the "market" to provide even the most basic care, except for the elderly and for those poor enough to be on welfare, whose medical care is partly subsidized by government. And indeed, the Medicare program for older adults— our only national-level, universal, publicly supported health care program—has long been one of the brighter sports in the otherwise distressing picture of American medical care. Since its establishment in the 1960s, after decades of opposition, Medicare has been one of our most successful social programs—providing predictable and affordable health care to older Americans as a matter of right. But despite its success, as Lillian Rubin points out in "The Untold Health Care Story," Medicare has faced systematic assaults in recent years. Inadequate budgets have led many doctors to trim the number of Medicare patients they are willing to see— or to drop them altogether. The failure to fully support the program is usually justified by the argument that "privatizing" the system would lead to better and more efficient care. That, however, would make Medicare look more like the *rest* of our failing—and mostly privatized—health care system: hardly a convincing solution to the endemic problems of medical care in America.

ENDNOTES

1. Report of the National Advisory Commission on Health Manpower, quoted in R. M. Titmuss, "Ethics and Economics of Medical Care," in *Commitment to Welfare* (New York: Pantheon, 1968), p. 268.

2. Vicki Kemper, "Study finds more lack health insurance," *Los Angeles Times*, March 5, 2003.

3. As this book went to press, Congress just passed comprehensive health care reform legislation that will ultimately extend health insurance coverage to most Americans who are now uninsured. But currently, millions remain without health insurance.

CHAPTER 30

Sick Out of Luck
The Uninsured in America

Susan Starr Sered
Rushika Fernandopulle

Francine is one tough lady. She has spent her life doing hard physical labor—what she calls "men's work"—in the tobacco fields and factories of the Mississippi Delta. Today, she is one of the lucky ones: The factory she works in has not yet moved to Mexico or Indonesia, so she still has health coverage. Her sister, Carlene, on the other hand, is not so fortunate. Carlene works as a home health-care aide, taking care of old people. Like many other African-American women in the region, and indeed many people all around the country whose work has moved from manufacturing to the service sector, Carlene cannot find a job that provides health insurance.

Carlene has multiple health problems, including a ferocious, persistent cough. Speaking on her diffident sister's behalf, Francine declares, "There should be a doctor somewhere so when you got no money, you can go to the doctor. There is no free clinic around here."

"So, what happens to uninsured people around here who don't have any money when they need to go to the doctor?" we ask her.

"They are shit out of luck."

During 2002–2003 we traveled to Texas, Mississippi, Idaho, Illinois, and Massachusetts, holding wide-ranging interviews with more than 120 uninsured Americans and approximately three dozen physicians, medical administrators, and health policy officials. In the course of our travels we met Americans who have seen loved ones die because they did not have medical coverage, Americans who have declared bankruptcy or were forced to sell their homes to pay for medical care, and Americans stuck in dead-end jobs because their health is too poor to allow them the career mobility available to Americans of earlier generations.

Unlike the health-care systems in most other Western countries, the core of America's health care is increasingly for-profit, employment-based, private insurance. This system flourished during the post–World War II era, when millions of blue-collar workers held long-term union contracts that guaranteed health-care benefits, and white-collar workers could expect to remain with—and rise up the ladder of—companies in which they built their careers.

In recent years, the connection between employment and health care has unraveled. As the nature of employment has changed globally, fewer people are able to stay in the same job for many years. As a result, jobs no longer serve as stable platforms for health-care arrangements. More than half of uninsured men and women work full-time throughout the year, and most of the others work part-time or for part of the year. They simply work at jobs without health benefits.

DOWN AND OUT IN DANVILLE

"When we find ourselves unable to provide for ourselves, and we've always been independent, it adds an emotional burden. You're trapped in a cycle you hate. I never in my life thought I would need this kind of help."

(Fran, Illinois)

Danville, Illinois, is a small city in the heart of the Midwestern Rust Belt. Like residents of manufacturing cities all over the country, Danville's citizens have had to learn a new vocabulary that includes terms like "corporate restructuring," "globalization of industry," "NAFTA and the WTO," "temp agencies," "outsourcing and downsizing," and "dislocated workers." As corporations such as General Motors have laid off American workers and moved their operations overseas, Danville has lost the jobs that had sustained this blue-collar community for many years.

The economic sea change that hit Danville has left its residents stunned, unsure where to assign blame—to themselves or to economic forces beyond their control. In Fran's words, "I had big plans, but circumstances kind of stepped in there for me and changed my plans. And I haven't been able to completely overcome the mindset. I was married for 28 years. I got divorced on Wednesday, lost my $18-an-hour job on Friday."

Fran, a petite, red-haired woman, had worked for seven years as an inventory-control supervisor at a large manufacturing plant. With three shifts of employees working for her, she had a job in which she felt accomplished and successful. She was caught by surprise when a foreign corporation purchased the plant. Like many other employees, she fell victim to general restructuring of the plant and to the new owners bringing in their own people from outside [central] Illinois.

"I was really making good money. I was up to almost $30,000 a year. And I have always taken care of myself. Even when I was married, I always worked full-time. We never, never took charity in any form. We always took care of ourselves.

"When I lost my job, I had no idea that was coming, blindsided there, and I kind of stepped back and said, what am I going to do now? I was 42 years old. I wasn't 20 anymore. I thought I would go back to junior college to get a degree. I was pretty excited at starting over fresh.

"I had plans for when I got out of school, I was studying local area networks on PCs. I was doing hardware parts, because I'd always done software and accounting-type work. And I was going to start my own business. I had a couple of people who were willing to back me. I wanted to go to college in a serious way. I started working part-time, and I went to school full-time."

Until 1992, when she was laid off and divorced, Fran had always had health insurance and had gone to the doctor for regular checkups. After that, "I paid for COBRA [a federally mandated insurance program offered to people leaving their jobs; COBRA allows them to continue their health insurance coverage, but at their own expense] for a while, but it was too expensive. I had never been sick; I was a really healthy and active person. So I figured it was a small gamble to go without insurance for two years while I went to college. I was getting along just fine until the middle of my second year when I was getting ready to graduate. That is when I started getting sick."

Thinking she had a hangnail on her finger, she went to a local physician who told her to soak it and squeeze it, and to come back in three or four weeks if it didn't heal. "You'll have to bring $200 in cash, because we don't do surgery without insurance," they told her. But Fran did not have insurance, she did not have the cash, and she did not return.

"By about April, it got to the point where I could hardly make it to school. I was just exhausted. I found out I had diabetes. I had no clue, had never been sick in any way, shape, or form before that. And that not only affected me physically, it affected me, depression, you know. It's a hard thing to deal with all of a sudden. I had several operations on my hand, and I was sick."

A resourceful woman, Fran took advantage of the free health-care options available in her community. Thus, several months after the hangnail incident, she went to the County Health Department for a free Pap smear. The nurse there told her to go right over to the Vermillion Area Health Center, a small, nonprofit, mostly volunteer-run, part-time clinic. Gangrene had set into her finger at the site of the small injury. The gangrene was symptomatic of osteomyelitis (a deep infection of the bone) resulting from undiagnosed and untreated diabetes.

From a medical standpoint, Fran learned that for this sort of severe complication to set in—neuropathy and circulatory problems—she most probably had been diabetic for more than two years before it was diagnosed. Without standard medical screenings, the kind she had received regularly before the layoff, the disease progressed silently in her body. Fran also learned that if her diabetes is not controlled, she could end up blind, with an amputated leg, and with kidney failure, all fairly common complications from uncontrolled diabetes.

At this point, Fran is healthy enough and eager to work full-time. She has applied for many full-time jobs, but "with the economic situation being what it is, there's not a big call for a 55-year-old woman." The part-time and freelance bookkeeping jobs she has picked up over the past twelve years have paid enough for her to scrape by, but none has provided health insurance. Fran explains that she is caught in something of a catch-22: If she were to take a full-time, unskilled job outside her profession of bookkeeping and business management, she would probably earn too much to remain eligible for charity services at the Vermillion County Health Center. However, as an unskilled worker, she would not earn enough to pay for medical care out of pocket, and she would be unlikely to be given health insurance, especially a plan that would cover her preexisting condition. With diabetes and a history of osteomeylitis, she cannot take the risk of being without medical care. For Fran, the link between employment and health care has turned out to be sickening indeed.

A MINER'S TALE

"We have worked all of our lives, even went to work sick."

(*Lenny, Idaho*)

The son of an Idaho logger, Lenny began working to help support himself and his two brothers when he was 14. By age 18, he said, "I hit the road building houses for International Home." Not liking living out of a suitcase, he took a job working underground at Sunshine Mine at the age of 23, where he mined silver for 30 years.

"Sunshine had a terrible reputation for being the hottest mine, and it was hot! I worked in a place that the average was probably 90 degrees with humidity probably 98 percent. There was no protective equipment against the heat in those days. They just gave you a fan so you could blow the hot air around, but, yeah, that was hot. I lost weight, and I found out what cramps were, muscle cramps. Every muscle in your body had a charley horse that made your hands buckle backwards. Your legs would all wad up so you couldn't walk. Usually what we did is one guy would do part of the work, and the other guy would just kind of sit back so he could carry the other guy out at the end of the shift. He might not be able to get out otherwise, and we did that for six months of the year."

Despite the dreadful heat, taking a job at the mine was an easy decision for Lenny. "Benefits were the reason people went to the mines. Sunshine was a good mine as far as pay, it paid well, and they had the best insurance. They covered you, your wife, and all your kids 100 percent—dental, optical, everything." Shortly after he began working at Sunshine, his wife became pregnant. Soon after they had another child, and then a third, and Sunshine's benefits—a union-negotiated package of health and retirement benefits—looked better and better.

Then in 1972 a fire broke out in the mine. Lenny was one of the lucky ones—he survived. "What happened was we had a fire underground, and it's a hard rock mine. See, the railroads were put down and all this wood stuff for the railroads burned and the smoke had nowhere to go. The smoke was so concentrated that you could hardly see even if you had a lamp on your forehead. We made it out at about 1 p.m., and there was nobody outside the mine, and I thought, 'Man, everybody beat me out.'" In fact, few beat him out—91 of his fellow workers died in the fire.

After the fire, Lenny went back to work at the mine. The other local employment option, logging, rarely provided health benefits and seemed to Lenny even more dangerous than working underground. Moreover, in the wake of the fire,

Sunshine had improved the ventilation system. Besides, Lenny had acquired some seniority at the mine.

In 1984, Lenny injured his back at work and underwent surgery. While the surgery helped some, his legs would give out from time to time. He managed to be reassigned to the less arduous position of shifter. As Lenny explains, "The shifter is the guy that goes underground. He takes a crew of 10 to 15 people down the mine shaft to a certain level, and he lines them all out. He also handles the motor, and he visits everybody at least once a day to make sure they are not hurt." After a few years as a shifter, he was made a mine foreman, which meant that he was in charge of the shifters and no longer had to go underground, a fortunate change because of his ongoing back troubles. "I didn't do this overnight. You know I spent 30 to 32 years there, so the last 10 years I had built up enough knowledge of the whole mine and all of the people that worked there that I was a natural for the position."

Things were better for a while, but then silver prices fell. In order to help save the mine and hold onto their jobs, the miners took cuts in pay and insurance and began paying part of their own premiums. For the first time in decades, they had to pay for their own optical care and for a variety of other medical treatments, though with the pay cuts few could afford it. Eventually, the price of silver fell below the cost of extracting it from the ground, and Sunshine closed for a year. When the mine reopened, management introduced more mechanization, took back only some of the employees, and decreased the benefits even further.

THE DEBTS PILE UP

In 2001, the mine closed permanently, and Lenny, along with his coworkers, lost his health insurance and other benefits. For thirty years at Sunshine—twenty years underground, often in stifling conditions—Lenny always felt that the trade-off was worthwhile. Good benefits and comprehensive health insurance for his family made up for the heat and danger. Now, still handicapped by the lingering effects of an injury on the job, Lenny found himself, at the age of 51, without health insurance.

Unemployment is high in northern Idaho, and finding another job was not easy. Calling on all his friends and relatives for help, he lined up a job installing telephone lines. "The job was okay, less money than the mines," and, as Lenny explains, "not the job that I spent 31 years learning. It is kind of hard, hanging upside down putting up the lines. It is hard to start at square one at my age. Some of the wires are underground, and you use a backhoe when you can. But when we get into where there are wires and stuff all together, you have to dig manually."

Still, he was relieved to find a job, and especially one that offered insurance. The rub was that it took 60 days on the job to get the insurance.

The luck that had made Lenny one of the survivors of the 1972 Sunshine fire had run out. Only 30 days after he began the job, he fell down on the pavement in full cardiac arrest. Paramedics flew him to Spokane, Washington, to a cardiac unit. Lenny's recovery was far better than anyone expected, but he was saddled with enormous medical bills. A year later, he was sent to the hospital for a bypass operation, angioplasty, and eventually open-heart surgery. The cardiologists saved his life, but Lenny is still suffering acute headaches as a result of falling to the pavement during the initial cardiac arrest. The cardiologist sent him to an ear, nose, and throat specialist, who then sent him to other specialists for treatments, none of which has eliminated his headaches.

The bill for his various surgeries, consultations, medications, and treatments is over $140,000—a sum that might as well be $1 billion, since Lenny will never be able to pay it. His sole income at this time is the $400 monthly pension he receives from Sunshine.

Lenny would like to go back to work, but he can no longer do the only kind of work he knows how to do—hard physical labor. After the injury to his head, he cannot climb telephone poles or bend over ditches; he is overcome by dizziness, which could be fatal from the top of a pole. "I can't get work, my doctor says I can't, so I have applied for Social Security [Disability]. But Social Security is one of those things, you know, it takes 10 years to get on it, so I don't know how that is going to work out."

According to the administrator of the Indigent Program in Shoshone County, Lenny is "emotionally at his wits' end because Social Security is not being kind to him. He's a loose cannon."

Fortunately, the County Indigent Program and the state of Idaho have been able to provide Lenny with some assistance: They have paid most of his outstanding hospital bills. As the administrator explains, the "only" cost to Lenny is that Shoshone County has taken a $10,000 lien on his house.

FROM CLASS TO CASTE

Fran and Lenny represent the millions of Americans affected by a fundamental change taking place in our society. In the wake of changes to the economy and the structure of work, they have been transformed from proud members of the working class—a social category that connotes what one does, using one's hands in a more or less skilled capacity, to members of a new caste known as the working poor—a term used to describe who one is. Marginally employed as temps, subs, part-timers, or contracted or contingent laborers, members of this new caste are locked in employment situations that do not offer medical benefits. Without consistent and reliable access to health care, they find themselves situated outside of the traditionally fluid class structure of American society. We know, of course, that we are not writing about a caste system in the same sense as traditional Indian society. Rather, we have chosen to use the language of caste to describe a social arrangement that is emerging de facto from the political economy of our country at this time.

What makes Fran's and Lenny's situations castelike is the permanent effect that delayed, patchy, and second-rate health care has on their bodies: Even if economic conditions improve in Illinois or Idaho, they no longer will be healthy enough to rejoin the stratum of the labor market that provides health benefits. As the cost of health care in America has soared far beyond the costs of care in Canada,

England, and other European countries, the millions who find themselves uninsured are now priced out of the health-care marketplace, potentially facing bankruptcy (of the record 1.57 million Americans who filed for personal bankruptcy in
2002, between one-third and one-half filed because of medical bills), and in substantially worse health than those who do have health insurance. Uninsured
Americans receive less preventive care, poorer treatments for both minor and serious chronic and acute illnesses, and they often live shorter lives than members of
comparable insured populations.

As in other caste systems, our new American caste system is characterized by
outward markings on the body. Indeed, illness itself constitutes a physical marker:
Rotten teeth, chronic coughs, bad skin, limps, sores that don't heal, obesity, hearing
or vision deficits that are not corrected, addiction to pain medication—all these
markings signal caste in very basic ways and often limit the employment opportunities available to those who have them. Several people we interviewed told of
being promised a job over the telephone, rushing over to the personnel office, and
then being told that the job was no longer available as soon as the hiring agent took
a look at them.

Echoing the classical Indian caste system, membership in the American caste
of the ill, infirm, and marginally employed carries a moral taint in addition to physical markings and occupational immobility. America has traditionally placed a
moral value on productive work and good health. Work, of course, has long been
construed as a moral virtue in America. We need only think of the generations of
American women who embroidered samplers proclaiming that "idle fingers are the
devil's playthings" and the moral disdain directed at so-called "welfare queens" for
remaining outside the system of paid employment.

Uninsured Americans around the country spoke to us of the stigma of lacking
health insurance—of medical providers who treated them like "losers" because
they are uninsured. Similarly, the providers we spoke to emphasized the problem of
"compliance" among the uninsured, complaining about "difficult" patients who do
not follow through with their doctors' instructions. Sickness increasingly seems to
be construed as a failure of ethical virtue, a failure to take care of oneself "properly,"
to eat the "right" foods or get "enough" exercise, to go for Pap smears; many con-
strue it also as a genetic failure, a failure of will, a failure of commitment. The new
media panic over obesity can only deepen caste-consciousness and exacerbate the
stigma associated with having a body that has not been sculpted through high-
priced gym memberships.

Speaking about what it means in her life to scrape by without health insurance, one of our respondents, a young college graduate in Massachusetts, said, "I
just feel that the way the system is set up is like a bizarre version of natural selection, where the people who are poorest can't afford to keep themselves healthy, and
so they die."

CHAPTER 31

Why Not the Best?
Results from the National Scorecard on U.S. Health System Performance, 2008

The Commonwealth Fund

INTRODUCTION

In the first decade of the 21st century, the nation's health care system faces challenges on multiple fronts. The number of uninsured has increased by 8.6 million since 2000, as employer-sponsored coverage continued to erode even during a period of economic expansion. There were 47 million uninsured Americans as of 2006.[1] Affordable insurance is of concern to families, employers, and public programs: as health care costs continue to rise far faster than incomes, financial protection and access to care for middle- as well as low-income families are increasingly at risk.[2]

U.S. health expenditures, already the highest in the world, are projected to double and reach 20 percent of the nation's gross domestic product (GDP) by 2017, with even higher shares of GDP going toward health care over the longer term.[3] The United States spends the most per person on health care—twice what other major industrialized countries spend—and has had rapid rates of cost growth over the past two decades (Exhibit 31.1).

Evidence continues to mount that the quality of care is uneven and often suboptimal.[4] Quality encompasses not only whether patients receive care that is safe and scientifically proven, but also whether physicians communicate well with patients and coordinate care effectively when patients transition from one place to another. Yet, providers' financial incentives typically encourage doing more rather than supporting high-quality, integrated care across settings, episodes, and conditions with more efficient use of resources. Too often, patients are left to cope with what is, in effect, a fragmented "non-system" of care. Reflecting broad public concerns with access, costs, and care experiences, the percentage of patients expressing dissatisfaction with the health care system doubled from 1998 to 2006.[5]

EXHIBIT 31.1

International Comparison of Spending on Health, 1980–2005

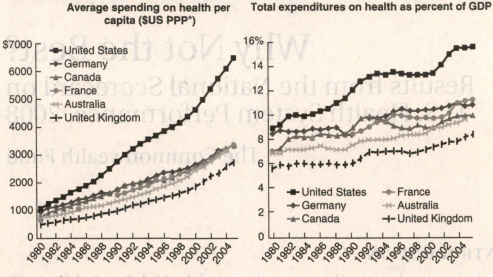

*PPP = Purchasing Power Parity.
Data: OECD Health Data 2007, Version 10/2007.
Source: Commonwealth Fund National Scorecard on U.S. Health System Performance, 2008.

Unlike virtually all other industrialized countries, the U.S. fails to ensure universal coverage of its population. This failing has serious consequences: poorer health from lack of timely access to care; health conditions that, left unchecked, become costlier to treat; premature death; and reduced economic output from a less productive, sicker workforce.[6] Other nations spend less on health care, achieve better health outcomes, and cover their entire populations. This indicates that the U.S. is not getting high value commensurate with its investment in the health care system.[7]

Developing policies to move the U.S. toward a higher-value health system over time, and evaluating the effects of particular health policies relative to goals, requires a means to monitor health system performance across all of its dimensions. To meet this need for a whole-system view, the Commonwealth Fund Commission on a High Performance Health System created a *National Scorecard on U.S. Health System Performance* in 2006.[8] Spanning healthy lives, quality, access, efficiency, and equity, the Scorecard found that U.S. health system performance fell far short of what should be attainable, based on benchmarks of achieved performance, and uncovered broad evidence of opportunities to improve.

The *National Scorecard on U.S. Health System Performance, 2008,* updates the analysis to assess current performance and changes over time, based on the most recent data available. By contrasting national performance with benchmarks, the

Scorecard provides targets for action and a yardstick against which to assess new policies over time. In the sections that follow, we describe how the Scorecard works and present overall findings and results for five core dimensions of health system performance. We conclude with an analysis of cross-cutting themes and implications for national policy and improvement initiatives.

HEALTHY LIVES

Overview.   Compared with top-performing countries and states, the U.S. as a whole is falling short in promoting healthy, long, and productive lives for everyone. The Scorecard includes five indicators in this dimension, including potentially preventable deaths, infant mortality, disability, and healthy life expectancy. From 2006 to 2008, average performance declined from 75 to 72, due to poor performance on two core indicators. The score reflects the growing gaps in health outcomes between average and top performance, particularly as the U.S. lags behind gains achieved by leading countries.

Preventable Mortality.   The U.S. fell into last place among 19 industrialized countries on national rates of mortality considered "amenable to health care."[9] These are deaths before age 75 caused by at least partially preventable or treatable conditions, such as bacterial infections, screenable cancers, diabetes, heart disease, stroke, and complications of common surgical procedures. While the U.S. rate improved 4 percent between 1997–1998 and 2002–2003 (from 115 to 110 deaths per 100,000), rates improved by 16 percent on average in the other countries (Exhibit 31.2). In fact, countries that began with considerably higher premature mortality rates than the U.S., including the United Kingdom, Ireland, and Portugal, now outperform the U.S. in preventing or delaying such deaths. At the same time, the top three countries (France, Japan, and Australia) have raised the bar of performance. As a result, U.S. death rates are now 59 percent higher than in countries with the lowest rates. Improving U.S. mortality from amenable causes to levels achieved by these leading countries would translate into 101,000 fewer deaths per year.

The rate of infants born in the U.S. who die before their first birthday improved slightly from 2002 to 2004 (from 7.0 to 6.8 deaths per 1,000 live births), thus returning to earlier levels. Yet, the U.S. average remains well above rates in the lowest states and countries. Rates of infant mortality in the worst-performing states are more than twice those in benchmark states. Of concern, the gap between the leading and lagging states grew wider in 2004, as states with the highest rates— primarily poor and located in the South—experienced an increase in infant mortality.[10] Moreover, the U.S. ranked last among eight industrialized countries that report infant mortality using the same methodology, with a national rate more than double the leading countries (2.8 to 3.1 deaths per 1,000 live births in Japan, Iceland, and Sweden in 2004).[11]

EXHIBIT 31.2 Healthy Lives

Mortality Amenable to Health Care
Deaths per 100,000 population*

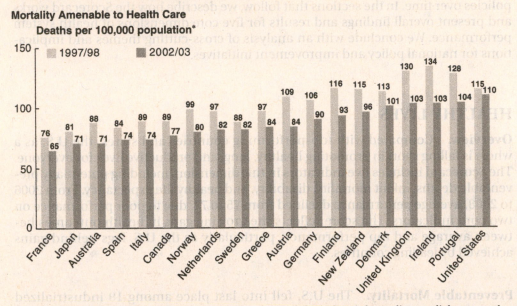

*Countries' age-standardized death rate before age 75; includes ischemic heart disease, diabetes, stroke, and bacterial infections.

Data: E. Nolte and C. M. McKee, London School of Hygiene and Tropical Medicine analysis of World Health Organization (WHO) mortality files (Nolte and McKee 2008).

Source: Commonwealth Fund National Scorecard on U.S. Health System Performance, 2008.

Impacts of Poor Health. *Healthy life expectancy.* Reflecting these mortality trends, life expectancy in the U.S. has not kept pace with other advanced countries, even as it reached a new high of almost 78 years in 2006.[12] The U.S. ranks poorly in terms of healthy life expectancy at age 60, as U.S. adults spend more of their lives in poor health than adults in other countries. Perhaps this is not surprising, given the greater burden of chronic health problems among older adults in the U.S., compared with adults abroad, and the adverse health consequences for older adults after long periods without insurance.[13]

Activity limitations. More than one of every six working-age adults (18%) reported being unable to work or carry out everyday activities because of health problems in 2006—up from 15 percent reporting limitations in 2004. Health-related limitations increased in both the top and bottom five states, but the deterioration was greatest in the bottom states. Previously reported rates at which children miss large numbers of school days because of illnesses or injuries vary more than twofold across states. These findings indicate the need for better prevention and treatment of chronic diseases to enhance quality of life and capacity to work, particularly among younger cohorts as they age. . . .

Patient-Centered and Timely Care.   Patient-centered care and timely access to care can increase adherence to treatment plans, help engage patients in care decisions, and improve outcomes of care.[14] The overall score for patient-centered and timely care declined from 72 to 69, as two indicators declined (one could not be updated). The Scorecard results indicate that there are major deficiencies in providing timely care and communicating effectively with patients. National scores on indicators are as much as 65 percent below benchmarks set by leading countries, health plans, or hospitals.

Rapid access to primary care. U.S. adults with health problems are significantly less likely than patients in five of the seven countries surveyed to get a rapid appointment with a physician—the same or the next day—when they are sick. Only 46 percent of patients reported having such rapid access in 2007, nearly the same as in 2005. The failure to improve highlights the slow pace of adoption of advanced access models of care in physician practices and clinics. The U.S. rate would need to improve by more than 75 percent to reach the benchmark rate (81%).

After-hours care. U.S. adults with health problems are also the most likely among adults in seven countries surveyed to report difficulty obtaining health care after hours without going to the emergency department. This rate increased from 61 percent to 73 percent from 2005 to 2007. Studies in the U.S. indicate that improved after-hours care and better access to primary care can reduce the need for relatively costly emergency department visits, particularly among higher-risk, low-income patients."[15]

Physician communication. Open and clear communication between doctors and their patients is a key component of patient-centered care. On average, just over half of U.S. patients in 2004 and 2002 (57% and 54%) said their doctors always listened carefully, explained things clearly, showed them respect, and spent enough time with them. Patient communication experiences vary widely by insurance status and source of coverage. The national rate in 2004 remained well below the 75 percent benchmark rate set by top-performing health plans. Interventions aimed at both physicians and patients may improve the quality of interpersonal medical interactions.[16] . . .

HEALTH CARE ACCESS

Overview.   Access to care is fundamental to high-quality care. Inadequate access can result in inefficient care from avoidable complications, reliance on emergency departments for primary care, duplication of services, and failure to follow-up on test results or preventive care. Rising numbers of uninsured as well as escalating health care costs and health insurance premiums create barriers to care and place financial strain on insured as well as uninsured patients.[17] Reflecting these trends, performance on four of five access indicators declined substantially, as increasing numbers of middle- as well as low-income families found themselves at risk of inadequate access to care. The overall score on this dimension dropped from 67 to 58—further from the goal of full participation and affordable access.[18]

EXHIBIT 31.3   Access: Participation

Percent of Adults Ages 18–64 Uninsured by State

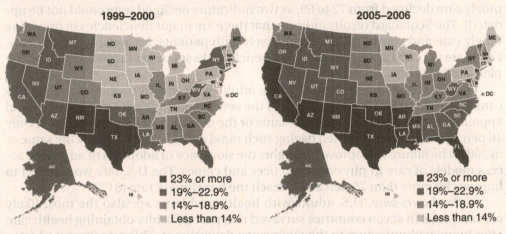

1999–2000   2005–2006

■ 23% or more   ■ 23% or more
■ 19%–22.9%   ■ 19%–22.9%
■ 14%–18.9%   ■ 14%–18.9%
■ Less than 14%   ■ Less than 14%

Data: Two-year averages 1999–2000, updated with 2007 Current Populations Survey correction, and 2005–2006 from the Census Bureau's March 2000, 2001, and 2006–2007 CPS.

Source: Commonwealth Fund National Scorecard on U.S. Heath System Performance, 2008.

Participation.   To date, most of the erosion in insurance coverage has occurred among working-age adults. Based on annual census data, from 1999–2000 to 2005–2006 the number of states where 23 percent or more of the working-age adult population is uninsured grew from two to nine, while the number of states with less than 14 percent uninsured declined from 22 to eight (Exhibit 31.3). Children fared better due to public coverage expansions. In 2005–2006, only five states had more than 16 percent of children uninsured, down from nine in 1999–2000. And in twelve states, fewer than 7% of children were uninsured.[19]

As the number of adults without insurance has steadily grown, so has the number of "underinsured"—those who are insured all year but have medical bills or deductibles that were high relative to their incomes.[20] In 2007, 25 million adults (14%) were underinsured, an increase of more than 60 percent since 2003 when 16 million were underinsured. This sharp jump was driven by a near tripling in the rate (from 4% to 11%) among those with moderate or higher incomes (200% of the federal poverty level or more). Another 50 million adults were uninsured during the year. As a result, as of 2007, more than 75 million adults—42 percent of all adults ages 19 to 64—were either uninsured during the year or underinsured, up from 35 percent in 2003 (Exhibit 31.4).

Although low-income adults remain most at risk, the increase in the percent uninsured or underinsured was greatest among those with incomes of 200 percent of poverty or higher.

The erosion in coverage undermines access to care. In 2007, more than one-third of U.S adults (37%) went without needed care, including prescription drugs,

EXHIBIT 31.4 Access: Participation

Uninsured and Underinsured Adults, 2007 Compared with 2003

Percent of adults (ages 19–64) who are uninsured or underinsured

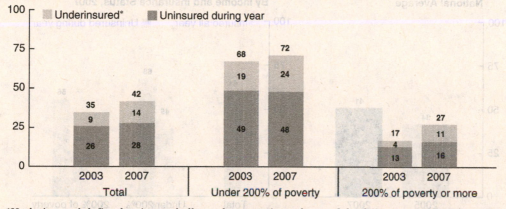

*Underinsured defined as insured all year but experienced one of the following: medical expenses equaled 10% or more of income; medical expenses equaled 5% or more of income if low income (<200% of poverty); or deductibles equaled 5% or more of income.

Data: 2003 and 2007 Commonwealth Fund Biennial Health Insurance Survey.

Source: Commonwealth Fund National Scorecard on U.S. Health System Performance, 2008.

because of costs. In contrast, only 5 percent of adults in the Netherlands, the benchmark country, reported such financial barriers to care. The Netherlands has universal coverage with a broad range of benefits and modest cost-sharing by U.S. standards.

Affordable Care. The costs of both health insurance and medical care have become less affordable. The average cost of family coverage obtained at employer group rates exceeded $12,000 a year in 2007.[21] With premiums rising faster than wages, the average cost of insurance premiums relative to income increased in almost all states. As a result, the percent of adults residing in a state where employer premiums averaged less than 15 percent of the median household income declined precipitously, from 58 percent to 25 percent over the most recent two years.

By 2005, nearly one of four adults under age 65 (23%) lived in families with high out-of-pocket health care costs, including premiums and direct spending for services, up from 19 percent in 2001. This increase was driven entirely by rising costs among those with private insurance. Financial burdens were especially steep among people who purchased insurance in the nongroup market: half faced high out-of-pocket burdens, compared with 40 percent in 2008.

Efforts to moderate premium growth have led to limits on benefits and higher cost-sharing. The resulting exposure to costs added to the share of families who

EXHIBIT 31.5   Access: Affordable Care

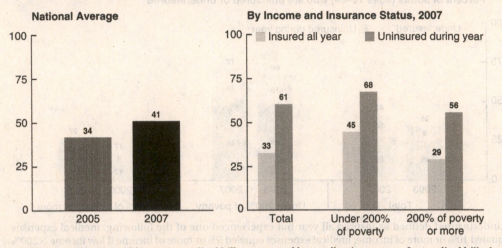

Medical Bill Problems or Medical Debt
Percent of adults (ages 19–64) with any medical bill problem or outstanding debt*

*Problems paying or unable to pay medical bills, contacted by a collection agency for medical bills, had to change way of life to pay bills, or has medical debt being paid off over time.

Data: 2005 and 2007 Commonwealth Fund Biennial Health Insurance Survey.

Source: Commonwealth Fund National Scorecard on U.S. Health System Performance, 2008.

struggle with medical debt and medical bills. By 2007, two of five U.S. adults (41%) reported having problems paying medical bills, being contacted by collection agencies, or paying medical debt over time, up from 34 percent in 2005 (Exhibit 31.5). Having insurance is no longer a guarantee of financial protection: one of three (33%) adults ages 19 to 64 who were continually insured faced medical bill problems; middle- and lower-income adults were the most at risk.

Access and Its Relationship to Quality and Efficiency.   Reduced access to care has serious implications for overall health system performance. Without adequate coverage and financial protection, there is diminished opportunity to receive high-quality care.[22] Uninsured people often fail to get timely and appropriate care when needed, leading to worse health outcomes and more costly emergency or acute care later on. When they do get care, the uninsured also experience more medical errors or coordination problems, such as delays in transferring medical records/test results and duplication of tests. A recent study estimates the death toll from being uninsured amounted to 137,000 from 2000 to 2006, including 22,000 deaths in 2006.[23]

Editors' Note: *Notes for this reading can be found in the original source.*

CHAPTER 32

The Untold Health Care Story
How They Crippled Medicare

Lillian B. Rubin

Until recently, my husband and I had been seeing one of those "Oh-I'm-so-glad-he's-my-doctor" physicians for two decades. Then one day the mail brought the announcement that the office was closing its doors and that the four doctors who had been in the practice were either retiring or leaving San Francisco. They enclosed a list of doctors who, they said, had indicated they had room in their practices. So started my search for a new primary-care physician.

I looked the list over, saw a familiar name, and dialed the number. "Yes," the receptionist assured me, "doctor is taking new patients." It was all very friendly; I made an appointment; she set about recording the necessary information, and then the crucial question. "What insurance do you have?" "Medicare and AARP" (one of the several medi-gap insurance plans to which those of us who can afford it subscribe), I replied. I heard a small intake of breath, a ten-second silence that felt like much more, and then, "Oh, you should have told me before that you're Medicare; doctor isn't taking new Medicare patients." And with that she severed the connection and, I assume, wiped my appointment off the book.

I was surprised at the brusque refusal, shaken a bit, but not yet worried. San Francisco is a city that seduces with its charms, and with a major medical school within its borders and two more less than an hour's drive away, we have plenty of well-trained physicians practicing here. How hard could it be to find a good internist? Very hard, it turned out, as I worked my way down a list of a dozen doctors—some referred by my retiring internist, some recommended by friends or friends of friends.

Since the medical community in the city knew of the shuttering of the office where I'd been cared for, they were prepared for calls like mine. Some announced on their voice mail: "The doctor isn't taking any new Medicare patients"; some asked the fatal question about insurance before responding to my request for an appointment; and a few waited until they had noted all my personal information before asking the question. Twelve calls; twelve refusals to take Medicare.

Stunned, I sat at my desk looking at the list and wondering, What happened to the Medicare I once knew, to the physicians for whom it was simply another part of their practice, to the government that once supported it fully before the right-wing mania for privatization set in? Big questions. But my immediate concern was to find a doctor who would be available when my husband or I needed her or him.

Because I'm reasonably well-known in this community, I decided to get past the front desk by writing to each of these physicians directly. I laid out my credentials and accomplishments as if I were applying for a grant or a job; I dropped some reputable names of people, lay and professional, who had given me permission to do so, while at the same time assuring the doctors to whom I was pleading my case that I continued to be very active and was in vigorous good health. It was an exercise in the absurd. There I was, looking for a doctor to oversee my health and at the same time assuring any who would listen that I wouldn't need them.

Two weeks later, I was getting desperate. The actual closure of the medical office was looming, and I still had not heard from a single physician on my list. I began to call the offices to ask if the doctor had received and read the letter I sent. I was brushed off in the first five with a curt reminder that "The doctor isn't taking new Medicare patients." Finally, on the sixth call, the woman on the other end of the line said she'd ask the doctor and call me back. An hour later, she called to say that he had read my letter, was "intrigued," and would like to meet me.

We met, he agreed to take us on, and finally we had a doctor. But what, I wondered, happens to ordinary folk who don't write letters and who, if they did, wouldn't "intrigue" the person at the other end? Was this just something happening here in San Francisco where some doctors are charging a thousand-dollar fee for the privilege of becoming a patient and an annual membership payment of $500 thereafter?

As my story got out, the answers came pouring in. Friends and acquaintances around the country had similar tales to tell, sometimes their own experiences, sometimes about a friend or family member. Doctors from New York to California were either refusing to take new Medicare patients or making it so hard to get into their offices that it was no better than a direct refusal.

While this Medicare drama played out in my own life, health care was center stage in the long, drawn-out political theater known as the Democratic Party's primaries. As Senators Barack Obama and Hillary Clinton argued about the fine points of their respective universal-health-care promises, President George W. Bush released plans to reduce budget deficits on the backs of America's old folks by calling for $208 billion in mandatory budget reductions, with Medicare taking the biggest hit. In addition to cutting services and doctors' payments, the administration seeks to slow the pace of Medicare growth from 7 percent to 5 percent over the next five years—cuts that come during the very period when Medicare rolls will grow exponentially as the first of the baby boomers become eligible for coverage, and about which no candidate of either party has expressed any outrage.

The history of the struggle for health care in the United States is a long and bitter one, going back to 1945 when President Harry Truman asked the Congress to enact a national insurance program "to assure the right to adequate medical care and protection from the economic fears of sickness." A coalition of conservative groups, led by the implacable opposition of the American Medical Association (AMA) and fueled by the insurance and pharmaceutical industries, denounced the Truman plan as "socialistic," stoked public fears about freedom and choice, and defeated the legislation.

By 1952, Truman, acknowledging that he couldn't win health care for all, tried softening the opposition with a compromise proposal, one that would provide care only for those age sixty-five and over who were receiving Social Security. But if the universal health care plan was outright socialism, the new, more limited legislation was nothing less than a foot in the socialist door, and the same forces that had fought so fiercely before joined once again to defeat the scaled-back proposal.

The same scenario was repeated in 1960 when, with the support of President John F. Kennedy, Medicare's backers introduced yet another bill to provide health care for America's aged. Only this time, the AMA, with the help of the wives of physicians across the country, organized what was known as "Operation Coffee Cup" and enlisted a B-movie actor named Ronald Reagan, who was then host of the popular Sunday night television program General Electric Theater, to warn, "One of the traditional methods of imposing statism or socialism on a people has been by way of medicine."

Reflecting on the campaign against Medicare, Drew Pearson, a well-known Washington columnist at the time, wrote

> Ronald Reagan of Hollywood has pitted his mellifluous voice against President Kennedy in the battle for medical aid for the elderly. As a result it looks as if the old folks would lose out. He has caused such a deluge of mail to swamp Congress that Congressmen want to postpone action on the medical bill until 1962. What they don't know, of course, is that Ron Reagan is behind the mail; also that the American Medical Association is paying for it. . . . Just how [Reagan's] background qualifies him as an expert on medical care for the elderly remains a mystery. Nevertheless, thanks to a deal with the AMA, and the acquiescence of General Electric, Ronald may be able to out influence the President of the United States with Congress.

It took President Lyndon Johnson, a former Senate leader who knew where all the congressional bodies were buried, to twist enough arms in Congress to stiffen its spine. On July 30, 1965, the years of struggle finally paid off. President Johnson signed into law Title XVIII of the Social Security Act establishing Medicare and its companion program, Medicaid, which insures indigent Americans. The nation had its first (and still only) government-sponsored, single-payer medical system. Former President Harry Truman was the first person to enroll in the program. The fee for Medicare Part B, which covers doctors visits (Part A covers hospital care), was $3 a month. Today, there's a deductible of $135 before Medicare picks up 80 percent of the bill, and a monthly premium of $96.40 for those earning up to $82,000 ($164,000 for a couple filing a joint return). After that, the premiums go up proportionate to income.

While Medicare was a bare-bones program at first, covering hospital and doctor visits, it was expanded repeatedly over the next twenty-five years to cover disabled persons of any age, people with end-stage renal disease, recipients of the Supplemental Security Income (SSI) program for the elderly and disabled poor, chiropractic services, home health care, hospice, and more.

Despite the immense popular support for Medicare, the program continued to grate on conservative sensibilities, and by the early 1980s the conservatism of the Reagan administration—its distaste for what it called "social engineering," which meant any federally financed benefit programs—began to make itself felt. But the same voices that were railing against entitlements like Medicare were silent when the program was amended to cover the federal judiciary, members of Congress, and the president. No cries of socialism arose, no concerns about the cost of entitlements, no jeremiads about freedom and choice were heard from the congressional opposition or President Reagan when it was their turn to get government-sponsored health care.

With all the controversy, however, it wasn't until 1995, after the Clinton administration's failed attempt at universal health care, that the Republican Congress, urged on by Speaker of the House Newt Gingrich and backed strongly by the insurance companies, passed the Medicare Reform Bill, which was much less a step toward reform than a walk toward privatization. But it couldn't have happened without the support from some Democrats and the signature of President Bill Clinton, who seemed to have lost his veto pen that day. True, he didn't have the votes to sustain a veto, but that hasn't stopped George W. Bush from sending back to Congress legislation that offends his principles, leaving those bills to languish on the stalemated congressional back burner with no hope of passage anytime soon.

Ultimately, the alleged reforms meant, among other things, an increased reliance on private insurance companies—subsidized by the federal government—for the delivery of care. It looked like a good deal at first, with grand promises from the insurance companies of more care for less money, and Medicare recipients flocked to the health maintenance organizations, my husband and I among them. But it wasn't long before many of us found out that an insurance company's public relations campaign has little relation to reality, and their promises melted away before the imperative of the bottom line. So, for example, when my husband developed a persistent urinary-tract infection that our primary care doctor kept treating unsuccessfully, I finally asked him why he wasn't referring the problem to a urologist. He hemmed and hawed, shifted his feet, dropped his eyes, and finally said almost shamefacedly, "These HMOs are making it harder and harder to make that kind of referral." I immediately switched back to Medicare, where a physician's judgment is still generally the deciding factor in specialist care.

By 1997, two years after the so-called reforms were instituted, Senator Ted Kennedy and Representative Richard Gephardt were so outraged by the continued assault on Medicare that they wrote in a *Washington Post* op-ed piece,

Republicans in Congress—and, unfortunately, a few Democrats too—want to go beyond the bipartisan budget agreement and subject Medicare to death by countless cuts by increasing the cost of care, skimming off the healthiest and wealthiest participants, raising the age of eligibility, means-testing the program and turning major parts of Medicare over to the tender mercies of private insurance companies and managed-care firms.

Then came the Bush years. From its earliest days, this administration's hostility to Medicare and Social Security has been no secret. It lost the fight to privatize Social Security, but the war against Medicare continues as it pushes people into HMOs by increasing the monthly cost for Medicare, cutting services, and reducing payments to hospitals and doctors until the very existence of the program is threatened. As long ago as 2005, an AMA survey reported that nearly 40 percent of 5,486 physicians said that if the projected 5 percent cuts were to pass, they would "curtail the number of new Medicare patients they accept into their practices."

In the intervening years the situation has only gotten worse. A recent national survey of a thousand practicing physicians, released by the Medical Group Management Association, reports that in anticipation of the proposed 10.6 percent further payment reductions to take effect on July 1, 2008, 60 percent of the respondents reported that they were either limiting the number of Medicare patients or refusing to accept them altogether. One Oregon physician reported that he was "routinely turning away Medicare patients so desperate to find a doctor that they offered to pay for excess charges out-of-pocket," a practice prohibited by Medicare law. Another whose Florida practice is made up of over 50 percent Medicare patients, agonized over dropping people who, he said, had become "like old friends after 28 years in practice." But if the payments are slashed again, he explained, "I'll have no choice. It's a business, and if I can't pay the bills, I can't survive." Chilling news for those of us now in Medicare, and worse yet for the Baby Boomers who will become eligible in the next few years.

True, some may argue that doctors already make more money than most Americans, and it's hard to listen to their grievances with much sympathy. But doctors are at the heart of the success of Medicare, and until the Bush administration's escalation of the war against the program, they took care of the nation's elders without complaint. Moreover, their grievances gain force and legitimacy when we notice that the administration's proposed budget cuts target doctors, hospitals, and a variety of patient services but don't lay a glove on payments to the private insurance companies and their HMOs, even though many independent experts say federal payments to those plans are far too high and the service they provide much too low.

Unfortunately, the election campaign now under way offers little hope of substantial improvement in the health care crisis that now afflicts this nation. For despite what the privatization of Medicare has taught us about the incompatibility of for-profit insurance companies with quality patient care, and despite the fact that federal subsidies to these corporations are substantially more costly to taxpayers than the government-run Medicare, no candidate dares to propose the only universal health care plan that will work: a government-sponsored, single-payer system along the lines of the original Medicare[1]—a program that worked just fine until a coalition of conservative forces, insurance companies, the pharmaceutical industry, and right-leaning and/or fearful Democrats disassembled it.[2]

ENDNOTES

1. Ironically, a recent study conducted by the Indiana University School of Medicine's Center for Health Policy and Professionalism Research Policy and published in the *Annals of Internal Medicine* (April 2008) reports that in a survey of 2,200 physicians, 59 percent now support legislation to establish national health insurance. Reflecting on his analysis of the data, Dr. Ronald Ackerman, co-author of the study, concluded that "across the board, physicians feel that our fragmented and for-profit insurance system is obstructing good patient care, and a majority now support national insurance as the remedy."

2. All this, and I haven't even mentioned the huge multi-billion-dollar boondoggle the federal government handed the insurance companies and the pharmaceutical industry with Medicare Part D, the prescription drug benefit that went into effect on January 1, 2006. It would take another whole article to discuss the many-tiered problems with this program.

PART TEN

The Schools

Hardly a year goes by without another dire report on the sad state of America's public schools. Although they are often reasonably satisfied with the schools their own children attend, many Americans believe that the schools in *general* are falling apart. Bad schools are routinely blamed for a host of our national problems, from uneven economic growth to youth violence.

As many commentators have pointed out, the popular image of the schools is more than a little misleading. *Overall*, the public schools are not as bad as they are often said to be. They are educating more children, from a wider range of backgrounds—and often with more difficult problems—than ever before. Scores on achievement tests, which fell disturbingly in the 1970s, aren't falling any more. More American students go on to college than those of most other industrial countries—and our system of higher education remains one of the best in the world, drawing students from every part of the globe.

Nevertheless, there are a number of serious problems with American schools, and the articles in this part help us to separate the real ones from those that are mostly mythical.

Perhaps the most fundamental of those problems is the persistence of deep inequalities in schooling that continue to divide America's schoolchildren into educational haves and have-nots. At their best, schools—both private and public— offer students high-quality teaching, substantial resources, and excellent facilities. But at their worst, American schools can be astonishingly bad—offering dilapidated and aging classrooms, few resources, and an educational experience that cannot possibly prepare the young for a productive role in society. Unsurprisingly, these "savage inequalities," in the words of the writer Jonathan Kozol, fall along lines of income and race.

In the selection we reprint here from his book, *The Shame of the Nation*, Kozol describes how these inequalities shape the educational experience of children in the New York City public schools and argues that, if anything, the educational disparities between affluent and poor children are growing. Not only do inner-city schools receive less funding per student than their counterparts in wealthier communities, but they have steadily lost many of the basics—like libraries, art and music programs, and medical care for students—that used to be taken for granted.

The problems Kozol describes are part of a broader pattern in which educational resources—like health care and other social goods—are increasingly distributed in markedly unequal ways. We have always prided ourselves on the inclusiveness of our system of public education, as a symbol and embodiment of fundamental American values. What has traditionally made college, for example, a way of moving upward for generations of lower-income Americans was that a college education could be had for free, or nearly so—meaning that the opportunity to gain a higher education was separated from one's ability to pay. But as Ellen Mutari and Melaku Lakew show, going to college today, even at many public universities, increasingly means long hours of outside work, the burden of taking on heavy student loans, or "maxing out" credit cards—a reality that may not be news to many readers of this book. As college becomes less and less affordable, it becomes that much harder for working people to achieve the American Dream through their own efforts.

The very real troubles of the schools have periodically led critics to blame them for most of our other social problems—from poverty to income inequality to international competitiveness—and to imply that improving the schools could be a panacea. As Lawrence Mishel and Richard Rothstein argue, however, the sources of these problems lie far beyond the schools, and expecting schools to solve them on their own is unrealistic. Enhancing the quality of education for everyone is certainly an important goal on its own merits, but it should not be seen as a quick fix for the inequality and distorted economic priorities that have trapped so many in poverty and thwarted opportunities. Strengthening our economy and raising the overall standard of living for Americans will require much more—including policies to ensure that the fruits of growing productivity are more fairly distributed.

Jennifer Washburn's discussion of the growing links between universities and private industry illustrates another troubling development in education—the blurring of the boundaries between education and the pursuit of profit. Traditionally, universities have been committed to the disinterested search for knowledge. But like many other institutions in America, they have become increasingly subject to the influence of private corporations, and the line between objective research and corporate public relations is now sometimes difficult to draw. Corporations not only fund important research, but often help to shape its conclusions. And in some areas—such as research on the safety and effectiveness of new drugs—the consequences are both unethical and dangerous.

CHAPTER 33

The Shame of the Nation
The Restoration of Apartheid Schooling in America

Jonathan Kozol

"Dear Mr. Kozol," said the eight-year-old, "we do not have the things you have. You have Clean things. We do not have. You have a clean bathroom. We do not have that. You have Parks and we do not have Parks. You have all the thing and we do not have all the thing. . . . Can you help us?"

The letter, from a child named Alliyah, came in a fat envelope of 27 letters from a class of third grade children in the Bronx. Other letters that the students in Alliyah's classroom sent me registered some of the same complaints. "We don't have no gardens," and "no Music or Art," and "no fun places to play," one child said. "Is there a way to fix this Problem?" Another noted a concern one hears from many children in such overcrowded schools: "We have a gym but it is for lining up. I think it is not fair." Yet another of Alliyah's classmates asked me, with a sweet misspelling, if I knew the way to make her school into a "good" school— "like the other kings have"—and ended with the hope that I would do my best to make it possible for "all the kings" to have good schools.

The letter that affected me the most, however, had been written by a child named Elizabeth. "It is not fair that other kids have a garden and new things. But we don't have that," said Elizabeth. "I wish that this school was the most beautiful school in the whole why world."

Elizabeth had very careful, very small, and neatly formed handwriting. She had corrected other errors in her letter, squeezing in a missing letter she'd initially forgotten, erasing and rewriting a few words she had misspelled. The error she had left unaltered in the final sentence therefore captured my attention more than it might otherwise have done.

"The whole why world" stayed in my thoughts for days. When I later met Elizabeth I brought her letter with me, thinking I might see whether, in reading it aloud, she'd change the "why" to "wide" or leave it as it was. My visit to her class, however, proved to be so pleasant, and the children seemed so eager to bombard me with their questions about where I lived, and why I lived there rather than New

297

York, and who I lived with, and how many dogs I had and other interesting questions of that sort, that I decided not to interrupt the nice reception they had given me with questions about usages and spelling. I left "the whole why world" to float around unedited and unrevised within my mind. The letter itself soon found a resting place up on the wall above my desk.

In the years before I met Elizabeth. I had visited many elementary schools in the South Bronx and in one northern district of the Bronx as well. I had also made a number of visits to a high school where a stream of water flowed down one of the main stairwells on a rainy afternoon and where green fungus molds were growing in the office where the students went for counseling. A large blue barrel was positioned to collect rain-water coming through the ceiling. In one make-shift elementary school housed in a former skating rink next to a funeral parlor in another nearly all-black-and-Hispanic section of the Bronx, class size rose to 34 and more; four kindergarten classes and a sixth grade class were packed into a single room that had no windows. Airlessness was stifling in many rooms; and recess was impossible because there was no outdoor playground and no indoor gym, so the children had no place to play.

In another elementary school, which had been built to hold 1,000 children but was packed to bursting with some 1,500 boys and girls, the principal poured out his feelings to me in a room in which a plastic garbage bag had been attached somehow to cover part of the collapsing ceiling. "This," he told me, pointing to the garbage bag; then gesturing around him at the other indications of decay and disrepair one sees in ghetto schools much like it elsewhere, "would not happen to white children."

A friend of mine who was a first-year teacher in a Harlem high school told me she had 40 students in her class but only 30 chairs, so some of her students had to sit on windowsills or lean against the walls. Other high schools were so crowded they were forced to shorten schooldays and to cut back hours of instruction to accommodate a double shift of pupils. Tens of thousands of black and Hispanic students were in schools like these, in which half the student body started classes very early in the morning and departed just before or after lunch, while the other half did not begin their schoolday until noon.

Libraries, once one of the glories of the New York City system, were either nonexistent or, at best, vestigial in large numbers of the elementary schools. Art and music programs had for the most part disappeared as well. "When I began to teach in 1969," the principal of an elementary school in the South Bronx reported to me "every school had a full-time licensed art and music teacher and librarian." During the next decade, he recalled, "I saw all of that destroyed."

School physicians were also removed from elementary schools during these years. In 1970, when substantial numbers of white children still attended New York City's schools, 400 doctors had been present to address the health needs of the children. By 1993, the number of doctors had been cut to 23, most of them part-time— a cutback that affected most acutely children in the city's poorest neighborhoods where medical provision was perennially substandard and health problems faced by children most extreme. During the 1990s, for example, the rate of pediatric asthma in the South Bronx, already one of the highest in the nation, was exacerbated when the city chose to build a medical waste incinerator in their neighborhood after a plan to build it on the East Side of Manhattan was abandoned in the face of protests from the parents of that area. Hospitalization rates for these asthmatic children in the Bronx were as much as 20 times more frequent than for children in the city's affluent communities. Teachers spoke of children who came into class with chronic wheezing and, at any moment of the day, might undergo more serious attacks, but in the schools I visited there were no doctors to attend to them.

Political leaders in New York tended to point to shifting economic factors, such as a serious budget crisis in the middle 1970s, rather than to the changing racial demographics of the student population, as the explanation for these steep declines in services. But the fact of economic ups and downs from year to year, or from one decade to the next, could not convincingly explain the permanent shortchanging of the city's students, which took place routinely in good economic times and bad, with bad times seized upon politically to justify these cuts while, in the good times, losses undergone during the crisis years had never been restored.

"If you close your eyes to the changing racial composition of the schools and look only at budget actions and political events," says Noreen Connell, the director of the nonprofit Educational Priorities Panel in New York, "you're missing the assumptions that are underlying these decisions." When minority parents ask for something better for their kids, she says, "the assumption is that these are parents who can be discounted. These are kids that we don't value."

The disrepair and overcrowding of these schools in the South Bronx "wouldn't happen for a moment in a white suburban school district like Scarsdale," says former New York State Commissioner of Education Thomas Sobol, who was once the superintendent of the Scarsdale schools and is now a professor of education at Teachers College in New York. "I'm aware that I could never prove that race is at the heart of this if I were called to testify before a legislative hearing. But I've felt it for so long, and seen it operating for so long, I know it's true. . . ."

During the 1990s, physical conditions in some buildings had become so dangerous that a principal at one Bronx school, which had been condemned in 1989 but nonetheless continued to be used, was forced to order that the building's windows not be cleaned because the frames were rotted and glass panes were falling in the street, while at another school the principal had to have the windows bolted shut for the same reason. These were not years of economic crisis in New York. This was a period in which financial markets soared and a new generation of free-spending millionaires and billionaires was widely celebrated by the press and on TV; but none of the proceeds of this period of economic growth had found their way into the schools that served the truly poor. . . .

I had, as I have noted, visited many schools in other cities by this time; but I did not know children in those schools as closely as I'd come to know, or soon would know, so many of the children in the New York City schools. So it would be these children, and especially the ones in elementary schools in which I spent the most time in the Bronx, whose sensibilities and puzzlements and understandings would impress themselves most deeply on my own impressions in the years to come, and it would be their question that became my questions and their accusations and their challenges, when it appeared that they were making challenges, that came to be my own.

This, then is the accusation that Alliyah and her classmates send our way: "You have. . . . We do not have." Are they right or are they wrong? Is this a case of naïve and simplistic juvenile exaggeration? What does a third grader know about these big-time questions about what is fair and what is not, and what is right and what is wrong? Physical appearances apart, how in any case do you begin to measure something so diffuse and vast and seemingly abstract as having more, or having less, or having not at all?

In a social order where it seems a fairly common matter to believe that what we spend to purchase almost anything we need bears some connection to the worth of what we get, a look at what we think it's in our interest to invest in children like Alliyah or Pineapple may not tell us everything we need to know about the state of educational fair play within our nation, but it surely tells us *something* about what we think these kids are worth to us in human terms and in the contributions they may someday make to our society. At the time I met Alliyah in the school-year 1997–1998, New York's Board of Education spent about $8,000 yearly on the education of a third grade child in a New York City public school. If you could have scooped Alliyah up out of the neighborhood where she was born and plunked her down within a fairly typical white suburb of New York, she would have received a public education worth about $12,000 every year. If you were to lift her up once more and set her down within one of the wealthiest white suburbs of New York, she would have received as much as $18,000 worth of public education every year and would likely have had a third grade teacher paid approximately $30,000 more than was her teacher in the Bronx.

The dollars on both sides of the equation have increased since then, but the discrepancies between them have not greatly changed. The present per-pupil spending level in the New York City schools is $11,700, which may be compared to a per-pupil spending level in excess of $22,000 in the well-to-do suburban district of Manhasset. The present New York City level is, indeed, almost exactly what Manhasset spent per pupil 18 years ago, in 1987, when that sum of money bought a great deal more in services and salaries than it can buy today. In dollars adjusted for inflation, New York City has not yet caught up to where its wealthiest suburbs were a quarter-century ago.

Gross discrepancies in teacher salaries between the city and its affluent white suburbs have remained persistent too. In 1997, the median salary for teachers in Alliyah's neighborhood was $43,000, as compared to $74,000 in suburban Rye, $77,000 in Manhasset, and $81,000 in the town of Scarsdale, which is only about 11 miles from Alliyah's school. Five years later, in 2002, salary scales for New York City's teachers rose to levels that approximated those within the lower-spending districts in the suburbs, but salary scales do not reflect the actual salaries that teachers typically receive, which are dependant upon years of service and advanced degrees. Salaries for first-year teachers in the city now were higher than they'd been four years before, but the differences in median pay between the city and its upper-middle-income suburbs had remained extreme. The overall figure for New York City in 2002–2003 was $53,000, while it had climbed to $87,000 in Manhassett and exceeded $95,000 in Scarsdale.

Even these numbers that compare the city to its suburbs cannot give an adequate impression of the inequalities imposed upon the children living in poor sections of New York. For, even within the New York City schools themselves, there are additional discrepancies in funding between schools that serve the poorest and the wealthiest communities, since teachers with the least seniority and least experience are commonly assigned to schools in the most deeply segregated neighborhoods. The median salary of teachers in Pineapple's neighborhood was less than $46,000 in 2002–2003, the lowest in the city, compared to $59,000 in one of Manhattan's recently gentrified communities, and up to $64,000 in some neighborhoods of Queens.

None of this includes the additional resources given to the public schools in affluent communities where parents have the means to supplement the public funds with private funding of their own, money used to build and stock a good school library for instance, or to arrange for art and music lessons or, in many of these neighborhoods, to hire extra teachers to reduce the size of classes for their children.

This relatively new phenomenon of private money being used selectively to benefit the children only of specific public schools had not been noted widely in New York until about ten years ago when parents of the students at a public school in Greenwich Village in Manhattan raised the funds to pay a fourth grade teacher, outside of the normal budget of the school, when class size in the fourth grade otherwise was likely to increase from 26 to 32, which was the average class size in the district at the time but which, one of the parents said, "would have a devastating impact" on her son. The parents, therefore, collected $46,000—two thirds of it, remarkably, in just one night—in order to retain the extra teacher.

The school in Greenwich Village served a population in which less than 20 percent of students were from families of low income, a very low figure in New York, compared, for instance, to Pineapple's neighborhood, where 95 percent of children lived in poverty. The Greenwich Village school, moreover, was already raising a great deal of private money—more than $100,000 yearly, it was now revealed—to pay for music, art, and science programs and for furniture repairs.

The chancellor of the New York City schools initially rejected the use of private funds to underwrite a teacher's pay, making the argument that this was not fair to the children in those many other schools that had much larger classes; but the district later somehow came up with the public funds to meet the cost of hiring the extra teacher, so the parents won their children the advantage they had sought for them in any case.

As it turned out, the use of private subsidies to supplement the tax-supported budgets of some schools in affluent communities was a more commonly accepted practice than most people in the city's poorest neighborhoods had known. The PTA at one school on the Upper West Side of Manhattan, for example, had been raising nearly $50,000 yearly to hire a writing teacher and two part-time music teachers. At a school in a middle-class section of Park Slope in Brooklyn, parents raised more than $100,000 yearly to employ a science teacher and two art instructors. In yet another neighborhood, parents at an elementary school and junior high had raised more than $1 million, mostly for enrichment programs for their children.

In principle, the parents in poor neighborhoods were free to do fund-raising too, but the proceeds they were likely to bring in differed dramatically. The PTA in one low-income immigrant community, for instance, which sponsored activities like candy sales and tried without success to win foundation grants, was able to raise less than $4,000. In the same year, parents at P.S. 6, a top-rated elementary school serving the Upper East Side of Manhattan, raised $200,000. The solicitation of private funds from parents in communities like this had come to be so common, said the president of the New York City Board of Education, "you almost expect a notice from the schools saying there's going to be tuition." A good deal of private money, moreover, as The Times observed, was "being collected under the table" because parents sometimes feared that they would otherwise be forced to share these funds with other schools. "We can do it," said the leader of the parent group at one of the schools where lavish sums of private money had been raised, "but it is sad that other schools that don't have a richer parent body can't. It really does make it a question of haves and have-nots."

In view of the extensive coverage of this new phenomenon not only by New York City papers but by those in other cities where the same trends are observed, it is apparent that this second layer of disparities between the children of the wealthy and the children of the poor is no secret to the public any longer. Yet, even while they sometimes are officially deplored, these added forms of inequality have been accepted with apparent equanimity by those who are their beneficiaries.

"Inequality is not an intentional thing" said the leader of the PTA in one of the West Side neighborhoods where parents had been raising private funds, some of which had been obtained as charitable grants. "You have schools that are empowered and you have schools that have no power at all. . . . I don't bear any guilt for knowing how to write a grant," he said, a statement that undoubtedly made sense to some but skirted the entire issue of endemic underbudgeting of public schools attended by the children of poor people who did not enjoy his money-raising skills or possible connections to grant makers.

A narrowing of civic virtue to the borders of distinct and self-contained communities is now evolving in these hybrid institutions which are public schools in that they benefit from the receipt of public funds but private in the many supplementary programs that are purchased independently. Boutique schools within an otherwise impoverished system, they enable parents of the middle class and upper middle class to claim allegiance to the general idea of public schools while making sure their children do not suffer gravely for the stripped-down budgets that have done great damage to poor children like Alliyah and Pineapple.

CHAPTER 34

Class Conflict
The Rising Costs of College

Ellen Mutari
Melaku Lakew

Brigit M. just graduated from a public college in southern New Jersey with a 4.0 GPA. Putting herself through college with a full course load, she worked 25 to 30 hours a week off campus as a waitress, plus 8 to 12 hours a week on campus as a writing and economics tutor. She had a scholarship, but, as she says, "You think a full scholarship is great, but it doesn't cover books, transportation, and health care costs." She was lucky to have a flexible employer who was willing to accommodate her course schedule. But the time juggle was still difficult: "It was hard to come home from work at 11:00 P.M. and still have to write a paper that was due for an 8:30 A.M. class."

Brigit is one of almost six million working students in the United States. Many of these students do much more than put in a few hours in the school cafeteria or library. They cannot afford a college education without working long hours at one or more off-campus jobs, taking on heavy student loans, and using credit cards to fill in the gaps. The costs of college have skyrocketed, increasing faster than inflation, family incomes, and taxpayer funding of public institutions and financial aid programs. Full-time annual tuition now ranges from an average of $1,627 for a public community college to $15,380 on average for a private college or university. Total costs—including books and fees—are much higher. The total cost of attending a public community college on a full-time basis averages $7,265 a year, while a four-year public university averages $10,889, and a private college or university typically costs $19,443. Today's college students face tremendous monetary pressures.

Many Americans believe in education as a way of ensuring economic opportunity. Politicians and business leaders trumpet college education as means out of poverty, a by-your-own-bootstraps way of attaining the American Dream. Yet college is becoming less and less affordable, especially for students from lower-income families. Tuition at public and private institutions is rising faster than most families' incomes, according to a 2002 study by the National Center for Public Policy and Higher Education. Consequently, families paying college tuition today are shelling out much larger percentages of their incomes than families did twenty years ago. In 1980, the poorest one-fifth, or quintile, of Americans could pay tuition at a public two-year college with only 6% of their family income. By 2000, this percentage had doubled to 12% of family income. Four-year colleges and universities, including public-sector ones, take an even bigger bite out of tight family budgets. Tuition at a private college represents 25% of the annual income of the poorest quintile of families—up from 13% in 1980. It is not only the poorest families that are losing ground. Middle-class incomes have also failed to keep pace with rising tuition. Only the wealthiest families, those in the top income quintile—who since the 1980s have benefited from inflated stock prices, as well as tax cuts and other economic policies skewed toward the rich—have soaring incomes to match escalating tuition costs.

Why is tuition rising so fast? One reason is that colleges and universities are receiving less funding of other kinds; tuition is replacing other revenue sources such as donations, grants, contracts, and perhaps most significantly, state government appropriations to public-sector institutions. In fact, state appropriations to public two-year colleges, four-year undergraduate schools with some graduate programs, and research universities actually fell between the 1988–89 and 1997–98 academic years, and stayed level for four-year bachelor's institutions. The anti-tax, anti-government, anti-public services rhetoric and policies of the past few decades have undermined states' financial support for public institutions of higher learning. Yet these are the institutions with the explicit mission of making college accessible to all. The short-sighted mentality of "tax cuts today" has eroded our nation's public investment in human capital, much as it has our public infrastructure of roads, schools, and bridges.

STUDENTS WORKING OVERTIME

The gap between total costs and aid for full-time students is significant, averaging $5,631 a year at public community colleges and $6,904 at public four-year institutions. For students attending private colleges and universities, the gap is over $10,000.

More and more, students make up this shortfall with paid work. Almost three-fourths of all full-time college students work while attending school, reports the U.S. Department of Education in its 1999–2000 National Postsecondary Student Aid Survey (NPSAS). This figure is up four percentage points since the 1995–96 survey, and accounts for both on- and off-campus jobs, as well as work-study positions. While we might expect to see older, non-traditional students working, the U.S. Bureau of Labor Statistics reports high rates of employment even among traditional-age college students (those between 16 and 24 years old). These are the students we would most expect to receive parental support so that they could focus on classes and social life. But over half of these college students were holding down jobs (see Figure 34.1). Even young people who are full-time students and those enrolled in four-year colleges are employed at high rates, 47.0% and

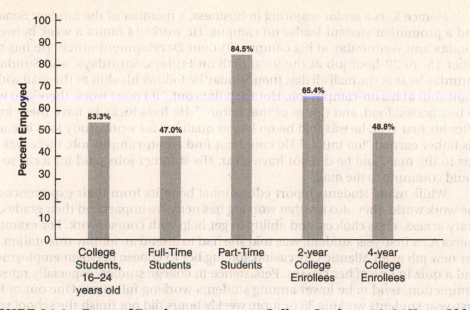

FIGURE 34.1   Rates of Employment among College Students 16–24 Years Old, October 2001

Source: U.S. Bureau of Labor Statistics, "College Enrollment and Work Activity of 2001 High School Graduates," News Release USDL 02-288.

48.8%, respectively. For part-time students, employment rates are substantially higher, at 84.5%. Is this because working people choose to attend college on a part-time basis? Or because the costs of college require so many work hours that students cannot take a full-time course load?

Students' work hours indicate that they are paying for more than an occasional pizza in the dorm. Some 71% of full-time students who work are putting in more than the 15 hours per week one might expect of an on-campus work-study job, according to a summary of the NPSAS findings by the State Public Interest Research Groups' (PIRGs) Higher Education Project (see Figure 34.2). One out of five of these students working over 15 hours per week holds down the equivalent of a full-time job—balancing 35 or more weekly hours of paid work against a full-time course load.

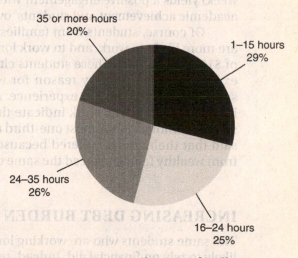

FIGURE 34.2   Distribution of Full-Time Students Who Work, by Hours Worked per Week, 1999–2000

Source: Tracey King and Ellynne Bannon, *At What Cost? The Price That Working Students Pay For A College Education,* The State PIRGs' Higher Education Project, 2002.

Horace K. is a senior majoring in business, a member of the Student Senate, and a prominent student leader on campus. He works 14 hours a week between Sunday and Wednesday at his campus Student Development office. He has another 15- to 20-hour job at the local mall on Fridays, Saturdays, and Sundays. Saturday he is at the mall all day, then Sunday he follows his shift at the mall with a night shift at his on-campus job. Horace points out, "If I don't work, there's no way to buy books, food, and things of that nature." He feels lucky to have these jobs. After his first year, he was told he no longer qualified for work-study jobs because his father earned "too much." He could not find an on-campus job, there was no bus to the mall, and he did not have a car. His summer jobs paid for a car so he could commute to the mall.

While many students report educational benefits from their experiences in the work world, they also say that working has negative impacts on their grades, library access, class choices, and ability to get help with course work. For example, Auliya A., a first-year student, was told she had to attend an all-day orientation for her new job at an Atlantic City casino, forcing her to choose between employment and a quiz in one of her classes. Persistence in college studies, especially rates of completion, tend to be lower among students working full-time. One out of five first-year students working 35 or more weekly hours did not finish the school year, compared with only one out of 17 students working fewer than 15 hours per week. According to the PIRG study, the longer a student's weekly work hours, the lower the benefits and the higher the drawbacks they report. The conclusion of the PIRG findings seems to be that a moderate amount of paid work (less than 16 hours per week) yields a positive engagement with the world, but that long work hours harm academic achievement and students' overall college experience.

Of course, students from families with annual incomes of less than $20,000 are more likely to work, and to work longer hours, than those with family incomes of $100,000 or more. These students cite necessities such as tuition, fees, or living expenses as the primary reason for working, while well-off students work for spending money and job experience. According to the PIRG report, half of low-income students who work indicate that they could not afford to continue their studies without a job. Almost one-third (32%) of students from low-income families said that their grades suffered because of their paid jobs, while 23% of students from wealthy families voiced the same concern.

INCREASING DEBT BURDEN

The same students who are working long hours to pay their rising tuition bills are likely to rely on financial aid. Indeed, seven out of ten full-time students receive financial aid. Unfortunately, financial aid does not help as much as it once did. Pell grants are the most important needs-based aid program for low-income college students. Growing out of the War on Poverty and Great Society initiatives of the 1960s, federal Pell grants were created in 1972 as the core program for low-income and working-class college students. Grant aid per student, though, has not kept pace with the rate of tuition increases. Consider how far a Pell grant stretches. The maximum Pell grant of $4,000 represents only 39% of the average cost of attending a four-year public institution. Back in 1975–76, by contrast, the maximum Pell grant was equivalent to 84% of that cost. Grant aid programs originally reflected a vision that higher education should be accessible to all students, but today Congress is undermining that vision by allowing funding to erode.

As grant programs have become stingier, student loans (including federally guaranteed loans) have come to comprise a greater portion of financial aid. Because she worked so many hours, Brigit managed to graduate with only around $5,000 of debt. But this is far less than average. Various studies estimate that average student debt upon completion of a four-year degree falls between $12,000 and $19,000, depending on research methodology. Students are graduating from college shouldering more than a gown: their monthly debt payments typically amount to $150 to $200, and last for 10 years.

At least student loans have reasonable interest rates. That makes them quite different from the high-interest credit card debts many students pile up. Credit card companies aggressively market their wares to college students they know are struggling to make ends meet. Issuers customize their standards for college students, lowering or eliminating experience ratings and income requirements. "When you're a freshman," explains Horace, "you apply and you can get any kind of credit you want." Concern about aggressive marketing to students who may not understand the implications of carrying debt has led some universities to put limits on how their students can be solicited. Nonetheless, approximately two-thirds of college students have at least one credit card; these students carry an average balance of $2,748, according to one study reported by the General Accounting Office. Approximately 15% of students with cards have balances over $1,000. The degree to which students use their cards for direct college costs is hard to pin down. The GAO found studies indicating that as many as 21% of card users paid tuition with their cards and 7% used them for room and board.

Horace's story is instructive. He is graduating with $17,000 in debt from a series of government-subsidized and unsubsidized loans. None of his financial aid was grant aid. At one time, he also had $6,000 in credit card debt. During his first year, he says, he would "walk down the hallways, sign up for a card, and get free t-shirts." Enticed by the aggressive marketing, he wound up with six cards that he used to pay for tuition and books until he found steady employment. He has gradually paid off four of the cards, but still owes $2,000 between two of them.

SOCIETY'S COSTS AND BENEFITS

There is a silver lining for students who struggle with course work and paid work, tuition bills and credit card bills. A college education brings tremendous benefits—both tangible economic gains and personal growth. College, as most students today recognize, is an "investment good," and the economic returns are substantial. The U.S. Census Bureau found that in 2000, college graduates earned 80% more than people with a high school diploma. As the U.S. economy has shifted from a manufacturing base, where jobs requiring only a high school diploma were plentiful, to a high-tech, "information-based" service economy, the demand for college graduates has escalated. Of course, the service economy also involves plenty of jobs in sectors like retail and food service. But even when a college degree is unnecessary for explicit job content, employers increasingly use it as a screening device to identify workers who they think will be hard-working and obedient.

So going to college is a little like buying a house: those who can afford the up-front costs reap great financial rewards later. This economic reality has boosted college enrollments despite the financial difficulties. The college enrollment rate of graduating high school students has risen for several decades, peaking in 1997 at 67%. There was a slight reversal as the rate fell to 63% for the high school class of 2000.

The market, however, now has the upper hand in determining who will have access to higher education. Both the federal government and the states have been shifting their responsibility for providing adequate resources for higher education to the private sector and students themselves. Markets allow the well-to-do to pay for tutors, college preparatory courses, and private college education for their children, who go on to keep the so-called "family tradition," while working-class and poorer students are more likely to be excluded from educational opportunities that can transform their lives.

Treating higher education like any other commodity to be distributed by market forces is a dangerous approach. Even the most narrow-minded economists agree that improving access to education generates benefits for society as a whole—it produces what economists call "positive externalities." Better access to education creates higher levels of skill and knowledge in the workforce, for instance. It also allows for the fuller use of one of our most valuable economic resources—our youth.

But restricting access to higher education is wrong for reasons much deeper than the fact that it "underutilizes" people. Education offers people an opportunity to expand their interests, understand human relationships, and develop a moral compass—it is not just job training, but a basis of human development. As Stanford education professor and feminist economist Myra Strober notes, economic theory is "ill suited to convey the complex and transformational goals" of education. It also fails to identify what is really wrong with leaving access to the market: education and development should be for everyone, not just those who can pay.

Viewed from this perspective, access to education should be considered a basic social right due to all people, like health care, child care, and adequate income. In most other highly-industrialized countries, people expect their government to guarantee the opportunities and material support needed to live decently: it is part of government's public purpose to provide for social rights. Access to an affordable education is one of those rights—but one that is now threatened as rising costs collide with declining aid.

CHAPTER **35**

Schools as Scapegoats
Our Increasing Inequality and Our Competitiveness Problems are Huge— But They Can't Be Laid at the Door of Our Education System

Lawrence Mishel
Richard Rothstein

Education is the answer. But, what's the question? Simple: What's the cure for any adverse economic condition?

Is your pay stagnant or declining? Quick, get more education.

Are workers failing to share in economic growth? Too bad, they should have gained more skills.

Are you worried about jobs offshored to low-wage countries? Blame schools for workers' lack of creativity.

Is the nation failing to compete globally? Raise education standards across the board.

Education as the cure-all is everywhere around us. But this contention exaggerates the role of schools in the economy, and it conflates two issues: First, how can American firms increase productivity to improve their ability to compete in the world? And second, how have the fruits of U.S. productivity growth been distributed, and what explains rising inequality?

Education can help in the first area, although it is far from a silver bullet. As to the second, education deficits have had very little to do with the changes in the distribution of wages. Fortunately, after more than two decades, the education-as-panacea argument is being overwhelmed by contradictory evidence. Perhaps we may now be able to face more clearly the separate challenges of enhancing competitiveness and reconnecting the link between productivity growth and pay.

The modern obsession with schools as the cause and cure of our economic problems began with President Ronald Reagan's 1983 report, *A Nation at Risk*. Increased market shares for Japanese automobiles, German machine tools, and Korean steel, the report charged, reflected the superior education of workers in those nations: "Our once unchallenged preeminence in commerce, industry, science, and technological innovation is being overtaken by competitors throughout the world . . . The educational foundations of our society are presently being eroded by a rising tide of mediocrity that threatens our very future as a Nation . . ."

In 1990, a group of prominent Democrats and Republicans, calling themselves the National Center on Education and the Economy, followed with another report, *America's Choice: High Skills or Low Wages*. It saw skills development as virtually the *only* policy lever for shaping the economy. It charged that inadequate skills attained at flawed schools had caused industrial productivity to "slow to a crawl" and would, without radical school reform, lead to permanently low wages for the bottom 70 percent of all Americans.

Leading public intellectuals, such as *Prospect* co-founder Robert Reich, focused attention on human capital solutions in a laissez-faire global system. In his book, *The Work of Nations*, Reich argued that international competition would be won by nations with the most (and best) "symbolic analysts," not "routine" workers. Lester Thurow's book, *Head to Head*, forecast that Western Europe would come to dominate the United States and Japan because European schools were superior. Many mainstream economists, both liberal and conservative, agreed that rising-wage and income inequality were caused by an acceleration of "skill-biased technological change," meaning that computerization and other advanced technologies were bidding up the relative value of education, leaving the less-skilled worse off.

Yet the response of American manufacturers to these analyses was curious. Automakers moved plants to Mexico, where worker education levels are considerably lower than those in the American Midwest. Japanese manufacturers pressed their advantage by setting up non-union plants in places like Kentucky and Alabama, states not known for having the best-educated workers. But high school graduates in those locations apparently had no difficulty working in teams and adapting to Japanese just-in-time manufacturing methods.

The ink was barely dry on the *America's Choice* report when Americans' ability to master technological change generated an extraordinary decade-long acceleration of productivity in the mid-1990s, exceeding that of other advanced countries. It was accomplished by the very same workforce that the experts claimed imperiled our future. Productivity advances created new wealth to support a steady increase in Americans' standard of living.

And for a brief period, standards of living did increase because the fruits of productivity growth were broadly shared. The late 1990s saw increasing wages for both high school and college graduates. Even wages of high school dropouts climbed. But no presidential commissions or distinguished experts were praising American education for producing widely shared prosperity. Instead, denunciations of public schools increased in intensity, often tied to calls for their privatization with vouchers.

Then, the collapse of the stock bubble in 2000, the recession of the early 2000s, and the intensification of policies hostile to labor, brought wage growth to a halt.

Living standards again began to decline and inequality zoomed—at the same time that workforce productivity continued to climb. White-collar offshoring to India, China, and other low-wage countries signaled that globalization was now taking its toll on computer programmers and other symbolic analysts of the information age. **Today, however, a new cast of doomsayers has resuscitated** an old storyline, picking up where *A Nation at Risk* left off. Forgetting how wrong such analyses were in the 1980s and 1990s, the contemporary cliché is that however good schools may once have been, the 21st century makes them obsolete. Global competition requires all students to graduate from high school prepared either for academic college or for technical training requiring an equivalent cognitive ability. We can only beat the Asians by being smarter and more creative than they are.

The argument got a boost from *New York Times* columnist Thomas Friedman's 2005 book, *The World is Flat*, and has been repeated by the same National Center on Education and the Economy in *Tough Choices or Tough Times*, a sequel to its 1990 report. The argument has also garnered support from influential foundations (Gates, for example, and its chairman, Bill Gates) and from education advocacy groups (such as the testing organization, ACT).

The *Tough Choices* report bemoans the fact that "Indian engineers make $7,500 a year against $45,000 for an American engineer with the same qualifications and concludes from this that we can compete with the Indian economy only if our engineers are smarter than theirs. This is silly: No matter how good our schools, American engineers won't be six times as smart as those in the rest of the world. Nonetheless, Mare Tucker, author of *Tough Choices* (and president of the group that produced the 1990 report as well), asserts, "The fact is that education holds the key to personal and national economic well-being, more now than at any time in our history."

Administration officials blame workers' education for the middle-class income stagnation that has occurred on Bush's watch. Treasury Secretary Henry Paulson contends that "market forces work to provide the greatest rewards to those with the needed skills in the growth areas. This means that those workers with less education and fewer skills will realize fewer rewards and have fewer opportunities to advance." Former Federal Reserve Chairman Alan Greenspan frequently blamed schools for inequality: "We have not been able to keep up the average skill level in our workforce to match the required increases of increasing technology . . ."

This view can be found on both the Republican right and the Democratic center. The American Enterprise Institute's Frederick Hess and former Clinton White House domestic policy staffer Andrew Rotherham jointly write in an AEI article that "study after study shows an America unprepared to compete in an increasingly global marketplace." They worry that the urgent "competitiveness agenda" could be derailed if we are distracted by a focus on equity-improving outcomes for disadvantaged students. Attention will now have to be turned, they conclude, to further improving the technological savvy of those already primed to succeed.

University of Chicago economists Kevin Murphy and Gary Becker (a Nobel laureate) recently wrote that there is an "upside" to income inequality because it encourages more people to go to college. They warn that raising taxes on high-income households and reducing them on low-income households is tantamount to "a tax on going to college and a subsidy for dropping out of high school." In this way of thinking, preserving the Bush tax cuts is the way to stimulate college enrollment.

But these 21st-century claims are as misguided as those of the last century. Of course we should work to improve schools for the middle class. And we have an urgent need to help more students from disadvantaged families graduate from good high schools. If those students do so, our society can become more meritocratic, with children from low-income and minority families better able to compete for good jobs with children from more privileged homes. But the biggest threats to the next generation's success come from social and economic policy failures, not schools. And enhancing opportunity requires much more than school improvement.

The misdiagnoses of the early 1990s were understandable. When *America's Choice* was written, when the Reich and Thurow books were best sellers, American productivity growth had, indeed, stagnated. These authors could not have known that explosive growth was just around the corner. But today's education scolds have no such excuse. Workforce skills continue to generate rising productivity. In the last five years, wages of both high school– and college-educated workers have been stagnant, while productivity grew by a quite healthy 10.4 percent.

Rising workforce skills can indeed make American firms more competitive. But better skills, while essential, are not the only source of productivity growth. The honesty of our capital markets, the accountability of our corporations, our fiscal-policy and currency management, our national investment in R&D and infrastructure, and the fair-play of the trading system (or its absence), also influence whether the U.S. economy reaps the gains of Americans' diligence and ingenuity. The singular obsession with schools deflects political attention from policy failures in those other realms.

But while adequate skills are an essential component of productivity growth, workforce skills cannot determine how the wealth created by national productivity is distributed. That decision is made by policies over which schools have no influence—tax, regulatory, trade, monetary, technology, and labor-market policies that modify the market forces affecting how much workers will be paid. Continually upgrading skills and education is essential for sustaining growth as well as for closing historic race and ethnic gaps. It does not, however, guarantee economic success without policies that also reconnect pay with productivity growth.

American middle-class living standards are threatened, not because workers lack competitive skills but because the richest among us have seized the fruits of productivity growth, denying fair shares to the working- and middle-class Americans, educated in American schools, who have created the additional national wealth. Over the last few decades, wages of college graduates overall have increased, but some college graduates—managers, executives, white-collar sales workers—have commandeered disproportionate shares, with little left over for scientists, engineers, teachers, computer programmers, and others with high levels of skill. No amount of school reform can undo policies that redirect wealth generated by skilled workers to profits and executive bonuses.

College graduates are, in fact, not in short supply. A background paper for the *Tough Choices* report (but not one publicized in the report itself) acknowledges that "fewer young college graduates have been able to obtain college labor market jobs, and their real wages and annual earnings have declined accordingly due to rising mal-employment." In plain language, many college graduates are now forced to take jobs requiring only high school educations.

In many high school hallways you can find a chart displaying the growing "returns to education"—the ratio of college to high school graduates' wages. The idea is to impress on youths the urgency of going to college and the calamity that will befall those who don't. The data are real—college graduates do earn more than high school graduates, and the gap is substantially greater than it was a few decades ago. But it is too facile to conclude that this ratio proves a shortage of college graduates.

Statistically, the falling real wages of high school graduates has played a bigger part in boosting the college-to-high-school wage ratio than has an unmet demand for college graduates. Important causes of this decline have been the weakening of labor market institutions, such as the minimum wage and unions, which once boosted the pay of high school–educated workers.

For the first time in a decade, the minimum wage was recently increased. The curious result will be a statistical decline in "returns to education." But we should not conclude from a minimum-wage increase that we need fewer college graduates, any more than we should have concluded from falling wages for high school graduates that college graduates are scarce and schools are failing.

Another too glib canard is that our education system used to be acceptable because students could graduate from high school (or even drop out) and still support families with good manufacturing jobs. Today, those jobs are vanishing, and with them the chance of middle-class incomes for those without good educations.

It's true that many manufacturing jobs have disappeared. But replacements have mostly been equally unskilled or semi-skilled jobs in service and retail sectors. There was never anything more inherently valuable in working in a factory assembly line than in changing bed linens in a hotel. What made semiskilled manufacturing jobs desirable was that many (though not most) were protected by unions, provided pensions and health insurance, and compensated with decent wages. That today's working class doesn't get similar protections has nothing to do with the adequacy of its education. Rather, it has everything to do with policy decisions stemming from the value we place on equality. Hotel jobs that pay $20 an hour, with health and pension benefits (rather than $10 an hour without benefits), typically do so because of union organization, not because maids earned bachelor's degrees.

It is cynical to tell millions of Americans who work (and who will continue to be needed to work) in low-level administrative jobs and in janitorial, food-service, hospitality, transportation, and retail industries that their wages have stagnated because their educations are inadequate for international competition. The quality of our civic, cultural, community, and family lives demands school improvement, but barriers to unionization have more to do with low wages than does the quality of education. After all, since 1973 the share of the workforce with college degrees has more than doubled; over 40 percent of native-born workers now have degrees beyond high school. Additionally, the proportion of native-born workers that has not completed high school or its equivalent has decreased by half to just 7 percent.

Indeed, Becker's and Murphy's own data confirm: The wage gap between college- and high school–educated workers was flat from 2001 to 2005. However, inequality surged in this period, a fact that can't be explained by something that didn't change! Moreover, other industrialized countries have seen a more rapid growth in college completion than the United States has, yet those nations accomplished this educational growth without increasing inequality.

Fortunately, the elite consensus on education as a cure-all seems now to be collapsing. Offshoring of high-tech jobs has deeply undercut the Clinton-era metaphor of an education-fueled transition to the information age, since it is all too apparent that college educations and computer skills do not insulate Americans from globalization's downsides. Former Clinton economic advisor (and Federal Reserve vice chairman) Alan Blinder has emerged as an establishment voice calling attention to the potentially large-scale impact of continued offshoring. Blinder stresses that the distinction between American jobs likely to be destroyed by international competition and those likely to survive is *not* one of workers' skills or education. "It is unlikely that the services of either taxi drivers or airline pilots will ever be delivered electronically over long distances . . . Janitors and crane operators are probably immune to foreign competition; accountants and computer programmers are not."

A growing number of other mainstream economists now also caution that blaming inadequate schooling for falling living standards and growing inequality might be too simplistic. In a series of papers, David Autor, Larry Katz, Melissa Kearney, Frank Levy, and Richard Murnane, mainstream Cambridge-based economists who promoted the story of a technology-based transition to the 21st century, now have revised their account. They assert that prior to the 1990s, technology increased demand for more educated workers across the board, but that now there is "polarization," where technology disadvantages middle-skilled workers relative to those with both more and less education. Their finding severely undercuts the suggestion that upgrading human capital is the solution to inequality.

Alan Greenspan's successor as Federal Reserve chairman, Ben Bernanke, has also adopted a less simplistic analysis. While concurring that skills matter, Bernanke also observes that a poorly educated workforce cannot explain "why the wages of workers in the middle of the distribution have grown more slowly in recent years than those of workers at the lower end of the distribution, even though, of the two groups, workers in the middle of the distribution are typically the better educated."

Prominent free-trade economists now also acknowledge that education reform cannot address Americans' economic insecurity nor solve globalization's political problems. In a recent analysis prepared for the financial services industry, two prominent former Bush administration economists (Grant Aldonas and Matthew Slaughter), and one from the Clinton administration (Robert Z. Lawrence), wrote that since 2000, "only a small share of workers at the very high end has enjoyed strong growth in incomes. The strong U.S. productivity growth of the past several years has not been reflected in wage and salary earnings, and instead has accrued largely to the earnings of very high-end Americans and to corporate profits. The bottom line is that today, many American workers feel anxious—about change and about their paychecks. Their concerns are real, widespread, and legitimate . . . For college graduates and those with non-professional master's degrees, this poor income performance is a new and presumably unwelcome development."

And Robert Reich no longer believes that being a symbolic analyst is adequate income protection. He now blogs, "The only people who are getting much out of this economy are in the top one percent—earning over $800 grand a year. They're taking home almost 20 percent of total income. Back in 1980, the top one percent took home 8 percent of total income."

In a paper recently posted on the National Bureau of Economic Research's Web site, Massachusetts Institute of Technology economists Frank Levy and Peter Temin wrote, "The current trend toward greater inequality in America is primarily the result of a change in economic policy that took place in the late 1970s and early 1980s." They went on to say that "the recent impacts of technology and trade have been amplified by the collapse of these institutions," by which they mean the suppression of unions and the abandonment of the norm of equality.

These are not problems that can be solved by charter schools, teacher accountability, or any other school intervention. A balanced human capital policy would involve schools, but would require tax, regulatory, and labor market reforms as well. To take only one example, in the daze of college-for-all, what used to be called "vocational" or "career" education has been discredited. It should be brought back. We recently analyzed a group of 21st-century occupations not requiring a college education that, at least for the time being, still provide middle-class incomes. These include firefighters, electricians, machinists, aircraft engine mechanics, electronic technicians, licensed practical nurses, and clinical laboratory technicians. We found that white non-college youth were 50 percent more likely to land one of these "good" jobs than black non-college youth. Equalizing this access will require a combination of stepped up anti-discrimination efforts, job placement services, and skills training directed at schools serving minority youth.

In their paper posted on the Web site of the National Bureau of Economic Research, Levy and Temin conclude, "No rebalancing of the labor force can restore a more equal distribution of productivity gains without government intervention and changes in private sector behavior."

We agree.

CHAPTER 36

Hired Education

Jennifer Washburn

Michael Wolfe, a gastroenterologist at Boston University, admits he was duped by the Pharmacia Corporation, the manufacturer of the blockbuster arthritis drug Celebrex. (In 2003, the company was purchased by Pfizer.) In the summer of 2000, *The Journal of the American Medical Association* asked Wolfe to write a review of a study showing that Celebrex was associated with lower rates of stomach and intestinal ulcers and other complications than two older arthritis medications, diclofenac and ibuprofen. Wolfe found the study, tracking 8,000 patients over a six-month period, persuasive, and penned a favorable review, which helped to drive up Celebrex sales.

But early the next year, while serving on the Food and Drug Administration's (FDA) arthritis advisory committee, Wolfe had occasion to review the same drug trial again and was flabbergasted by what he saw. Pharmacia's study had run for one year, not six months, as the company had originally led both Wolfe and the *Journal* to believe. When the complete data was considered, most of Celebrex's advantages disappeared because the ulcer complications that occurred during the second half of the study were disproportionately found in patients taking Celebrex.

"I am furious," Wolfe told *The Washington Post* in 2001. "I looked like a fool. But . . . all I had available to me was the data presented in the article." Remarkably, none of the *Journal* study's 16 authors, including eight university professors, had spoken out publicly about this egregious suppression of negative data. All the authors were either employees of Pharmacia or paid consultants of the company.

Celebrex, an anti-inflammatory drug similar to Vioxx, is once again in the news due to concerns that it may be associated with the same cardiovascular risks that caused Vioxx to get yanked from the market. In recent months, we've heard a great deal about conflicts of interest at both the FDA, the agency that approves drugs for public safety, and the National Institutes of Health, where publicly funded scientists moonlight as consultants for the very companies that manufactured the drugs they are testing. Still largely ignored, however, is the role played by the once-autonomous ivory tower and the university scientists who, either knowingly or unknowingly, facilitate the pharmaceutical industry's manipulation of drug testing by lending it an aura of objectivity.

Today, market forces are dictating what is happening in the world of higher education as never before, causing universities to look and behave more and more like business enterprises. Instead of honoring their traditional commitment to teaching, disinterested research, and the broad dissemination of knowledge, universities are aggressively striving to become research arms of private industry. Faced with declining government funding, they are avidly seeking to enhance their role as "engines" of economic growth, promising state legislators and governors that they will help drive regional economic development by pumping out commercially valuable inventions.

This radical redefinition of the university's mission can be traced back to the economic stagnation of the 1970s. Propelled by heightened competition from Germany and Japan, Congress passed landmark legislation in 1980 that allowed universities to automatically retain the rights to intellectual property stemming from taxpayer-financed research. The intent of the legislation, popularly known as the Bayh-Dole Act (its sponsors were Senators Birch Bayh and Bob Dole), was to stimulate innovation and speed the transfer of federally financed research to industry. What it accomplished in the process was the introduction of a dangerous new profit motive into the heart of the university.

As a result, schools now routinely operate expensive patenting and licensing operations to market their faculty's inventions, extracting royalty income and other fees in return. They invest their endowment money in risky startup firms founded by their professors. They run their own industrial parks and venture capital funds. They publish newsletters encouraging faculty members to commercialize new research by launching independent, faculty-owned companies. Star professors consult for, or hold equity in, the same firms that manufacture the drugs they are studying, while also often accepting generous fees to join corporate advisory boards and speakers' bureaus. Sometimes these professors even hold the patent to the drug or device being tested. In a study of 800 scientific papers published in leading journals of medicine and molecular biology, Sheldon Krimsky, a professor of public policy at Tufts University, found that slightly more than a third of the lead authors based at research institutions in Massachusetts had a significant financial interest in their own reports. So pervasive are such ties that journal editors now frequently complain that they can no longer find academic experts who do not have a financial interest in a drug or therapy the journal would like to review.

Research suggests that publicly funded science, most of it performed at universities, was a critical contributor to the discovery of nearly all of the 25 most important breakthrough drugs introduced between 1970 and 1995. If university scientists lose their independence, who will perform this pathbreaking research and objectively evaluate the safety and effectiveness of drugs already on the market? Conflicts of interest are more than an academic concern. When it comes to health policy, they pose a serious threat to public health.

With the possible exception of business schools, the nation's medical schools have been more infiltrated by industry than any other sector of the university. Pharmaceutical companies sponsor daily lunches for medical students at which they market their latest drugs; they ply professors with fancy dinners, gifts, luxurious trips, and free prescriptions designed to influence medical decisions and prescribing habits. The drug industry also spends millions of dollars financing clinical drug research at the academy, but increasingly this money comes with many more strings attached. After conducting a thorough review of the medical literature for *The New England Journal of Medicine* in 2000, Thomas Bodenheimer, an internist at the University of California, San Francisco, concluded that academic investigators were rapidly ceding to industry control over nearly every stage of the clinical research process.

In the past, for example, it was common for university scientists to initiate the research protocol. Now, studies are frequently conceived and designed in the company's own pharmacological and marketing departments, thus removing this formative stage of the research from academic hands almost entirely. The company then shops the study around to various academic institutions (and a growing number of competing for-profit subcontractors that run clinical trials) in search of investigators to conduct the research. As university medical schools have grown more dependent on industry grants to sustain their operations, their professors have become increasingly willing to accept an industry-initiated protocol without modification, even though the study may be largely designed to secure a company's market position. Should a professor reject the study or insist on changes, another university scientist will very likely be more solicitous.

Industry also encourages the use of ghostwriters on scientific papers. This means an article or review bylined by a prominent academic might in fact have been written by a medical-communications company working for the drugmaker, with the "author" paid an honorarium to attach his or her name to it. When Wyeth-Ayerst sought to boost market demand for Redux, one part of the once highly popular "fen-phen" diet-drug combination, the company hired a company called Excerpta Medica to help draft the manuscripts and pay doctors to review and sign the articles. One of the many doctors who signed Excerpta's papers was Richard Atkinson, a renowned obesity expert at the University of Wisconsin–Madison. Atkinson denied having any knowledge of Excerpta's connection to Wyeth, but as an independent academic, he nonetheless agreed to lend his name to a company he apparently knew little about. (Excerpta maintains that all its authors were told of the company's association with the manufacturer.) In a deposition on January 15, 1999, Wyeth-Ayerst executive Jo Alene Dolan admitted that her company had written the article for Atkinson, stressing that all drug companies ghostwrite articles. Shortly before the article could be published, Redux was pulled from the market because of its association with serious heart and lung problems.

Scientists who perform industry-sponsored research are also asked routinely to sign legal contracts requiring them to keep both the methods and the results of their work secret for a period of time. Research conducted by David Blumenthal and Eric Campbell, health-policy researchers at Harvard University, suggests that data withholding and publication delays have become far more common over the last 25 years, particularly in molecular biology, medicine, and other life-science disciplines, where commercial relationships have grown dramatically in recent years. In a survey of 2,167 life-science faculty, Blumenthal found that nearly one in five of them had delayed publication for more than six months to protect proprietary information.

Industry also manipulates academic research by suppressing negative studies altogether. Recently, it came to light that a whole class of popular antidepressants—including such heavily prescribed drugs as Paxil, Zoloft, and Prozac—are largely ineffectual in treating childhood depression and actually increase the risk of suicide. One of the main reasons this information was not available to doctors and the broader public, it turns out, is that the academic investigators who led these studies either allowed industry to bury their research or were complicit in downplaying negative findings in their own published papers. How prevalent is such corporate meddling? The question has received surprisingly little scholarly attention, but what research does exist is not encouraging. One survey of major university-industry research centers in the field of engineering, for example, found that 35 percent would allow corporate sponsors to delete information from papers prior to publication.

But all the blame for the eroding objectivity of university researchers does not rest with industry. Universities themselves are complicit: They are so financially invested in their professors' research through patents, equity, and other financial holdings that their disinterested pursuit of knowledge has been gravely compromised. For instance, when the Harvard Center for Risk Analysis' longtime director, Professor John D. Graham, was nominated by President George W. Bush to become the government's "regulatory czar" at the Office of Information and Regulatory Affairs (part of the Office of Management and Budget), it helped to expose just how extensive Harvard's financial conflicts really were. Congressional hearings revealed that Graham's center solicited tobacco money and worked with the tobacco industry to disparage the risks of secondhand smoke. (Harvey Fineberg, a dean at the Harvard School of Public Health, demanded that one check from Philip Morris be returned. In response, Graham wrote to the company asking if it might send the $25,000 back to the Harvard center via the Philip Morris subsidiary Kraft Foods instead.) Graham's center also argued that cell-phone use by drivers should not be restricted, even though its own research, which was funded by AT&T Wireless Communications, showed that such use could lead to a thousand additional highway deaths a year. As a member of the Environmental Protection Agency's scientific advisory board subcommittee on dioxin, a known human carcinogen, Graham argued that reducing dioxin levels might "do more harm . . . than good." His Harvard center, meanwhile, was heavily funded by dioxin producers.

Worse yet, the universities' loyalties are now so conflicted that schools are increasingly willing to cave in to narrow commercial demands rather than defend their own professors' academic freedom or the public interest. When researchers at the University of Utah discovered an important human gene responsible for hereditary breast cancer, for example, they didn't make it freely available to other scientists, even though we—the U.S. taxpayers—paid $4.6 million to finance the research. The university raced to patent it, then granted the monopoly rights to Myriad Genetics Inc., a startup company founded by a University of Utah professor, which proceeded to hoard the gene and prevent other academic scientists from using it.

Professors, too, are increasingly driven by the bottom line. More and more, they not only accept industry grants to support their research but also hold stock in or have other financial ties to the companies funding them. Many experts fear this skewing of professors' research toward short-term commercial goals will impede long-term scientific and technological innovation. Financial entanglements between researchers and corporations have grown so common that the Securities and Exchange Commission (SEC) has investigated numerous academic researchers suspected of engaging in insider trading. In a case filed in Pennsylvania, the SEC charged Dale J. Lange, a Columbia University neurologist, with pocketing $26,000 in profits after Lange bought stock in a company that was about to release promising new findings concerning a drug to treat Lou Gehrig's disease. Lange had good reason to expect the stock to soar because he had conducted the confidential clinical trials himself. In 2000, an investigation by *USA Today* found that more than half the experts hired to advise the U.S. government on the safety and effectiveness of drugs—a large number of whom are academics—now have financial links to companies that will be affected by their conclusions.

When Wyeth-Ayerst was trying to get its diet drug, Redux, approved for sale in the United States, for example, it faced a serious hurdle: Patients in Europe who had taken a drug virtually identical to Redux had an increased chance of getting a rare, life-threatening lung ailment known as pulmonary hypertension. To combat this negative health profile, the company packed an FDA hearing room with a who's who list of the nation's top academic obesity experts, all of whom were *also* paid consultants to Wyeth-Ayerst or other companies involved in the sale of Redux. In addition, the company recruited expert "opinion leaders," such as George Blackburn, a renowned obesity expert at Harvard, to testify before the Medical Society of Massachusetts for approval of the drug. Blackburn and other academic luminaries further participated in the company's "Visiting Important Professors Program" and were paid thousands of dollars in honoraria to fly to fancy resorts and promote Redux at medical conferences. Not surprisingly, the drug handily won market approval, and prescriptions in the United States began to soar.

Soon, however, evidence of the drug's association with lung damage surfaced once again, and the company turned to leading university scientists to do damage control. In the summer of 1996, an internal company memo revealed that the company was planning to spend $5.8 million to pay for more university-based studies, noting that that money was needed to "establish and maintain relationships with opinion leaders at the local and national level to communicate to their colleagues the benefits of Redux and to encourage its use." Among the many doctors willing to heed the company's call was Atkinson, the obesity expert at the University of Wisconsin, whose name appeared on a company-authored article.

"Let me congratulate you and your writer," wrote Atkinson in a thank-you letter to the ghostwriting firm that was one of numerous company documents that became public during subsequent legal proceedings. "Perhaps I can get you to write all my papers for me!"

So how does this growing web of academic-industry ties affect research outcomes? A vast body of work suggests that industry-funded research is far from impartial. In 1996, Stanford researcher Mildred Cho co-authored a study in the *Annals of Internal Medicine* that found that 98 percent of papers based on industry-sponsored research reflected favorably on the drugs being examined, compared with 79 percent of papers based on research not funded by industry. An analysis published in *The Journal of the American Medical Association* in 1999 found that studies of cancer drugs funded by the pharmaceutical industry were nearly eight times less likely to reach unfavorable conclusions than similar studies funded by non-profit organizations. More recently, a systematic review of 1,140 clinical trial studies, published by researchers at Yale in 2003, concluded that, from cancer to arthritis to cholesterol, the evidence is overwhelming that when research is industry-sponsored, it is "significantly more likely to reach conclusions that [are] favorable to the sponsor" than non–industry-funded research.

In the area of health and drug research, of course, the results of such manipulation can be deadly. Running down the list of drugs recently pulled from the market or subject to increased health warnings—Rezulin, the diabetes drug; Redux (or fen-phen), the diet drug; Retin-A, the anti-wrinkle cream; Neurontin, the epilepsy drug; Paxil, Zoloft, and the many other antidepressants now deemed ineffective for children—one finds that a remarkable number of prominent university professors with close financial ties to the manufacturers played a central role in lobbying for these drugs to be approved, recommending them to other doctors, and, in many cases, urging that they remain on the market long after the problems or lack of effectiveness became known. Not infrequently, the university scientists who shill for the drug companies most aggressively are also the biggest-name professors in their fields.

Universities have gone out of their way to assure the public that their clinical trials meet the highest standards of "scientific excellence" and "academic rigor." But over the last 20 years, public dismay over the growing financial entanglements in clinical research has prompted the federal government to impose tougher conflict-of-interest regulations, only to encounter fierce university opposition. In 1995, the federal government finally succeeded in pushing through rules that would apply to all academic researchers funded by the Department of Health and Human Services (HHS) or the National Science Foundation (NSF). But the rules, which remain in place today, were not tough enough to be effective. Although they mandate that serious conflicts of interest must be managed and/or eliminated, they leave the determination of what action is to be taken, if any, entirely up to the university. The policy also doesn't provide any guidance on which conflicts warrant serious attention, nor does it impose any prohibitions, such as banning financial conflicts outright in the area of human-subject research. Significantly, the policy also says nothing about institutional conflicts of interest.

The result, not surprisingly, is that university conflict-of-interest rules vary widely. One comprehensive 2000 survey of the written policies at 100 academic institutions found that only 55 percent of schools required disclosure of conflicts of interest from all faculty, and only 19 percent specified any limits on researchers' financial ties to corporate sponsors. Worse yet, under this fragmented system, there is enormous pressure on universities to keep their policies lax. Schools with tighter restrictions run the risk of losing talented faculty to competing schools with more permissive policies, where the financial rewards and commercial prospects are likely to be greater.

Another conspicuous problem with the HHS/NSF policy is that it does not require universities to make any of the information they compile on faculty financial conflicts available to the public. Many academic journals do require their authors to disclose corporate financial ties. But in practice, reporting is astonishingly poor. In a 2001 study, Tufts' Krimsky found that a mere 0.5 percent of the 61,134 papers appearing in 181 peer-reviewed journals contained statements about the authors' financial ties. More recent studies have found similarly low levels of reporting.

In some respects, the whole debate reflects how far the academic world remains from dealing seriously with the issue; disclosure of potential conflicts of interest is, after all, a far cry from eliminating them outright, as many professions not only recommend but also require. In the legal profession, for example, attorneys are prohibited from taking on cases in which they have a financial interest or other explicit conflicts that might be seen to compromise their professional integrity. The same is true of judges. But when it comes to academia, neither the medical community nor the government (whether through Congress or the regulatory agencies) has taken up the task, instead proceeding under the assumption that universities can be trusted to manage these commercial interactions themselves. It's a nice idea. But are academic institutions really capable of performing this function? There is good reason to be skeptical: Far from being independent watchdogs capable of dispassionate inquiry, universities are increasingly joined at the hip to the very market forces the public has entrusted them to check, creating problems that extend far beyond the research lab.

■■■■■

PART ELEVEN

Crime and Justice

We've seen that the United States stands out among the advanced industrial societies in many ways—in our rates of poverty, our extremes of inequality, and our lack of a universal health care system, among others. Crime—and the system we have established to control it—is another. The United States has the highest rates of serious violent crime of any advanced industrial nation, and at the same time confines a greater proportion of its people in jails and prisons—six times the proportion in the United Kingdom, nine times that in Sweden, twelve times that of Japan. And though levels of violent crime are not as high as they were at their peak in the early 1990s, they remain higher than they were before the dramatic increases in imprisonment of the past 40 years.

The scope of America's outsized prison system is illustrated in the Pew Foundation's report, "1 in 100". That is the proportion of adults currently locked up in jails and prisons in the United States. That figure is troubling enough in itself, but it tells only part of the story. The figures are much worse for some groups, especially young minority men. One in 36 Hispanic men, and fully 1 in 15 black men, are now behind bars in America. And the growth of the prison system has siphoned off vast amounts of public funds that could have been used for schools, health care, and othr services that could help to prevent crime in the first place.

Yet despite the swelling of the prison population to levels seen nowhere else in the world, many people believe that we have been shockingly lenient with criminals. In the excerpt we reprint here, Elliott Currie argues that this is a myth, and examines the factual underpinnings of this myth—as well as the belief that our investments in prisons are cost effective and efficacious. The reality is that we tend to be quite punitive with those "street" criminals we actually catch—considerably more so than most other countries. And, with more than two million people in our jails and prisons on any given day, we are becoming more so all the time.

Politicians, however, looking for quick fixes to the crime problem, have passed a variety of even more punitive measures in recent years—including so-called three strikes and you're out laws, mandating 25-year to life sentences for criminals convicted of three felonies. In California, the third felony may be a relatively minor offense, such as stealing a bicycle or possessing a small amount of drugs. Despite the harshness of this law, it has been recently upheld by the U.S. Supreme Court, which ruled in 2003 that a sentence of 25 years to life for stealing three golf clubs did not constitute the "cruel and unusual punishment" prohibited by our constitution.

As of December 2008, there were more than 8,400 inmates in California prisons sentenced to 25 years to life as "third strikers," and another 32,680 "second strikers." Though the law was promoted as being targeted at the state's worst violent offenders, more than three times as many third strikers had been sentenced for drug possession as for murder and rape combined. The law has also generated sharp racial disparities: at last count, only 25 percent of second and third strike inmates were white, while more than 70 percent were black or Hispanic.[1]

One result of locking up so many prisoners for such long terms will be the aging of the state's prison population: it's estimated that there will be more than 30,000 inmates over the age of 60 by the year 2020, whose need for extra care will cost the state's taxpayers roughly a billion dollars a year.[2] (This did not prevent the state's voters from defeating, in 2004, a modest proposal to soften the law's harsh provisions.)

These laws are surely "tough," but are they effective? Jerome H. Skolnick calls California's three-strikes law a "wild pitch"—arguing that the law is too rigid and will result in a vast and costly expansion of the prison system into a home for aged and low-level offenders. In response, John J. DiIulio maintains that, as a nation, we are actually soft on criminals, allowing some of the most dangerous to bargain their way into lesser charges at the front end of the system, while releasing them early to parole and community supervision at the back. In his reply, Skolnick says that DiIulio's generalizations are inaccurate and offers data to show why.

The three strikes laws, like our criminal justice system generally, most often sweep up people from the lower end of the social and economic spectrum—especially the minority poor. At the other end of the scale is another kind of criminal—the affluent offenders, often corporate executives, who commit so-called white-collar crimes. The term was coined by an American criminologist, Edwin Sutherland, in the 1930s to mean crimes committed by otherwise "respectable" people in the course of their business. It has long been understood that these "respectable" offenders are treated very differently by the criminal justice system than the "ordinary" offenders who now pack the jails and prison. They are far less likely to ever see the inside of a prison or jail, and unlikely, on the whole, to stay long if they do. But the article here by Ken Silverstein shows something more: that even companies that are repeat offenders, whose crimes kill and injure people and who may receive substantial fines as a result, are often rewarded by billions of dollars in government contracts. Indeed, some of the biggest government contractors in America are also among the worst and most persistent violators of federal environmental and health and safety laws. In this case, if in few others, we are indeed lenient in our treatment of criminals.

ENDNOTES

1. California Department of Corrections and Rehabilitation, *Second and Third Striker Felons in the Adult Institution Population*, Sacramento, CA, December 31, 2008.

2. Sandra Kobrin, "Dying on Our Dime," *Los Angeles Times Magazine*, June 26, 2005.

CHAPTER 37

The Myth of Leniency

Elliott Currie

Many Americans believe that the main reason we remain a frighteningly violent country is that we are shockingly lenient with criminals. That would seem, at first glance, a difficult position to maintain in the country that boasts the developed world's highest imprisonment rate. And, in fact, the idea that serious, violent criminals are treated leniently in the United States *is* a myth. But it is a myth that is deeply entrenched in the public imagination. How is it possible to maintain that America is "soft" on criminals in the face of the enormous increases in punishment in recent years?

One way to make this case is simply to downplay the magnitude of our recent increases in incarceration. Thus James Q. Wilson speaks of our "inching up" the costs of offending in recent years, a jarringly peculiar way to describe the quintupling of the prison population. Others simply sidestep the extraordinary growth of imprisonment and argue that misguided liberal policies allow most offenders to go unpunished and vast numbers of "known violent predators," in the phrase of the conservative Council on Crime in America, to run loose. William Bennett, John J. DiIulio, and James P. Walters, the authors of the leading recent conservative tract on crime, put it this way in the course of arguing for "more incarceration":

> Today and every day the "justice" system permits known, convicted, violent and repeat criminals, adult and juvenile, to get away with murder and mayhem on the streets. Criminals who have repeatedly violated the life, liberty, and property of others are routinely set free to do it all over again.

The myth of leniency is propped up by several "facts" that have been recycled repeatedly in popular and academic publications across the country in recent years. It is common to read, for example, that the overwhelming majority of violent criminals are let off without punishment, and that indeed "only 1 in 100" violent crimes results in a prison sentence; that in the rare cases when offenders are punished, the sentences they receive, even for heinous crimes, are shockingly, even ludicrously, short and that most violent criminals are not put in prison at all but are "community-based"—that is, on pretrial release, probation, or parole—an arrangement that allows them to commit further heinous crimes. All of these "facts" carry the same basic message: the heart of our crime problem lies in misguided leniency—"the failure to restrain known violent offenders," as the Council on Crime in America puts it. Contrary to what the figures on the swollen prisons would seem to tell us, the reality is that we are letting most criminals off with little or no punishment—and they are repaying us by murdering, raping, and robbing with impunity.

The prescription that follows from this diagnosis is short on specifics, but its general direction is clear. "Our view," writes the Council,

> is that America needs to put more violent and repeat criminals, adult and juvenile, behind bars longer, to see to it that truth-in-sentencing and such kindred laws as are presently on the books are fully and faithfully executed, and to begin reinventing probation and parole agencies in ways that will enable them to supervise their charges, enforce the law, and enhance public safety.

It is important to be clear: no one denies that serious offenders are sometimes let off lightly, or that we should do all we can to prevent such miscarriages of justice. But these critics are saying something more: that lenient sentencing and "revolving-door justice" are the norm in America and are responsible for America's continuing crime problem. What do we make of this argument? How do we square this picture of dramatic leniency with the reality of bursting prisons?

We can't. All of these claims are at best disingenuous, at worst painfully transparent distortions of the way criminal justice in America really works.

Consider first the statement, repeated over and over again by John DiIulio and the Council and picked up by opinion-page editors around the country, that "only 1 in 100 violent crimes results in a prison sentence." The figure itself is technically correct. In 1992, for example, there were over 10 million crimes of violence recorded in the annual survey of criminal victimization carried out by the U.S. Bureau of Justice Statistics; and, as Bennett, DiIulio, and Walters put it, "only about 100,000 persons convicted of a violent crime went to state prison." But do the numbers really tell us that "revolving-door justice" lets the wicked off with a slap on the wrist, or less?

Not at all. To begin with, it is important to understand that the majority of violent crimes are not serious ones. Thus, in 1995, 6.2 million were "simple assaults"; almost 5 million—more than half of all violent crimes—"simple assaults without injury." We are talking here about schoolyard fights or minor barroom altercations, which few would argue should result in a state prison sentence. (Most assaults, too, are "attempted" or "threatened," not "completed.") Another bit of sleight of hand is that the figure of 100,000 sent to state prison conveniently leaves out those who go to local jails, federal prisons, or juvenile institutions—implying that not going to state prison means that the offender is set free, which distorts the picture considerably.

But there is a much more fundamental problem. It is indeed true that most crimes—including many very serious ones—don't result in punishment. As every serious student of crime knows, however, that isn't primarily because the justice system is lenient with offenders; it is because the vast majority of crimes do not enter the criminal justice system at all. The Council on Crime in America provides the basic figures itself: of the more than 10 million violent crimes picked up in the national victim survey in 1992, only a little over 4 million were even *reported* to police. To be sure, more serious crimes of violence (as well as crimes like auto theft, which are reported in order to collect insurance) are more often reported. But even for robbery and assault the percentages are relatively low, and they are lower still for rape and domestic violence (more than 9 in 10 motor vehicle thefts, but only two-thirds of robberies, half of aggravated assaults, and one third of rapes are reported to the police, according to the victim surveys). And of those violent crimes that *are* reported, other than homicide, the majority do not result in an arrest (are not "cleared," in the language of criminal justice). Of those 10 million violent victimizations, just 641,000 led to an arrest at all. Hence, that "1 in 100" figure has already been transformed beyond recognition—for only 6 in 100 even enter the system. And once in the system, more offenses are dropped for lack of evidence, or otherwise dismissed, or the defendant is acquitted. The result is that the 10 million crimes are followed by only about 165,000 *convictions*—meaning that most offenses never arrive at the stage of sentencing at all.

A recent analysis, conducted by the *Los Angeles Times,* of 32 homicides that took place in the course of one week in the summer of 1994 in Los Angeles County illustrates how difficult it can be to bring a crime to the sentencing stage—even for a crime that is among those *most* likely to result in arrest and conviction. Nearly half of the 32 murder cases in that week did not result in an arrest; of those that did, a fifth were dismissed, or the suspects released or acquitted. A look at the circumstances of these cases shows some of the reasons why:

> Francisco Robert Vasquez, 20, is shot numerous times in an East Los Angeles alley. Vasquez may have been killed by fellow gang members, police say. Empty shell casings are found at the scene. But no gun is found and no suspects are arrested.

> Near MacArthur Park, at a drug sales corner controlled by 18th Street gang members, Louie Herrera, 27, is killed in a burst of gunfire. A suspect is identified, but charges are dropped after a witness becomes uncooperative, then disappears.

As these cases show, homicides that take place in the murky world of urban gangs and drugs are hard to solve. And the difficulty of achieving solid arrests and convictions is even greater for most other serious offenses. It follows that if we can improve our ability to make good arrests, and to convict those arrested, we might be able to make significant inroads against violent crime—an issue to which we'll return (indeed, the proportion of violent-crime cases that result in convictions has already increased in recent years). But it is *not* true that the gap between the large number of violent crimes committed and the much smaller number that are punished results from our leniency toward convicted offenders—from the fact that, as DiIulio puts it, "our criminal justice system is not handing down sentences to fit the crimes."

If our concern is whether we are encouraging crime by failing to punish known offenders, the real question is how many of those who are actually caught and convicted are then put behind bars. And here the evidence is unequivocal. We've already seen that the chances of incarceration for violent offenses have risen sharply in recent years in the United States; as a result, the probability that a convicted violent offender will go behind bars is very high indeed, and for repeat offenders a virtual certainty. In 1994, 77 percent of offenders convicted of felony robbery went to prison; another 11 percent went to jail, making the total incarcerated almost 9 in 10. Similarly, 88 percent of felons convicted of rape were incarcerated, four out of five of them in prison. Keep in mind that these are *averages* that lump together first-time offenders with repeaters, and less serious versions of these crimes with more serious ones. The kinds of offenders that critics like DiIulio say are now allowed to roam free—serious, violent repeaters—have been going behind bars routinely for many years, and the proportion has risen substantially since the 1970s.

But what about the *severity* of their sentences? Isn't it true that even those we do send to prison get out after a laughably short time—thus both subverting justice and encouraging predators? Here too the myth of leniency is widespread. Many Americans believe that we generally let convicted criminals off with a slap on the wrist, even those guilty of heinous offenses; John DiIulio insists that "hard time for hardened criminals is rare." Once again, that view would seem hard to reconcile with the enormous increases in imprisonment over the past twenty-five years. How is it possible to make this argument? What evidence is offered in its support?

Here is one example. In 1993 Senator Phil Gramm, later to run for president, wrote an op-ed piece in the *New York Times* entitled "Don't Let Judges Set Crooks Free." Gramm wrote that America was "deluged by a tidal wave of crime," and he identified the "main culprit" as "a criminal justice system in which the cost of committing crimes is so shamelessly cheap that it fails to deter potential criminals." Years of "soft sentencing" had brought "a dramatic decline in the cost of committing a crime and a dramatic increase in crime." As evidence, Gramm pointed to a study by an economist named Morgan Reynolds, of Texas A&M University, which has been widely cited by proponents of the myth of leniency. Reynolds's study purported to estimate the amount of time offenders committing various kinds of crimes could "expect to serve" in prison as of 1990. And the calculations are indeed startling. According to Gramm, a murderer can "expect" to spend just 1.8 years in prison. A rape earns 60 days. A robbery, according to these "findings," results in 23 days behind bars, and a car theft just a day and a half. Proof positive, according to Gramm, that a "soft" justice system is responsible for the tidal wave of crime.

The figures have been used over and over again to demonstrate the extraordinary leniency of the American justice system. And were the implications drawn from them even remotely true it would indeed be a scandal. If judges were in fact sentencing rapists to just two months behind bars and letting robbers free in less than a month, we would have a bizarre justice system indeed. But anyone who has ever followed a serious criminal trial, or known anyone who was actually sentenced to prison, knows instantly that there is something very wrong with these figures.

The standard data on the length of sentences for various crimes are published by the U.S. Bureau of Justice Statistics on the basis of periodic surveys of prison systems across the country. There are complexities involved in measuring the length of the time prisoners actually serve; it makes a considerable difference, for example, whether we try to measure it by looking at average time served by prisoners who are *released* or by estimating the time that will be served by offenders now going *into* prison. The figures on time served by released prisoners reflect the sentencing and parole policies in force some years before, when they were sentenced, while the expected time to be served for new admissions is what a convicted offender can *now* expect—which, under current conditions, will be longer. But however we measure it, the average time serious offenders spend behind bars bears no resemblance to the numbers cited by Gramm.

Among offenders sentenced in 1994—the most recent year available—the estimated time to be served in prison for murder was 127 months, or about 10 years. That figure, it should be noted, markedly understates the penalties for murder, for two reasons. First, it includes what in most states is called "nonnegligent manslaughter," a lesser offense that carries a far lower sentence than murder, and thus brings down the average. Even more importantly, the figure of 10 years does *not* include the roughly 27 percent of murderers who are sentenced to life imprisonment or death, which reduces the average far more. But even with these sentences excluded, the current penalty for murder is still many times higher than the figure Gramm provides. The same disparity holds true for the other crimes as well. The average expected time to be served for a convicted rapist in 1994 was not 60 days but 85 *months,* or just over 7 years. For robbery it was not 23 days but 51 *months,* or well over 4 years.

These figures on expected time to be served also put into perspective the frequent complaint that because of parole and "good time" provisions, most prisoners serve only a fraction of the sentence handed down in court—another sign of leniency run wild. In 1994, the Justice Department estimated that offenders sentenced for violent crimes would serve on average about 46 percent of their sentences, 54 percent for rape. But whether this is an indication of leniency obviously depends on the length of the original sentence. If all first-time robbers were sentenced to fifty-year terms, the fact that they wound up serving just half of that sentence would probably not trouble even the most punitive among us. The United States, as we've seen, generally imposes very harsh sentences by international standards; the widespread use of sentence reductions serves only to bring our average time served for serious violent crimes roughly into line with some (but not all) other advanced industrial countries. Robbers sentenced in 1994 received an average term of not quite 10 years, of which they would probably serve 4 years and 3 months. Rapists received over 13 years on average and could expect to serve over 7.

Note too that the time that offenders are likely to serve behind bars for some offenses has risen with stunning rapidity in recent years, as sentences have gotten harsher and as parole and "good time" provisions have increasingly come under siege. In just four years, from 1990 to 1994, the estimated time to be served in state prison for murder went up by two years and for rape by eleven months. Among newly committed state prison inmates generally, the estimated minimum time to be served rose from an average of thirty-one months in 1985 to forty-three months in 1995.

It is sometimes claimed that average prison sentences have *decreased* in recent years—proof, again, that we have in fact become "softer," not harder, on criminals. The U.S. Bureau of Justice Statistics, during the Bush administration, released statistics purporting to show that "there is no evidence that the time served in prison, prior to the first release on a sentence, has been increasing"—that indeed the median time served by state prison inmates had dropped from 17 months in 1981 to 13 months in 1988. The implication was that despite the "get tough" campaigns of the 1970s and 1980s we were, oddly enough, more lenient at the end of the period than at the beginning. That was highly unlikely on the face of it, and the bureau's own chart showed that time served had risen for robbery and sexual assault and stayed level for homicide—while falling for lesser crimes, notably drug offenses and larceny. And there lies the key to the overall drop in the average time served in prison. Drug offenders were 8 percent of the inmate population in 1980 and 26 percent by 1993; violent offenders fell from 57 to 45 percent of the total. Since, with some important exceptions, drug offenders were being sentenced to shorter terms, that meant a flood of inmates with less severe sentences entering the persons, bringing down the average. Think of what happens when a river floods: say the usual depth of the river is twenty feet. The flood submerges hundreds of square miles of surrounding countryside under five feet of water. The *average* depth of the water has accordingly fallen considerably—small comfort, of course, to those whose homes and farms are now underwater.

Now, reasonable people may disagree about whether the existing sentences for violent crimes are appropriate. Some may feel that an average of seven years in prison for a rape is too little. But these actual sentence lengths are light-years away from the figures cited by Gramm (and others) to demonstrate that "soft sentencing" has flooded the nation with crime. What accounts for this wide disparity? Where did Reynolds get his numbers? The trick, again (as with the "1 in 100" figure) is that the numbers have very little to do with how "toughly" or "leniently" we are treating offenders in the courts—with "soft sentencing"—but primarily with the low rates of *arrest* for most offenses. Reynolds's figure of 23 days for robbery is derived by dividing the average time served by the robbers who are arrested and convicted *by the total number of robberies committed*, whether anyone is ever caught or not, much less convicted. It is true that, by this calculation, the "average cost" of a robbery is low—but that is because the average robbery isn't followed by an arrest, much less a conviction. Thus in 1994 about 1.3 million robberies took place, of which about 619,000 were reported to the police. But there were fewer than 46,000 adult felony convictions for robbery, of which almost all—more than 40,000—resulted in some incarceration in a jail or prison; and as we've seen, robbers who went to prison could expect to stay for well over 4 years. Again, if we could improve our ability to catch robbers in the first place, we might substantially increase the "average cost" of robberies. But it is pure sleight of hand to argue, as Gramm and others do, that weak *sentencing* practices account for the numbers, or that we treat the robbers we catch with shocking leniency.

Indeed, what the figures on the relatively low percentage of crime resulting in punishment really add up to is a profound argument for a greater emphasis on crime *prevention*—as opposed to punishment after the fact. For even if we assume that we could boost our capacity to apprehend robbers, no one seriously argues that we will ever arrive at the point where most robberies result in an arrest; and therefore no amount of increasing punishment will make as much difference as its proponents hope. That is surely not the conclusion that the purveyors of the "1 in 100" figure intended. But it is the only one that stands the test of hard scrutiny.

The fact that we already give relatively lengthy sentences to violent criminals—especially repeaters—helps explain why the rash of "three strikes and you're out" laws passed in recent years have in practice had much less impact than many people expected. Critics of these laws thought states would go broke trying to accommodate a flood of new prisoners; supporters thought large drops in violent crime were sure to come as huge numbers of violent predators roaming the streets finally got their just desserts. What has actually happened confounds both expectations, especially in those jurisdictions—which include most of the states as well as the federal government—where three-strikes laws are aimed solely at violent repeat offenders. As a study by the Campaign for an Effective Crime Policy has shown, none of those states has put many violent offenders away under their new laws. That is surely not because prosecutors are unwilling to charge offenders under the "tough" statutes. It may be in part because some judges, in some jurisdictions, are still managing to sentence offenders in ways that circumvent the harshest provisions of these laws. But it is *mainly* because most repeat violent offenders who come before the courts in these states would have been sentenced to "hard" time under the laws that already existed.

In California, where the three-strikes law was broadly drawn to target relatively low-level property and drug offenders as well as violent repeaters (any felony can trigger a third strike, leading to a mandatory sentence of twenty-five years to life), the number of people sentenced under the law has, unsurprisingly, been higher. But the proportion of *violent* offenders sentenced has still been relatively low. As of 1995, more people had been sentenced under California's three-strikes law for simple marijuana possession than for murder, rape, and kidnapping combined, and more for drug possession generally than for *all* violent offenses. Even in that state, where legislators led a stampede to pass the three-strikes law by arguing that hordes of violent repeaters were roaming the streets unpunished, the number of offenders given third *or second* "strikes" for a violent offense was fewer than 3,000 over the first two years of the law. And most of those violent offenders would have gone to prison *without* the new law. Before the passage of the three-strikes law, California already had on the books a mandatory five-year "enhancement" for the second conviction for many felonies, as well as a "habitual offender" statute providing for life imprisonment (with a minimum of twenty years before parole) for violent offenders who had caused "great bodily harm" to victims and had already served two prison sentences for similar offenses. In short, California's prisons have not been flooded with repeat violent offenders by the three-strikes law, mainly because such offenders were already being sentenced to relatively "tough" terms *before* the new law.

Again, no one denies that truly dangerous people sometimes slip out of the system. But to acknowledge that mistakes do occur is not the same as believing that the system as a whole is "soft" on serious violent criminals. And ironically, the wholesale return of genuinely "bad apples" to the streets has sometimes happened precisely because of unreflective efforts to "get tough," notably in states where dangerous criminals have been released to make room in overcrowded prisons for far less serious offenders incarcerated under mandatory sentences. The most studied case is Florida, where—despite the addition of 25,000 new prison beds—a huge influx of drug offenders during the 1980s resulted in massive prison overcrowding, forcing the state to establish an early-release program, which deposited tens of thousands of offenders who did *not* have mandatory sentences onto the streets. That number included a great many violent criminals, even robbers and rapists, most of whom received little serious supervision once in the community. (The state legislature has recently shifted its policy, to target incarceration on violent offenders and seek out alternatives for the nonviolent.)

With occasional exceptions, then, it remains true that serious, violent criminals, especially if they are repeaters, are likely to do hard time if caught and convicted. But what about the fact that so many violent criminals are out on bail, or on probation or parole? Doesn't that show that we are shockingly "soft"? Wouldn't cracking down on such people by abolishing parole altogether—and putting many of those now on probation behind bars—have a dramatic effect on the crime rate?

Probably not. Here the problems are more genuine. But they are more complicated, and more difficult to solve, than critics like the Council on Crime in America would have us believe. Their argument begins with the undisputed observation that, at any given point, more people who have committed crimes are under some form of "community" supervision than in prison and that the number of "community-based" offenders has grown along with the rise in the prison population. (Between 1980 and 1994, the number of prison inmates increased at an annual average of 8.4 percent, the parole population by 8.5 percent, and the probation population by 7.2 percent.) But it is not apparent why this should be taken as evidence of a "weak" justice system. John DiIulio, for example, argues that the fact that in 1991, 590,000 people who had been convicted of a violent crime were "residing in our communities" on parole or probation, while only 372,000 were in prison, represents "another sobering example of how the scales are tipping" toward the criminal. But that conclusion doesn't follow. Unless we believe that everyone accused of a crime ought to be detained until trial, that everyone convicted of an offense—no matter how minor—should be sent to jail or prison, and that all of those sent to prison should stay there for the rest of their lives, it is not clear why the sheer fact of growth in the number of people on pretrial release, probation, or parole is a sign of either leniency or bad policy.

The real issue is whether we are allowing the *wrong* people to remain free—whether large numbers of "known violent predators" who ought to be behind bars are being released into the community. The Council on Crime in America insists that they are and points to statistics showing that large proportions of violent crimes (up to a third, depending on the jurisdiction and the offense) are committed by offenders who are on probation, parole, or pretrial release. Many Americans likewise believe that large numbers of predators are routinely released to community supervision, and their belief is fed by sensational media anecdotes about horrible crimes committed by parolees and offenders released on bail. Again, no one denies that such tragedies happen, or that we should do all we can to prevent them. But do these figures really tell us that we are typically lenient with "known, violent predators"?

No. To begin with, the numbers, though (usually) technically correct, are, once again, misleadingly presented. The Washington-based Sentencing Project offers this useful example: suppose in a given county there are a thousand offenders under pretrial release. There are also three murders, one of which was committed by an offender under pretrial supervision. Thus the *proportion of murders* accounted for by pretrial releasees is a substantial one-third. But the other side of the coin is that *only one in one thousand* pretrial releasees committed a murder—which suggests that trying to prevent that murder by incarcerating all the offenders we now release before trial would be extraordinarily expensive and indeed, for practical purposes, probably impossible.

There is another, even more fundamental, problem with the assertion that we are letting hordes of violent offenders go free even though we *know* they are dangerous characters. Consider this example. A young man is arrested in a big, crime-ridden city for a minor drug deal. Because he has no prior arrests and no known history of violence, he is given a year's probation. While on probation he kills an acquaintance in a fight. Is it meaningful to say the murder resulted from the "failure to restrain" a known violent offender? Not really, because it is hard to conceive of a reasonable argument that would have justified putting him in prison for a long time on the strength of what was known about him. Could we improve our capacity to *predict* which among the vast pool of minor offenders who come into the courts are truly dangerous—thus ensuring that the violent do not elude our control? Maybe. But it is important to remember that our criminal justice systems *already* try to do just that, and many have adopted elaborate risk-assessment procedures, backed by considerable research and experience, to guide those decisions. Hence, realistically, our ability to get *much* better at predicting which of those offenders poses a high enough risk to justify lengthy incarceration is limited.

What holds for probation also applies to parole. Many people believe that if we abolished parole altogether, we could sharply reduce violent crime, and that belief is based in part on the reality that heinous crimes are sometimes committed by people on parole. But unless we believe that everyone convicted of a crime of violence—of whatever seriousness—should stay in prison for the rest of their lives, most *will* at some point be released to the community—and it is not clear why it would be better for them to be in the community *without* supervision than with it.

The real question, for both probation and parole, is whether we can do a better job than we now do of monitoring and supervising offenders in the community and thereby reduce the risks that they will do harm. And here the answer is certainly yes. Many probation and parole agencies in the United States, especially in the big cities, are stretched well past the point of effectiveness, their ability to provide meaningful supervision of offenders drastically eroded by years of fiscal starvation and caseloads that can run into the hundreds. The Council on Crime in America, to their credit, reject the idea that all offenders necessarily belong behind bars and suggest that improving the capacity of parole and probation agencies to supervise them outside prison walls makes eminent sense. What they do *not* say, however, is that one of the main reasons why the effectiveness of the probation and parole systems has been so badly compromised is that we have systematically disparaged what they do as "soft" on crime while diverting the money we could have used to improve them into the prisons. We desperately need better community supervision of offenders. But we are unlikely to get it unless we rein in the rush toward indiscriminate incarceration.

As importantly, if we want to prevent crimes committed by "community-based" offenders, we will need to invest more in programs to provide those we *do* incarcerate with a better chance of succeeding on the outside when they are released, as nearly all of them will be. But it should be obvious that if we make no effort to improve the capacity of ex-offenders to live and work productively outside prison walls, we shouldn't profess great surprise when many of them fail—especially if they are also returning to communities with few and perhaps diminishing opportunities for success. And we should not blame that failure on the leniency of the justice system.

CHAPTER 38

Wild Pitch
"Three Strikes, You're Out" and Other Bad Calls on Crime

Jerome H. Skolnick

According to the pundits, the polls, and the politicians, violent crime is now America's number one problem. If the problems were properly defined and the lessons of past efforts were fully absorbed, this could be an opportunity to set national crime policy on a positive course. Instead, it is a dangerous moment. Intuition is driving the country toward desperate and ineffectual responses that will drive up prison costs, divert tax dollars from other vital purposes, and leave the public as insecure and dissatisfied as ever.

The pressures pushing federal and state politicians to vie for the distinction of being toughest on crime do not come only from apprehensive voters and the tabloid press. Some of the leading organs of elite opinion, notably the *Wall Street Journal,* have celebrated gut-level, impulsive reactions. In one *Journal* column ("Crime Solution: Lock 'em Up"), Ben J. Wattenberg writes that criminologists don't know what works.

What works is what everyone intuitively knows: "A thug in prison cannot shoot your sister." In another *Journal* column ("The People Want Revenge"), the conservative intellectual Paul Johnson argues that government is failing ordinary people by ignoring their retributive wishes. Ordinary people, he writes, want neither to understand criminals nor to reform them. "They want them punished as severely and cheaply as possible."

Johnson is partly right and mostly wrong. Ordinary people want more than anything to walk the streets safely and to protect their families and their homes. Intuitively, like Wattenberg, many believe that more prisons and longer sentences offer safety along with punishment. But, especially in dealing with crime, intuition isn't always a sound basis for judgment.

The United States already has the highest rate of imprisonment of any major nation. The prisons have expanded enormously in recent years in part because of get-tough measures sending low-level drug offenders to jail. Intuitions were wrong:

the available evidence does not suggest that imprisoning those offenders has made the public safer.

The current symbol of the intuitive lock-'em-up response is "three strikes and you're out"—life sentences for criminals convicted of three violent or serious felonies. The catchy slogan appears to have mesmerized politicians from one coast to the other and across party lines. Three-strikes fever began in the fall of 1993 in the wake of the intense media coverage of the abduction and murder of a 12-year-old California girl, Polly Klaas, who was the victim, according to police, of a criminal with a long and violent record. California's Republican Governor Pete Wilson took up the call for three strikes, and on March 7 the California legislature overwhelmingly approved the proposal. Even New York Governor Mario Cuomo endorsed a three strikes measure. The U.S. Senate has passed a crime bill that adopts three strikes as well as a major expansion of the federal role in financing state prisons and stiffening state sentencing policy. In his 1994 State of the Union address, President Clinton singled out the Senate legislation and three strikes for praise.

But will three strikes work? Teenagers and young men in their twenties commit the vast majority of violent offenses. The National Youth Survey, conducted by Colorado criminologist Delbert S. Elliott, found that serious violent offenses (aggravated-assault, rape, and robbery involving some injury or weapon) peak at age 17. The rate is half as much at age 24 and declines significantly as offenders mature into their thirties.

If we impose life sentences on serious violent offenders on their third conviction—after they have served two sentences—we will generally do so in the twilight of their criminal careers. Three strikes laws will eventually fill our prisons with geriatric offenders, whose care will be increasingly expensive when their propensities to commit crime are at the lowest.

Take the case of "Albert," described in the *New York Times* not long ago by Mimi Silbert, president of the Delancey Street Foundation in San Francisco. At age 10, Albert was the youngest member of a barrio gang. By the time he was sent to San Quentin at the age of 19, he had committed 27 armed robberies and fathered two children. Now 36, he is a plumber and substitute teacher who has for years been crime-free, drug-free, and violence-free. According to Silbert, the Delancey Street program has turned around the lives of more than 10,000 Alberts in the past 23 years.

To imprison the Alberts of the world for life makes sense if the purpose is retribution. But if life imprisonment is supposed to increase public safety, we will be disappointed with the results. To achieve that purpose, we need to focus on preventing violent crimes committed by high-risk youths. That is where the real problem lies.

The best that can be said of some three-strikes proposals is that they would be drawn so narrowly that they would have little effect. The impact depends on which felonies count as strikes. Richard H. Girgenti, director of the New York State Division of Criminal Justice Services, says that the measure supported by Governor Cuomo would affect only 300 people a year and be coupled with the release of nonviolent prisoners. President Clinton is also supporting a version of three strikes that is more narrowly drawn than California's. Proposals like California's, however, will result in incarcerating thousands of convicts into middle and old age.

REGRESSING TO THE MEAN

Before Governor Wilson signed the most draconian of the three-strikes bill introduced in the legislature, district attorneys across the state assailed the measure, arguing that it would clog courts, cost too much money, and result in disproportionate sentences for nonviolent offenders. So potent is the political crime panic in California that the pleas of the prosecutors were rebuffed.

The prospect in California is ominous. Even without three-strikes legislation, California is already the nation's biggest jailer, with one out of eight American prisoners occupying its cells. During the past 16 years, its prison population has grown 600 percent, while violent crime in the state has increased 40 percent. As Franklin E. Zimring and Gordon Hawkins demonstrate in a recent issue of the *British Journal of Criminology,* correctional growth in California was "in a class by itself" during the 1980s. The three next largest state prison systems (New York, Texas, and Florida) experienced half the growth of California, and western European systems about a quarter.

To pay for a five-fold increase in the corrections budget since 1980, Californians have had to sacrifice other services. Education especially has suffered. Ten years ago, California devoted 14 percent of its state budget to higher education and 4 percent to prisons. Today it devotes 9 percent to both.

The balance is now expected to shift sharply in favor of prisons. To pay for three strikes, California expects to spend $10.5 billion by the year 2001. The California Department of Corrections has estimated that three strikes will require the state to add 20 more prisons to the existing 28 and the 12 already on the drawing board. By 2001, there will be 109,000 more prisoners behind bars serving life sentences. A total of 275,621 more people are expected to be imprisoned over the next 30 years—the equivalent of building an electric fence around the city of Anaheim. By the year 2027 the cost of housing extra inmates is projected to hit $5.7 billion a year.

But will California be better off in 2027—indeed, will it have less crime—if it has 20 more prisons for aging offenders instead of 20 more college campuses for the young?

Of course, Wilson and other politicians are worrying about the next elections, not the next century. By the time the twice-convicted get out of prison, commit a third major offense, and are convicted and sentenced to life terms, Wilson and the others supporting three strikes will be out—that is, out of office, leaving future generations a legacy of an ineffectual and costly crime policy. To avoid that result, political leaders need to stop trying to out-tough one another and start trying to out-reason each other.

THE LIMITS OF INTUITION

H. L. A. Hart, the noted legal philosopher, once observed that the Enlightenment made the form and severity of punishment "a matter to be *thought* about, to be *reasoned* about, and *argued*, and not merely a matter to be left to feelings and sentiment." Those aspirations ought still to be our guide.

The current push to enact three strikes proposals is reminiscent of the movement in the 1970s to enact mandatory sentencing laws, another effort to get tough, reduce judicial discretion, and appease the public furies. But mandatory sentencing has not yielded any discernible reduction in crime. Indeed, the result has been mainly to shift discretionary decision-making upstream in the criminal justice system since the laws have continued to allow great latitude in bringing charges and plea bargaining.

Ironically, mandatory sentencing allowed the serial freedom of Richard Allen Davis, the accused murderer of Polly Klaas. Before 1977, California had a system of indeterminate prison sentencing for felony offenders. For such felonies as second-degree murder, robbery, rape, and kidnapping, a convict might receive a sentence of 1 to 25 years, or even one year to life. The objective was to tailor sentences to behavior, to confine the most dangerous convicts longer, and to provide incentives for self-improvement. However, in 1977, declaring that the goal of imprisonment was punishment rather than rehabilitation, the state adopted supposedly tougher mandatory sentences. Richard Allen Davis benefited from two mandated sentence reductions, despite the prescient pre-sentencing report of a county probation officer who warned of Davis's "accelerating potential for violence" after his second major conviction. Under indeterminate sentencing, someone with Davis's personality and criminal history would likely have been imprisoned far longer than the mandated six years for his first set of offenses.

Most criminologists and policy analysts do not support the reliance on expanded prisons and the rigidities of habitual offender laws. Some, like David Rothman, have apologized for their naiveté joining the movement to establish determinate sentencing in the 1970s and now recognize that it has been a failure.

Others, like John J. DiIulio, Jr., take a harder line, although the hardness of DiIulio's line seems to depend on his forum. In a January 1994 column appearing—where else?—in the *Wall Street Journal*, DiIulio supported the superficially toughest provisions of the Senate crime bill. (The *Journal*'s headline writers called the column "Let 'em Rot," a title that DiIulio later protested, though his own text was scarcely less draconian.) But writing in *The American Prospect* in the fall of 1990 ("Getting Prisons Straight") and with Anne Thomson Piehl in the fall of 1991 for the *Brookings Review*, DiIulio's message was more tempered.

The Brookings article reviews the debate over the cost-effectiveness of prisons. Imprisonment costs between $20,000 to $50,000 per prisoner per year. But is that price worth the benefit of limiting the crimes that could have been committed by prisoners if they were on the street? "Based on existing statistical evidence," write DiIulio and Piehl, "the relationship between crime rates and imprisonment is ambiguous." This is hardly a mandate for "letting 'em rot." DiIulio and Piehl recognize that the certainty of punishment is more effective than the length and that "even if we find that 'prison pays' at the margin, it would not mean that every convicted criminal deserves prison; it would not mean that it is cost effective to imprison every convicted felon." I agree and so do most criminologists. Does DiIulio read DiIulio?

THE RISE OF IMPRISONMENT

Two trends are responsible for the increase in imprisonment. First, the courts are imposing longer sentences for such nonviolent felonies as larceny, theft, and motor vehicle theft. In 1992 these accounted for 60.9 percent of crime in America, according to the Federal Bureau of Investigation's Uniform Crime Reports.

Second, drugs have become the driving force of crime. More than half of all violent offenders are under the influence of alcohol or drugs (most often alcohol) when they commit their crimes. The National Institute of Justice has shown that in 23 American cities, the percentage of arrested and booked males testing positive for any of ten illegal drugs ranged from a low of 48 percent in Omaha to 79 percent in Philadelphia. The median cities, Fort Lauderdale and Miami, checked out at 62 percent.

There has been an explosion of arrests and convictions and increasingly longer sentences for possessing and selling drugs. A Justice Department study, completed last summer but withheld from the public until February this year, found that of the 90,000 federal prison inmates, one-fifth are low-level drug offenders with no current or prior violence or previous prison time. They are jamming the prisons.

The federal prison population, through mandated and determinate sentences, has tripled in the past decade. Under current policy, it will rise by 50 percent by the century's turn, with drug offenders accounting for 60 percent of the additional prisoners. Three-strikes legislation will doubtless solidify our already singular position as the top jailer of the civilized world.

THE FEAR FACTOR

The lock-'em-up approach plays to people's fear of crime, which is rising, while actual crime rates are stabilizing or declining. This is by no means to argue that fear of crime is unjustified. Crime has risen enormously in the United States in the last quarter-century, but it is no more serious in 1994 than it was in 1991. The FBI's crime index declined 4 percent from 1991 to 1992.

In California, a legislative report released in January indicates that the overall crime rate per 100,000 people declined slightly from 1991 to 1992, dropping from 3,503.3 to 3,491.5. Violent crimes—homicide, forcible rape, robbery, and aggravated assault—rose slightly, from 1,079.8 to 1,103.9. Early figures for 1993 show a small decline.

On the other coast, New York City reported a slight decline in homicides, 1,960 in 1993, compared with 1,995 in 1992, and they are clustered in 12 of the city's 75 police districts, places like East New York and the South Bronx. "On the east side of Manhattan," writes Matthew Purdy in the *New York Times,* "in the neighborhood of United Nations diplomats and quiet streets of exclusive apartments, the gunfire might as well be in a distant city."

So why, when crime rates are flat, has crime become America's number one problem in the polls? Part of the answer is that fear of crime rises with publicity, especially on television. Polly Klaas's murder, the killing of tourists in Florida, the roadside murder of the father of former basketball star Michael Jordan, and the killing of commuters on a Long Island Railroad train sent a scary message to the majority of Americans who do not reside in the inner cities. The message seemed to be that random violence is everywhere and you are no longer safe—not in your suburban home, commuter train, or automobile—and the police and the courts cannot or will not protect you.

A recent and as yet unpublished study by Zimring and Hawkins argues that America's problem is not crime per se but random violence. They compare Los Angeles and Sydney, Australia. Both cities have a population of 3.6 million, and both are multicultural (although Sydney is less so). Crime in Sydney is a serious annoyance but not a major threat. My wife and I, like other tourists, walked through Sydney at night last spring with no fear of being assaulted.

Sydney's crime pattern explains the difference. Its burglary rate is actually 10 percent higher than L.A.'s, and its theft rate is 73 percent of L.A.'s. But its robbery and homicide rates are strikingly lower, with only 12.5 percent of L.A.'s robbery rate and only 7.3 percent of L.A.'s homicide rate.

Americans and Australians don't like any kind of crime, but most auto thefts and many burglaries are annoying rather than terrifying. It is random violent crime, like a shooting in a fast-food restaurant, that is driving fear.

Violent crime, as I suggested earlier, is chiefly the work of young men between the ages of 15 and 24. The magnitude of teenage male involvement in violent crime is frightening. "At the peak age (17)," Delbert Elliott writes, "36 percent of African-American (black) males and 25 percent of non-Hispanic (white) males report one or more serious violent offenses." Nor are young women free of violence. One in five African-American females and one in ten white females report having committed a serious violent offense.

Blacks are more likely than whites to continue their violence into their adult years. Elliott considers this finding to be an important insight into the high arrest and incarceration rates of young adult black males. As teenagers, black and white males are roughly comparable in their disposition to violence. "Yet," Elliott writes, "once involved in a lifestyle that includes serious forms of violence, theft, and substance use, persons from disadvantaged families and neighborhoods find it very difficult to escape. They have fewer opportunities for conventional adult roles, and they are more deeply embedded in and dependent upon the gangs and the illicit economy that flourish in their neighborhoods."

The key to reformation, Elliott argues, is the capacity to make the transition into conventional adult work and family roles. His data show that those who successfully make the change give up their involvement in violence. Confinement in what will surely be overcrowded prisons can scarcely facilitate that transition, while community-based programs like Delancey Street have proven successful.

Just as violent crime is concentrated among the young, so is drug use. Drug treatment must be a key feature of crime prevention both in prisons and outside. There is some good news here. In early 1994, President Clinton and a half-dozen cabinet members visited a Maryland prison that boasts a model drug-treatment program to announce a national drug strategy that sharply increases spending for drug treatment and rehabilitation. Although the major share of the anti-drug budget, 59 percent, is still allocated to law enforcement, the change is in the right direction. A number of jurisdictions across the country have developed promising court-ordered rehabilitation programs that seem to be succeeding in reducing both drug use and the criminality of drug-using offenders.

Drugs are one area where get-tough policies to disrupt supply have been a signal failure, both internationally and domestically. Interdiction and efforts to suppress drug agriculture and manufacture within such countries as Peru and Colombia have run up against what I have called "the Darwinian Trafficker Dilemma." Such efforts undercut the marginally efficient traffickers, while the fittest—the most efficient, the best organized, the most ruthless, the most corrupting of police and judges—survive. Cocaine prices, the best measure of success or failure, dropped precipitously in the late 1980s. They have recovered somewhat, but likely more from monopolistic pricing than government interference.

Domestically, get-tough intuitions have inspired us to threaten drug kingpins with long prison terms or death. Partly, we wish to punish and incapacitate them, but mostly we wish to deter others from following in their felonious paths. Unfortunately, such policies are undermined by the "Felix Mitchell Dilemma," which I named in honor of the West Coast's once notorious kingpin, who received a life sentence in the 1980s, albeit a short one since he was murdered in federal prison. Mitchell's sentence and early demise did not deter drug sellers in the Bay Area. On the contrary, drug sales continued and, with Mitchell's monopolistic pricing eliminated, competition reduced the price of crack. The main effect of Mitchell's imprisonment was to destabilize the market, lower drug prices, and increase violence as rival gang members challenged each other for market share. Drug-related drive-by shootings, street homicides, and felonious assaults increased.

Recently, two of Mitchell's successors, Timothy Bluitt and Marvin Johnson, were arrested and sent to prison. So will peace finally come to the streets? "When a guy like Bluitt goes down, someone takes his place and gets an even bigger slice of the pie," an anonymous federal agent told the *San Francisco Chronicle* this past January. "The whole process is about consolidating turf and power."

Youngsters who sell drugs in Oakland, Denver, Detroit, South Central Los Angeles, Atlanta, and New York are part of generations who have learned to see crime as economic opportunity. This does not excuse their behavior, but it does intensify our need to break the cycle of poverty, abuse, and violence that dominates their lives. Prisons do not deter criminals partly because the Mitchells and Bluitts do not rationally calculate choices with the same points of reference that legislators employ. Drug dealers already face the death penalty on the streets.

History reminds us that gang violence is not novel, but it has not always been so lethal. The benchmark sociological study of the urban gang is Frederick Thrasher's research on 1,313 Chicago gangs published in 1927. The disorder and violence of these gangs appalled Thrasher, who observed that they were beyond the ordinary controls of police and other social agencies. He described gang youth, of which only 7.2 percent were "Negro," as "lawless, godless, wild." Why didn't more of them kill each other? They fought with fists and knives, not assault weapons.

PREVENTING VIOLENT CRIME

If violent crime prevention is our strategic aim, we need to test tactics. We need to go beyond the Brady Bill and introduce a tight regulatory system on weapons and ammunition, and we need more research and analysis to figure out what control system would be most effective. Successful gun and ammunition control would do far more to stem the tide of life-threatening violence than expensive prisons with mandated sentences.

The Senate crime bill, however, promises to increase the nation's rate of imprisonment. Besides its three strikes provisions, the legislation incorporates Senator Robert Byrd's $3 billion regional prison proposal. If enacted, states can apply to house their prisoners in 10 regional prisons, each with a capacity of 2,500 inmates.

To qualify, states must adopt "truth in sentencing" laws mandating that offenders convicted of violent crimes serve "at least 80 percent of the sentence ordered," the current average served by federal offenders. They also must approve pretrial detention laws similar to those in the federal system. And the states must ensure that four categories of crime—murder, firearms offenses resulting in death or serious bodily injury, sex offenses broadly defined, and child abuse—are punished as severely as they are under federal law. In effect, the Senate crime bill federalizes sentencing policy.

According to H. Scott Wallace of the National Legal Aid and Defender's Association, the mandate will add about 12,000 prisoners to the average state's correctional population but will offer only about 3 percent of the space needed to house them.

The most costly provision of the Senate crime bill—$9 billion worth—is its proposal for 100,000 more police, a measure endorsed by the administration. Its potential value in reducing crime is unclear. We need more research on constructive policing, including community policing, which can be either an effective approach or merely a fashionable buzzword. We need to address the deficiencies of police culture revealed in the corruption uncovered by New York City's Mollen Commission and the excessive force revealed on the Rodney King beating videotape. More police may help in some places but not much in others. And they are very expensive.

A leading police researcher, David H. Bayley, has explained the ten-for-one rule of police visibility: ten cops must be hired to put one officer on the street. Only about two-thirds of police are uniformed patrol officers. They work three shifts, take vacation and sick leave, and require periodic retraining. Consequently 100,000 new officers will mean only about 10,000 on the street for any one shift for the entire United States.

Even if we were to have more and better police, there is no guarantee they will deter crime. Criminologists have found no marginal effect on crime rates from putting more cops on the street. Indeed, Congress and the president need look no farther than down their own streets to discover that simply increasing police doesn't necessarily make the streets safe. Washington, D.C., boasts the highest police-per-resident ratio in the nation with one cop for every 150 civilians. It is also America's homicide capital.

We might get more bang for the patrolling buck by investing in para-police, or the police corps, or private police, rather than by paying for more fully sworn and expensive officers. Under the leadership of former Chief Raymond Davis, Santa Ana, California, had the most effective community-oriented policing department in the nation. Davis, who faced a weak police union, could innovate with community- and service-oriented civilians who wore blue uniforms but carried no guns— a new and cost-effective blue line.

The crime bill allocates approximately $3 billion for boot camps, another get-tough favorite. Criminologist Doris MacKenzie has found, contrary to intuition, no significant difference between camp graduates and former prison inmates in the rate at which they return to prison. Similarly, a General Accounting Office report concluded that there is no evidence that boot camps reduce recidivism.

If the public wants boot camps primarily for retribution, it doesn't matter whether they work. Under the Eighth Amendment's bar on cruel and unusual punishment, we're not permitted to impose corporal punishment with whips and clubs. In boot camps, however, we can require painful exercises and hard and demeaning labor to teach these miscreant youth a message of retribution. But if correctional boot camps are intended to resocialize youth and to prepare for them noncriminal civilian life, the camps are inadequate.

We need to experiment with boot camps plus—the "plus" including skills training, education, jobs, community reconstruction. Conservatives who stress moral revitalization and family values as an antidote to youth crime have the right idea. Yet they rarely if ever, consider how important are the structural underpinnings— education, opportunity, employment, family functioning, community support—for developing such values.

Eventually, we are going to have to choose between our retributive urges and the possibilities of crime prevention. We cannot fool ourselves into thinking they are the same. One punishment meted out by criminal law is a blunt and largely ineffectual instrument of public protection. It deters some, it incapacitates others, and it does send a limited moral message. But if we want primarily to enhance public safety by preventing crime, we need to mistrust our intuitions and adopt strategies and tactics that have been researched, tested, and critically evaluated. In short, we need to embrace the values of the enlightenment over those of the dark ages.

Instant Replay

Three Strikes Was the Right Call

John J. DiIulio Jr.

Jerome H. Skolnick's essay on crime policy ("Wild Pitch: 'Three Strikes, You're Out' and Other Bad Calls on Crime," Spring 1994) omitted some important facts and ignored several valid arguments.

Echoing the anti-incarceration consensus within criminology, Skolnick asserts that life without parole for thrice-convicted violent felons is a bad policy idea, a "wild pitch." Actually, it's more of an underhanded lob to career criminals, most of whom would hardly be affected by it. In 1991 there were about 35,000 new court commitments to federal prisons. Less than 6 percent of federal prisoners were sentenced for violent crimes. About 30 percent of the 142,000 persons committed to state prisons were sentenced for violent crimes. If 10 percent of all prisoners sentenced for violent crimes were on their "third strike," then the law would have affected some 4,500 persons in a corrections population of nearly 4.5 million. Love it or hate it, "three strikes" would have little impact on the size of prison populations, and would do nothing to plug the worm's hole of phoney "mandatory minimum" laws. These laws have put about three-quarters of all convicts—over 3 million criminals—on the streets under "supervision" that in most cases means a monthly chat with an overworked, underpaid probation or parole agent.

Millions of crimes are committed each year by convicted offenders whom the system didn't keep behind bars. Within three years of their release, persons convicted of property crimes are about as likely to commit a violent crime as persons convicted of violent crimes in the first place. And please, no more nonsense about "intermediate sanctions." Recent studies show that fully half of all probationers don't even comply with the basic terms of their sentences (pay fines, do community service, accept drug treatment) before being released from custody, and only one-fifth of the violators are ever disciplined in any way. Meanwhile, repeat criminals who beat the system inflict hundreds of billions of dollars in damages on their victims and society each year.

Skolnick may think the Polly Klaas tragedy is mere sensationalism, but all the data show that the system routinely permits known predatory criminals to plea bargain their way to lesser charges at the front end, only to give them numerous get-out-of-jail-free cards at the back end. In 1991 thirty-four states released more than 325,000 prisoners combined, 90 percent of them to community-based supervision. About half of these offenders had served *a year or less* in prison before their releases. On average, they served 35 percent of their time in confinement. This average held pretty well for all types of offenders. Thus, murderers received a maximum sentence of 20 years but served under 8 years (below 40 percent of their sentences) in prison, while drug traffickers (organized traffickers, *not* mere possessors) received an average of 4 years and served about 14 months (35 percent of their sentence) before release. The state-level data paint the same bleak picture in finer detail. In New Jersey, for example, the typical prisoner had 9 arrests, and 6 convictions, committed over a dozen serious crimes (excluding *all* drug crimes) in the year prior to his incarceration, had about a 50–50 chance of victimizing again after his release, and was most likely to victimize poor and minority citizens.

No Americans suffer more from permissive penal practices than the law-abiding minority citizens of inner city neighborhoods. Middle-class and affluent Americans are spending record amounts on private security devices, rent-a-cops, and other measures intended to make the environments in which they live relatively impervious to crime. That spending, in conjunction with now commonplace danger-avoidance behaviors (don't walk alone or ride the subway at night, don't drive through "bad neighborhoods"), help explain the recent decrease in crime rates nationally. But poor folks can't afford private security measures. Instead, they rely mainly on a "justice system" that virtually invites the criminally deviant to prey upon the truly disadvantaged.

Like most criminologists, Skolnick obscures the public protection value of imprisonment behind criminologically *de rigueur* rhetoric about the steep increase in the rate of incarceration, the U.S. having the highest incarceration rate in the world, etc. But he doesn't mention that the rate increase in community-based supervision has been even steeper. Nor does he note that only 6 percent of state prisoners are nonviolent first-time offenders. The federal system, in which prisoners must serve at least 85 percent of their time behind bars, consists largely of "non-violent" drug dealers with multiple convictions. My Princeton colleague, Ethan Nadelmann, has made a number of powerful arguments for decriminalizing drugs. He's persuaded me on some points, but not all, and not on the bottom line of legalization. But most criminologists who balk at mandatory prison terms for drug merchants lack the courage of their criminological convictions. Rather than asserting that we're locking up too many harmless people for too long, criminologists ought to get specific—identify these people, and tell us, on a jurisdiction-by-jurisdiction basis, precisely what classes of criminals they would like to let out sooner.

I agree with Skolnick that it is irrational to wait until career criminals are drifting into their less crime-prone years before slapping them with long sentences. James Q. Wilson and others made that case years ago. But there are at least four other considerations. First, the differences among the criminal classes in prison today are not that wide. We're not talking about criminals—we're talking about plea-bargain-gorged *convicted and imprisoned criminals*—the vast majority of whom carry a criminal portfolio featuring multiple property crimes, multiple violent crimes, or both.

Second, it's true that older criminals commit fewer and less serious crimes than do younger criminals. But less crime isn't no crime and we don't have any reliable way of predicting which prisoners are harmless "geriatric inmates" and which are still dangerous. (Ask the Massachusetts authorities who recently got burnt by a 61-year-old released prisoner who murdered again.)

Third, if we're really so concerned about waiting too long before hammering repeat criminals with heavy sentences, why not support "two strikes" laws that incarcerate them while they're hot—if not for life, then for 15- to 20-years with no good time and no parole? California and dozens of other states are moving in this direction. Godspeed to them. Of course, when pressed most criminologists want only "violent" crimes to count as a "strike"—major drug felonies, carjacking at knifepoint, etc., aren't supposed to count. These folks have to stop decriminalizing things without admitting it, and without telling the rest of us why. This goes especially for all their hypocritical cheers for gun control. New Jersey, like many states, has dozens of tough gun laws. But the penalties for gun law violations aren't strictly enforced. Would those who want more restrictions on guns also favor making serious gun-law violations a "strike"? I would.

Fourth, society has a right not only to protect itself from convicted criminals but to express its moral outrage at their acts by, among other things, keeping them behind bars. For example, what is the right moral posture when it comes to cases like the 73-year-old man recently sentenced to life without parole for the 1963 murder of civil rights worker Medgar Evers? In my view, the public and their elected leaders have a better grasp of the moral *and* empirical issues at stake than do most of our country's criminologists.

Skolnick and most other criminologists are sure that prison is not the answer. But what, precisely, is the question? If the question's how to solve America's crime problem, plus all the rest of its urban problems, then prison is no answer. But if the question is what can protect the public from violent and repeat criminals, then prison is a very good answer indeed. Professionally, criminologists should not ignore the data on how little time most violent and repeat criminals spend behind bars. Morally they should not ignore the pleas of a majority of Americans of every demographic description. Nor should they belittle the lived experiences of the Klaas family and others that, like my own, have suffered the murder of a loved one at the hands of a released repeat criminal, or had their lives and property trifled with or ruined by thugs whom the system let loose. We can forgive the public, which has become so frustrated with America's revolving door justice that it applauds Singapore's institutionalized canings.

As Skolnick noted, the "100,000 cops" provision of the crime bill would actually mean about 10,000 around-the-clock cops distributed by Congress among hundreds of jurisdictions. The federal bucks are just seed dollars that will dry up in a half-decade, leaving the states and cities to bite the bullet. Still, with artful administration by the Office of Justice Programs (read: not the 1970s saga of the Law Enforcement Assistance Administration revisited), there is still the chance that the community policing provisions of the bill could be married to its manpower provisions. At least that's what the academics (including David Bayley, author of the 10-for-1 rule cited by Skolnick) and government officials who joined me at Brookings for a session with the Justice Department hope will happen.

In the 1980s Skolnick and other criminologists made excellent arguments for community policing. But community policing was oversold as a do-more-with-less strategy. You can't just retrain cops and put more of them on foot patrol. Many big city police forces have contracted. The thin blue line is stretched too thin, especially in the underserved inner city where crime is out of control. Community policing should be embraced for what it is—a do-better-with-more strategy. The cheap talk's over, the bill's due, and it includes more money for more cops. The public is willing to pay; criminologists should belly up to the bar, too, and endorse more police.

Skolnick has cited my January 1994 op-ed on crime for the *Wall Street Journal*, which had also recently run pieces on crime by syndicated columnist Ben Wattenberg, historian Paul Johnson, and several others. In that op-ed, I supported what President Clinton said on crime in his State of the Union address, and condemned Attorney General Reno and other liberal elites who respond with double-speak to the public's legitimate calls for tougher anti-crime measures. Skolnick compares this op-ed to a 1990 article I published in *The American Prospect*, and a 1991 article I co-authored for the *Brookings Review*. Finding my "message" to be "more tempered" in these essays than it was in the op-ed, he writes that the "hard-ness of DiIulio's line seems to depend on his forum." He concludes by asking, "Does DiIulio read DiIulio?"

For the record, my *TAP* article was mainly about prison rehabilitation pro-grams, including drug treatment. I have continued to write on that issue, done what I could to encourage Senate Republicans and others not to throw the drug treat-ment baby out with the crime bill bath water, and accepted a public tribute on that score from Democratic Congressman Charles Schumer of New York. I'm for more prisons, stiffer and enforced sentences, and whatever rehabilitation programs work to cut costs and reduce recidivism. But there's no need to genuflect at the prisoner rehabilitation altar in an op-ed that calls for tougher sentencing.

Whether or not imprisoning Peter keeps Paul honest, with Peter locked up, so-ciety saves itself from the crimes he might have continued to commit. And by keep-ing him behind bars for all or most of his term, society spares itself the crimes that might have followed his early release. For example, between 1987 and 1991 Florida parolees committed some 25,000 new crimes, including 5,000 violent crimes and 346 murders. The *Brookings Review* article referenced by Skolnick was a cost-benefit analysis of imprisonment based on official criminal records and prisoner self-report data, which revealed that in the year prior to incarceration, the typical prisoner committed about a dozen serious offenses, excluding all drug crimes. The study found that for most prisoners "prison pays" (i.e., the social benefits of incar-ceration are nearly 1.4 times the social costs).

Last year I completed another major prisoner self-report survey. The results, which will be published this year, indicate that the benefits of imprisonment are even greater than reported in the *Brookings* study. Still, as I wrote in the first study, "the relationship between imprisonment rates and crime rates is ambiguous." Finding that prison pays at the margin does "not mean that it is cost-effective to imprison every convicted felon."

Amazingly, however, Skolnick and other criminologists have repeatedly cited those obvious cautions and ignored the major finding of the study—namely, that contrary to all their assertions, *prison pays*. Incarcerating a greater fraction of convicted felons would yield positive social benefits, and quite dramatic ones if we factored in even a small deterrence benefit and included even a tiny fraction of all drug crimes.

Skolnick notes that the *Journal* tagged my January 1994 article "Let 'em Rot." As I made clear in my blistering top-of-the-letters-page response, the *Journal* editors' title has everything to do with the casual callousness of some conservative elites and nothing to do with either the public's concerns about crime or my views, backed by extensive research, on the practical attainability and moral necessity of humane (not luxurious) prison administration. Still, Skolnick asserted that my "message" in the piece was as "draconian" as the title.

If criminologists like Skolnick think it's "draconian" to want most violent and repeat criminals to spend most of their time behind bars, to be fed up with fake get-tough measures, to condemn liberal elites who just don't get it, and to want what majorities of every demographic group in America wants in the way of effective justice, then so be it. That says more about the perversity of the criminologists' message (prisons are teeming with petty criminals, Americans are a punitive people, voters are fools, politicians are weathervanes, drugs ought to be decriminalized, and the "experts" always know best) than it does about any venue-sensitive changes in my writing. And since Skolnick liked tarring me with a title against which I had publicly protested, let me note that last November I wrote an op-ed for, if I may imitate Skolnick—where else?—*The New York Times*. My loud, clear, and on-the-record "message" on prisons (more!) was exactly the same there as in the criminologically incorrect *Journal* piece. But the *Times* billed the article "Save the Children."

Jerome H. Skolnick Replies

John DiIulio's response is shot through with overheated generalizations. His first paragraph contains his first big—no, colossal—error, namely that three strikes "would have little impact on the size of prison populations." That's not true in California, the nation's most populous state, where three strikes is currently on the books.

DiIulio assumes that only "violent" felonies count as "strikes," but the California law itemizes "serious" felonies as well. Consequently, California is expected to imprison an additional 3,850 as a result of the Three Strikes law next year.

DiIulio estimates that three strikes will affect a total of only 4,500 felons in all state prisons in a given year based on 1991 estimates of prison population. Subtract 3,850 from 4,500 and you have only 650 additional felons incarcerated for life, in a given year, as a result of the three strikes laws impending in other states. That's not believable.

DiIulio's point would be better made as follows: the impact of three strikes laws on the size of prison populations will depend on how legislatures define third offenses that count as "strikes." DiIulio himself doesn't see much difference between property offenders and violent offenders. He mistrusts intermediate sanctions as well, although he fails to mention how starved parole and probation services are in comparison to prisons. DiIulio disavows "Let 'em rot" as his maxim, but "Lock 'em up" seems to be advised.

California's legislature has plenty of DiIulio-like thinkers. Consequently, the Department of Corrections expects significant increases in prison population as a result of three strikes, and so will other states if they follow California's lead. Moreover, since these are life sentences, their impact on prison population increases with time.

Even before three strikes legislation passed in California, the Department of Corrections predicted that its 1999 population would be more than seven times what it was in 1980. The CDC now predicts that three strikes will enlarge this number by more than half again.

The CDC estimates that three strikes will require at least 20 new prisons, in addition to the dozen already under construction. Eventually, in 2027–28, California is expected to incarcerate 272,438 criminals—the equivalent of building an electric fence around the city of Anaheim.

Interestingly, nobody, including three strikes supporters such as Governor Pete Wilson, disputes these figures. What they warrant instead is that prisons save money.

In New Jersey, where the Senate unanimously approved a three strikes law on May 12, Louis F. Kosco, the bill's sponsor, echoed this theme to a *New York Times* reporter who questioned how cash-strapped governments will cover the cost of booming prison populations. "Each time they go through the revolving door, repeat offenders cost the state a great deal in legal and parole expenses," he said. "And we must take into account the economic and social costs. . . ." George Romero, Chief Economist of the California Governor's Office of Planning and Research, issued a report in late February which estimates the amount of these savings. The average criminal, he says, hits the rest of us up for around $200,000 a year.

Consequently, although Californians will spend $383 million to imprison an estimated additional 3,580 under the three strikes law now in effect, the state will save, Romero computes, $716 million. California will really strike it rich in 2027, when the state can count on imprisoning 272,438 at a whopping savings of $54 billion compared to a measly $6.3 billion in prison costs. But three false assumptions undermine the report's conclusions:

First, the report assumes a finite group of criminals. If we keep them locked up for life or close to it, crime, the report assumes, will tumble significantly. The fallacy is this: serious violent crime is committed primarily by 15–24 year old males. The rate declines when they move into their thirties, as DiIulio acknowledges.

As Gottfredson and Hirschi assert convincingly in their recent *A General Theory of Crime*, the serious, predatory offenses said to be associated with career criminals are actually committed by young people "some of whom go on committing them for awhile, but most of whom spend their . . . late twenties running afoul of the authorities over alcohol, drugs and family squabbles." Even Sheldon and

Eleanor Glueck, after a lifetime of research, report a substantial reduction in serious criminality in the 25–31 age range. If we lock them up for life as three strikes demands, they will be replaced by younger criminals. Geriatric cases will fill the prisons, while offenders will remain youthful. In the end, the public is no safer.

Second, there is no such animal as "the average criminal" or an "average murderer." The eight-year figure supplied by DiIulio includes premeditated murderers, and those who kill accidentally while driving under the influence. Both deserve punishment, but criminal law sensibly distinguishes their respective moral culpability. Sensible public policy should not penalize all felons, even violent felons, with equal, mandated, discretionless severity. Three strikes laws, and Romero's analysis, tend to treat all felons equally. This is neither morally justified nor fiscally sound.

Finally, prison costs are certain while savings are speculative. While shelling out for the five-fold increase in corrections since 1980, Californians have had to sacrifice other services in education, health, and welfare. California's public schools, which once ranked near the top, now rank near the bottom, close to Mississippi's. Its higher education system has been ravaged by the need to offer a generous retirement package to many of its most distinguished faculty because it can no longer afford to pay them without firing twice as many junior faculty.

Three strikes will shift the budget balance sharply in favor of prisons and away from educational and social services, in the absence of which teenage crime will flourish. Vast "savings" from expanded prisons are the 1994 crime control version of voodoo economics.

Even without three strikes legislation, California is already the nation's biggest jailer, with one out of eight American prisoners occupying its cells. California's prison system has grown twice as much as the systems in the next three largest states (New York, Texas, and Florida) and four times as much as Western Europe's.

If high rates of imprisonment (recall DiIulio wants "more prisons, stiffer and enforced sentences") lead to feelings of public safety, Californians should feel twice as safe as New Yorkers, Texans, and Floridians and four times as safe as citizens of France. They don't. As Joan Petersilia and Peter Reuter conclude in their RAND book *Urban America: Policy Choices for Los Angeles and the Nation*, California locks up too many people, often for the wrong offenses (drug offenders accounted for 26 percent of California prisoners in 1990, up from 11 percent in 1980) and has too little to show for it in enhanced public safety.

As reports of these facts are filtering through, the public and the press are beginning to reconsider. For example, a 70-year-old San Francisco woman refused to testify against an addict-burglar who had broken into her car. She didn't think he deserved a life sentence and called the Three Strikes law "a holocaust for the poor" in a local newspaper.

Even the Klaas family has come out against the current law, saying they were bamboozled into supporting it in a time of grief. They support a more moderate bill that eliminates household burglaries as strikes. The California three strikes law is tough and dumb, and anyone remotely familiar with the criminal justice system understands that.

According to DiIulio, I and other criminologists are out of touch with the concerns of middle class Americans. This is hyperbolic nonsense. Granted, most criminologists are skeptical that expanding imprisonment by mandating life sentences is a solution to America's crime problem. But we are skeptical for the very reason that DiIulio is: "If the question's how to solve America's crime problem ... then prison is no answer." If we starve education and social services to pay for excessively long prison sentences, if we concentrate on building prisons at the expense of schools, crime will increase and public safety will suffer.

The criminal sanction is both an expression of moral outrage and a method of controlling crime. Unfortunately, the two goals are not always in sync. The call for long, mandated prison sentences is a response to moral outrage. Some criminals should be locked up for decades, even for life, to protect the public. For that goal we need more, rather than less, discretion from judges and parole boards.

Likewise, it makes no sense to mandate five-year sentences for an 18-year-old caught selling drugs, unless we simply want to express moral outrage. Someone else will almost certainly take his place. (See Daniel Feldman, "Imprisoner's Dilemma," *TAP* Summer 1993.)

Yes, time served for violent felonies has decreased in the last ten years. Two trends are responsible. We've been sending more nonviolent offenders to state prison because local jails are overcrowded, and we've been locking up parolees who flunk their drug tests. The latter account for about 25 percent of California's prison population.

DiIulio's rantings about criminologists as "elitists" belie a central truth. Criminologists are deeply concerned with controlling crime, especially in communities of disadvantage. I didn't write, as DiIulio claims, that the Polly Klaas tragedy is "mere sensationalism." I did say that had supposedly "soft-on-crime" indeterminate sentencing been in effect, Richard Allen Davis would not have been released.

I also tried to account for the fact that at a time when crime rates are flat or declining in California (and the nation), crime has become America's number one concern. Klaas's murder, plus a number of other highly publicized crimes, I wrote, "have sent a scary message to the majority of Americans who do not live in the inner city." Polly was an especially lovely, vivacious girl with a winning smile. And she was white and became "America's daughter." But the fact remains, a teenager's chances of being murdered in east Oakland or southeast Washington D.C. are considerably higher than in Petaluma, a bucolic northern California suburb.

What most criminologists question are policies directing funds away from crime prevention measures in disadvantaged communities and toward the expensive financing of mandated life sentences, especially for those convicted of nonviolent felonies. If crime control is the issue, criminologists have a lot to contribute. If moral outrage is what it's all about, the ranters and ravers will win the day.

Nor are criminologists opposed to appropriate, just, and effective incapacitation. When thoughtfully applied, it can protect the public against repeatedly violent criminals. True, we will make mistakes. The answer, however, is not to eliminate discretion, but to use it wisely, as is done in Minnesota's widely acclaimed sentencing guideline system.

Even DiIulio agrees imprisoning criminals for decades when they are beyond their high crime years makes no sense. He wants to hammer them while they're hot. The issue then becomes what does it mean to hammer, for which offenses, and how hot?

I agree that prosecutors will soften the impact of three strikes in California and other states. Prosecutors are the most powerful actors in the criminal justice system. They can and will bargain, no matter what the legislation says. Even so, California and other states that follow its model will experience a vast expansion of imprisonment.

Let me conclude on a personal note. This business of argument by "elite" name calling (including Janet Reno in that category, no less) scarcely advances the debate. Besides, how can a Princeton professor and contributor to the *Brookings Review* and *The American Prospect* classify others as elites and himself as an ordinary working stiff? C'mon, let's be real. If the cultural revolution were to come to America, John DiIulio and I would be sentenced to plow the fields together side by side.

CHAPTER **39**

One in 100

Behind Bars in America 2008

Pew Foundation

A SNAPSHOT OF PRISON GROWTH

The United States incarcerates more people than any country in the world, including the far more populous nation of China. At the start of the new year, the American penal system held more than 2.3 million adults. China was second, with 1.5 million people behind bars, and Russia was a distant third with 890,000 inmates, according to the latest available figures. Beyond the sheer number of inmates, America also is the global leader in the rate at which it incarcerates its citizenry, outpacing nations like South Africa and Iran. In Germany, 93 people are in prison for every 100,000 adults and children. In the U.S. the rate is roughly eight times that, or 750 per 100,000.[2]

To produce a fresh portrait of incarceration levels at the start of 2008, Pew conducted a survey of inmate counts from the states and the federal government. Our finding: the U.S. prison population rose by more than 25,000 inmates in 2007— a 1.6 percent rate of growth that brought the national prison census to 1,596,127. Although the 2007 expansion didn't match the 3.1 percent hike during 2006, the growth tracks projections[3] and continues a pattern of steady expansion that has characterized the U.S. penal system for more than 30 years.

1 in 100 Adults Behind Bars.   The consequences of that upward trend are many, but few can rival this: more than 1 in 100 adults is now locked up in America. With 1,596,127 in state or federal prison custody, and another 723,131 in local jails, the total adult inmate count at the beginning of 2008 stood at 2,319,258. With the number of adults just shy of 230 million, the actual incarceration rate is 1 in every 99.1 adults.

That statistic masks far higher incarceration rates by race, age and gender. A separate analysis of midyear 2006 data from the U.S. Department of Justice shows that for Hispanic and black men, for instance, imprisonment is a far more

Between 1987 and 2007, the national prison population has nearly tripled.

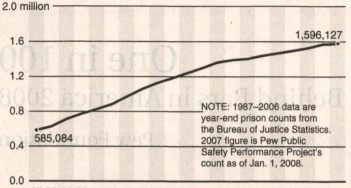

FIGURE 39.1   Prison Count Pushes Up

Sources: Bureau of Justice Statistics: Pew Public Safety Performance Project

prevalent reality than it is for white men.[4] The young, meanwhile, are disproportionately more likely to wind up in prison than their elders. While one in every 15 black males aged 18 or older is in prison or jail, for black men over 55, the rate is one in 115. . . .

Florida: A Case Study in Growth.   For policy makers keen on understanding the dynamics of prison growth, Florida serves as a compelling case. Between 1993 and 2007, the state's inmate population has increased from 53,000 to over 97,000. While crime and a growing resident population play a role, most of the growth, analysts agree, stemmed from a host of correctional policies and practices adopted by the state.

One of the first came in 1995, when the legislature abolished "good time" credits and discretionary release by the parole board, and required that all prisoners—regardless of their crime, prior record, or risk to recidivate–serve 85 percent of their sentence. Next came a "zero tolerance" policy and other measures mandating that probation officers report every offender who violated any condition of supervision and increasing prison time for these "technical violations." As a result, the number of violators in Florida prisons has jumped by an estimated 12,000.[5] Crime in Florida has dropped substantially during this period, but it has fallen as much or more in some states that have not grown their prison systems, or even have shrunk them, such as New York.

Without a change of direction, Florida is expected to reach a peak of nearly 125,000 inmates by 2013. Based on that projection, the state will run out of prison capacity by early 2009 and will need to add another 16,500 beds to keep pace.[6]

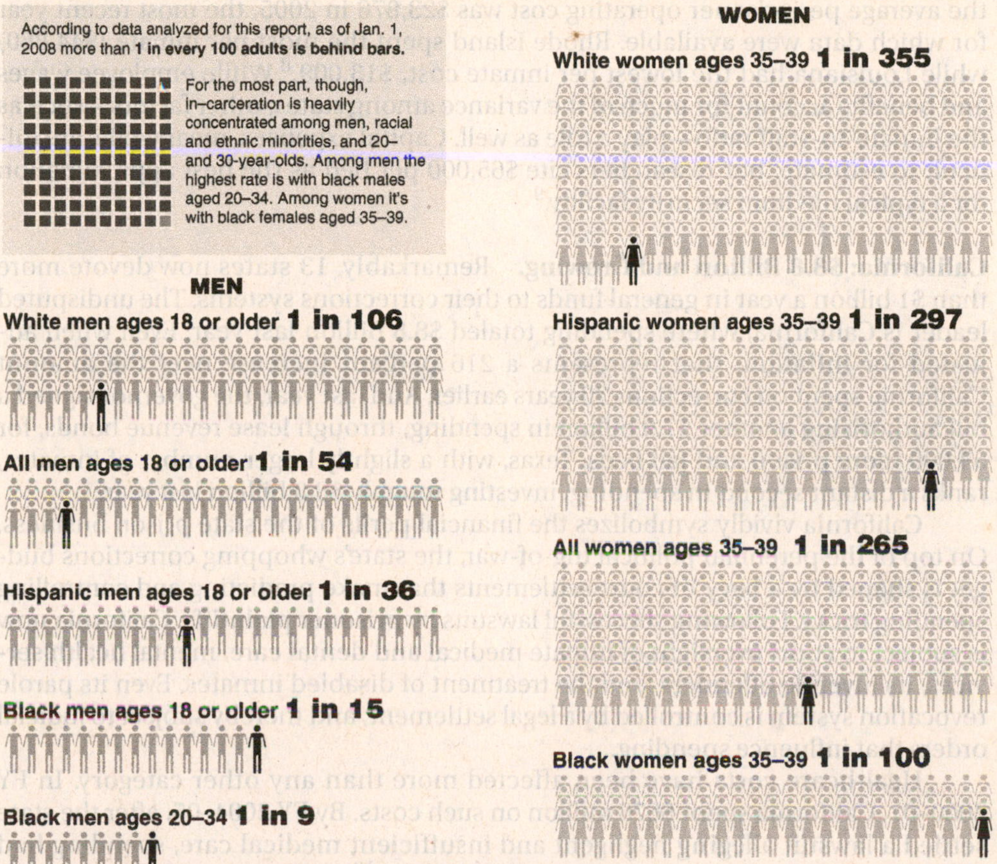

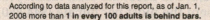

According to data analyzed for this report, as of Jan. 1, 2008 more than **1 in every 100 adults is behind bars.**

For the most part, though, in–carceration is heavily concentrated among men, racial and ethnic minorities, and 20– and 30-year-olds. Among men the highest rate is with black males aged 20–34. Among women it's with black females aged 35–39.

WOMEN

White women ages 35–39 1 in 355

MEN

White men ages 18 or older 1 in 106

All men ages 18 or older 1 in 54

Hispanic women ages 35–39 1 in 297

Hispanic men ages 18 or older 1 in 36

All women ages 35–39 1 in 265

Black men ages 18 or older 1 in 15

Black women ages 35–39 1 in 100

Black men ages 20–34 1 in 9

FIGURE 39.2   Who's Behind Bars

A sampling of incarceration rates by various demographics.

Source: Analysis of "Prison and Jail Inmates at Midyear 2006," published June 2007 by the U.S. Department of Justice, Bureau of Justice Statistics. All demographic statistics, with exception of "1 in every 100 adults" are midyear 2006, not 2008 figures.

THE COSTS—HIGH AND CLIMBING FAST

Prisons and Jails are "24-7" Operations. They require large, highly trained staffs. Their inhabitants are troubled, aging and generally sicker than people outside prison walls. Even absent continued growth, the cost of keeping the nation's lock-ups running safely is staggering. Total state spending on corrections—including bonds and federal contributions—topped $49 billion last year, up from $12 billion in 1987. By 2011, continued prison growth is expected to cost states an additional $25 billion.[7]

The primary catalyst behind the increase is obvious: prison growth means more bodies to feed, clothe, house and supervise. While figures vary widely by state, the average per prisoner operating cost was $23,876 in 2005, the most recent year for which data were available. Rhode Island spent the most per inmate ($44,860) while Louisiana had the lowest per inmate cost, $13,009.[8] While employee wages and benefits account for much of the variance among states, other factors—such as the inmate-to-staff ratio—play a role as well. Capital expenses, meanwhile, are difficult to estimate, but researchers cite $65,000 per bed as the best approximation for a typical medium security facility.[9]

California: $8.8 Billion and Growing.   Remarkably, 13 states now devote more than $1 billion a year in general funds to their corrections systems. The undisputed leader is California, where spending totaled $8.8 billion last year. Even when adjusted for inflation, that represents a 216 percent increase over the amount California spent on corrections 20 years earlier. And last year, the governor signed a bill authorizing another $7.9 billion in spending, through lease revenue bonds, for 53,000 more prison and jail beds. Texas, with a slightly larger number of inmates, ranks a distant second in spending, investing roughly $3.3 billion last year.

California vividly symbolizes the financial perils of the state prison business. On top of the perennial political tug-of-war, the state's whopping corrections budget is shaped by a bevy of court settlements that make predicting and controlling spending tricky. Following successful lawsuits by prisoner plaintiffs, California now is subject to court oversight of inmate medical and dental care, mental health services, its juvenile offenders, and the treatment of disabled inmates. Even its parole revocation system is controlled by a legal settlement, and thereby subject to judicial orders that influence spending.

Healthcare costs have been affected more than any other category. In FY 2000–01, California spent $676 million on such costs. By FY 2004–05, after the state settled a lawsuit alleging negligent and insufficient medical care, spending had soared to $1.05 billion, an increase of 55 percent.[10] And that was before a judge appointed a federal receiver to run prison healthcare, a move that is driving such spending up even more dramatically. It now stands at $2.1 billion annually, a 210 percent increase since 2000.

Health Care, Geriatrics Drive Costs.   As California has learned, medical care is one of the principal cost drivers in corrections budgets today. From 1998 to 2001, healthcare spending in state prisons grew 10 percent annually, a 2004 report by the Council of State Governments found. At the time of the study, medical care costs totaled $3.7 billion annually and accounted for about 10 percent of correctional spending.[11]

Under the 1976 U.S. Supreme Court ruling *Estelle v. Gamble*, states are compelled to provide a constitutionally adequate level of medical care, or care that generally meets a "community standard." Beyond that mandate, the rise in medical outlays largely stems from mushrooming costs associated with special needs populations, including HIV-positive prisoners and geriatric inmates.

Communicable diseases are a particular concern, spreading quickly in a crowded prison environment where risky behaviors such as tattooing and piercing, unprotected sex, fighting and intravenous drug use are not uncommon.[12]

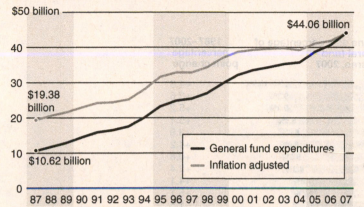

Between fiscal years 1987 and 2007, total state general fund expenditures on corrections rose 315 percent.

FIGURE 39.3   Twenty Years of Rising Costs

Source: National Association of State Budget Officers, "State Expenditure Report" series; Inflation adjusted figures are based on a reanalysis of data in this series.

Note: These figures represent state general funds. They do not include federal or local government corrections expenditures and typically do not include funding from other state sources.

Hepatitis C, a blood-borne, life-threatening disease, is the biggest worry. The latest Hepatitis C treatments cost as much as $30,000 per inmate annually. At one California prison, in Vacaville, the chief medical officer estimates that half of the 3,200 inmates have been infected with Hepatitis C.[13] Other states put the in-prison prevalence at between 25 and 40 percent.[14]

Increasingly, the graying of the nation's prisons is causing costs to swell. While crime remains overwhelmingly a young man's game, between 1992 and 2001, the number of state and federal inmates aged 50 or older rose from 41,586 to 113,358, a staggering jump of 173 percent, a 2004 National Institute of Corrections report found.[15] And older inmates are gradually making up a larger proportion of the overall count. In the federal prisons, for example, about one-quarter of the population was over 50 in 1989. By 2010, that proportion is forecast to grow to one-third. On the state level, Oklahoma recently found that 16 percent of newly admitted inmates were over 45 years old—more than double the rate in 1990.[16]

While aging decreases criminal activity, it brings a multitude of challenges in a prison setting. Because they are often preyed upon by younger, stronger inmates, older convicts may require special housing.[17] Hearing and visual impairments, incontinence, dietary intolerance, depression and the early onset of chronic diseases are other complicating management factors. As a result, the average cost associated with an older prisoner is $70,000—two to three times that of a younger prisoner.[18]

The bottom line: Some crimes are so heinous they warrant a lifetime behind bars. But states are spending more and more on inmates who are less and less of a threat to public safety.

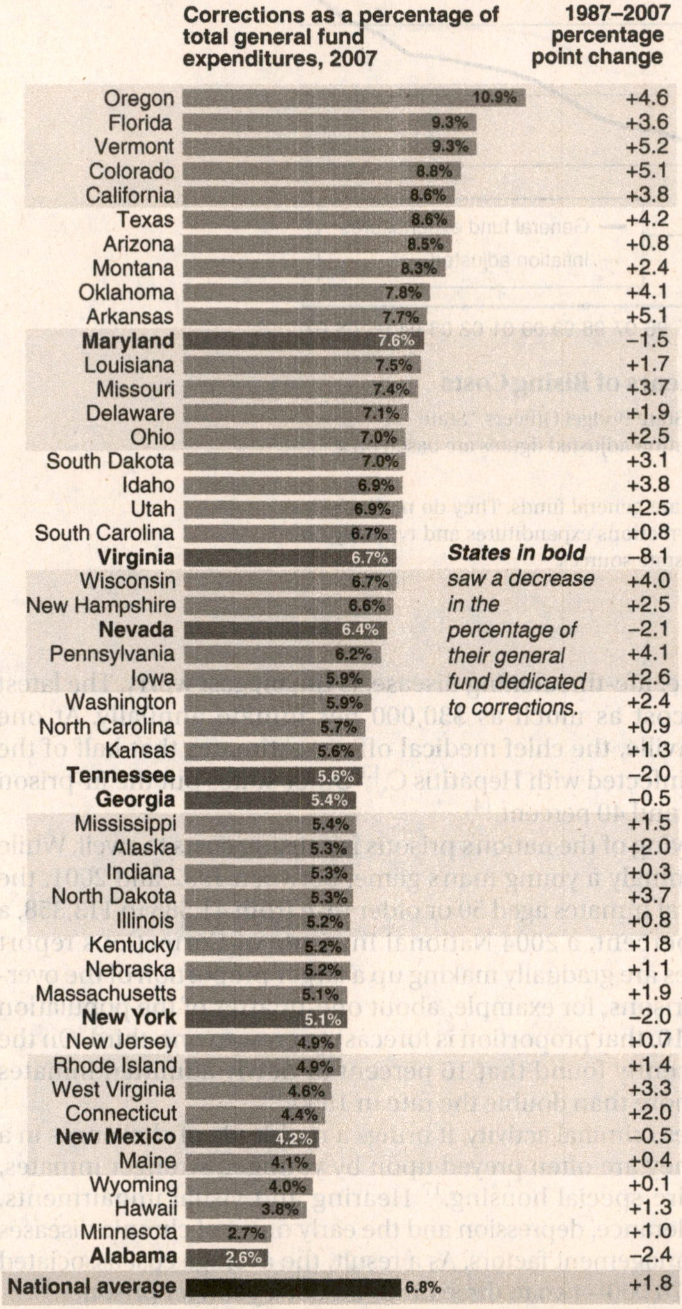

	Corrections as a percentage of total general fund expenditures, 2007	1987–2007 percentage point change
Oregon	10.9%	+4.6
Florida	9.3%	+3.6
Vermont	9.3%	+5.2
Colorado	8.8%	+5.1
California	8.6%	+3.8
Texas	8.6%	+4.2
Arizona	8.5%	+0.8
Montana	8.3%	+2.4
Oklahoma	7.8%	+4.1
Arkansas	7.7%	+5.1
Maryland	7.6%	−1.5
Louisiana	7.5%	+1.7
Missouri	7.4%	+3.7
Delaware	7.1%	+1.9
Ohio	7.0%	+2.5
South Dakota	7.0%	+3.1
Idaho	6.9%	+3.8
Utah	6.9%	+2.5
South Carolina	6.7%	+0.8
Virginia	6.7%	−8.1
Wisconsin	6.7%	+4.0
New Hampshire	6.6%	+2.5
Nevada	6.4%	−2.1
Pennsylvania	6.2%	+4.1
Iowa	5.9%	+2.6
Washington	5.9%	+2.4
North Carolina	5.7%	+0.9
Kansas	5.6%	+1.3
Tennessee	5.6%	−2.0
Georgia	5.4%	−0.5
Mississippi	5.4%	+1.5
Alaska	5.3%	+2.0
Indiana	5.3%	+0.3
North Dakota	5.3%	+3.7
Illinois	5.2%	+0.8
Kentucky	5.2%	+1.8
Nebraska	5.2%	+1.1
Massachusetts	5.1%	+1.9
New York	5.1%	−2.0
New Jersey	4.9%	+0.7
Rhode Island	4.9%	+1.4
West Virginia	4.6%	+3.3
Connecticut	4.4%	+2.0
New Mexico	4.2%	−0.5
Maine	4.1%	+0.4
Wyoming	4.0%	+0.1
Hawaii	3.8%	+1.3
Minnesota	2.7%	+1.0
Alabama	2.6%	−2.4
National average	6.8%	+1.8

States in bold saw a decrease in the percentage of their general fund dedicated to corrections.

FIGURE 39.4 Taking a Bigger Cut

In fiscal year 2007, an estimated 1 in every 15 state general fund dollars was spent on corrections.

Source: National Association of State Budget Officers, "State Expenditure Report" series; Percentage point increases are based on a reanalysis of data in this series.

Note: Michigan does not have a comparable figure because of the state's general fund definition. See Jurisdictional Notes.

Crowding Out Other Priorities.   Year by year, corrections budgets are consuming an ever larger chunk of state general funds, leaving less and less in the pot for other needs. Collectively, correctional agencies now consume 6.8 percent of state general funds, 2007 data show.[24] That means one in every 15 dollars in the states' main pool of discretionary money goes to corrections. Considering all types of funds, corrections had the second fastest rate of growth in FY 2006. With a 9.2 percent jump, it trailed transportation but outpaced increases in spending on education and Medicaid.[25]

Some states spend an even larger proportion of their budgets on corrections. Oregon, for example, directed one in every 10 dollars to corrections, while Florida and Vermont spent one in 11. Minnesota and Alabama are at the other extreme, spending less than 3 percent of their general fund dollars on corrections. Over the past 20 years, corrections spending took up a larger share of overall general fund expenditures in 42 states.

Some policy makers are questioning the wisdom of devoting an increasingly large slice of the budget pie to incarceration, especially when recidivism rates have remained discouragingly high. Are we getting our money's worth? Is our investment in this system returning sufficient dividends for victims, taxpayers and society at large?

On average, corrections is the fifth-largest state budget category, behind health, elementary and secondary education, higher education and transportation. But nearly all corrections dollars come from the states' own coffers; healthcare, by contrast, draws a majority of funding from the federal government, primarily through Medicaid. For some public officials, that distinction highlights the effect of corrections spending on other priorities.

Pre-K, Higher Ed Funding Lags.   Higher education is of particular concern. Higher education spending accounts for a roughly comparable portion of state expenditures as corrections, and other than tuition is paid for almost entirely out of state rather than federal funds. States don't necessarily make explicit choices between higher education and corrections funding, but they do have to balance their budgets. So, unlike the federal government, a dollar spent in one area is unavailable for another.

In 1987, states collectively spent $33 billion of their general funds on higher education. By 2007, they were spending $72.88 billion, an increase of 121 percent. Adjusted to 2007 dollars, the increase was 21 percent. Over the same timeframe, inflation-adjusted corrections spending rose 127 percent, from $10.6 billion ($19.4 billion in 2007 dollars) to more than $44 billion.

Some regional differences were more dramatic. While inflation-adjusted prison spending rose 61 percent in the Northeast in the last 20 years, higher education spending went the other way, dropping by 5.5 percent. In the West, meanwhile, the number of dollars allocated to prisons skyrocketed by 205 percent. At the same time, higher education spending rose just 28 percent.

Corrections spending also competes with the funding many states want to devote to early childhood education, one of the most proven crime prevention strategies. Research shows that attending a high-quality pre-kindergarten influences

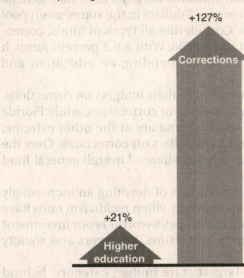

Between 1987 and 2007, the amount states spent on **corrections** more than doubled while the increase in **higher education** spending has been moderate.

+127%

Corrections

+21%

Higher education

FIGURE 39.5   Of Books and Bars

Source: National Association of State Budget Officers, "State Expenditure Report" series: Inflation adjusted general fund figures are based on a reanalysis of data in this series.

a child's success both in school and in life. One rigorous study that followed severely disadvantaged children into adulthood showed that participation in pre-kindergarten dramatically reduced participation in juvenile and adult crime, and increased high school graduation, employment and earnings, with a total benefit-cost ratio of 16 to 1.[26]

Backed with such evidence of success, states have substantially increased support for high-quality, voluntary pre-kindergarten. New state pre-k funding exceeded $525 million in FY 2008, an increase of more than 12 percent over FY07 expenditures, bringing total state investments in early education across the country to $4.8 billion.[27]

Increasingly, state policy makers are finding that a dollar spent for pre-k classes now can forestall many more dollars for prison beds down the road.

A FINAL WORD

As a nation, the United States has long anchored its punishment policy in bricks and mortar. The tangible feel of a jail or prison, with its surefire incapacitation of convicts, has been an unquestioned weapon of choice in our battle against crime. Recent studies show, however, that a continual increase in our reliance on

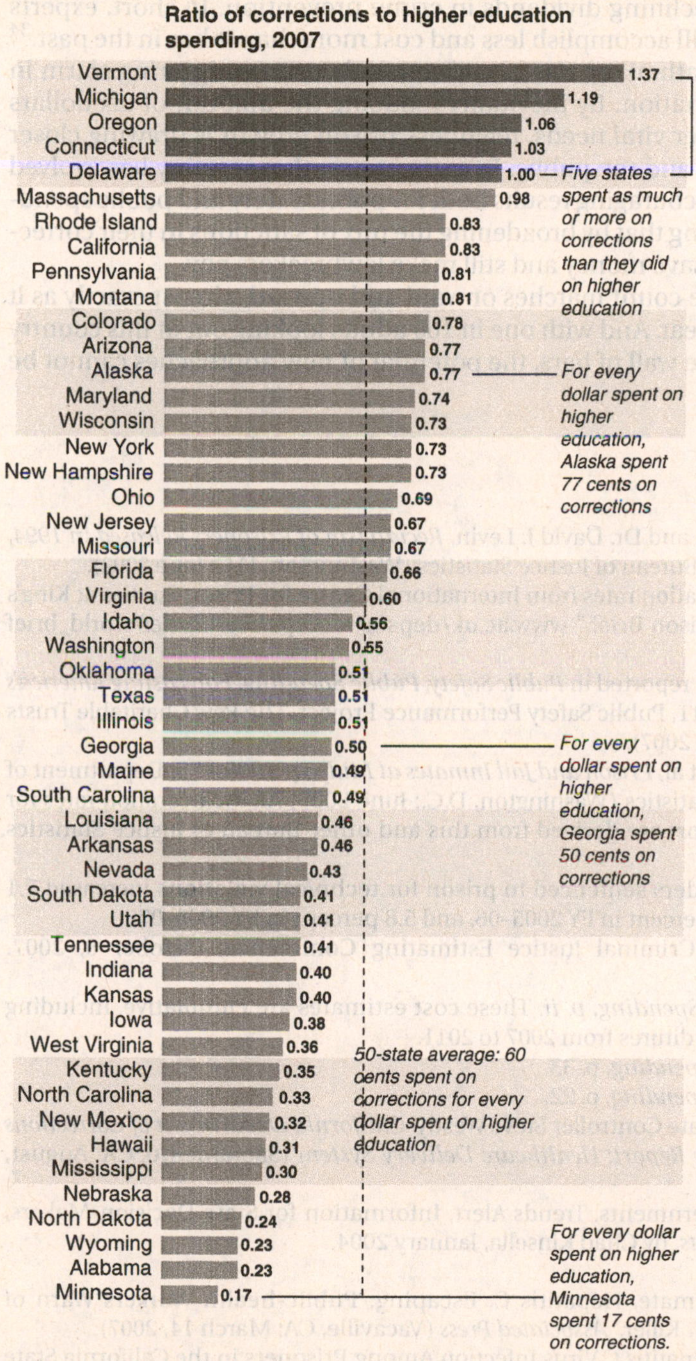

Ratio of corrections to higher education spending, 2007

Vermont	1.37
Michigan	1.19
Oregon	1.06
Connecticut	1.03
Delaware	1.00
Massachusetts	0.98
Rhode Island	0.83
California	0.83
Pennsylvania	0.81
Montana	0.81
Colorado	0.78
Arizona	0.77
Alaska	0.77
Maryland	0.74
Wisconsin	0.73
New York	0.73
New Hampshire	0.73
Ohio	0.69
New Jersey	0.67
Missouri	0.67
Florida	0.66
Virginia	0.60
Idaho	0.56
Washington	0.55
Oklahoma	0.51
Texas	0.51
Illinois	0.51
Georgia	0.50
Maine	0.49
South Carolina	0.49
Louisiana	0.46
Arkansas	0.46
Nevada	0.43
South Dakota	0.41
Utah	0.41
Tennessee	0.41
Indiana	0.40
Kansas	0.40
Iowa	0.38
West Virginia	0.36
Kentucky	0.35
North Carolina	0.33
New Mexico	0.32
Hawaii	0.31
Mississippi	0.30
Nebraska	0.28
North Dakota	0.24
Wyoming	0.23
Alabama	0.23
Minnesota	0.17

Five states spent as much or more on corrections than they did on higher education

For every dollar spent on higher education, Alaska spent 77 cents on corrections

For every dollar spent on higher education, Georgia spent 50 cents on corrections

50-state average: 60 cents spent on corrections for every dollar spent on higher education

For every dollar spent on higher education, Minnesota spent 17 cents on corrections.

FIGURE 39.6
Making Decsions Where to Spend
While states don't necessarily choose between higher education and corrections, a dollar spent in one area is unavailable for another.

Source: Reanalysis of data presented in the National Association of State Budget Officers. "State Expenditure Report" series.

incarceration will pay declining dividends in crime prevention. In short, experts say, expanding prisons will accomplish less and cost more than it has in the past.[34]

Meanwhile, the breathtaking rise in correctional costs is triggering alarm in statehouses around the nation. By inevitably reducing the amount of tax dollars that are available for other vital needs, relentless prison growth is drawing closer scrutiny from lawmakers and the public. In some states, that scrutiny has evolved into action, producing encouraging results both for public safety and public spending. These states are finding that by broadening the mix of sanctions in their correctional tool box, they can save money and still make lawbreakers pay.

The national inmate count marches onward and upward, almost exactly as it was projected to do last year. And with one in 100 adults looking out at this country from behind an expensive wall of bars, the potential of new approaches cannot be ignored.

ENDNOTES

1. Langan, Dr. Patrick A., and Dr. David J. Levin, *Recidivism of Prisoners Released in 1994*, U.S. Department of Justice, Bureau of Justice Statistics (Washington, D.C.: June 2002).

2. International incarceration rates from International Centre for Prison Studies at King's College, London, "World Prison Brief." www.ac.uk/depsta/rel/icps/worldbrief/world_brief.html

3. State projections were reported in *Public Safety, Public Spending: Forecasting America's Prison Population*, 2007–2011, Public Safety Performance Project, The Pew Charitable Trusts (Washington, D.C: February 2007).

4. Sabol, Dr. William J., et al, *Prison and Jail Inmates at Midyear 2006*. U.S. Department of Justice, Bureau of Justice Statistics (Washington, D.C.: June 2007) All incarceration rates for subpopulations in this report are derived from this and other Bureau of Justice Statistics reports.

5. The number of offenders sentenced to prison for technical violations increased 7.1 percent in FY 2004–05, 4.3 percent in FY 2005–06, and 5.8 percent in FY 2006–07.

6. Workpapers of the Criminal Justice Estimating Conference, October 8, 2007. Tallahassee, FL: EDR.

7. *Public Safety, Public Spending, p. ii.* These cost estimates are cumulative, including operating and capital expenditures from 2007 to 2011.

8. *Public Safety, Public Spending*, p. 33.

9. *Public Safety, Public Spending*, p. 22.

10. Office of California State Controller Steve Westly, *California Department of Corrections and Rehabilitation, Review Report: Healthcare Delivery System* (Sacramento, CA: August, 2006).

11. Council of State Governments, Trends Alert, Information for State Decision-Makers, *Corrections Health Care Costs*, by Chad Kinsella, January 2004.

12. *Ibid.*

13. Prison's Deadliest Inmate, Hepatitis C, Escaping: Public-health Workers Warn of Looming Epidemic of 'Silent Killer,' *Associated Press* (Vacaville, CA: March 14, 2007).

14. Fox, Rena K. et al, "Hepatitis C Virus Infection Among Prisoners in the California State Correctional System," *Clinical Infectious Diseases* (June 2005).

15. Anno, Jaye B., et al., *Addressing the Needs of Elderly, Chronically Ill, and Terminally Ill Inmates*, U.S. Department of Justice, National Institute of Corrections, Criminal Justice Institute (Middleton, CT: February, 2004).

16. Turley, Jonathan, George Washington University Law School professor. Testimony before the House Judiciary Committee, Dec. 6, 2007.

17. *Addressing the Needs of Elderly, Chronically Ill, and Terminally Ill Inmates.*

18. *Ibid.*

19. U.S. Census Bureau, State Government Employment and Payroll data: http://www .census.gov/govs/www/apesst.html. For more, see Appendix A-5.

20. Marley, Patrick, "Prison officers rack up overtime," Milwaukee Journal Sentinel, December 12, 2007.

21. Chorneau, Tom, "$500 million in OT at state prisons," San Francisco Chronicle, July 15, 2007.

22. Thoennes, Dr. Nancy, *Child Support Profile: Massachusetts Incarcerated and Paroled Parent,* Center for Policy Research (Denver, CO: May 2002).

23. Florida Department of Corrections, *Restitution and Other Monetary Obligations Collected from Offenders Under Supervision in FY 2004–05*, available online at http://www .dc.state.fl.us/oth/ccmyths.html

24. National Association of State Budget Officers, "State Expenditure Report FY 2006," December 2007. http://www.nasbo.org/Publications/PDFs/fy2006er.pdf

25. *Ibid.*

26. Schweinhart, L. J., Montie, J., Xiang, Z., Barnett, W. S., Belfield, C. R., & Nores, M. (2005). *Lifetime effects: The High/Scope Perry Preschool study through age 40.* (Monographs of the High/Scope Educational Research Foundation, 14). Ypsilanti, MI: High/Scope Press.

27. Prek Now, *Votes Count, Legislative Action on Prek Fiscal Year 2008* (Washington, D.C.: September 2007). www.preknow.org

28. In the latest Gallup Poll, only 2 percent of Americans volunteered "crime" as the most important problem facing the country. In March 1977, by contrast, 15 percent of Americans polled by Gallup volunteered "crime" as the most important problem facing the country. Cited in Sam Roberts, "All Crime Is Local In '08 Politics," The New York Times, Sept 16, 2007.

29. For more detail on Texas and the legislators who helped advance this legislation, see the following reports: Council of State Governments Justice Center, *Justice Reinvestment State Brief: Texas,* and Public Safety Performance Project, The Pew Charitable Trusts, *Changing Direction: A Bipartisan Team Paves a New Path for Sentencing and Corrections in Texas.*

30. Vera Institute of Justice, *Managing State Prison Growth: Key Trends in Sentencing Policy* (New York, January 2008).

31. *Prison and Jail Inmates at Midyear 2006.*

32. *Ibid.*

33. For more detail on Kansas and a national discussion of the issues surrounding parole violators, see the following reports: Council of State Governments Justice Center, *Justice Reinvestment State Brief: Kansas,* and Public Safety Performance Project, The Pew Charitable Trusts, *When Offenders Break the Rules: Smart Responses to Parole and Probation Violations.*

34. Vera Institute of Justice, Reconsidering Incarceration: New Directions for Reducing Crime, by Don Stemen (New York: January 2007).

CHAPTER 40

Unjust Rewards

Ken Silverstein

In 1989, an explosion ripped through a Phillips Petroleum chemical plant in Pasadena, Texas, killing 23 workers and injuring more than 100. Federal officials fined the company $4 million, citing "clear evidence that the explosion was avoidable had recognized safety practices been followed." In 1999 and 2000, two more explosions at the plant left another 3 workers dead and 73 injured. Phillips was hit with an additional $2.3 million in fines for ignoring safety hazards.

In 1994, a worker was killed in an explosion at an Arizona factory run by TRW, the nation's leading maker of air bags. The company, which had a record of violating workplace laws at the plant, settled criminal charges in the case for $1.7 million. Officials later discovered that TRW, in a move "clearly approved by management," was illegally dumping chemical waste from the plant at landfills in three states. Last year, the company paid a record $24 million in civil and criminal penalties.

In 1999, a jury found Koch Industries guilty of negligence in the deaths of two teenagers killed in a fire caused by a corroded pipeline. The following year, the Kansas-based energy giant paid $30 million—the largest civil penalty in the history of the Clean Water Act—for illegally discharging 3 million gallons of crude oil in six states. Last year, Koch paid $25 million to settle charges that it lied about how much oil it was pumping out of federal lands, cheating the government in nearly 25,000 separate transactions.

Phillips, TRW, and Koch have more in common than a history of repeatedly violating workplace and environmental laws. They also rank among the nation's largest government contractors. Between 1995 and 2000, the three corporations received a combined total of $10.4 billion in federal business—at the same time that regulatory agencies and federal courts were citing the companies for jeopardizing the safety of their employees, polluting the nation's air and water, and even defrauding the government.

That's not supposed to happen. Federal contracting officers are charged with reviewing the record of companies that do business with the government and barring those that fail to demonstrate "a satisfactory record of integrity and business ethics." But officials are given no guidelines to follow in making such decisions, and there's no centralized system they can consult to inform them of corporate wrongdoing. As a result, a government report concluded in 2000, those responsible for awarding federal contracts are "extremely reluctant" to take action, even when they are aware of violations. And in the rare instances when the rule is enforced, it is almost always employed against small companies with little clout in Washington.

Shortly before leaving office, President Clinton issued a new order to provide clear guidelines for deciding which firms share in the roughly $200 billion in federal contracts awarded each year. The new "contractor responsibility rule"—championed by Vice President Al Gore and developed after two years of congressional testimony and public hearings—specified that federal officials should weigh "evidence of repeated, pervasive, or significant violations of the law." Officials were told to consider whether a company has cheated on prior contracts or violated laws involving the environment, workplace safety, labor rights, consumer protection, or antitrust activities.

The measure was never implemented. In one of his first acts as president, George W. Bush put the rule on hold after only 11 days in office, saying the issue needed further study. With big business suing to block the new guidelines, Bush revoked the rule 11 months later.

Some 80,000 contractors do at least $25,000 in business with the federal government each year, and the great majority comply with the law. But a six-month investigation by *Mother Jones* of the nation's 200 largest contractors found that the government continues to award lucrative contracts to dozens of companies that it has repeatedly cited for serious violations of workplace and environmental laws. The government's own database of contractors was matched with lists of the worst violations documented by the Environmental Protection Agency (EPA) and the Occupational Safety and Health Administration (OSHA) between 1995 and 2000. Among the findings:

- Forty-six of the biggest contractors were prosecuted by the Justice Department and ordered to pay cleanup costs after they refused to take responsibility for dumping hazardous waste and other environmental violations. General Electric—which received nearly $9.8 billion from the government, making it the nation's 10th-largest contractor—topped the list with 27 cases of pollution for which it was held solely or jointly liable.

- Fifty-five of the top contractors were cited for a total of 1,375 violations of workplace safety law that posed a risk of death or serious physical harm to workers. Ford Motor, which ranks 177th among contractors with $442 million in federal business, led the OSHA list with 292 violations deemed "serious" by federal officials. In 1999, six workers were killed and dozens injured when a boiler exploded at Ford's River Rouge Complex in Dearborn, Michigan. The company was hit with a $1.5 million fine after an internal memo revealed that Ford had decided not to replace safety equipment on the aging boilers because it would then have to fully upgrade them to meet "all present safety standards."

TABLE 40.1   The Dirty Dozen: Federal Contractors with Both EPA and OSHA Violations, Ranked by Penalties (1995–2000)

	Contracts (in millions)	Rank as Contractor	EPA Violations	OSHA Violations	Total Penalties
Ford Motor	$442	177	12	292	$6,082,271
TRW	10,267	9	3	79	5,745,234
Archer Daniels Midland	471	168	4	93	1,676,850
ExxonMobil	2,173	43	20	5	1,481,400
E.J. DuPont de Nemours	446	175	17	23	956,700
Avondale Industries	1,347	66	1	73	759,100
General Motors	4,854	18	21	14	418,393
General Electric	9,777	10	27	48	369,363
Olin Corp.	1,310	68	7	4	168,500
Atlantic Richfield	675	138	10	1	150,600
DaimlerChrysler	1,575	54	7	166	130,121
Textron	5,507	17	4	78	111,215

ABOUT THE DATA

The "contractor responsibility rule" revoked by President Bush required officials to review a company's recent history of violating federal laws. To determine which contractors have the worst records in two significant areas covered by the rule—the environment and workplace safety—*Mother Jones* compiled a list of 200 corporations that did the most business with the government between 1995 and 2000. The list was then matched to two federal databases: a list of companies prosecuted by the Justice Department and found liable for environmental violations, and a list of firms cited by the Occupational Safety and Health Administration for posing a serious risk of injury or death to workers. Database work was conducted by Ron Nixon of Investigative Reporters and Editors, a nonprofit organization based in Columbia, Missouri. Additional reporting was provided by George Sanchez, with documentation from the Project on Government Oversight, a research group based in Washington, D.C. A complete list of violations committed by the top 200 contractors is available online at *www.motherjones.com*.

- Thirty-four leading contractors were penalized for violating both environmental and workplace safety rules. The firms were hit with a total of $12.6 million in EPA penalties and $5.9 million in OSHA fines—costs more than covered by the $229 billion in federal contracts they were awarded during the same period.

"It is clear that, in many cases, the government continues to do business with contractors who violate laws, sometimes repeatedly," concludes a 2000 report by the Federal Acquisition Regulatory Council, the agency that oversees federal contractors. Others put it more bluntly. "Government should not do business with crooks," says Rep. George Miller (D-Calif.), who has demanded that the White House make public any closed-door meetings it had with corporate lobbyists to discuss killing the contractor responsibility rule. Bush's decision, Miller says, "sends a message to contractors that the government doesn't care if you underpay your workers, or expose them to toxic hazards, or destroy the public lands—the government will do business with you anyway."

During Bill Clinton's second term in office, a coalition of labor, civil rights, and consumer groups lobbied the government to crack down on contractor misconduct. Backed by Miller and other congressional allies, they pointed to numerous studies documenting the extent of the problem. A 1995 report by the Government Accounting Office revealed that 80 major federal contractors had violated the National Labor Relations Act by seeking to suppress unions. Another GAO report found that in 1994 alone, OSHA imposed fines of $15,000 or more on each of 261 companies that had received a combined $38 billion in federal contracts. Noting that some contractors place workers "at substantial risk of injury or illness," the report added that the "prospect of debarment or suspension can provide impetus for a contractor to undertake remedial measures to improve working conditions."

In July 1999, Clinton declared his support for the reform coalition and announced plans to revise the rule. What emerged ever the next two years was a set of specific guidelines for federal contracting officers to follow in determining a company's eligibility. The new rule created a hierarchy of violations to be considered, topped by convictions for contract fraud. It stipulated that only repeated and serious wrongdoing, not administrative complaints, should be weighed. And it acknowledged a need for flexibility, noting that companies with serious violations might continue to receive contracts if they "correct the conditions that led to the misconduct."

"We view this fundamentally as empowering the government to do what every business in the world does, which is not to be forced to do business with people it doesn't trust," said Joshua Gotbaum, who helped draft the rule as controller of the Office of Management and Budget.

Clinton's move generated a fast and furious reaction from business and industry. The Business Roundtable, the U.S. Chamber of Commerce, and the National Association of Manufacturers launched a fierce lobbying campaign against the new rule. Despite a provision stating that only a pattern of "pervasive" and "significant" abuses would be considered, business opponents argued that the guidelines gave contracting officers excessive discretion to arbitrarily torpedo a contractor. "The proposed rules would allow contract officers to blacklist firms without regard to the number, nature, or severity of violations," said the National Center for Policy Analysis, a business-backed think tank. "Suspicions raised by rivals or disgruntled employees could cost firms millions, if not billions, of dollars."

To fight the measure, the business coalition hired Linda Fuselier of the Capitol Group, a high-powered lobbyist who had previously helped insurance firms avoid cleanup costs at Superfund waste sites. Opponents flooded officials with hundreds of comments opposing the guidelines. And when Clinton formally issued the new rule in December 2000, they went to federal court seeking to get the provision thrown out.

The court never had to decide the issue. A month later, when Bush took office, he immediately moved to postpone the rule. On January 31, 2001, federal agencies were quietly ordered to delay implementing it for six months—without issuing a public notice or soliciting comment. The Congressional Research Service issued an opinion concluding that the secret suspension of the rule was probably illegal, but the move went virtually unreported in the media. When Bush finally revoked the rule while vacationing at his Texas ranch last December, corporate executives and their allies in Congress hailed the decision. "There was never any rational basis or need for additional standards, since existing regulations already ensure the government does not do business with unethical companies," declared Rep. Thomas Davis III, a Republican from Virginia.

In reality, the government makes little effort to review contractors' records—and even the most diligent contracting officer would find it almost impossible to do so. The government does not maintain a central database to store information on contractors' records of compliance with the law. The EPA and OSHA maintain their own lists of corporate violations, but parent companies are not linked to their subsidiaries, which can number in the hundreds. OSHA makes some of its records available online, but the EPA and many other agencies do not. "There's no process built into the review system," says Gary Bass, executive director of OMB Watch, a Washington-based advocate of government accountability. "Just finding the right information is complicated and time-consuming."

As a result, even contractors that commit the most obvious violations are never suspended or debarred. One GAO study found that the government continues to award business to defense contractors that have committed fraud on prior contracts. General Dynamics, the nation's fifth-largest contractor, paid the government nearly $2 million in 1995 to resolve charges that it falsified employee time cards to bill the Pentagon for thousands of hours that were never worked on a contract for testing F-16 fighters. Northrop Grumman, the nation's fourth-largest contractor, paid nearly $6.7 million in 2000 to settle two separate cases in which it was charged with inflating the costs of parts and materials for warplanes. Yet the two defense giants continue to receive federal contracts, collecting a combined total of $38 billion between 1995 and 2000.

Opponents argue that the government already has the power to force contractors to clean up their act, without cutting them off from federal business. In addition, some contractors can be difficult to replace. The Pentagon, for example, maintains that it cannot afford to ban large defense contractors who provide specialized services and products, and the government is reluctant to take away contracts from nursing homes that commit Medicare fraud, fearing that patients will be hurt. "Debarment and suspension isn't practical," says Steven Schooner, a lawyer in the Office of Federal Procurement Policy under Clinton. "If the government needs the goods they produce, it's the only one that loses."

But while big contractors are all but immune from scrutiny, the government has no qualms about denying business to smaller operations that violate the law. Some 24,000 contractors are currently barred from government work, and almost all are small firms or individuals like Kenneth Hansen, a Kansas dentist banned from receiving federal funds to provide care for low-income patients because he defaulted on $164,800 in student loans. "We never take down the big guys," concedes Schooner, now a government-contracts law professor at George Washington University.

The review of environmental and workplace violations by *Mother Jones* reveals that many big contractors could have been forced to forfeit federal business had Bush not interceded on their behalf. Consider the record of ExxonMobil, which became the nation's 43rd-largest contractor when the two oil giants merged in 1999. Between 1995 and 2000, the firms received a total of $2.2 billion from the government for everything from renting fuel storage space to the Pentagon to selling oil to the Commerce Department. At the same time, they were openly disregarding the law. ExxonMobil has been held liable, either on its own or with other companies, in 20 cases in which it refused to clean up Superfund sites or take responsibility for air and water violations. The company is a partner in Colonial Pipeline, an Atlanta-based firm that the Justice Department sued in 2000 for multiple spills in nine states. In one incident, a pipeline rupture poured 950,000 gallons of diesel fuel into the Reedy River in South Carolina, killing 35,000 fish and other wildlife. In 1995, Mobil was hit with a $98,500 fine for its failure to inspect equipment at a refinery in Torrance, California, where 28 workers were injured in an explosion. In 1999, authorities discovered that Exxon had knowingly contaminated water supplies near a refinery in Benicia, California, with benzene and toluene, both of which cause cancer and birth defects.

One of the federal contractors with the worst record of workplace violations is Avondale Industries, which builds ships for the Navy. Between 1990 and 1996, nine workers died at Avondale's shipyard outside New Orleans, a death rate nearly three times that at other Navy shipyards. In 1999, OSHA inspectors uncovered hundreds of violations of safety and health standards, including Avondale's failure to provide safe scaffolding or training for employees who work at dangerous heights. OSHA hit the company with $717,000 in fines, among the largest ever imposed on a shipbuilder. "The stiff penalties are warranted," said then-Secretary of Labor Alexis Herman. "Workers should not have to risk their lives for their livelihood."

Yet just a month after the fines, the government awarded Avondale $22 million to work on amphibious assault ships at the New Orleans yard. The following year, three more workers were killed in accidents at the Avondale yard. One of the victims, 33-year-old Faustino Mendoza, died of head injuries when he fell 80 feet from scaffolding that lacked required safety features—the same problem that had been found during the most recent inspection. OSHA fined Avondale $49,000 for the "repeat" violation, but the penalty amounted to a tiny fraction of the $1.3 billion the firm received in federal business between 1995 and 2000. (Last year, Avondale became a subsidiary of Northrop Grumman.)

Another contractor with a pattern of workplace abuses is Tyson Foods, which received more than $163 million between 1995 and 2000, mostly for supplying poultry to government agencies. In 1999, seven workers died at plants run by Tyson or its independent operators. One of the victims was a 15-year-old boy—hired in violation of child-labor laws—who was electrocuted at a Tyson plant in Arkansas. The company has also attempted to buy influence with federal officials. In 1997, Tyson pleaded guilty to giving former Agriculture Secretary Michael Espy more than $12,000 in "gratuities" while the firm had issues before his department.

Even though the current federal rule requires contractors like Tyson, Avondale, and ExxonMobil to demonstrate "integrity and business ethics," they are in no danger of being barred from receiving federal business under the current standard. Indeed, the government continues to award major contracts to companies that have both defrauded the government *and* violated environmental and workplace laws.

TRW, the nation's ninth-largest contractor, supplies the government with everything from military satellites and spacecraft to auto parts and hand tools. Yet the company's subsidiaries have been cited for cheating the government on defense contracts, and last year it settled two cases in which it forced its employees to work off the clock and mishandled pension payments. In 1997, TRW was also listed in a "rogues' gallery" of OSHA violators in a study by *Business and Management Practices.* In just two years, the magazine found, the company racked up 67 violations and $113,202 in fines. In a single inspection in December 1999, OSHA cited TRW for 43 serious and repeat violations at an auto-parts plant in Michigan.

Some of TRW's most egregious offenses took place at two air-bag plants that lie at the foot of the Superstition Mountains near Mesa, Arizona. Within two years after they opened in 1989, the factories had experienced dozens of fires and explosions and were the target of at least six investigations by state regulators. "There were explosions so big that they felt like earthquakes," says Bunny Bertleson, who lives less than two miles from one of the plants. "Then clouds would come blowing out of the stacks."

The cause of the blasts was sodium azide, a highly volatile chemical that triggers the explosion that inflates air bags upon impact. Sodium azide is also highly toxic. It can damage the heart, kidneys, and nervous system if it is inhaled or comes into contact with the skin or eyes. Acute exposure can cause death.

A string of injuries suffered by workers at the Mesa plants drew the attention of state regulators. Employees frequently reported feeling queasy and dizzy, a condition they dubbed the "azide buzz," but say the company failed to address the problem. "There was constant pressure to get the production numbers up," recalls Felipe Chavez, a former employee. "That was the only priority." TRW insists that such exposure is rare, and that employee safety is "our highest priority." But in 1994, a spark detonated a small quantity of sodium azide, killing one worker and injuring six. The following year, the Mesa fire chief shut down one of the plants for two days, calling it an "imminent threat to both life and property."

The Arizona attorney general's office had already taken TRW to court and won consent orders requiring it to halt the fires, which were releasing sodium azide into the air, and to properly manage hazardous waste at the plants. In 1995, after the company failed to take safety steps it had promised to make to settle prior charges, a state superior court ordered TRW to pay $1.7 million—the largest corporate criminal consent judgment in state history.

But neither court-ordered fines nor injuries to workers prompted TRW to clean up its act. In 1997, an anonymous caller informed a state environmental agency that TRW was illegally storing wastewater laced with sodium azide at one of its Mesa plants. Following up on the tip, state investigators discovered that the company had illegally disposed of hundreds of thousands of gallons of chemical wastewater at landfills in Arizona, Utah, and California. The Arizona attorney general's office determined that the dumping was not "the work of low-level employees" but involved the "approval or acquiescence" of management.

Given the scope of the illegal dumping and TRW's history of breaking its promises, the state pressed criminal charges against the company. In a statement, TRW said that "the errors that occurred did not result in harm to the environment, local residents, or our employees." But last year, the company agreed to pay $24 million to the government for the illegal dumping—the largest such consent agreement in history.

Yet the company's pattern of lawbreaking has not harmed its ability to do business with the government. Between 1995 and 2000, when most of the illegal dumping and other abuses took place, TRW received nearly $10.3 billion in federal contracts—more than 400 times the amount it agreed to pay for its environmental crimes. After the company was caught dumping sodium azide, federal officials reviewed its violations and decided that it should remain eligible to work for the government. Last year, TRW received another $2.5 billion in federal contracts.

PART TWELVE

America in the World

The terrorist attacks on September 11, 2001, drove home for Americans the reality that we are part of a global community that is connected, for better or
worse, in multiple and intricate ways—and that what happens in our own
country cannot be divorced from what happens in the rest of the world. To an
important extent, of course, that has always been true. America has never existed in
pristine isolation from the rest of the globe. We are, for one thing, a nation of immigrants, and we cannot understand our history without understanding the importance of the international slave trade in the eighteenth and nineteenth centuries,
for example, or the impact of social changes in countries as diverse as Ireland,
Poland, and Mexico on our development as a society.

But the world is even more tightly connected today than in the past, with the
increasing speed of transportation and communication and the continued movement of vast numbers of people across nations and continents because of war,
oppression, or economic insecurity. More than ever, it is impossible to think about
many social problems in America without setting them in the context of the
changes that are reshaping the wider world. In this section, we introduce some of
the most important of them.

In the excerpt from his book *Blowback*, Chalmers Johnson argues that the
spread of American power around the world has bred a host of troubling, unforeseen consequences. We do not always recognize those consequences as being the
results of our own intervention, of course—but, Johnson argues, they often are.
American economic policies, for example, imposed partly through international
agencies such as the International Monetary Fund, can undermine economies
halfway around the world: when this happens, it is often assumed to be the natural
effect of an abstract process of "globalization." Johnson argues that we have created
a global "empire" based on extending American military and economic power
"to every corner of the world." But we have paid far too little attention to the
consequences—especially the effect on how we are viewed by the people around
the world whose lives are being shaped by these policies. We may, as a result, be

breeding a global crisis of massive proportions. The growth of international terrorism, Johnson argues, is only the most dramatic expression of that crisis.

Blowback was written before the events of September 11, 2001, but they only confirm the importance of his disturbing analysis. The report of the national commission launched to study the lessons of those events, part of which we reprint here, concludes that if we want to prevent terrorism in the future, we will need to adopt a more thoughtful and more socially aware approach to our relations with the world beyond our borders. Combating terrorism is not, they insist, just a military or political problem: It will require serious efforts to change the way America operates and is perceived in the rest of the world. Perhaps most importantly, it must include what the Commission calls an "agenda of opportunity"—a commitment to increasing educational and economic options in vulnerable countries, especially for the young. No one can guarantee that such a strategy will succeed in reducing the threat of global terrorism—but *not* tackling those issues virtually guarantees that we will fail.

But if our policies toward other countries have often backfired, causing problems that routinely come back to haunt us, why have we followed them? The record suggests that these policies are hardly random: from the beginning, they have been influenced by complex and shifting economic and political interests. As Michael Klare shows, one of the most important motives behind America's foreign policy (and that of many other countries) has been the desire to ensure a steady supply of energy—which, in our petroleum-driven economy, prominently includes oil. Concern over securing oil supplies helped to shape the political landscape of the contemporary Middle East, with all its volatility and tragedy; helped precipitate World War II; and, more recently, has been a backdrop for our two wars with Iraq. And as oil reserves inevitably dwindle, Klare points out, conflict over them is likely to increase.

CHAPTER 41

Blowback

Chalmers Johnson

Northern Italian communities had, for years, complained about low-flying American military aircraft. In February 1998, the inevitable happened. A Marine Corps EA-6B Prowler with a crew of four, one of scores of advanced American jet fighters and bombers stationed at places like Aviano, Cervia, Brindisi, and Sigonella, sliced through a ski-lift cable near the resort town of Cavalese and plunged twenty people riding in a single gondola to their deaths on the snowy slopes several hundred feet below. Although marine pilots are required to maintain an altitude of at least one thousand feet (two thousand, according to the Italian government), the plane had cut the cable at a height of 360 feet. It was traveling at 621 miles per hour when 517 miles per hour was considered the upper limit. The pilot had been performing low-level acrobatics while his copilot took pictures on videotape (which he later destroyed).

In response to outrage in Italy and calls for vigorous prosecution of those responsible, the marine pilots argued that their charts were inaccurate, that their altimeter had not worked, and that they had not consulted U.S. Air Force units permanently based in the area about local hazards. A court-martial held not in Italy but in Camp Lejeune, North Carolina, exonerated everyone involved, calling it a "training accident." Soon after, President Bill Clinton apologized and promised financial compensation to the victims, but on May 14, 1999, Congress dropped the provision for aid to the families because of opposition in the House of Representatives and from the Pentagon.[1]

This was hardly the only such incident in which American service personnel victimized foreign civilians in the post–Cold War world. From Germany and Turkey to Okinawa and South Korea, similar incidents have been common—as has been their usual denouement. The United States government never holds politicians or higher-ranking military officers responsible and seldom finds that more should be done beyond offering pro forma apologies and perhaps financial compensation of some, often minimal, sort.

On rare occasions, as with the Italian cable cutting, when such a local tragedy rises to the level of global news, what often seems strangest to Americans is the level of national outrage elsewhere over what the U.S. media portray as, at worst, an apparently isolated incident, however tragic to those involved. Certainly, the one subject beyond discussion at such moments is the fact that, a decade after the end of the Cold War, hundreds of thousands of American troops, supplied with the world's most advanced weaponry, sometimes including nuclear arms, are stationed on over sixty-one base complexes in nineteen countries worldwide, using the Department of Defense's narrowest definition of a "major installation"; if one included every kind of installation that houses representatives of the American military, the number would rise to over eight hundred.[2] There are, of course, no Italian air bases on American soil. Such a thought would be ridiculous. Nor, for that matter, are there German, Indonesian, Russian, Greek, or Japanese troops stationed on Italian soil. Italy is, moreover, a close ally of the United States, and no conceivable enemy nation endangers its shores.

All this is almost too obvious to state—and so is almost never said. It is simply not a matter for discussion, much less of debate in the land of the last imperial power. Perhaps similar thinking is second nature to any imperium. Perhaps the Romans did not find it strange to have their troops in Gaul, nor the British in South Africa. But what is unspoken is no less real, nor does it lack consequences just because it is not part of any ongoing domestic discussion.

I believe it is past time for such a discussion to begin, for Americans to consider why we have created an empire—a word from which we shy away—and what the consequences of our imperial stance may be for the rest of the world and for ourselves. Not so long ago, the way we garrisoned the world could be discussed far more openly and comfortably because the explanation seemed to lie at hand—in the very existence of the Soviet Union and of communism. Had the Italian disaster occurred two decades earlier, it would have seemed no less a tragedy, but many Americans would have argued that, given the Cold War, such incidents were an unavoidable cost of protecting democracies like Italy against the menace of Soviet totalitarianism. With the disappearance of any military threat faintly comparable to that posed by the former Soviet Union, such "costs" have become easily avoidable. American military forces could have been withdrawn from Italy, as well as from other foreign bases, long ago. That they were not and that Washington instead is doing everything in its considerable powers to perpetuate Cold War structures, even without the Cold War's justification, places such overseas deployments in a new light. They have become striking evidence, for those who care to look, of an imperial project that the Cold War obscured. The by-products of this project are likely to build up reservoirs of resentment against all Americans—tourists, students, and businessmen, as well as members of the armed forces—that can have lethal results.

For any empire, including an unacknowledged one, there is a kind of balance sheet that builds up over time. Military crimes, accidents, and atrocities make up only one category on the debit side of the balance sheet that the United States has been accumulating, especially since the Cold War ended. To take an example of quite a different kind of debit, consider South Korea, a longtime ally. On Christmas

Eve 1997, it declared itself financially bankrupt and put its economy under the guidance of the International Monetary Fund, which is basically an institutional surrogate of the United States government. Most Americans were surprised by the economic disasters that overtook Thailand, South Korea, Malaysia, and Indonesia in 1997 and that then spread around the world, crippling the Russian and Brazilian economies. They could hardly imagine that the U.S. government might have had a hand in causing them, even though various American pundits and economists expressed open delight in these disasters, which threw millions of people, who had previously had hopes of achieving economic prosperity and security, into the most abysmal poverty. At worst, Americans took the economic meltdown of places like Indonesia and Brazil to mean that beneficial American-supported policies of "globalization" were working—that we were effectively helping restructure various economies around the world so that they would look and work more like ours.

Above all, the economic crisis of 1997 was taken as evidence that our main doctrinal competitors—the high-growth capitalist economies of East Asia—were hardly either as competitive or as successful as they imagined. In a New Year's commentary, the columnist Charles Krauthammer mused, "Our success is the success of the American capitalist model, which lies closer to the free market vision of Adam Smith than any other. Much closer, certainly, than Asia's paternalistic crony capitalism that so seduced critics of the American system during Asia's now-burst bubble."[3]

As the global crisis deepened, the thing our government most seemed to fear was that contracts to buy our weapons might now not be honored. That winter, Secretary of Defense William Cohen made special trips to Jakarta, Bangkok, and Seoul to cajole the governments of those countries to use increasingly scarce foreign exchange funds to pay for the American fighter jets, missiles, warships, and other hardware the Pentagon had sold them before the economic collapse. He also stopped in Tokyo to urge on a worried Japanese government a big sale not yet agreed to. He wanted Japan to invest in the theater missile defense system, or TMD, antimissile missiles that the Pentagon has been trying to get the Japanese to buy for a decade. No one knew then or knows now whether the TMD will even work—in fifteen years of intercept attempts only a few missiles in essentially doctored tests have hit their targets—but it is unquestionably expensive, and arms sales, both domestic and foreign, have become one of the Pentagon's most important missions.

I believe the profligate waste of our resources on irrelevant weapons systems and the Asian economic meltdown, as well as the continuous trail of military "accidents" and of terrorist attacks on American installations and embassies, are all portents of a twenty-first-century crisis in America's informal empire, an empire based on the projection of military power to every corner of the world and on the use of American capital and markets to force global economic integration on our terms, at whatever costs to others. To predict the future is an undertaking no thoughtful person would rush to embrace. What form our imperial crisis is likely to take years or even decades from now is, of course, impossible to know. But history indicates that, sooner or later, empires do reach such moments, and it seems reasonable to assume that we will not miraculously escape that fate.

What we have freed ourselves of, however, is any genuine consciousness of how we might look to others on this globe. Most Americans are probably unaware of how Washington exercises its global hegemony, since so much of this activity takes place either in relative secrecy or under comforting rubrics. Many may, as a start, find it hard to believe that our place in the world even adds up to an empire. But only when we come to see our country as both profiting from and trapped within the structures of an empire of its own making will it be possible for us to explain many elements of the world that otherwise perplex us. Without good explanations, we cannot possibly produce policies that will bring us sustained peace and prosperity in a post–Cold War world. What has gone wrong in Japan after half a century of government-guided growth under U.S. protection? Why should the emergence of a strong China be to anyone's disadvantage? Why do American policies toward human rights, weapons proliferation, terrorism, drug cartels, and the environment strike so many foreigners as the essence of hypocrisy? Should American-owned and -managed multinational firms be instruments, beneficiaries, or adversaries of United States foreign policy? Is the free flow of capital really as valuable as free trade in commodities and manufactured goods? These kinds of questions can only be answered once we begin to grasp what the United States really is.

If Washington is the headquarters of a global military-economic dominion, the answers will be very different than if we think of the United States as simply one among many sovereign nations. There is a logic to empire that differs from the logic of a nation, and acts committed in service to an empire but never acknowledged as such have a tendency to haunt the future.

The term "blowback," which officials of the Central Intelligence Agency first invented for their own internal use, is starting to circulate among students of international relations. It refers to the unintended consequences of policies that were kept secret from the American people. What the daily press reports as the malign acts of "terrorists" or "drug lords" or "rogue states" or "illegal arms merchants" often turn out to be blowback from earlier American operations.

It is now widely recognized, for example, that the 1988 bombing of Pan Am flight 103 over Lockerbie, Scotland, which resulted in the deaths of 259 passengers and 11 people on the ground, was retaliation for a 1986 Reagan administration aerial raid on Libya that killed President Muammar Khadaffi's stepdaughter. Some in the United States have suspected that other events can also be explained as blowback from imperial acts. For example, the epidemic of cocaine and heroin use that has afflicted American cities during the past two decades was probably fueled in part by Central and South American military officers or corrupt politicians whom the CIA or the Pentagon once trained or supported and then installed in key government positions. For example, in Nicaragua in the 1980s, the U.S. government organized a massive campaign against the socialist-oriented Sandinista government. American agents then looked the other way when the Contras, the military insurgents they had trained, made deals to sell cocaine in American cities in order to buy arms and supplies.[4] . . .

Needless to say, blowback is not exclusively a problem faced by Americans. One has only to look at Russia and its former satellites today to see exactly how devastating imperial blowback can be. The hostage crisis of 1996–97 at the Japanese embassy in Lima, in which a handful of Peruvian revolutionaries took virtually the entire diplomatic corps hostage, was probably blowback from Japan's support for the antiguerrilla policies of President Alberto Fujimori and for the operations of Japanese multinational corporations in Peru. Israel's greatest single political problem is the daily threat of blowback from the Palestinian people and their Islamic allies because of Israeli policies of displacing Palestinians from their lands and repressing those that remain under their jurisdiction. The United States, however, is the world's most prominent target for blowback, being the world's lone imperial power, the primary source of the sort of secret and semisecret operations that shore up repressive regimes, and by far the largest seller of weapons generally.

It is typical of an imperial people to have a short memory for its less pleasant imperial acts, but for those on the receiving end, memory can be long indeed. Among the enduring sources of blowback, for instance, are the genocidal cruelties some nations have perpetrated during wartime. Japan to this day is trying to come to grips with the consequences of its actions in China during World War II. Japanese reactionaries are still reluctant to face atrocities committed in China and Korea: the rape of Nanking, conscription of conquered women to serve as prostitutes for frontline troops, and gruesome medical experimentation on prisoners of war are but the better known of these. But given the passage of time and some payment of compensation, many Chinese would probably accept a sincere apology for these events. However, Japanese armies also terrorized and radicalized an essentially conservative peasant population and thereby helped bring the Chinese Communist Party to power, leading to thirty million deaths during the Great Leap Forward and savaging Chinese civilization during the Cultural Revolution. There are many educated Chinese who can never forgive Japan for contributing to this outcome.

Today, we know of several similar cases. In pursuing the war in Vietnam in the early 1970s, President Richard Nixon and his national security adviser Henry Kissinger ordered more bombs dropped on rural Cambodia than had been dropped on Japan during all of World War II, killing at least three-quarters of a million Cambodian peasants and helping legitimize the murderous Khmer Rouge movement under Pol Pot. In his subsequent pursuit of revenge and ideological purity Pol Pot ensured that another million and a half Cambodians, this time mainly urban dwellers, were murdered.

Americans generally think of Pol Pot as some kind of unique, self-generated monster and his "killing fields" as an inexplicable atavism totally divorced from civilization. But without the United States government's Vietnam-era savagery, he could never have come to power in a culture like Cambodia's, just as Mao's uneducated peasant radicals would never have gained legitimacy in a normal Chinese context without the disruption and depravity of the Japanese war. Significantly, in its calls for an international tribunal to try the remaining leaders of the Khmer

Rouge for war crimes, the United States has demanded that such a court restrict its efforts to the period from 1975 to 1979—that is, after the years of carpet bombing were over and before the U.S. government began to collaborate with the Khmer Rouge against the Vietnamese Communists, who invaded Cambodia in 1978, drove the Khmer Rouge from power, and were trying to bring some stability to the country.

Even an empire cannot control the long-term effects of its policies. That is the essence of blowback. Take the civil war in Afghanistan in the 1980s, in which Soviet forces directly intervened on the government side and the CIA armed and supported any and all groups willing to face the Soviet armies. Over the years the fighting turned Kabul, once a major center of Islamic culture, into a facsimile of Hiroshima after the bomb. American policies helped ensure that the Soviet Union would suffer the same kind of debilitating defeat in Afghanistan as the United States had in Vietnam. In fact, the defeat so destabilized the Soviet regime that at the end of the 1980s it collapsed. But in Afghanistan the United States also helped bring to power the Taliban, a fundamentalist Islamic movement whose policies toward women, education, justice, and economic well-being resemble not so much those of Ayatollah Khomeini's Iran as those of Pol Pot's Cambodia. A group of these mujahideen, who only a few years earlier the United States had armed with ground-to-air Stinger missiles, grew bitter over American acts and policies in the Gulf War and vis-à-vis Israel. In 1993, they bombed the World Trade Center in New York and assassinated several CIA employees as they waited at a traffic light in Langley, Virginia. Four years later, on November 12, 1997, after the Virginia killer had been convicted by an American court, unknown assailants shot and killed four American accountants, unrelated in any way to the CIA, in their car in Karachi, Pakistan, in retaliation.

It is likely that U.S. covert policies have helped create similar conditions in the Congo, Guatemala, and Turkey, and that we are simply waiting for the blowback to occur. Guatemala is a particularly striking example of American imperial policies in its own "backyard." In 1954, the Eisenhower administration planned and the CIA organized and funded a military coup that overthrew a Guatemalan president whose modest land reform policies were considered a threat to American corporations. Blowback from this led to a Marxist guerrilla insurgency in the 1980s and so to CIA- and Pentagon-supported genocide against Mayan peasants. In the spring of 1999, a report on the Guatemalan civil war from the U.N.-sponsored Commission for Historical Clarification made clear that "the American training of the officer corps in counterinsurgency techniques" was a "key factor" in the "genocide. . . . Entire Mayan villages were attacked and burned and their inhabitants were slaughtered in an effort to deny the guerrillas protection."[5] According to the commission, between 1981 and 1983 the military government of Guatemala—financed and supported by the U.S. government—destroyed some four hundred Mayan villages in a campaign of genocide in which approximately two hundred thousand peasants were killed. José Pertierra, an attorney representing Jennifer Harbury, an American lawyer who spent years trying to find out what happened to her "disappeared" Guatemalan husband and supporter of the guerrillas, Efraín Bámaca Velásquez, writes that the Guatemalan military officer who arrested, tortured, and murdered Bámaca was a CIA "asset" and was paid $44,000 for the information he obtained from him.[6]

Visiting Guatemala in March 1999, soon after the report's release, President Clinton said, "It is important that I state clearly that support for military forces and intelligence units which engaged in violence and widespread repression was wrong, and the United States must not repeat that mistake. . . . The United States will no longer take part in campaigns of repression."[7] But on virtually the day that the president was swearing off "dirty tricks" in other people's countries, his government was reasserting its support for Turkey in its war of repression against its Kurdish minority.

The Kurds constitute fifteen million people in a Turkish population estimated at fifty-eight million. Another five million Kurds live largely within reach of Turkey's borders in Iraq, Iran, and Syria. The Turks have discriminated against the Kurds for the past seventy years and have conducted an intense genocidal campaign against them since 1992, in the process destroying some three thousand Kurdish villages and hamlets in the backward southeastern part of the country. Former American ambassador to Croatia Peter W. Galbraith comments that "Turkey routinely jails Kurdish politicians for activities that would be protected speech in democratic countries."[8] The Europeans have so far barred Turkey from the European Union because of its treatment of the Kurds. Because of its strategic location on the border of the former Soviet Union, however, Turkey was a valued American ally and NATO member during the Cold War, and the United States maintains the relationship unchanged even though the USSR has disappeared.

After Israel and Egypt, Turkey is the third-highest recipient of American military assistance. Between 1991 and 1995, the United States supplied four-fifths of Turkey's military imports, which were among the largest in the world. The U.S. government, in turn, depends on the NATO base at Incirlik, Turkey, to carry out Operation Provide Comfort, set up after the Gulf War to supply and protect Iraqi Kurds from repression by Saddam Hussein—at the same time that the United States acquiesces in Turkish mistreatment of its far larger Kurdish population. One obvious reason is that communities like Stratford and Bridgeport, Connecticut, where Black Hawk and Comanche helicopters are made, depend for their economic health on continued large-scale arms sales to countries like Turkey. At the time of the Gulf War, a senior adviser to the Turkish prime minister said to John Shattuck, assistant secretary of state for human rights, "If you want to stop human rights abuses do two things—stop IMF credits and cut off aid from the Pentagon. But don't sell the weapons and give aid and then complain about the Kurdish issue. Don't tell us about human rights while you're selling these weapons."[9]

The capture in February 1999 of the Kurdish guerrilla leader Abdullah Ocalan exposed the nature of American involvement with Turkey, in this case via a CIA gambit that holds promise as a rich source of future blowback. The CIA term for this policy is "disruption," by which it means the harassment of terrorists around the world. The point is to flush them out of hiding so that cooperative police forces or secret services can then arrest and imprison them. According to John Diamond of the Associated Press, "The CIA keeps its role secret, and the foreign countries that actually crack down on the suspects carefully hide the U.S. role, lest they stir up trouble for themselves." There are no safeguards at all against misidentifying "suspects," and "the CIA sends no formal notice to Congress." Disruption is said to be a preemptive, offensive form of counterterrorism. Richard Clarke, President Clinton's antiterrorism czar, likes it because he can avoid "the cumbersome Congressional reporting requirements that go with CIA-directed covert operations" and because "human rights organizations would have no way of identifying a CIA role." The CIA has carried out disruption operations in at least ten countries since September 1998. In the case of Ocalan's capture, the United States "provided Turkey with critical information about Ocalan's whereabouts." This was the first time some of the details of a "disruption" campaign were made public.[10]

In a sense, blowback is simply another way of saying that a nation reaps what it sows. Although people usually know what they have sown, our national experience of blowback is seldom imagined in such terms because so much of what the managers of the American empire have sown has been kept secret. As a concept, blowback is obviously most easy to grasp in its most straightforward manifestation. The unintended consequences of American policies and acts in country X are a bomb at an American embassy in country Y or a dead American in country Z. Certainly any number of Americans have been killed in that fashion, from Catholic nuns in El Salvador to tourists in Uganda who just happened to wander into hidden imperial scenarios about which they knew nothing. But blowback, as demonstrated in this [reading], is hardly restricted to such reasonably straightforward examples.

From the hollowing out of key American industries due to Japan's export-led economic policies to refugee flows across our southern borders from countries where U.S.-supported repression has created genocidal conditions or where U.S.-supported economic policies have led to unbearable misery, blowback can hit in less obvious and more subtle ways and over long periods of time. It can also manifest itself domestically in ways that are often not evident, even to those who created or carried out the initial imperial policies.

Because we live in an increasingly interconnected international system, we are all, in a sense, living in a blowback world. Although the term originally applied only to the unintended consequences for Americans of American policies, there is every reason to widen its meaning. Whether, for example, any unintended consequences of the American policies that fostered and then heightened the economic collapse of Indonesia in 1997 ever blow back to the United States, the unintended consequences for Indonesians have been staggering levels of suffering, poverty, and loss of hope. Similarly, the unintended consequences of American-supported coups and bombing in Cambodia in the early 1970s were unimaginable chaos, disruption, and death for Cambodians later in the decade.

Our role in the military coup in Chile in 1973, for example, produced little blowback onto the United States itself but had lethal consequences for liberals, socialists, and innocent bystanders in Chile and elsewhere. On the nature of American policies in Chile, journalist Jon Lee Anderson reports, "The plan, according to declassified United States government documents, was to make Chile ungovernable under [elected socialist president Salvador] Allende, provoke social chaos, and bring about a military coup. . . . A CIA cable outlined the objectives clearly to the station chief in Santiago: 'It is firm and continuing policy that Allende be overthrown by a coup. . . . We are to continue to generate maximum pressure toward this end utilizing every appropriate resource. It is imperative that these actions be implemented clandestinely and securely so that United States Government and American hand be well hidden.'"[11]

No ordinary citizen of the United States knew anything about these machinations. The coup d'état took place on September 11, 1973, resulting in the suicide of Allende and the seizure of power by General Augusto Pinochet, whose military and civilian supporters in their seventeen years in power tortured, killed, or "disappeared" some four thousand people. Pinochet was an active collaborator in Operation Condor, a joint mission with the Argentine militarists to murder exiled dissidents in the United States, Spain, Italy, and elsewhere. This is why, when Pinochet traveled to England in the autumn of 1998 for medical treatment, Spain tried to extradite him to stand trial for genocide, torture, and state terrorism against Spanish citizens. On October 16, 1998, the British police arrested Pinochet in London and held him pending his possible extradition.

Although few Americans were affected by this covert operation, people around the world now know of the American involvement and were deeply cynical when Secretary of State Madeleine Albright opposed Pinochet's extradition, claiming that countries like Chile undertaking a "transition to democracy" must be allowed to guarantee immunity from prosecution to past human rights offenders in order to "move forward."[12] America's "dirty hands" make even the most well-intentioned statement about human rights or terrorism seem hypocritical in such circumstances. Even when blowback mostly strikes other peoples, it has its corrosive effects on the United States by debasing political discourse and making citizens feel duped if they should happen to take seriously what their political leaders say. This is an inevitable consequence not just of blowback but of empire itself.

ENDNOTES

1. "Some Aid Canceled for Gondola Deaths," *Los Angeles Times*, May 15, 1999.
2. Department of Defense, "U.S. Military Installations" (updated to July 17, 1998), *DefenseLINK,* on-line at http://www.defenselink.mil/pubs/installations/foreignsummary. htm; and John Lindsay-Poland and Nick Morgan, "Overseas Military Bases and Environment," *Foreign Policy in Focus* 3.15 (June 1998), on-line at http://www.foreignpolicy-infocus.org/briefs/vol13/v3n15mil.html. According to one report, when the Soviet Union collapsed in 1991, the United States had 375 military bases scattered around the globe staffed by more than a half million personnel. Joel Brinkley, "U.S. Looking for a New Path as Superpower Conflict Ends," *New York Times*, February 2, 1992.
3. Charles Krauthammer, "What Caused Our Economic Boom?" *San Diego Union-Tribune,* January 5, 1998.
4. For documentary evidence, including Oliver North's notebooks, see "The Contras, Cocaine, and Covert Operations," *National Security Archive Electronic Briefing Book,* no. 2, online at http://www.seas.gwu.edu/nsarchive. Also see James Risen, "C.I.A. Said to Ignore Charges of Contra Drug Dealing in '80's," *New York Times*, October 10, 1998.

5. Mireya Navarro, "Guatemala Study Accuses the Army and Cites U.S. Role," *New York Times,* February 26, 1999; Larry Rohter, "Searing Indictment," *New York Times,* February 27, 1999; Michael Shifter, "Can Genocide End in Forgiveness?" *Los Angeles Times,* March 7, 1999; "Coming Clean on Guatemala," editorial, *Los Angeles Times,* March 10, 1999; and Michael Stetz, "Clinton's Words on Guatemala Called 'Too Little, Too Late,'" *San Diego Union-Tribune,* March 16, 1999.

6. José Pertierra, "For Guatemala, Words Are Not Enough," *San Diego Union-Tribune,* March 5, 1999.

7. John M. Broder, "Clinton Offers His Apologies to Guatemala," *New York Times,* March 11, 1999. Also see Broder, "Clinton Visit in Honduras Dramatizes New Attitude," *New York Times,* March 10, 1999; and Francisco Goldman, "Murder Comes for the Bishop," *New Yorker,* March 15, 1999.

8. Peter W. Galbraith, "How the Turks Helped Their Enemies," *New York Times,* February 20, 1999.

9. John Tirman, *Spoils of War: The Human Cost of America's Arms Trade* (New York: Free Press, 1997), p. 236.

10. John Diamond, "CIA Thwarts Terrorists with 'Disruption'; It's Prevention by Proxy," *San Diego Union-Tribune,* March 5, 1999; and Tim Weiner, "U.S. Helped Turkey Find and Capture Kurd Rebel," *New York Times,* February 20, 1999.

11. Jon Lee Anderson, "The Dictator," *New Yorker,* October 19, 1998; Peter Kronbluth, "Chile and the United States: Declassified Documents Relating to the Military Coup," *National Security Archive Electronic Briefing Book,* no. 8, on-line at http://www.seas.gwu.edu/nsarchive; and Philip Shenon, "U.S. Releases Files on Abuses in Pinochet Era," *New York Times,* July 1, 1999.

12. Michael Ratner, "The Pinochet Precedent," *Progressive Response* 3.3 (January 28, 1999).

CHAPTER 42

Oil, Geography, and War

Michael T. Klare

O f all the resources discussed in this book, none is more likely to provoke conflict between states in the twenty-first century than oil. Petroleum stands out from other materials—water, minerals, timber, and so on—because of its pivotal role in the global economy and its capacity to ignite large-scale combat. No highly industrialized society can survive at present without substantial supplies of oil, and so any significant threat to the continued availability of this resource will prove a cause of crisis and, in extreme cases, provoke the use of military force. Action of this sort could occur in any of the major oil-producing areas, including the Middle East and the Caspian basin. Lesser conflicts over petroleum are also likely, as states fight to gain or retain control over resource-rich border areas and offshore economic zones. Big or small, conflicts over oil will constitute a significant feature of the global security environment in the decades to come.

Petroleum has, of course, been a recurring source of conflict in the past. Many of the key battles of World War II, for example, were triggered by the Axis Powers' attempts to gain control over petroleum supplies located in areas controlled by their adversaries. The pursuit of greater oil revenues also prompted Iraq's 1990 invasion of Kuwait, and this, in turn, provoked a massive American military response. But combat over petroleum is not simply a phenomenon of the past; given the world's ever-increasing demand for energy and the continuing possibility of supply interruptions, the outbreak of a conflict over oil is just as likely to occur in the future.

The likelihood of future combat over oil is suggested, first of all, by the growing buildup of military forces in the Middle East and other oil-producing areas. Until recently, the greatest concentration of military power was found along the East-West divide in Europe and at other sites of superpower competition. Since 1990, however, these concentrations have largely disappeared, while troop levels in the major oil zones have been increased. The United States, for example, has established a permanent military infrastructure in the Persian Gulf area and has "prepositioned" sufficient war matériel there to sustain a major campaign. Russia, meanwhile, has shifted more of its forces to the North Caucasus and the Caspian Sea basin, while China has expanded its naval presence in the South China Sea. Other countries have also bolstered their presence in these areas and other sites of possible conflict over oil.

Geology and geography also add to the risk of conflict. While relatively abundant at present, natural petroleum does not exist in unlimited quantities; it is a finite, nonrenewable substance. At some point in the future, available supplies will prove inadequate to satisfy soaring demand, and the world will encounter significant shortages. Unless some plentiful new source of energy has been discovered by that point, competition over the remaining supplies of petroleum will prove increasingly fierce. In such circumstances, any prolonged interruption in the global flow of oil will be viewed by import-dependent states as a mortal threat to their security—and thus as a matter that may legitimately be resolved through the use of military force. Growing scarcity will also result in higher prices for oil, producing enormous hardship for those without the means to absorb added costs; in consequence, widespread internal disorder may occur.

Geography enters the picture because many of the world's leading sources of oil are located in contested border zones or in areas of recurring crisis and violence. The distribution of petroleum is more concentrated than other raw materials, with the bulk of global supplies found in a few key producing areas. Some of these areas—the North Slope of Alaska and the American Southwest, for example—are located within the borders of a single country and are relatively free of disorder; others, however, are spread across several countries—which may or may not agree on their common borders—and/or are located in areas of perennial unrest. To reach global markets, moreover, petroleum must often travel (by ship or by pipeline) through other areas of instability. Because turmoil in these areas can easily disrupt the global flow of oil, any outbreak of conflict, however minor, will automatically generate a risk of outside intervention.

That conflict over oil will erupt in the years ahead is almost a foregone conclusion. Just how much violence, at what levels of intensity, and at which locations, cannot be determined. Ultimately, the frequency and character of warfare will depend on the relative weight and the interplay of three key factors: (1) the political and strategic environment in which decisions over resource issues are made; (2) the future relationship between demand and supply; and (3) the geography of oil production and distribution.

THE POLITICS OF OIL SECURITY

Many resources are needed to sustain a modern industrial society, but only those that are viewed as being vital to national security are likely to provoke the use of military force when access to key supplies is placed in jeopardy.* There is no

*In 1998, the U.S. National Security Council defined "vital interests" as those interests "of broad, overriding importance to the survival, safety, and vitality of our nation. Among these are the physical security of our territory and that of our allies, the safety of our citizens, our economic well-being, and the protection of our critical infrastructures. We will do what we must to defend these interests, including—when necessary—using our military might unilaterally and decisively" (*A National Security Strategy for a New Century,* October 1998).

question that oil has enjoyed this distinctive status in the past. Ever since the introduction of oil-powered warships at the beginning of the twentieth century, petroleum has been viewed as essential for success in war. Before that time, petroleum
had largely been used to provide illumination, most commonly in the form of
kerosene. (Indeed, many of the major oil companies of today, including Exxon,
Mobil, and Royal Dutch/Shell, were initially established in the nineteenth century
to produce and market kerosene to the growing urban populations of Europe and
North America.) The critical turning point came in 1912, when the British
Admiralty—then led by First Lord of the Admiralty Winston Churchill—decided to
convert its combat vessels from coal to oil propulsion.[1]

The transition from coal to oil provided British ships with a significant advantage in speed and endurance over the coal-powered vessels of its adversaries, especially Germany. But it also presented London with a significant dilemma: while rich
in coal, Britain possessed few domestic sources of petroleum and so was vitally
dependent on imported supplies. With a war about to begin, and the reliability of
overseas suppliers in question, the cabinet decided—on a strict national security
basis—to endow the government with direct responsibility for the delivery of oil.
On June 17, 1914, Parliament voted to approve the government's acquisition of a
majority stake in the Anglo-Persian Oil Company (APOC), a London-based firm
that had recently discovered petroleum in southwestern Persia. With this vote, it
became British policy to protect APOC's oil concession area in Persia—thus, for
the first time, making the security of overseas petroleum supplies a major state
responsibility.[2]

The link between oil and military policy was made even more substantial during World War I itself, when all of the major belligerents employed oil-driven
vehicles for combat, reconnaissance, and logistics. The airplane and the tank—
oil-powered machines that were to revolutionize the conduct of warfare—were
introduced during the conflict. Scarcely less important was the widespread use of
motor vehicles to carry troops and supplies to the battlefield: over the course of the
war, the British army's fleet of trucks grew from 10,000 to 60,000; the American
Expeditionary Force brought with it another 50,000 motor vehicles.[3] It is with this in
mind that Lord Curzon, former viceroy of India and soon-to-be foreign secretary,
told a group of government and industry officials in London that the Allies had
"floated to victory upon a wave of oil."[4]

This perception continued to influence strategic thinking after World War I
and in the years leading up to World War II. Believing that the next major conflict
would see an even greater reliance on oil-powered weapons than the last, many
governments followed the British example by creating state-owned oil companies
and by seeking control over foreign sources of petroleum. Britain, for its part, expanded its oil interests in the Persian Gulf area and strengthened its dominant
position in Iran (the new name for Persia). France established a state-owned firm,
the Compagnie Française des Pétroles, and obtained concessions in the Mosul area
of northwest Iraq. Germany and Japan—both of which lacked domestic sources of
petroleum—laid plans to acquire their supplies from Romania and the Dutch East
Indies, respectively.[5]

Once war broke out, the competitive pursuit of oil by all sides had a significant impact on the tempo and trajectory of battle. In the Pacific, Japanese efforts to gain control over the petroleum supplies of the Dutch East Indies produced mounting alarm in Washington and led, in 1941, to the imposition of a U.S. embargo on oil exports to Japan. This, in turn, persuaded Japanese officials that a war with the United States was inevitable, propelling them to seek an initial advantage through a surprise attack on the U.S. naval base at Pearl Harbor. In the European theater, Germany's desperate need for oil helped trigger its 1941 invasion of Russia. Along with Moscow and Leningrad, a major target of the invasion was the Soviet oil center at Baku (in what is now Azerbaijan). Both efforts ended in failure: the Japanese plan to import East Indian oil was foiled by American air and submarine attacks on tanker ships, while the German drive on Baku was thwarted by stubborn Soviet resistance. With their supplies of oil becoming increasingly scarce, Japan and Germany were unable to mount effective resistance to Allied offensives and so were eventually forced to concede defeat.[6]

After the war, petroleum continued to be seen by military planners as a vital combat necessity. With military organizations placing even greater emphasis on the role of airpower and armored forces, the need for reliable oil supplies became more critical than ever. This influenced the strategic thinking not only of the European powers, which had long been dependent on imported supplies, but also of the United States, which for the first time began to acquire significant supplies of petroleum from outside the country. Fearing that the Soviet Union would seek control over the Persian Gulf area—rapidly becoming the leading source of Western oil imports—Washington established a modest military presence in the region and sought to integrate Iran, Iraq, Saudi Arabia, and other key oil-producing states into the Western alliance. Both the Truman Doctrine (1947) and the Eisenhower Doctrine (1957) included promises of U.S. military aid to any state in the region that came under attack from Soviet or Soviet-backed forces.[7]

Initially, American moves in the Middle East were governed by classical military considerations: to prevent a hostile power from gaining control over a vital resource needed for the effective prosecution of war. With the outbreak of the October 1973 Arab-Israeli conflict, however, the perception of oil as a strategic commodity took on an entirely new meaning. To punish Washington for its support of Israel and to build worldwide pressure for an acceptable outcome to the conflict, the Arab states cut off all petroleum deliveries to the United States and imposed rolling cutbacks on deliveries to other countries. At the same time, the Organization of Petroleum-Exporting Countries (OPEC) announced a fourfold increase in the price of oil. Occurring at a time when petroleum supplies were already under pressure from rapidly growing demand, the oil embargo and OPEC price increase sent a powerful shock wave through the global economy: oil shortages developed in many areas, industrial output declined, and the world plunged into a prolonged economic recession. From this time on, oil was seen not only as an essential military commodity but also as a prerequisite for global economic stability.[8]

The Arab oil embargo was rescinded in March 1974, and the economic crisis gradually receded. Nevertheless, the events of 1973–74 left a profound and lasting impact on the perceived link between oil and the national security of the major in-dustrialized powers. Worried that significant supply disruptions could occur again, the oil-importing countries sought to minimize their vulnerability by searching for new petroleum deposits in more secure locations (the North Sea and the North Slope of Alaska, for example) and by storing large quantities of oil in special reser-voirs. The United States, for its part, stored hundreds of millions of barrels of oil in its newly established Strategic Petroleum Reserve.

The American response to the "oil shocks" of 1973–74 was not limited to de-fensive measures. For the first time, senior officials began talking of using force to protect vital petroleum supplies in peacetime, to guarantee the health of the econ-omy. Specifically, policy makers began to consider American military intervention in the Middle East to prevent any interruption in the flow of Persian Gulf oil. Initially private, these deliberations became public in 1975 when Henry Kissinger, then secretary of state, told the editors of *Business Week* that the United States was prepared to go to war over oil. Although reluctant to employ force in a dispute over prices alone, he stated, Washington would have no such hesitation "where there's some actual strangulation of the industrialized world."[9]

This formulation of Western security interests has governed American military planning ever since. When, in 1979, the shah of Iran was overthrown by militant Islamic forces and the world experienced a second major "oil shock," President Carter was quick to threaten the use of force against any adversary that might seek to impede the flow of oil from the Persian Gulf area. On January 23, 1980, Carter declared that any attempt by a hostile power to constrict the flow of oil in the Gulf "will be repelled by any means necessary, including military force."[10] In line with this principle, known since as the Carter Doctrine, the United States commenced a military buildup in the Persian Gulf area that has continued to this day. This principle has, moreover, periodi-cally been put to the test. During the Iran–Iraq war of 1980–88, when the Iranians stepped up their attacks on oil shipping in the Gulf (presumably to punish Kuwait and Saudi Arabia for their financial support of Iraq), the United States agreed to "reflag" Kuwaiti tankers with American flags and provide them with a U.S. naval escort.[11]

The Carter Doctrine was next invoked in August 1990, when Iraqi forces occu-pied Kuwait and positioned themselves for an assault on Saudi Arabia. Concluding that Iraqi control of both Kuwaiti and Saudi oil fields would pose an intolerable threat to Western economic security, President Bush quickly decided on a tough military response—dispatching large numbers of American forces to defend Saudi Arabia and, if need be, to drive the Iraqis out of Kuwait. "Our country now imports nearly half the oil it consumes and could face a major threat to its economic inde-pendence," he told the nation on August 7. Hence, "the sovereign independence of Saudi Arabia is of vital interest to the United States."[12] A number of other concerns, including Iraq's burgeoning weapons capabilities, also figured in the U.S. decision to employ force in the Gulf, but senior administration officials always placed particu-lar emphasis on the threat to Western oil supplies and the continued health of the American economy.[13]

Since Desert Storm, American leaders have continued to stress the impor-tance of unhindered oil deliveries to the health and stability of the global economy.

"America's vital interests in the [Persian Gulf] region are compelling," General J. H. Binford Peay III, commander in chief of the U.S. Central Command (CENTCOM), declared in 1997. "The unrestricted flow of petroleum resources from friendly Gulf states to refineries and processing facilities around the world drives the global economic engine."[14] In accordance with this outlook, the United States has beefed up its forces in the Gulf and taken other steps to protect friendly powers in the area. At the same time, Washington has enhanced its capacity to intervene in the Caspian Sea region and in other areas holding large supplies of oil.

A similar perspective regarding the role of oil in maintaining economic stability also governs the security policies of other states, including China and Japan. Both of these countries have bolstered their capacity to protect vital petroleum supplies: China has tightened its hold on Xinjiang (a potential source of oil and the site of a rebellion by members of the Muslim Uighur ethnic group) and the islands of the South China Sea (another potential source of oil); Japan has extended the reach of its air and naval forces to better protect its sealanes.

For oil-importing countries, the safe delivery of oil is the basis of their economic security. For oil exporters, however, the *possession* of oil dominates economic thinking. Even at the depressed prices of the late 1990s, the sale of oil was enormously lucrative for those countries; as demand grows and prices rise, the monetary value of oil reserves will climb even higher. In 1997, for instance, the U.S. Department of State placed the value of untapped Caspian Sea oil supplies at a staggering $4 trillion—and oil prices were then considerably lower than they are today.[15] It is therefore not surprising that any state possessing some piece of this latent wealth will view its protection as a vital aspect of national and economic security. . . .

THE INESCAPABLE CONSTRAINTS OF GEOGRAPHY

As older fields are depleted, the global competition for oil will focus increasingly on those few areas of the world that still contain significant supplies of petroleum. These areas will automatically acquire increased strategic importance, as will the transit routes used for carrying oil to distant markets. Clearly, any instability or disorder in these critical areas could impede the continued flow of oil, thus provoking outside intervention. The relative likelihood of conflict is therefore closely related to the geography of oil distribution and to the political environment in key producing and transit regions.

The most significant fact about petroleum, from a world security point of view, is that so much of it is concentrated in a few major producing areas. As shown by Table 42.1, fourteen countries—Saudi Arabia, Iraq, the United Arab Emirates (UAE), Kuwait, Iran, Venezuela, Russia, Mexico, the United States, Libya, China, Nigeria, Norway, and the United Kingdom—jointly possess all but 10 percent of the known world supply. Among these fourteen, the possession of oil is even more highly concentrated, with the five leading producers—Saudi Arabia, Iraq, the UAE, Kuwait, and Iran—together holding nearly two-thirds of global reserves.

TABLE 42.1 Global Reserves and Production of Petroleum (as calculated in 1999)

Producer (in order by reserves)	Estimated Reserves (bbl)	Percent of World Reserves	Production, 1998 (mbd)
Saudi Arabia	261.5	24.8	9.2
Iraq	112.5	10.7	2.2
United Arab Emirates	97.8	9.3	2.7
Kuwait	96.5	9.2	2.2
Iran	89.7	8.5	3.8
Venezuela	72.6	6.9	3.3
Russia	48.6	4.6	6.2
Mexico	47.8	4.5	3.5
United States	30.5	2.9	8.0
Libya	29.5	2.8	1.4
China	24.0	2.3	3.2
Nigeria	22.5	2.1	2.2
Norway/United Kingdom (North Sea)	16.1	1.5	6.0
Total	949.6	90.1	53.9

Source: BP Amoco, *Statistical Review of World Energy 1999.*
bbl = billion barrels
mbd = million barrels per day

The high concentration of petroleum in a handful of major producing areas means that the global availability of oil is closely tied to political and socioeconomic conditions within a relatively small group of countries. When war or political turmoil erupts in these countries, and the global flow of oil is subsequently disrupted, the rest of the world is likely to experience significant economic hardship.[16] This was made painfully evident in 1973–74, when the Arab oil embargo produced widespread fuel shortages and triggered a prolonged economic recession; the same message was delivered again in 1979–80, following the revolution in Iran. A close look at Table 42.1 suggests, moreover, that such traumas can occur again in the future: a majority of the countries listed in this group have experienced war or revolution during the past ten to twenty years, and many continue to face internal or external challenges.

The epicenter of all this disorder is, of course, the Middle East. That so many of the world's leading oil producers are located in this fractious region has long been a matter of grave concern for leaders of the major importing nations. Even before the discovery of oil, the states in this region were torn by internal divisions along ethnic and political lines, and by the historic rift between Sunni and Shiite Muslims. Once the flow of petroleum began, these divisions were further strained by disputes over the ownership of oil fields and the distribution of oil revenues. This fiery cauldron has been further heated in recent years by the rise of Islamic fundamentalism, the endurance of authoritarian regimes, and deep frustration (among many Arabs) over Israel's treatment of the Palestinians.[17]

Because the Middle East has so often been convulsed by social and political unrest, the major consuming nations have sought to reduce their dependence on Persian Gulf oil by developing alternative sources elsewhere. This is the impulse that led to the rapid development of North Sea and North Slope reserves in the 1970s and, more recently, to the establishment of new production areas in Africa, Latin America, and the Caspian region. "We are undergoing a fundamental shift away from reliance on Middle East oil," the National Security Council optimistically reported in 1998. "Venezuela [has become] our number one foreign supplier and Africa supplies 15 percent of our imported oil."[18]

But while shifting production to these other areas may diminish the importers' reliance on the Middle East, this does not guarantee that the new sources of petroleum will be any less free of disorder and conflict. Colombia and Nigeria, for example, have experienced considerable internal violence over the past few years, while Venezuela is going through a painful and potentially disruptive political transition. Nor is the Caspian Sea area likely to prove any less unstable than the Persian Gulf.

It is true that the development of multiple producing areas allows consuming nations to switch from one source of oil to another when a crisis erupts in any individual area, but the number of such sources are few, and those among them that are entirely free of conflict (or the risk of conflict) are fewer still.

It is clear, then, that a strategy of diversification can succeed for only so long. Ultimately, the oil-importing countries will be forced to rely on the same group of unreliable suppliers in the Persian Gulf, the Caspian, Latin America, and Africa. Like it or not, major importing countries will have to pay close attention to political developments in key producing areas and will have to intervene—in one way or another—whenever local and regional turmoil threatens to disrupt the flow of petroleum.

ENDNOTES

1. For background on the decision to switch from coal to oil, see Geoffrey Jones, *The State and the Emergence of the British Oil Industry* (London: MacMillan, 1981), pp. 9–31.

2. For background and discussion, see ibid., pp. 129–76.

3. Ibid., p. 177. See also Daniel Yergin, *The Prize* (New York: Touchstone, Simon and Schuster, 1993), pp. 167–83.

4. This was said to a celebratory meeting of the Inter-Allied Petroleum Council in London on November 21, 1918. Cited in Yergin, *The Prize*, p. 183.

5. For background on this period, see Jones, *The State and the Emergence of the British Oil Industry*, pp. 208–44; Yergin, *The Prize*, pp. 184–206, 260–308.

6. See Yergin, *The Prize*, pp. 308–88.

7. For background on these endeavors, see David S. Painter, *Oil and the American Century* (Baltimore: Johns Hopkins University Press, 1986), and Michael B. Stoff, *Oil, War, and American Security* (New Haven: Yale University Press, 1980). On the Nixon Doctrine, see James H. Noyes, *The Clouded Lens* (Stanford, Calif.: Hoover Institution Press, 1979), and U.S. Congress, House, Committee on Foreign Affairs, Subcommittee on the Near East and South

Asia, *New Perspectives on the Persian Gulf,* Hearings, 93rd Congress, 1st session (Washington, D.C.: Government Printing Office, 1973).

8. For background on these events, see Yergin, *The Prize,* pp. 588–632.

9. Interview in *Business Week,* January 13, 1975, p. 69.

10. From the transcript of Carter's address in *The New York Times,* January 24, 1980.

11. For background on this episode, see Anthony H. Cordesman and Abraham R. Wagner, *The Lessons of Modern War,* volume II, *The Iran-Iraq War* (Boulder: Westview Press, 1990), pp. 277–80, 295–302, 317, 329.

12. From the transcript of Bush's speech in *The New York Times,* August 8, 1997.

13. Alluding to Kissinger's earlier comments, Defense Secretary Richard Cheney told the Senate Armed Services Committee in September 1990 that Washington could not allow Saddam Hussein to acquire "a stranglehold on our economy." U.S. Congress, Senate, Committee on Armed Services, *Crisis in the Persian Gulf Region: U.S. Policy Options and Implications,* Hearings, 101st Congress, 2d Session (1990), pp. 10–11. These hearings represent one of the best sources for information on U.S. security thinking at the time.

14. U.S. Central Command (CENTCOM), *1997 Posture Statement* (MacDill Air Force Base, Fla.: CENTCOM, n.d.), p. 1.

15. U.S. Department of State, *Caspian Region Energy Development Report,* p. 3.

16. For further discussion of this point, see Edward R. Fried and Philip H. Trezise, *Oil Security: Retrospect and Prospect* (Washington, D.C.: Brookings Institution, 1993).

17. For discussion, see the essays in Gary G. Sick and Lawrence G. Potter, eds., *The Persian Gulf at the Millennium* (New York: St. Martin's Press, 1997).

18. U.S. National Security Council, *A National Security Strategy for a New Century* (Washington, D.C.: White House, October 1998), p. 32.

CHAPTER 43

What to Do?
A Global Strategy against Terrorism

The 9/11 Commission

REFLECTING ON A GENERATIONAL CHALLENGE

Three years after 9/11, Americans are still thinking and talking about how to protect our nation in this new era. The national debate continues.

Countering terrorism has become, beyond any doubt, the top national security priority for the United States. This shift has occurred with the full support of the Congress, both major political parties, the media, and the American people.

The nation has committed enormous resources to national security and to countering terrorism. Between fiscal year 2001, the last budget adopted before 9/11, and the . . . fiscal year 2004, total federal spending on defense (including expenditures on both Iraq and Afghanistan), homeland security, and international affairs rose more than 50 percent, from $354 billion to about $547 billion. The United States has not experienced such a rapid surge in national security spending since the Korean War.[1]

This pattern has occurred before in American history. The United States faces a sudden crisis and summons a tremendous exertion of national energy. Then, as that surge transforms the landscape, comes a time for reflection and reevaluation. Some programs and even agencies are discarded; others are invented or redesigned. Private firms and engaged citizens redefine their relationships with government, working through the processes of the American republic.

Now is the time for that reflection and reevaluation. The United States should consider *what to do*—the shape and objectives of a strategy. Americans should also consider *how to do it*—organizing their government in a different way.

Defining the Threat.   In the post–9/11 world, threats are defined more by the fault lines within societies than by the territorial boundaries between them. From terrorism to global disease or environmental degradation, the challenges have become transnational rather than international. That is the defining quality of world politics in the twenty-first century.

National security used to be considered by studying foreign frontiers, weighing opposing groups of states, and measuring industrial might. To be dangerous, an enemy had to muster large armies. Threats emerged slowly, often visibly, as weapons were forged, armies conscripted, and units trained and moved into place. Because large states were more powerful, they also had more to lose. They could be deterred.

Now threats can emerge quickly. An organization like al Qaeda, headquartered in a country on the other side of the earth, in a region so poor that electricity or telephones were scarce, could nonetheless scheme to wield weapons of unprecedented destructive power in the largest cities of the United States.

In this sense, 9/11 has taught us that terrorism against American interests "over there" should be regarded just as we regard terrorism against America "over here." In this same sense, the American homeland is the planet. . . .

Engage the Struggle of Ideas.   The United States is heavily engaged in the Muslim world and will be for many years to come. This American engagement is resented. Polls in 2002 found that among America's friends, like Egypt—the recipient of more U.S. aid for the past 20 years than any other Muslim country—only 15 percent of the population had a favorable opinion of the United States. In Saudi Arabia the number was 12 percent. And two-thirds of those surveyed in 2003 in countries from Indonesia to Turkey (a NATO ally) were very or somewhat fearful that the United States may attack them.[23]

Support for the United States has plummeted. Polls taken in Islamic countries after 9/11 suggested that many or most people thought the United States was doing the right thing in its fight against terrorism; few people saw popular support for al Qaeda; half of those surveyed said that ordinary people had a favorable view of the United States. By 2003, polls showed that "the bottom has fallen out of support for America in most of the Muslim world. Negative views of the U.S. among Muslims, which had been largely limited to countries in the Middle East, have spread. . . . Since last summer, favorable ratings for the U.S. have fallen from 61% to 15% in Indonesia and from 71% to 38% among Muslims in Nigeria."[24]

Many of these views are at best uninformed about the United States and, at worst, informed by cartoonish stereotypes, the coarse expression of a fashionable "Occidentalism" among intellectuals who caricature U.S. values and policies. Local newspapers and the few influential satellite broadcasters—like al Jazeera—often reinforce the jihadist theme that portrays the United States as anti-Muslim.[25]

The small percentage of Muslims who are fully committed to Usama Bin Ladin's version of Islam are impervious to persuasion. It is among the large majority of Arabs and Muslims that we must encourage reform, freedom, democracy, and opportunity, even though our own promotion of these messages is limited in its effectiveness simply because we are its carriers. Muslims themselves will have to reflect upon such basic issues as the concept of jihad, the position of women, and the place of non-Muslim minorities. The United States can promote moderation, but cannot ensure its ascendancy. Only Muslims can do this.

The setting is difficult. The combined gross domestic product of the 22 countries in the Arab League is less than the GDP of Spain. Forty percent of adult Arabs are illiterate, two-thirds of them women. One-third of the broader Middle East lives on less than two dollars a day. Less than 2 percent of the population has access to the Internet. The majority of older Arab youths have expressed a desire to emigrate to other countries, particularly those in Europe.[26]

In short, the United States has to help defeat an ideology, not just a group of people, and we must do so under difficult circumstances. How can the United States and its friends help moderate Muslims combat the extremist ideas?

Recommendation: The U.S. government must define what the message is, what it stands for. We should offer an example of moral leadership in the world, committed to treat people humanely, abide by the rule of law, and be generous and caring to our neighbors. America and Muslim friends can agree on respect for human dignity and opportunity. To Muslim parents, terrorists like Bin Ladin have nothing to offer their children but visions of violence and death. America and its friends have a crucial advantage—we can offer these parents a vision that might give their children a better future. If we heed the views of thoughtful leaders in the Arab and Muslim world, a moderate consensus can be found.

That vision of the future should stress life over death: individual education and economic opportunity. This vision includes widespread political participation and contempt for indiscriminate violence. It includes respect for the rule of law, openness in discussing differences, and tolerance for opposing points of view.

Recommendation: Where Muslim governments, even those who are friends, do not respect these principles, the United States must stand for a better future. One of the lessons of the long Cold War was that short-term gains in cooperating with the most repressive and brutal governments were too often outweighed by long-term setbacks for America's stature and interests.

American foreign policy is part of the message. America's policy choices have consequences. Right or wrong, it is simply a fact that American policy regarding the Israeli–Palestinian conflict and American actions in Iraq are dominant staples of popular commentary across the Arab and Muslim world. That does not mean U.S. choices have been wrong. It means those choices must be integrated with America's message of opportunity to the Arab and Muslim world. Neither Israel nor the new Iraq will be safer if worldwide Islamist terrorism grows stronger.

The United States must do more to communicate its message. Reflecting on Bin Ladin's success in reaching Muslim audiences, Richard Holbrooke wondered, "How can a man in a cave outcommunicate the world's leading communications society?" Deputy Secretary of State Richard Armitage worried to us that Americans have been "exporting our fears and our anger," not our vision of opportunity and hope.[27]

Recommendation: Just as we did in the Cold War, we need to defend our ideals abroad vigorously. America does stand up for its values. The United States defended, and still defends, Muslims against tyrants and criminals in Somalia, Bosnia,

Kosovo, Afghanistan, and Iraq. If the United States does not act aggressively to define itself in the Islamic world, the extremists will gladly do the job for us.

- Recognizing that Arab and Muslim audiences rely on satellite television and radio, the government has begun some promising initiatives in television and radio broadcasting to the Arab world, Iran, and Afghanistan. These efforts are beginning to reach large audiences. The Broadcasting Board of Governors has asked for much larger resources. It should get them.
- The United States should rebuild the scholarship, exchange, and library programs that reach out to young people and offer them knowledge and hope. Where such assistance is provided, it should be identified as coming from the citizens of the United States.

An Agenda of Opportunity.   The United States and its friends can stress educational and economic opportunity. The United Nations has rightly equated "literacy as freedom."

- The international community is moving toward setting a concrete goal—to cut the Middle East region's illiteracy rate in half by 2010, targeting women and girls and supporting programs for adult literary.
- Unglamorous help is needed to support the basics, such as textbooks that translate more of the world's knowledge into local languages and libraries to house such materials. Education about the outside world, or other cultures, is weak.
- More vocational education is needed, too, in trades and business skills. The Middle East can also benefit from some of the programs to bridge the digital divide and increase Internet access that have already been developed for other regions of the world.

Education that teaches tolerance, the dignity and value of each individual, and respect for different beliefs is a key element in any global strategy to eliminate Islamist terrorism.

Recommendation: The U.S. government should offer to join with other nations in generously supporting a new International Youth Opportunity Fund. Funds will be spent directly for building and operating primary and secondary schools in those Muslim states that commit to sensibly investing their own money in public education.

Economic openness is essential. Terrorism is not caused by poverty. Indeed, many terrorists come from relatively well-off families. Yet when people lose hope, when societies break down, when countries fragment, the breeding grounds for terrorism are created. Backward economic policies and repressive political regimes slip into societies that are without hope, where ambition and passions have no constructive outlet.

The policies that support economic development and reform also have political implications. Economic and political liberties tend to be linked. Commerce, especially international commerce, requires ongoing cooperation and compromise, the exchange of ideas across cultures, and the peaceful resolution of differences through negotiation or the rule of law. Economic growth expands the middle class, a constituency for further reform. Successful economies rely on vibrant private sectors, which have an interest in curbing indiscriminate government power. Those who develop the practice of controlling their own economic destiny soon desire a voice in their communities and political societies.

The U.S. government has announced the goal of working toward a Middle East Free Trade Area, or MEFTA, by 2013. The United States has been seeking comprehensive free trade agreements (FTAs) with the Middle Eastern nations most firmly on the path to reform. The U.S.–Israeli FTA was enacted in 1985, and Congress implemented an FTA with Jordan in 2001. Both agreements have expanded trade and investment, thereby supporting domestic economic reform. In 2004, new FTAs were signed with Morocco and Bahrain and are awaiting congressional approval. These models are drawing the interest of their neighbors. Muslim countries can become full participants in the rules-based global trading system, as the United States considers lowering its trade barriers with the poorest Arab nations.

Recommendation: A comprehensive U.S. strategy to counter terrorism should include economic policies that encourage development, more open societies, and opportunities for people to improve the lives of their families and to enhance prospects for their children's future.

Turning a National Strategy into a Coalition Strategy. Practically every aspect of U.S. counterterrorism strategy relies on international cooperation. Since 9/11, these contacts concerning military, law enforcement, intelligence, travel and customs, and financial matters have expanded so dramatically, and often in an ad hoc way, that it is difficult to track these efforts, much less integrate them.

Recommendation: The United States should engage other nations in developing a comprehensive coalition strategy against Islamist terrorism. There are several multilateral institutions in which such issues should be addressed. But the most important policies should be discussed and coordinated in a flexible contact group of leading coalition governments. This is a good place, for example, to develop joint strategies for targeting terrorist travel, or for hammering out a common strategy for the places where terrorists may be finding sanctuary.

Presently the Muslim and Arab states meet with each other, in organizations such as the Islamic Conference and the Arab League. The Western states meet with each other in organizations such as NATO and the Group of Eight summit of leading industrial nations. A recent G-8 summit initiative to begin a dialogue about reform may be a start toward finding a place where leading Muslim states can discuss—and be seen to discuss—critical policy issues with the leading Western powers committed to the future of the Arab and Muslim world.

These new international efforts can create durable habits of visible cooperation, as states willing to step up to their responsibilities join together in constructive efforts to direct assistance and coordinate action.

Coalition warfare also requires coalition policies on what to do with enemy captives. Allegations that the United States abused prisoners in its custody make it harder to build the diplomatic, political, and military alliances the government will need. The United States should work with friends to develop mutually agreed-on principles for the detention and humane treatment of captured international terrorists who are not being held under a particular country's criminal laws. Countries such as Britain, Australia, and Muslim friends, are committed to fighting terrorists. America should be able to reconcile its views on how to balance humanity and security with our nation's commitment to these same goals.

The United States and some of its allies do not accept the application of full Geneva Convention treatment of prisoners of war to captured terrorists. Those Conventions establish a minimum set of standards for prisoners in internal conflicts. Since the international struggle against Islamist terrorism is not internal, those provisions do not formally apply, but they are commonly accepted as basic standards for humane treatment.

Recommendation: The United States should engage its friends to develop a common coalition approach toward the detention and humane treatment of captured terrorists. New principles might draw upon Article 3 of the Geneva Conventions on the law of armed conflict. That article was specifically designed for those cases in which the usual laws of war did not apply. Its minimum standards are generally accepted throughout the world as customary international law.

Proliferation of Weapons of Mass Destruction.   The greatest danger of another catastrophic attack in the United States will materialize if the world's most dangerous terrorists acquire the world's most dangerous weapons. . . . [A]l Qaeda has tried to acquire or make nuclear weapons for at least ten years. . . . [O]fficials worriedly discuss[ed], in 1998, reports that Bin Ladin's associates thought their leader was intent on carrying out a "Hiroshima."

These ambitions continue. In the public portion of his February 2004 worldwide threat assessment to Congress, DCI Tenet noted that Bin Ladin considered the acquisition of weapons of mass destruction to be a "religious obligation." He warned that al Qaeda "continues to pursue its strategic goal of obtaining a nuclear capability." Tenet added that "more than two dozen other terrorist groups are pursuing CBRN [chemical, biological, radiological, and nuclear] materials."[28]

A nuclear bomb can be built with a relatively small amount of nuclear material. A trained nuclear engineer with an amount of highly enriched uranium or plutonium about the size of a grapefruit or an orange, together with commercially available material, could fashion a nuclear device that would fit in a van like the one Ramzi Yousef parked in the garage of the World Trade Center in 1993. Such a bomb would level Lower Manhattan.[29]

The coalition strategies we have discussed to combat Islamist terrorism should therefore be combined with a parallel, vital effort to prevent and counter the proliferation of weapons of mass destruction (WMD). We recommend several initiatives in this area.

Strengthen Counterproliferation Efforts.   While efforts to shut down Libya's illegal nuclear program have been generally successful, Pakistan's illicit trade and the nuclear smuggling networks of Pakistani scientist A. Q. Khan have revealed that the spread of nuclear weapons is a problem of global dimensions. Attempts to deal with Iran's nuclear program are still underway. Therefore, the United States should work with the international community to develop laws and an international legal regime with universal jurisdiction to enable the capture, interdiction, and prosecution of such smugglers by any state in the world where they do not disclose their activities.

Expand the Proliferation Security Initiative.   In May 2003, the Bush administration announced the Proliferation Security Initiative (PSI): nations in a willing partnership combining their national capabilities to use military, economic, and diplomatic tools to interdict threatening shipments of WMD and missile-related technology.

   The PSI can be more effective if it uses intelligence and planning resources of the NATO alliance. Moreover, PSI membership should be open to non-NATO countries. Russia and China should be encouraged to participate.

Support the Cooperative Threat Reduction Program.   Outside experts are deeply worried about the U.S. government's commitment and approach to securing the weapons and highly dangerous materials still scattered in Russia and other countries of the Soviet Union. The government's main instrument in this area, the Cooperative Threat Reduction Program (usually referred to as "Nunn-Lugar," after the senators who sponsored the legislation in 1991), is now in need of expansion, improvement, and resources. The U.S. government has recently redoubled its international commitments to support this program, and we recommend that the United States do all it can, if Russia and other countries will do their part. The government should weigh the value of this investment against the catastrophic cost America would face should such weapons find their way to the terrorists who are so anxious to acquire them.

Editors' Note: *Notes for this reading can be found in the original source.*

Credits

pp. 20–26: From *Take the Rich off Welfare* by Mark Zepezauer, pp. 1, 82–89. Reprinted by permission of South End Press.

pp. 27–32: "Tax Cheats and Their Enablers" by Robert S. McIntyre, Citizens for Tax Justice, 2005. Reprinted by permission.

pp. 33–39: "The Commercial" from *How to Watch TV News* by Neil Postman and Steve Powers. Copyright © 1992 by Neil Postman and Steve Powers. Used by permission of Viking Penguin, a division of Penguin Group (USA) Inc.

pp. 40–46: "Water for Profit" by John Luoma from *Mother Jones*, November/December 2002. © 2003, Foundation for National Progress. Reprinted by permission.

pp. 50–61: "Nickel-and-Dimed: On (Not) Getting by in America" by Barbara Ehrenreich from *Harper's*, January 1999, pp. 37–44. Copyright © 1999 by Barbara Ehrenreich.

pp. 62–71: "Generation Broke" by Tamara Draut and Javier Silva. Reprinted by permission of Demos.

pp. 72–78: "Retirement's Unraveling Safety Net" by Dale Russakoff. From *The Washington Post*, May 15, 2005. Copyright © 2005, The Washington Post. Reprinted by permission.

pp. 79–82: From *The Squandering of America: How the Failure of Our Politics Undermines Our Prosperity* by Robert Kutter, copyright © 2007 by Robert Kutter. Used by permission of Alfred A. Knopf, a division of Random House, Inc.

pp. 86–90: "*Increasing Inequality in the United States*" by Dean Baker. Reprinted by permission of the Friedrich Ebert Foundation, Washington Office.

pp. 91–97: "From Poverty to Prosperity: A National Strategy to Cut Poverty in Half" by the Center for American Progress. This material was created by the Center for American Progress www.americanprogress.org.

pp. 98–106: "Day by Day: the Lives of Homeless Women" from *Tell Them Who I Am: The Lives of Homeless Women* by Elliot Liebow. Copyright © 1993 by Elliot Liebow. Reprinted with the permission of The Free Press, a Division of Simon & Schuster, Inc.

pp. 107–112: "As Rich-Poor Gap Widens in the U.S., Class Mobility Stalls" by David Wessel from *The Wall Street Journal*, May 13, 2005. Copyright © 2005 Dow Jones & Co. Reprinted by permission of Dow Jones & Co. via Copyright Clearance Center.

pp. 116–121: "The Roots of White Advantage" by Michael K. Brown, et. al., from *Whitewashing Race: The Myth of a Color-Blind Society*, pp. 66, 77–79, 26–30. Reprinted by permission of The University of California Press via Copyright Clearance Center.

pp. 122–127: "Schools and Prisons: Fifty Years after *Brown v. Board of Education*" by the Sentencing Project. Reprinted by permission of The Sentencing Project.